Colección Támesis

SERIE A: MONOGRAFÍAS, 261

# THE *COMEDIA* IN ENGLISH

## TRANSLATION AND PERFORMANCE

# THE *COMEDIA* IN ENGLISH

## TRANSLATION AND PERFORMANCE

Edited by

Susan Paun de García and Donald R. Larson

TAMESIS

First published 2008 by Tamesis, Woodbridge

ISBN 978–1–85566–169–1

Tamesis is an imprint of Boydell & Brewer Ltd
PO Box 9, Woodbridge, Suffolk IP12 3DF, UK
and of Boydell & Brewer Inc.
668 Mt Hope Avenue, Rochester, NY 14620, USA
website: www.boydellandbrewer.com

A CIP catalogue record for this book is available
from the British Library

This publication is printed on acid-free paper

Printed in Great Britain by
Antony Rowe Ltd, Chippenham, Wiltshire

# CONTENTS

# PREFACE

One of the significant developments in recent years in studies of Spanish Golden Age theatre has been an increase of interest in how the plays of that astonishingly rich genre have been, are being, and might be performed. No longer are plays examined only as literary texts, but also as living works of theatre, combining spoken words, gesture, movement, music, and spectacle. Analyses written from that point of view are now quite common in the professional journals, and there is even a new periodical – entitled, appropriately enough, *Comedia Performance* – that concentrates exclusively on matters of performance. Many of the articles that have appeared in the last fifteen years that may broadly be categorized as performance-oriented discuss theatre practices, both of the early modern and modern periods; others attempt to imagine virtual representations of individual works; still others comment on productions of specific plays. Surprisingly, however, very few of those studies deal with the performance of Spanish plays in English translation, the focus of this volume.

Such an omission is all the more remarkable in that Spanish *comedias* – verse plays in three acts with a wide range of themes and characters, and a blending of comic and tragic tonalities – have appeared on the stages of the English-speaking world with increasing frequency in recent years. One may point to numerous student and amateur productions, but in addition to these there have been notable professional stagings, including those incorporated into the internationally known Siglo de Oro Drama Festival, held annually at the Chamizal National Memorial in El Paso, Texas, and those that were mounted by the Royal Shakespeare Company during its "Spanish Season" in the summer of 2004. Considered as a whole, all these productions, whether undertaken by professional or non-professional organizations, suggest a fascinating array of questions. What is the best way to translate the language of the Spanish original texts into modern English? Are verse translations preferable to those written in prose, and if so, what kind of verse? Should translations be "faithful" or should they aim at conveying the "spirit" of the original? Which kinds of plays "work" particularly well on the contemporary stages of English-speaking countries, and which "work" less well? Which values and customs of the earlier period can be assumed to present no difficulties for modern audiences, and which require some kind of decoding on the part of translators, directors, and actors? Which kinds of staging are suitable, and which are not? To what degree, if any, should one aim for authenticity? And so on.

In this volume, we include seventeen essays, all of them heretofore unpublished, that deal with these and related matters. About a third of them are authored by individuals who have translated Spanish *comedias* into English; another third are written by those who have served as directors or dramaturges of particular productions; and the final third come from critics and scholars who have attended, and reflected upon, specific performances. The contributors represent a number of different countries – principally, the United States, but also Canada, the United Kingdom, Ireland, and Israel. Among them are both university professors and practicing theatre professionals, all widely known in their fields. Some essays are theoretical in nature, while others are analytical; in contrast, some pieces are more recollective, even anecdotal. The individual essays of the contributors reflect their own experience and opinions, as well as their own tones and registers in writing. While many articles are in agreement with one another, others suggest varying, even opposite opinions about translation, production, and perception of the *Comedia* in general and the particular plays they discuss. It is our hope that the diversity of voices and multiplicity of points of view that they bring to the subject of Spanish classical theatre in English will appeal to a variety of readers beyond the limits of academic circles.

The range of plays covered in the volume is limited in part by the experiences and interest of the contributors, resulting in what may be perceived as an overlap of some essays. Rather than regard this as repetition, we hope that the reader will enjoy and benefit from the multiple points of view of directors, translators, and viewers of the same works, even of the same performances.

While we have grouped the essays in four sections – Overview, Translating and Adapting, Directing and Contextualizing, Viewing and Reviewing – we imagine that readers may wish to read them at random and not necessarily in the order in which we present them. For those who are not conversant with the vagaries of Spanish verse forms used in the *Comedia*, however, we suggest that they turn first to Dakin Matthews's essay, which contains a useful and succinct survey of those forms.

## The Spanish *Comedia* in English: An Overview of Translation and Performance

By way of a general orientation, we begin the volume with a survey of translation and performance of the *Comedia* in the English-speaking world over the centuries, from the early seventeenth to the present. While of necessity such a review must be selective and not exhaustive, the essay attempts to identify and discuss obvious trends, some of which flourish and then wither, others of which persist across time and space. In this introduction, we discuss significant translations and professional performances, in the British Isles, the United States, and Canada.

## Translating and Adapting the *Comedia*

This section contains six essays by translators of the *Comedia*, some veterans and some newcomers. While the approaches to the task differ widely, all of the writers wrestle with the same fundamental issues or problems: that the original plays are in verse, that they are texts meant to be performed, and that they are from another culture and another time.

In *Translating* Comedias *into English Verse for Modern Audiences*, Dakin Matthews shares his insights into these and other questions, offering an explanation of the decisions he has taken in terms of translating into poly-metric verse, translating for performance, and translating culture in the five versions he has created of plays by Tirso de Molina, Juan Ruiz de Alarcón, and Agustín Moreto.

Also concerned with verse translations is Victor Dixon's piece, *Translating the Polymetric* Comedia *for Performance (with Special Reference to Lope de Vega's Sonnets)*. Dixon posits the supreme importance to the *Comedia* of polymetric poetry, and specifically the sonnet, both sonnets in general, and in particular those of Lope de Vega, who set the model by example. For Dixon, sonnets are much more than ornamental "arias"; they are windows into character, feelings, and motives,

In *Lope de Vega in English: The Historicised Imagination*, David Johnston discusses plays by Lope as well, but focuses on the problems, challenges, and opportunities of translating historical theatre. For Johnston, a play's existence in time becomes an itinerary between past and present, rather than the exca-vation of a bounded site, and the series of translations that form this itinerary take place in and across these various temporal engagements. Johnston's discussion focuses on the issues of translating the language of the *Comedia* so that it can be performed and experienced as precisely such an itinerary.

In her essay *Found in Translation: María de Zayas's* Friendship Betrayed *and the English-Speaking Stage*, Catherine Larson examines two interrelated aspects of the staging of Zayas's *La traición en la amistad* on the English-speaking stage. The first treats the task of translation itself, from lexical issues to metaphoric "translations" of a seventeenth-century Spanish context into one that can be understood and appreciated by twenty-first-century United States audiences. The second has to do with the ways that the words on the page come alive in production, illustrating the distance between academic understandings and those of theatre practitioners.

Dawn L. Smith's essay *Transformation and Fluidity in the Translation of Classical Texts for Performance: The Case of Cervantes's* Entremeses is a reflection on the nature of translating Golden Age dramatic texts for perform-ance in English. Based on her personal experience of translating Miguel de

Cervantes's *Ocho entremeses*, this study focuses on some key questions: How does the process of translating for performance evolve to reflect the "sensibilities" of successive audiences? How "true" can a translated version remain to the original text? How do recent translations compare with other versions of the *Entremeses*?

In *Translation as Relocation*, Ben Gunter discusses the importance of location as a way of exposing the dramatic possibilities and performance cues encoded within Golden Age plays' geographical, political, and social settings. For Gunter, translating location can forge connections between seventeenth-century playwriting conventions and twenty-first-century staging practices. Practicing translation as relocation offers translators a concrete way to use "given circumstances" to get in touch with characters and bring them to life precisely, vividly, and completely.

Directing and Contextualizing the *Comedia*

This section offers five essays by directors, dramaturges, or translators who have been intimately involved with a performance of a *comedia* in English. While some discussions focus on the praxis of bringing a play from the page to the stage, others expose challenges that must be faced in presenting early modern works to (post)modern audiences.

Michael Halberstam's *Rehearsing* Spite for Spite discusses the process of putting together a production of Dakin Matthews's adaptation of Moreto's *El desdén con el desdén*. Halberstam chronicles the tension, challenges, and rewards of breathing new life into an old text. He recalls the difficulties he and his company encountered in preparing for and staging the work, and reflects on the similarities and differences between working with the Spanish *Comedia* and Shakespeare.

In *Directing* Don Juan, The Trickster of Seville, Anne McNaughton discusses her experiences in staging Tirso's play for a modern, English-speaking audience in North Hollywood, generally unacquainted with seventeenth-century Spanish drama. She addresses the problems involved and resolved in the process of making the "Trickster" and his world come alive. As well, she defends some of her directorial decisions that have been challenged.

Isaac Benabu's essay, *Directing the* Comedia: *Notes on a Process*, discusses two *comedias* that he has directed, both involving advanced drama students. In his commentary on Pedro Calderón de la Barca's *The Surgeon of His Honour* he focuses on pragmatic issues such as blocking a classical text that has few explicit stage directions, and how movement and placement affect the audience's interpretation of the work. Benabu compares some of his experiences in staging this play and those encountered with a production (in Spanish) of Tirso's *El burlador de Sevilla*.

Jonathan Thacker's essay, *Tirso's Tamar Untamed: A Lesson of the Royal*

*Shakespeare Company's Production*, examines the character of Tamar in the light of past criticism and productions, but focuses on how it was specifically Simon Usher's direction of *Tamar's Revenge,* a production in English, that enabled a radical re-presentation of the Biblical character to emerge. Thacker sustains that one could not easily imagine such a staging in Spain, with its lack of a performance tradition in classical theatre.

In *The Loss of Context and the Traps of Gender in Sor Juana's* Los empeños de una casa / House of Desires Catherine Boyle studies the translation, production, and performance of *Los empeños de una casa / House of Desires* by the Royal Shakespeare Company in 2004. As translator of the playtext, Boyle examines how Sor Juana Inés de la Cruz plays with and subverts gender, and how codes of modern performances can direct the audience towards an easier interpretation of gender roles, particularly masculinity.

### Viewing and Reviewing the *Comedia*

This section presents five essays by literary critics who reflect on specific performances of four Golden Age plays in English: Tirso's *Don Juan*, Lope's *Capulets & Montagues* and *Peribáñez*, and Zayas's *Friendship Betrayed*.

James A. Parr's *Tirso's* Burlador de Sevilla *as Playtext in English* compares two notable translations of the original Don Juan play, both of which have been used in connection with recent stagings: Gwynne Edwards's earlier rendering and Dakin Matthews's more recent version. Parr compares key passages to the Spanish original, using Luis Vázquez's critical edition, to see how well these translations – one British, one American – capture the sense and sensibility of the original, and whether a rendering in prose or in verse offers a more stage-worthy product.

In *Anne McNaughton's* Don Juan: *A Rogue for All Seasons*, A. Robert Lauer observes that in his experience modern renditions of Don Juan, whether theatrical, cinematographic, or operatic, tend to disappoint. For an early modern work to be successful on the contemporary stage, at least two things must be in place: a poetic text that is true to the spirit of the work, and a production that manages to express it. Lauer offers as an example of such success the 2006 staging of Tirso de Molina's *El burlador de Sevilla*, translated into English by Dakin Matthews and directed by Anne McNaughton. In his review of the performance, Lauer analyzes, among other things, the delivery of long soliloquies and the characterization of royal figures.

Susan L. Fischer's *Aspectual, Performative, and "Foreign" Lope / Shakespeare:* Staging Capulets & Montagues *and* Peribáñez *in English and* Romeo and Juliet *in "Sicilian"* applies some of the ideas of Jonathan Bate and W. B. Worthen to (post)modern performance of the *Comedia* in English. Fischer considers the question: How do our ideas about the *Comedia* inform our understanding of the limits of performance? The notion of the text as a fixed site of authority has become controversial; nonetheless, our understanding of *Comedia* performance – in the work of actors and directors, as well as of performance scholars – retains a surprising sense of the possibility of being "faithful" to *the* text.

In *Zayas's Comic Sense: The First Performance in English of* La traición en la amistad Sharon D. Voros considers María de Zayas's sense of comedy as reflected through secondary characters in the play. While Zayas includes the traditional *gracioso* role (León), Voros contends that the character Belisa is his female counterpart. Voros remarks on the ways that in a recent Chamizal production director David Pasto highlights Belisa's evolution from subservient companion to aggressor who physically attacks her rival Fenisa. Voros comments on the significance of Belisa's argument with the *gracioso,* and highlights the controversial fight scene with Fenisa, as well as the use of stage props that often work at cross purposes with the text.

Barbara Mujica's *María de Zayas's* Friendship Betrayed *à la Hollywood: Translation, Transculturation, and Production* comments on the complexities involved in decoding and reconstructing a play from a different century and culture and by an atypical playwright – in this case, a woman. Mujica examines the theoretical and practical challenges faced, and how the Washington Women's Playwrights' production of *Friendship Betrayed* attempted to solve them. Special attention is given to: making the context (a seventeenth-century homo-social environment) intelligible to modern Americans; bringing pertinence to the moral issues raised by the play; staging the play in a non-*corral* space; and the use of props, music, and other paralinguistic elements.

These essays, while different in their approach and focus, all reflect on the same questions of faithfulness and freedom, of constraints and communication, of theory and practice. Clearly, in view of the current interest in performing Spanish *comedias* on the English-speaking stage, the time is ripe to examine the various issues involved. Among those who will sit up and listen, we fully expect, will be not only students and teachers of Spanish and English classical theatre, but also directors, producers, actors, and general readers of all sorts.


## Note to the Reader

In the text that follows, all quotations in foreign languages are followed by an English translation, except in those instances where the meaning is obvious. We have likewise given an English equivalent for all Spanish titles, normally only the first time that a title appears within a given essay. In some cases, the same play may appear with variant English titles, depending on the preference of the author of the essay.

We have elected not to standardize spelling, preferring to allow authors to maintain their individual American or British voice.

Rather than provide a glossary of terms related to Golden Age theatre, we have included these within the index, where we have indicated pages where the reader can find explanations or definitions.

# CONTRIBUTORS

Isaac Benabu is a Professor in the Department of Theatre Studies at The Hebrew University, Jerusalem. He has published widely on such topics as the public theatre in Renaissance Europe, Spanish tragedy, performance theory, and reading the playtext for performance. His most recent book is *Reading for the Stage: Calderón and His Contemporaries*. Among the many productions that he has directed are several Spanish *comedias*, both in Spanish and in English, notably Calderón's *The Surgeon of His Honour,* which was presented at the Chamizal Siglo de Oro Festival in El Paso, Texas, in 1997.

Catherine Boyle is Professor of Latin American Cultural Studies at King's College London. She is the author of *Chilean Theatre, 1973–1985: Marginality, Power, Selfhood*, as well as of numerous articles dealing with Latin American theatre, music, and culture. She has also worked with professional theatre companies in the translation and production of Spanish and Spanish American drama. Notably, her translation of Sor Juana Inés de la Cruz's *House of Desires* was produced by the Royal Shakespeare Company in 2004. She is currently working on issues of cultural transmission and translation, while maintaining research into memory, cultural expression, and political change.

Victor Dixon is Professor of Spanish, Emeritus, at Trinity College, Dublin. An actor and director, as well as a scholar, he has written extensively on Spanish theatre, both of the early modern and modern periods. Among his many publications are translations of Lope de Vega's *Fuenteovejuna* and *El perro del hortelano*, as well as a critical edition of the latter. Along with David Johnston, he has edited *El teatro de Buero Vallejo: homenaje del hispanismo británico e irlandés*, and he is the author of the entry on Spanish Renaissance Theatre in *The Oxford Illustrated History of Theatre*. To date, he has directed or acted in some twenty productions of Spanish plays.

Susan L. Fischer is Professor of Spanish and Comparative Literature at Bucknell University. She has written extensively on the Spanish *comedia* and Shakespeare, with special attention to translation and performance studies. She has lectured widely in the United Kingdom, the United States, and mainland Europe, on both the Spanish Golden Age and Shakespeare. She serves on the editorial board of the *Bulletin of Comediantes* and *Comedia Perform-ance*, and has edited two volumes of essays: *"Comedias del Siglo de Oro" and Shakespeare* and *Self-Conscious Art: A Tribute to John W. Kronik.*

Ben Gunter holds a PhD in dramaturgy from Florida State University, where he uses *comedias* in English to revolutionize courses in acting, play anal-ysis, theatre appreciation, and theatre history. His passion for translation has sparked workshops in university and community theatres, and inspired pres-entations at national theatre conferences. An experienced actor, musician, and artistic director, he has worked with professional companies in the US, Canada, and the UK.

Michael Halberstam is Artistic Director and co-founder of Writers' Theatre (Chicago) for whom he has directed or acted in over twenty-five produc-tions. He taught Shakespeare at The Theatre School (Depaul University) for two years. His directing credits include Illinois Shakespeare, American Theatre Company, Northlight, Chicago Opera Theatre, Peninsula Players, Ravinia Festival and Milwaukee Repertory. In New York he has directed Off-Broadway for Jean Cocteau Repertory (*Candida*) and in 2007 a highly acclaimed adaptation of *Crime and Punishment*. Numerous awards include the Crystal Award and honors from Lawyers for the Creative Arts and the Arts and Business Council.

David Johnston is Professor of Spanish and Head of the School of Languages, Literatures and Performing Arts at Queen's University Belfast. He has published numerous books on Spanish culture, theatre, and translation, including *Stages of Translation* and *Translation and Performance: The Practice of Theatre*. An award-winning translator for the stage, with over twenty versions performed and a dozen published, his adaptation of Lope de Vega's *The Dog in the Manger* was performed by the Royal Shakespeare Company during its 2003/4 season, the third time he has been commissioned by the RSC. He has just finished a six-year stint as Chair of Belfast's Lyric Theatre.

Catherine Larson is Professor of Spanish at Indiana University. Her research specializations are in early modern Spanish literature (especially the *Comedia*), Spanish American theatre, and Gender Studies. She is the author of *Language and the Comedia: Theory and Practice, Games and Play in the Theater of Spanish American Women*, and co-editor of two collections of essays: *Brave New Words: Studies in Spanish Golden Age Literature* (with Edward H. Friedman) and *Latin American Women Dramatists* (with Marga-rita Vargas). Her prose translation of María de Zayas's *La traición en la amistad* was recently performed by Washington Women in Theater.

Donald R. Larson has taught at Princeton University and the University of California at Berkeley, and is currently Associate Professor of Spanish at The

Ohio State University. He is the author of *The Honor Plays of Lope de Vega*, as well as numerous articles dealing with Spanish theatre of the early modern period. His introduction to Luis Vélez de Guevara's *Reinar después de morir* will appear in a forthcoming critical edition of the play. He is presently at work on a book on visual aspects of Golden Age theatre.

A. Robert Lauer is Professor of Spanish at The University of Oklahoma. A scholar of Golden Age literature, he has authored many studies dedicated to the works of Cervantes, as well as books and essays about the theatre of early modern Spain. He has served as Presenter and Discussant for the Siglo de Oro Drama Festival in El Paso, Texas, and as the official reviewer of the festival for the press. He is General Editor of Ibérica, a monograph series on the theatre of the Renaissance and the Baroque in Spain, Portugal, and Colonial Ibero-America.

Dakin Matthews is an actor, scholar, playwright, and translator. He is an Associate Artist and Shakespearean dramaturge at the Old Globe Theatre in San Diego and a Professor Emeritus of English at California State University, East Bay. He has translated plays by Goldoni, Sophocles, Musset, and Plautus, and most recently has completed five rhyming verse translations from the Golden Age: Moreto's *Spite for Spite*, Tirso's *Don Juan, the Trickster of Seville*, and Ruiz de Alarcón's *The Truth Can't Be Trusted*, *The Proof of the Promise*, and *The Walls Have Ears*. His adaptation of Shakespeare's *Henry IV* won a Tony Award in 2004 in the category of Best Revival.

Anne McNaughton was a member of the first graduating class of the Drama Division of The Juilliard School, and a founding member of John Houseman's Acting Company. She was the Artistic Director of the Valley Shakespeare Festival in Northern California, and an Associate Director at the Berkeley Shakespeare Festival, California Actors Theatre, San José Repertory Theatre, and Berkeley Stage Company. She is a founding member of both the Antaeus Company and the Andak Stage Company in Los Angeles. There she has directed four Spanish *comedias*, all of which were subsequently brought to the Siglo de Oro Drama Festival in El Paso, Texas.

Barbara Mujica is a Professor of Spanish at Georgetown University, past President of the Association for Hispanic Classical Theater (AHCT), and Editor-in-Chief of *Comedia Performance*, a journal devoted to early modern Spanish theatre. She has written extensively on mysticism, the pastoral novel, and seventeenth-century theatre, has published a number of novels and short story collections, and is currently working on an anthology of early modern Spanish theatre. She has edited several collections of essays dedicated to the *Comedia*, and she is the director of El Retablo, a Spanish-language theatre group.

James A. Parr is Professor of Hispanic Studies at the University of California, Riverside. A former president of the Cervantes Society of America, he also served for many years as editor-in-chief of the *Bulletin of the Comediantes*. Author of several books on *Don Quijote*, including *Don Quixote: A Touchstone for Literary Criticism,* he has also written widely on Spanish early modern theatre, and other topics centered on the Golden Age. Among his many interests are the life and work of Juan Ruiz de Alarcón. He has recently published a critical edition of Tirso's *El burlador de Sevilla y convidado de piedra.*

Susan Paun de García is Associate Professor of Spanish at Denison University. She has written articles on María de Zayas, on the seventeenth-century *Comedia*, and the post-baroque *Comedia* of the early eighteenth century, particularly the work of José de Cañizares, of whose *Don Juan de Espina* plays she published a critical edition. As Second Vice President of the Association for Hispanic Classical Theater, she also oversees the Association's committee for the *Comedia* in English.

Dawn L. Smith, Professor Emeritus of Hispanic Studies at Trent University, Ontario, Canada, is the author of numerous articles on the Spanish *Comedia* and co-editor, with Anita K. Stoll, of *The Perception of Women in Spanish Theater of the Golden Age* and *Gender, Identity, and Representation in Spain's Golden Age.* She has also edited a critical edition of Tirso de Molina's *La mujer que manda en casa.* Her English translation of Cervantes's *Ocho entremeses,* with introduction and critical notes, is frequently used for performance.

Jonathan Thacker is Faculty Lecturer at University of Oxford, and Fellow and Tutor in Spanish at Merton College, Oxford. Adviser to the Royal Shakespeare Company during their 2004 season of Spanish Golden Age plays, he is the author of *Role-Playing and the World as Stage in the Comedia,* the recently published *A Companion to Golden Age Theatre,* and numerous articles dealing with early modern Spanish literature. He has also translated Cervantes's *Exemplary Novels* and Tirso de Molina's *Damned for Despair* (in collaboration with Laurence Boswell).

Sharon D. Voros, Professor of Spanish and French at the United States Naval Academy, is the author of *Petrarch and Garcilaso: A Linguistic Approach to Style* (published under the name Sharon Ghertman), *Looking at the Comedia in the Quincentennial,* with Barbara Mujica, and *Aquel breve sueño: Dreams on the Early Modern Spanish Stage,* with Ricardo Saez. She is currently conducting research on Leonor de la Cueva y Silva and has written on Lope de Rueda, Calderón, Lope de Vega, Ana Caro, and María de Zayas. She is Treasurer of the Association for Hispanic Classical Theater and book review editor for *Comedia Performance.*

# ACKNOWLEDGEMENTS

In an endeavor such as this one, there are undoubtedly many to whom we should acknowledge our gratitude for their assistance. Primary among these are Salvador García Castañeda, Fernando Unzueta, and Ellie Ferguson, all of whom have given us inspiration, help, and support at various stages of this project.

In addition, we wish to express our thanks to the Denison University Research Foundation for their generosity in supporting this publication.

# Introduction
## The *Comedia* in English: An Overview of Translation and Performance

SUSAN PAUN DE GARCÍA AND DONALD R. LARSON

The *Comedia* in English is hardly a new phenomenon. Soon after appearing on the boards in Spain, many plays found their way across the Channel, some directly, others by way of France. Given the popularity of Spanish plays in the seventeenth century, it seems ironic that reviewers today consistently marvel at the fact that the rich dramatic tradition of the Golden Age is little known and rarely performed. The two favorites, *Fuenteovejuna* and *Life Is a Dream*, have of course been included habitually in modern anthologies for study, but until recently even they had little presence on the English-speaking stage, either in translation or adaptation. However, as we will show in this brief overview of translation and performance, the turn of the millennium saw a marked increase in interest, and consequently a proliferation in productions by professional companies not only of these two standbys but of a surprising number of other *comedias* as well. Many of the same reasons that attracted seventeenth-century playwrights and audiences to the genre can help to explain its reemergence of late. What we will emphasize in the present discussion is not only the sameness, then and now, of the process of creating an English playtext from a Spanish original, but also the newness of some of the trends that have led to a number of successful productions in the last twenty-five years.

Despite this success, the inconvenient truth of the matter is that the *Comedia* is still produced infrequently in the English-speaking world. Four centuries ago, however, it was a source for more English plays than we might suppose. A few of these come from the first half of the seventeenth century. The vast majority, however, are products of the second half. Interestingly, virtually none of these plays, whether of the first part of the century or the last, derive from works of the dark and brooding sort that many modern audiences associate with Spanish theatre. Rather they spring from *comedias de capa y espada*, amusing cloak and sword plays, with their plethora of plots and fast-paced action. It is these plays of "Spanish plot," to use Dryden's term, that initiated what John Loftis has called the "the Spanish strain in [English] drama" (*Plays* 3).[1]

What is it about Spanish theatre that allowed it to be assimilated with relative ease into English theatre? We should note, first of all, that the conventions of Spanish and English plays (and the stages upon which those plays were performed) were strikingly similar in their periods of formation.[2] Both dramatic traditions played to the *mobile vulgus* (although performances were attended by all social classes). Both favored dual and even multiple plots. Both – concomitantly – early on jettisoned the Unities. Clearly, there are many parallels, and they have been widely noted over the centuries, particularly by the British themselves and by the French. In his *Of Dramatick Poesie*, for example, Dryden remarked that both Spanish and British plays had more plot than their French counterparts.[3] Taking up the same point, but less sympathetically, Voltaire commented that the two traditions, as exemplified by their leading figures, were equally barbarous: "Calderón est aussi barbare que Shakespeare" (quoted in Besterman 83).[4] Later, Shelley would also make identification between the two: "a kind of Shakespeare is this Calderon" (quoted in Jones 115).

Nevertheless, while similarities between the two dramatic traditions abound, there are also significant differences that often make translation less satisfying than adaptation. For one, the *Comedia* is a polymetric verse drama, with particular stanza forms that have few equivalents in the English tradition. The favored eight-syllable line of the *Comedia* is shorter and quicker

---

[1]   In the discussion that follows regarding the influence of Spanish theatre upon English theatre in the seventeenth century it will be very evident that we are greatly indebted to the work of others. We should mention, particularly, the pioneering study of John Loftis, *The Spanish Plays of Neoclassical England,* his later "La comedia española en la Inglaterra del siglo XVII," and G. E. Bentley's monumental *The Jacobean and Caroline Stage*. Other studies that we have drawn from will be noted in the appropriate places.

[2]   For a detailed discussion of the parallels between Spanish and English theatres in this period, as well as the social, political, literary, and theatrical contexts that shaped them, see, particularly, Cohen, *Drama of a Nation*. Also useful is Cañadas, *Public Theaters*, especially pages 1–75. Specific aspects of the points of contact between Spanish and English theatres are treated in various essays in the collections edited by Louise and Peter Fothergill-Payne, Fischer (*Comedias*), and Sullivan, Galoppe, and Stoutz.

[3]   "Another thing in which the French differ from us and from the Spaniards, is, that they do not embarrass, or cumber themselves with too much plot; they only represent so much of a story as will constitute one whole [...]" (quoted in Loftis, *Plays* 13).

[4]   Writing to the members of the Académie Française in 1776, Voltaire seemingly laid the blame for the barbarism in Shakespeare on Calderón's predecessor, Lope de Vega: "La vérité, qu'on ne peut déguiser devant vous, m'ordonne de vous avouer que ce Shakespeare, si sauvage, si bas, si effréné, et si absurde avait des étincelles de génie. [...] Vous savez qu'alors l'esprit de l'Espagne dominait en Europe, et jusque dans l'Italie. Lope de Vega en est un grand exemple" (quoted in Loftis, *Comedia* 102).

than the ten or eleven syllables typical of English drama, making it difficult for the translator to reproduce the original metrics without sounding stilted, even unspeakable. (As evidenced by the essays included in this volume, some modern translators have attempted to maintain an eight-syllable line and/or original rhyme schemes, while others have opted for prose.)

Another difficulty for translators – and their audiences – is the pervasive presence in Spanish seventeenth-century drama of the theme of honor, defined not as conscience, or a sense of right and wrong, but as the esteem of others or public reputation.[5] As we will see, adaptors of Spanish plays, for whom such an understanding is irrelevant or even repugnant, frequently either downplayed considerations of honor when producing their own works or eliminated them altogether. The result, of course, is a text with a considerably altered moral structure.

A final problem for translators is the predilection of Spanish dramatists for long sections of exposition and other kinds of monologue, passages that today are often deemed "unactable." Sometimes in the seventeenth century these were cut altogether when creating an English play; at other times they were folded in pieces into the dialogue. Either way, what came of the modification was a more frenzied pace, with a less reasoned development of character and/or a less suspenseful plot.

As is the case today, in earlier periods turning Spanish plays (or in some cases their French or German derivatives) into English plays often involved two steps: first, a literal translation and then a literary transformation. In this process the literary author-adapter is faced with some key decisions, the chief of which is the degree to which she or he will be "faithful" to the original. Many authors stray into the realm of the "refundición," modernizing or adapting to accord with the taste of the audience. (Of course, modern directors and producers can do this to the source text in the original language as well, adjusting, cutting, changing the time frame through costuming in order to achieve a dynamic new production.) Others stay closer to the original.

We have said that the great majority of English plays that owe their genesis to Spanish theatre come from the second half of the seventeenth century. That is not to say that there are no works from earlier decades that derive from *comedias*.[6] *Love's Cure, or The Martial Maid* (pub. 1647)[7] is an example of

---

5   This concept of honor is examined extensively in Péristiany, ed., *Honor and Shame*, and, more recently, Bowman, *Honor*. For a brief discussion, see Donald R. Larson, *Honor Plays* 1–16.

6   Unfortunately, none of the plays that can be related to Spanish sources are from the pen of Shakespeare. Despite many efforts over the years to assert such a connection, the project today remains what Henry Thomas called it in his Taylorian Lecture of 1922: "Much Ado about Nothing."

7   John Fletcher, to whom the play is sometimes attributed, at least in part, died in 1625, but his works were not published until twenty-two years after his death. As Darby has explained,

such a work (Bentley, III 363–6). A play of uncertain authorship and indeterminate dating, although evidently of the first part of the century, its principal plot is taken from Guillén de Castro's *La fuerza de la costumbre (The Force of Habit)*.[8] Another work indebted to Spanish originals is Philip Massinger's tragicomedy *The Renegado, or The Gentleman of Venice* (lic. 1624; pub. 1630 [Bentley, IV 811–15]), which draws upon two works of Cervantes that were inspired by his imprisonment in North Africa: "The Captive's Tale," a novella intercalated in the First Part of *Don Quixote*, and *Los baños de Argel (The Bagnios of Algiers)*. The second of these is regarded as Massinger's major source. Finally, James Shirley based two of his plays on *comedias*. They are *The Young Admiral* (lic. 1633, pub. 1637 [Bentley, V 1168–70]), drawn from Lope de Vega's *Don Lope de Cardona*, and *The Opportunity* (lic. 1634, pub. 1640 [Bentley, V 1060–2]), taken from Tirso de Molina's *El castigo del penseque (The Penalty for Jumping to Conclusions)*. *The Opportunity* is a particularly interesting work, illustrating a modality of translation/adaptation that in the second half of the century would become standard practice. Shirley translated many of Tirso's passages literally and maintained the plot intact, but he eliminated monologues and asides, with the resulting effect of quickening the pace of the action and heightening the comicity. At the same time, he maintained many marks of the Spanish comedies: nocturnal scenes, rapid succession of incidents, and plot devices such as false identity, coincidences, and intrigue. Other elements of "Spanishness," however, are eliminated or "Englished."[9]

Aside from these four works there appear to be no others from the first part of the seventeenth century that can be said with assurance to derive from *comedias*.[10] To be sure, many works from the period have been dubbed "Spanish plays," or "Spanish romances," but these were derived not from theatrical sources but from prose fiction. In 1665, Loftis reminds us, Sir Robert Howard had dismissed the "Spanish Plays" as "nothing but so many Novels put into

---

information about the authorship of plays in this period comes from two principal sources, although neither was necessarily accurate: the title-page of the published text, and the Register of the Stationers' Company (425).

[8]    Bentley says that "nearly everything about the play is in a state of confusion" ( III, 364). The convoluted history of the scholarship on *Love's Cure* is discussed in Erickson.

[9]    On the sources of *The Renegado*, see Rice, but also Edwards and Gibson II, 2–4. The parallels between the texts of *Love's Cure, The Renegado, The Young Admiral*, and *The Opportunity* and their Spanish counterparts are discussed extensively in Loftis, "Comedia," which also has helpful bibliographic notes regarding the sources of the four plays.

[10]    One must, of course, tread carefully in these matters, because given the sheer quantity of Golden Age plays, many of them unknown or virtually unknown in modern times, one cannot ever be entirely certain that no works that have served as models for English plays have escaped detection. Sleuthing the sources is, of course, complicated by the fact that English playwrights in the seventeenth century very seldom acknowledged their indebtedness to earlier works, foreign or otherwise.

Acts and Scenes, without the least attempt or design of making the Reader more concern'd than a well-told Tale might do" (*Plays* 13n36). Howard's slighting tone aside, there is much truth in what he says. As Rudolph Schevill, Gerald E. Bentley, and, more recently, Trudi Darby and Agapita Jurado Santos have shown, English theatre, particularly during the reigns of James I and Charles I, did draw heavily on Spanish novels and novellas, coming to them often through French translations. An early example is John Fletcher's *The Fair Maid of the Inn*, a work based on Cervantes's *La ilustre fregona* (*The Illustrious Kitchen Maid*) that was acted at Blackfriars in 1622.[11] Later examples abound, including plays by Massinger and William Rowley, as well as others that resulted from the collaboration of Fletcher and Francis Beaumont. Of all these, it was Fletcher in particular who had a predilection for plots borrowed from Spanish stories, especially those of Cervantes. Indeed, of some fifty plays that he is estimated to have written, alone or with others, possibly as many as seventeen are derived from Spanish works, either through translations or directly.[12] Among these *Rule a Wife and Have a Wife* (1624; based on *El casamiento engañoso [The Deceitful Marriage]*) and *The Chances* (1625; based on *La señora Cornelia*) were extraordinarily popular, the latter appearing on the boards consistently from its debut until the end of the eighteenth century, the former almost never NOT playing from 1659 to 1800.

Loftis notes that since novels and novellas in prose are easier to read than plays in verse, it is not surprising that playwrights drew more widely upon the former (*Plays* 26–7). Evidently, their extensive borrowing from those texts had to do also with the fact that many of them were available in English translations. As Dale B. J. Randall has pointed out, between 1543 and 1657 over "a hundred titles, editions, and issues" of translated fiction appeared, averaging about one per year (5). While there is evidence that early influence of Spanish prose was courtly in nature, after the defeat of the Armada interest in Spain and in Spanish literature increased substantially, as witnessed by the greater numbers of works translated directly from the original and read by all levels of society, from romances of chivalry to picaresque novels. Perhaps the richest period in the Anglo-Spanish literary relationship is the final years of James I, a period marked not only by an increased interest in the study

11  Also based on Cervantes's tale was the play, sometimes attributed to Lope, which bears the same title as its source. Some have thought that it, too, entered into the composition of *The Fair Maid of the Inn*. The matter hinges on whether or not Fletcher knew Spanish, for, at the time he wrote, the play had not been translated either into French or into English. See E. M. Wilson.

12  Fletcher's indebtedness to his sources, both in those plays that he wrote alone and those that he wrote in collaboration with others, is examined in the introductions that accompany the collected works in the multi-volume edition for which Fredson Bowers served as general editor.

of Spanish but also more translations, as well as a number of Spanish text-books.

Heightened English attention to Spanish literature in the early years of the seventeenth century also had to do with greater travel between the two countries,[13] especially after the establishment of an English embassy in Madrid. Under the Catholic Stuarts, relations with Spain, interrupted during the reign of Elizabeth I, were reestablished in the person of the Duke of Nottingham who, in 1605, took a five-hundred-person entourage to Spain to ratify a peace treaty with Phillip III (Stoye 325–90). A permanent embassy was established at the Spanish court, with Sir Charles Cornwallis as the first ambassador. Cornwallis was succeeded as ambassador by Sir John Digby, whose secretary was James Mabbe (1571/2–1642?), like Digby, a former student at Magdalen College, Oxford.[14] Arriving in Spain in 1611, Mabbe subsequently spent several years there, acquiring a command of Spanish such that he became the most successful translator of Spanish literature of the period, producing most famously *Guzman de Alfarache* (1622), *Celestina* (1631),[15] and six of Cervantes's *Exemplary Novels* (1640).

A somewhat later visitor to Madrid was Sir Richard Fanshawe, who, according to the memoirs of his wife, Lady Ann Fanshawe, first came in 1632 and then returned in 1635 when he was appointed secretary to the new ambassador, Lord Aston. Lady Ann writes that Sir Richard – who in the future was also to serve as ambassador to the Spanish court – was one of several young Englishmen who came to Spain in the early 1630s for the specific purpose, at least initially, of learning the language (*Memoirs* 113). Since the period when they were in Madrid coincided with the final years of Lope's career and the high tide of Calderón's fame, it is not unreasonable to assume that they would have returned to England with reports of plays that they had seen in the city's *corrales,* or open-air theatres. Nevertheless, with the few exceptions already mentioned, and despite a great interest in Spanish literature in general, those reports did not immediately stimulate adaptations

[13] Some of the best-known translators from the Spanish either toured Spain or lived there for a time. See Randall 17n35 for interesting sources regarding seventeenth-century travel to Spain.

[14] "It is not astonishing [...] to learn that James Mabbe [...] was first a student and later an administrator at Oxford. More specifically, he was of Magdalen, a college which seems to have shown a particular Hispanic interest" (Randall 15). For an account of Mabbe and his life, see Russell.

[15] In a 1634 edition containing both his *Guzmán* and *Celestina,* Mabbe's dedicatory epistle is signed: "Don Diego Puede-ser," a literal translation of the name James Mabbe. In these preliminary materials, he provides the following evaluation of his translation: "I have in the undergoing of this translation, shewn more boldness than judgment. For though I doe speak like Celestina, yet come I short of her; for she is so concisely significant, and indeede so differing is the idiome of the Spanish from the English, that I may imitate it but not come neere it. Yet have I made it as naturall, as our language will give leave" (quoted in Allison 159).

of *comedias* on English soil. And, of course, after 1642, when the Puritan-controlled government closed theatres by Act of Parliament, there was little or no incentive to do so. Eighteen years later, however, when the theatres reopened, the situation was quite different. Now English playwrights began increasingly to look to the *Comedia* for inspiration, centering their attention, as we have pointed out, particularly on the *comedias de capa y espada* that enjoyed tremendous popularity in Spain throughout the entire seventeenth century. As Loftis has shown, this new-found interest in Spanish theatre can be directly related to Charles II and his travels in the 1650s (*Plays* 30–63).

Forced to flee the British Isles in 1651, following the turbulent period of the English Civil Wars that resulted in the execution of his father, Charles I, at the hands of his Parliamentary enemies, and the subsequent abolition of the monarchy, Charles spent the next nine years in penurious exile on the Continent.[16] He resided first in Paris, then in Cologne, Bruges and Brussels in the Spanish Netherlands, and, for a brief period, in Spain itself. Attending him at various times were his brothers, a number of soldiers attached to the Royalist cause, and a band of loyal courtiers, among whom were several men who were later to play a role in the importation of Spanish *comedias* to the English stage, including Lord Bristol, Sir Richard Fanshawe, Thomas Killigrew, Sir William Davenant, and Sir Samuel Tuke.

Charles's stay in Paris coincided with the pervasive influence of Spanish theatre upon French theatre, and it is logical to assume that, as an avid lover of the stage, he saw there at least some of the many adaptations by, among others, Antoine Le Métel d'Ouville, Paul Scarron, and Thomas Corneille of Spanish plays, among them works of Lope, Tirso, Calderón, Pérez de Montalbán, Ruiz de Alarcón, and Rojas Zorrilla.[17] Charles would have had no difficulty with the language of these plays, for he spoke it fluently, having as a youth spent extended periods in France. How well he knew Spanish is another question, although it is likely that he had at least some facility, for Spanish was the language of the court in Brussels during Charles's residence there, and he must have heard it on a daily basis.

It is also possible that, while there, he attended theatrical performances in Spanish, because, as Rennert has noted, companies from Spain were touring in the Netherlands at that time (339).[18] Even had he not, Charles could not have escaped becoming aware that Spanish influence upon the theatre in the Low Countries was nearly as great as its influence upon French theatre, with

---

16 On Charles's wanderings on the Continent between 1651 and 1660, see, among other sources, Hutton.

17 Le Métel had actually lived in Spain, and it was he who blazed the path that was followed by his French contemporaries. On Spanish contributions to French theatre at this time, see Lancaster, Parts 2 and 3, passim.

18 See also Sullivan, *German Lands* 45–7.

many Dutch plays of the time resulting from translations or adaptations of works by Lope, Calderón, and others.[19] Did Charles also see some of those works in Spain during his visit there in 1659? We do not know, but it is tempting to speculate that he did, for on his return to England, he displayed an intense and abiding interest in Spanish theatre.

Charles's return was made possible by the restoration of the monarchy in 1660, following the death of Oliver Cromwell and the subsequent disappearance of the Protectorate he had headed. Shortly after Charles's coronation, he received petitions from Sir William Davenant and Thomas Killigrew for permission to form theatrical companies, and he promptly granted their requests (Nicoll 276, *London Stage Pt 1*: xxi–xxx). The resulting companies were known, respectively, as the Duke's Company and the King's Company, and within a short time they came to enjoy a monopoly on the presentation of theatre in London. As is to be expected, the majority of the works mounted by the two groups were, in their first years of existence, revivals of plays that had been introduced before the closing of the theatres in 1642. Often, of course, they were considerably adapted to reflect both the changing tastes of the public and the evolving conditions of performance: covered theatres, moveable scenery, women actors, and so on (Dobson 44–5). Interestingly, one of the plays that was revived when the theatres reopened was Shirley's *The Opportunity*, presented by the King's Company at the Vere Street Theatre in London in November, 1660; another was his *The Young Admiral*, performed by a group called the Red Bull players, at Oxford during July, 1661; the latter play was also performed at court in November 1662, apparently by the King's Company.[20]

A flourishing theatre cannot exist primarily on revivals, however, and there soon came to be a steady demand for new works. One consequence of this demand was that English playwrights and companies, interested in supplying their public with something truly novel, began increasingly to look for inspiration at the *Comedia*, and in particular, at *comedias de capa y espada*. Thus it was that the plays of "Spanish plot" came into being.[21] Works of this nature, which were very much in the vein of the French adaptations of Spanish works that Charles might have seen in Paris during his exile there, have been characterized by the editors of *The London Stage* in the following succinct fashion: a "kind of play, based upon a Spanish source, [that] placed its emphasis upon

---

[19]    See van Praag, passim.

[20]    Dates of performances of Restoration plays are taken from *The London Stage, Part 1* and *Index to the London Stage*. Information in the former is arranged chronologically (i.e., theatre seasons are covered year-by-year), and in the latter alphabetically.

[21]    For a brief discussion of the development of plays of "Spanish Plot" in this period, see Hume, especially pages 369–71 and 378–80. The matter is treated in greater detail in Loftis, "Comedia española," and extensively in Loftis, *Plays*, passim.

a rigid code of conduct, had a plot filled with intrigue, and emphasized one or more high-spirited women in the *dramatis personae*" (*Pt 1*: cxxiii). The editors might have added that the works were normally set in Spain, that the complications of the action typically turned on matters of honor (rather than on efforts to gain or preserve wealth, as in many later Restoration plays), and that their happy endings, like those of most Spanish romantic comedies, were characterized by the working out of poetic justice (Casines 27–39).

The first of the plays of "Spanish plot" to appear on the London stage, and one of the most consequential, was Sir Samuel Tuke's *The Adventures of Five Hours*. An adaptation of *Los empeños de seis horas*, today generally assumed to be by Antonio Coello although in the seventeenth century attributed to Calderón, *The Adventures* is sometimes said to have been written at the suggestion of Charles II himself (Nicoll 180). If the story is true, then Charles's suggestion was an excellent one, for the work proved to be enormously successful, possibly because it fit snugly into the mold of Fletcherian comedy, still very popular at the time (Corman 57–9). It was premiered by the Duke's Company at Lincoln's Inn Fields on 8 January 1663, and by the end of that month had achieved a run of thirteen performances.[22] One of those in attendance, both at the play's opening and at a later performance, was Samuel Pepys who, in his *Diary*, pronounced it "the best, for the variety and the most excellent continuance of the plot to the very end, that ever I saw" (quoted in *London Stage, Pt 1*: 61). In subsequent years, *The Adventures of Five Hours* was performed twice at court, and was given numerous revivals, including one as late as 1767.

How well Tuke knew Spanish is a matter of conjecture, although he could have learned it during the time that he spent in Flanders with Charles. It is likely, nevertheless, that in making his adaptation of *Los empeños* he received at least some assistance from his friend, George Digby, Lord Bristol, who did indeed know Spanish very well, having spent his first twelve years in Madrid where his father served as ambassador. Lord Bristol was himself responsible for one surviving adaptation from the Spanish, *Elvira, or The Worst Not Always True*, from Calderón's *No siempre lo peor es cierto*, as well as two lost works that would also seem to have been adapted from Calderón: *'Tis Better than It Was*, presumably based on *Mejor está que estaba*; and *Worse and Worse*, probably derived from *Peor está que estaba* (Loftis, *Plays* 78–83). The production history of *Elvira* is unclear, although the editors of the *London Stage* suppose that it might have premièred in late November 1664. As for *Worse and Worse* and *'Tis Better than It Was,* in his *Roscius*

---

22 Tukes's text of 1663, along with a later revision (1671), was published in 1927, along with Coello's *Empeños de seis horas*, in an edition prepared by A. E. H. Swaen. For the role of *Adventures* in establishing the vogue of the "Spanish plot" on the English stage, see Corman, 55–9.

*Anglicanus* (1708) John Downes affirms that they were presented by the Duke's Company between 1662 and 1665, while Pepys, for his part, speaks in his *Diary* of attending a performance of the former play at Lincoln's Inn Fields in July, 1664 (*London Stage Pt 1*: 78). There was a further performance of *Worse and Worse* at court in November, 1666. Neither of the two plays appears to have been printed.

A play that is sometimes said to be an adaptation of a Spanish original is Thomas Porter's *The Carnival*, which was probably premiered in the spring of 1664, and thereafter achieved some popularity. As Loftis has shown (*Plays*, 83–7), the plot of the work does indeed resemble that of a standard *comedia de capa y espada*, but no specific source has as yet been identified. Better known today is *Tarugo's Wiles; or The Coffee House*, by Thomas Sysderf who, like many of the Cavalier dramatists, may have learned Spanish while serving in the Spanish Netherlands. An adaptation of Moreto's *No puede ser el guardar una mujer (There's No Guarding a Woman)*, it combines elements of the cloak and sword play with others that typify the *comedia de figurón* (similar to the Jonsonian comedy of "humours"). Presented by the King's Company at Lincoln's Inn Fields on 7 October 1667, it thereafter enjoyed a modest run, although Pepys considered it "insipid" (quoted in *London Stage, Pt 1*: 120).

As Allardyce Nicoll has pointed out, it was Moreto who, after Calderón, had the "nearest ties of kinship to the Restoration playwrights" (180). Another dramatist who looked to him for inspiration was John Leanard. A playwright of modest gifts, he was the author of *The Counterfeits*, an adaptation of Moreto's *La ocasión hace al ladrón (Opportunity Makes the Thief)* that follows the original so closely as to be little more than a translation. Unfortunately, Leanard's play fails completely to convey the sparkle of its source, and after being introduced by the Duke's Company at the Dorset Garden Theatre in May of 1678, it seems to have disappeared from the stage entirely.

The most successful version of a Moreto play in the Restoration period is John Crowne's masterpiece *Sir Courtly Nice; or It Cannot Be*, another adaptation of *No puede ser*. A prolific and popular playwright, Crowne's career bridged the Atlantic, for in his youth he lived in Massachusetts for several years, during which time he attended Harvard College. Undertaken at the suggestion of Charles II himself (Loftis, *Plays* 157), *Sir Courtly Nice* is a freer reworking of its source than Sysderf's *Tarugo's Wiles*, shifting the locale of the action from Spain to London and broadening the comicity of the heroine's jealous older brother, turning him into a quintessential English fop. The result was one of the most popular and witty of all Restoration plays, boasting clever twists of plot and dialogue that Bevis characterizes as "tasty" (96). Intended for performance by the United Company, an amalgamation of the King's Company and the Duke's Company, in February 1685, *Sir Courtly*'s première was of necessity postponed because of the death of

Charles on the 6th of that month. The first performance finally took place on 9 May 1685, at the Drury Lane Theatre. Subsequently, it was presented at court in November 1685, and again in November 1686, and it was revived innumerable times throughout the late seventeenth and eighteenth centuries.

*Sir Courtly Nice* is something of an anomaly, for it comes relatively late in the Restoration period and is substantially and directly derived from its Spanish source. Most other plays of the final decades of the century that show indebtedness to Spanish plays (not prose) either take only certain elements of their plots from them or, if they borrow more substantially, it is indirectly, by means of intermediaries, such as earlier English adaptations of *comedias*, or, as frequently happened, French plays and novellas based on *comedias* and *novelas*. At the same time, many plays of the time that relate in some fashion to Spanish models reveal the increasing influence in those years of neo-classical dramatic theory which urged, among other things, the simplification of intrigue and greater attention to characterization.[23] Such measures supposedly served the didactic function of theatre, so important to the neo-classicists, but instruction cannot be provided without delight, one especially pleasing form of which, as the dramatists were discovering, is witty repartee. The result of this new approach is that plays that in the early 1660s would have been cast in the mold of "Spanish plot" were now being conceived, like *Sir Courtly Nice*, as comedies of manners or wit. The new model, clearly, was Molière.[24]

The various tendencies mentioned are already evident in several plays of the late 1660s and early 1670s. The first of these was William Davenant's *The Man's the Master*, an adaptation of Paul Scarron's *Jodelet, ou le maître valet*, which was in turn based on Rojas Zorrilla's *Donde hay agravios no hay celos (Where There Is Offense There Can Be No Jealousy)*. It was premièred on 26 March 1668 by the Duke's Company at Lincoln's Inn Fields, and was performed several other times that spring. Although Pepys was not impressed – "most of the mirth was sorry, poor stuffe" (quoted in *London Stage, Pt 1*: 132) – others must have been, for it was revived later in the century, and even on three occasions in the eighteenth century.[25]

Of greater importance, nevertheless, in the history of English theatre were four other works of these years, two of them by John Dryden, the best-known

---

23  These and other related matters can possibly help to explain the popularity of Moreto, whose plays were more akin to the English comedy of manners than Calderón's.

24  On the influence of Molière on English theatre in this period, see Wilcox, Suckling, and Hughes (117–22). On the overall development of Restoration comedy, see, particularly, Nicoll (168–235) but also Bevis (71–102) and Hughes (30–77, 113–51, 185–239, 331–57, 377–423).

25  On the relation between *The Man's the Master*, and the French and Spanish works from which it derives, see Rundle, "D'Avenant's *The Man's the Master*." Rundle's contention that Davenant was directly acquainted with *Donde hay agravios* is disputed by Loftis (*Plays* 95).

dramatist of the period, and two by William Wycherley, almost equally prominent. The former's *An Evening's Love; or The Mock Astrologer* derives ultimately from Calderón's *El astrólogo fingido*, which Dryden may in fact have known, but his major sources seem to have been French adaptations of Calderón: Thomas Corneille's play *Le Feint astrologue* and a story by Mlle de Scudéry. He also drew upon an earlier English translation of Corneille's work. Somewhat surprisingly, perhaps, this complicated genesis resulted in one of Dryden's most popular plays. After its premiere by the King's Company at the Bridges Theatre on 12 June 1668, it enjoyed a run of eight performances, and was revived numerous times thereafter in the late seventeenth and early eighteenth centuries.[26]

Notably less successful was Dryden's *The Assignation; or, Love in a Nunnery*, whose second plot – although not the first – was drawn, possibly directly, from Calderón's *Con quien vengo, vengo (I Am What I Am)*. (The play's risqué elements, alluded to in the subtitle, obviously have nothing to do with Calderón.) It was performed by the King's Company at Lincoln's Inn Fields in the fall of 1672, although the date of its première is not known. In any event, it failed to please, as the preface to the printed edition (1673) attests – "It succeeded ill in the representation" (quoted in *London Stage, Pt. 1*: 200) – and was very rarely performed thereafter.[27]

Most critics assume that Dryden knew Spanish fairly well. Wycherley probably knew it even better, for there is reason to believe that he accompanied Sir Richard Fanshawe on his embassy to Madrid in 1664 (Loftis, *Plays* 121). If he was indeed in Spain in that year, that may have been when he became acquainted with the two plays by Calderón to which he was indebted in his own playwriting. The first of these is *Mañanas de abril y mayo (Mornings of April and May)*, the source of the subplot in *Love in a Wood*. In this instance the borrowing must have been direct, because at the time of composition of Wycherley's comedy, Calderón's play had not been translated either

---

[26] Other works from this period that derive from Spanish plays by way of French adaptations are John Corye's *The Generous Enemies; or, The Ridiculous Lovers* (1671), from Rojas Zorrilla's *Entre bobos anda el juego (It's a Fool's Game)*; and Edward Ravenscroft's *The Wrangling Lovers; or, The Invisible Mistress* (1676), from Calderón's *Los empeños de un acaso (The Consequences of an Accident)* and *Casa con dos puertas mala es de guardar (A House with Two Doors is Difficult to Guard)*. A later play that also depends on a French intermediary is John Vanbrugh's, *The False Friend* (1702), from Rojas Zorrilla's *La traición busca el castigo (Treachery Punished)*. Thomas Durfey's *The Banditti* (1686) owes something to *Peor está que estaba (Worse and Worse)*, but it would seem to be based on Bristol's English adaptation rather than on Calderón's text.

[27] On the sources of *The Mock Astrologer*, see Allen's article "*The Mock Astrologer*," which contains a bibliography of earlier studies. On the sources of *The Assignation*, see Rundle, "Comic Plot," which likewise discusses previous studies. Still valuable are the earlier books of Allen (*The Sources*) and Gaw. A more recent discussion of the pertinent questions is found in Moore.

into French or English. Despite close parallels, nevertheless, the two plays
are strikingly different. Wycherley has eliminated much of the exposition
of his source and slowed down and simplified its action in order to allow
room both for character development and for sardonic commentary on the
manners of contemporary London society. In this he may have gone too far,
for Bevis comments that "[o]ne has to go back to *Volpone* to find a nastier
lot of knaves and fools" (81). Despite its effort at accommodation to the
conventions and taste of the time, however, *Love in a Wood* seems not to
have been a great success. The play was presented by the King's Company
at the Bridges Theatre in 1671, and although the precise date of its première
is unknown, it may have been as early as March of that year. It enjoyed few
subsequent performances.

As its title clearly indicates, the second of Wycherley's "Spanish" plays,
*The Gentleman Dancing Master*, stems from Calderón's *El maestro de danzar*,
which itself is an adaptation of Lope's play of the same name. Here, however,
the borrowings are much less thorough-going and systematic, reduced to
a few scattered scenes. As in the case of *Love in a Wood*, the tone of the
play is markedly different from that of its inspiration: concern with honor
is burlesqued, and there is a sexual permissiveness that would have shocked
Calderón. The work was performed by the Duke's Company at the Dorset
Garden Theatre on 6 February 1672, but it is not clear whether or not that
was the premiere. According to Downes, "it lasted but 6 Days, being like't
but indifferently" (quoted in *London Stage, Pt 1*: 192).[28]

In addition to the works just mentioned, a number of other plays from
the period might have been drawn in some degree from *comedias*. These
include Dryden's *The Indian Emperour* (1667), alleged to have been based
on *El príncipe constante*, and Shadwell's *The Libertine* (1675), supposedly
indebted to Tirso's *El burlador de Sevilla (The Trickster of Seville)*. In both
of these instances, however, the evidence for such attributions is inconclusive
at best. A somewhat different case is that of Aphra Behn's *The Young King*
(1679), the subplot of which, dealing with the secret and unjust imprisonment
of a young prince, offers evident parallels with *La vida es sueño (Life Is a
Dream)*. Since the latter work had not been translated either into English or
French at the time of the writing of *The Young King*, Behn clearly borrowed
from it. Nevertheless, given that the resemblances between the two works are
situational and not verbal, Loftis suggests that Behn may have been working
not directly from Calderón's text but from a prose summary that had been

---

[28] On Wycherley's borrowings from Calderón, see, in addition to Loftis, *Plays* 121–30,
Rundle, "Wycherley," and Vernon.

supplied to her, or even from accounts of performances of *La vida es sueño* seen by travelers to Spain or the Spanish Netherlands (*Plays* 136–7).[29]

One of the last of the Restoration plays that was apparently derived from the *Comedia* was Colley Cibber's *She Would and She Would Not*, which premièred on 26 November 1702, at Drury Lane.[30] This play was popular throughout the entire eighteenth century and into the nineteenth; revived often, with never more than a two-year lapse between runs at Drury Lane, Covent Garden and the Haymarket, it became a classic in the repertory. Derived from Tirso's *Don Gil de las calzas verdes (Don Gil of the Green Breeches)*,[31] the first production followed closely after the English victory at Vigo Bay (12 October 1702), and the play was thereafter associated in the public mind with victory and positive feelings, eventually becoming a work of national celebration (Saglia 340–2).

While Cibber's play proved attractive to the public, Richard Steele's *The Lying Lover; or, The Ladies Friendship* was one of his least successful endeavors. Based on Pierre Corneille's *Le menteur* (Burling 11), itself an adaptation of Ruiz de Alarcón's *La verdad sospechosa*, the play was performed at Drury Lane for a week in December of 1703, and was revived at the same theatre in 1746 for four performances. In contrast, another adaptation of *Le menteur* (Cooke 65), Samuel Foote's *The Lyar*, was much more successful, playing at Covent Garden in late 1761 and the first part of 1762, as well as the second half of that year at the Haymarket. Thereafter, it appeared virtually every year on the boards of these two theatres or at Drury Lane until the end of the century. Its popularity was not limited to London, for the play, billed as "a favorite Comedy," formed part of the first dramatic event ever seen in Portland, Maine, on 17 October 1794.[32]

Perhaps one of the greatest "hits" derived from Spanish *Comedia,* although not directly, was Susanna Carroll Centlivre's *The Wonder: A Woman Keeps a*

---

[29] In her "Notes on Thirty-One English Plays and Their Spanish Sources" Floriana T. Hogan has suggested that two other plays of Aphra Behn, *The Dutch Lover* (1673) and *The Rover*, Part I (1677) derive in some degree from Calderón. She relates parts of the former to *No siempre lo peor es cierto* and *Peor está que estaba* and parts of the latter to *Mejor está que estaba*. Loftis believes, however, that in her borrowing Behn was probably not working with Calderón's plays directly, but rather with Lord Bristol's adaptations, *Elvira,* and the two lost works, *Better 'Tis than It Was* and *Worse and Worse* (*Plays* 139–50).

[30] Information on this and all other premieres during the eighteenth century can be found in Burling, *New Plays.* Runs are documented in *The London Stage,* organized chronologically. Individual plays are easily located in the *Index to the London Stage.* Loftis traces the complicated trail of sources for *She Would* in "Spanish Drama."

[31] Loftis sketches the striking parallels between the two texts in "Spanish Drama" 33–4. See also Saglia.

[32] Portland was inspired by the fact that nearby Boston had, in February 1794, violated a 1750 Massachusetts law (not repealed until 1797) prohibiting "Stage Plays and other Theatrical Entertainments" (Moreland 331–2).

*Secret.* Burling (33) lists the play as partly based on Edward Ravenscroft's *The Wrangling Lovers; or The Invisible Mistress* (1676), which, according to James Rundle, shows phraseology found in several plays by Calderón.[33] First performed in 1714 at Drury Lane, it was revived in 1733, and played almost yearly for the rest of the century in London and on into the early years of the next century in the United States. It was performed in Virginia at the Mount Vernon Theatre on 20 July 1803, and in New York's New Theatre on 21 April 1806, and again on 23 January 1811, and 14 October 1812 (*Early American Playbills*). After a hiatus of almost two hundred years, Centlivre's play has returned to the boards on both sides of the Atlantic, first in New York and then in London. Directed by Elizabeth Swain in January and February of 2001, the New York production at the Gloria Maddox Theatre did not win over David Lohrey, reviewer of *CurtainUp.com*,[34] who found the play dated and who wondered that *The Wonder*, as it was billed, was done at all (although he did find the wigs "to die for"). The press release from The Other Company's November 2006 production in London described the play as "A wonderfully silly early 18th century farce, where jealous lovers, tyrannical fathers and dashing soldiers struggle to keep their swords in their sheaths, their children under control and their secrets in the cupboard." Evidently more to the taste of British than American audiences, the production, which played at the White Bear in November 2006, garnered the Critics' Choice "Show of the Week" for two weeks running. Alastair Macaulay of the *Financial Times* observed that "as the play proceeds, both cast and audience seem to have a better and better time."[35]

Two years after the première of Centlivre's *The Wonder,* Christopher Bullock's *A Woman is a Riddle* was performed on 4 December 1716, at Lincoln's Inn Fields. Based on Calderón's *La dama duende (The Phantom Lady)*,[36] the play enjoyed numerous runs from its opening until 1788, although it was evidently "extensively altered for performance on 12 March 1776" at Covent Garden (Burling 40). As well, the play inspired several reworkings.

---

[33] During the 1930s and 1940s, a spirited debate ensued between Rundle and H. C. Lancaster over the derivation of *The Wrangling Lovers,* the latter sustaining that Ravenscroft followed Edmé Boursault, and the former maintaining that he borrowed directly from Calderón's *Casa con dos puertas, Los empeños de un acaso*, and possibly *Fuego de dios en el querer bien (Woe to Those Who Love Too Well)*. Loftis found Lancaster's arguments more convincing (*Plays* 161n43).

[34] For complete citations of all reviews mentioned in this introduction, see Works Cited under the reviewer's name.

[35] Following a successful run at the White Bear, *The Wonder! A Woman Keeps A Secret* transferred to Battersea Arts Centre as part of the Critics' Choice Season, from 27 February to 11 March 2007.

[36] Burling (40) cites several source studies for this play, one of which (Tracy 38–40) suggests that Richard Savage may have had a hand in the script. See also Prettiman.

Prettiman notes that in 1742 Bullock's play was reduced to a farce called *The Litigious Suitor Defeated; or, A New Trick to Get a Wife* and was included in the collection *The Stroller's Pacquet* (34n1). Burling suggests two offshoots, first a 1778 anonymous adaptation entitled *The Macaroni Adventure*, and in the same year, an anonymous farce, *The Invisible Mistress* (40).

Another popular play of the time, possibly indebted both to Lope's *El mejor alcalde el rey (The King, the Greatest Alcalde)* and to Calderón's *El alcalde de Zalamea*, is Robert Dodsley's *The King and the Miller of Mansfield* (Lundeberg). A satire on court life of the time, the play was first performed at Drury Lane on 29 January 1737, and enjoyed considerable success thereafter. Revived yearly until 1765, the play was still performed frequently for the rest of the century at Drury Lane, Haymarket, Covent Garden, and many other London theatres.

Other less successful comedies of the early eighteenth century were also taken from Calderón. Richard Savage's *Love in a Veil*, based, like Lord Bristol's *Elvira*, on *No siempre lo peor es cierto*, premièred at Drury Lane on 17 June 1718 (Burling 48). Performed only four days that year, it was revived in 1784 for a single night (19 April) at Drury Lane. Isaac Bickerstaffe's *'Tis Well It's No Worse*, possibly adapted from Calderón's *El escondido y la tapada (The Hidden Gallant and the Veiled Lady)* (Burling 265–6), was performed at Drury Lane for an eleven-day run in 1770; it was revived in 1771, 1785, and 1788.

Although, as we have seen, the drama of Spain had been a wellspring of attractive and entertaining plots for English theatre in the seventeenth-century, in the eighteenth the turn from plot towards character development and interaction, features heightened by the neo-classical emphasis on unities and decorum, as well as an increasing interest in tragedy, led to a waning of the "Spanish plot." As the years passed, French form and critical precepts increasingly undermined English interest in the *Comedia*, and its fortunes were further prejudiced by the persistence of the *leyenda negra*; there still remained the perception that Spain was "a country of fanatical Catholicism, the perpetrator of atrocities practiced in the name of religion" (Loftis, *Plays* 256). Perhaps as a result, new translations and adaptations in the eighteenth century were few, while some old favorites were revived or recast, and enjoyed long runs. An example of recasting would be Thomas Hull's 1767 *The Perplexities*, a refashioning of Tuke's *The Adventures of Five Hours* (Burling 246), or Elizabeth Griffith's 1766 comedy, *The Double Mistake*, an alteration of Bristol's *Elvira* (Burling 243). Other plays of the "Spanish romance" sort, although not derived from *comedias*, continued to be popular. One of these was an anonymous 1749 reworking of Massinger and Fletcher's *The Spanish Curate*, taken from Gonzalo Céspedes y Meneses's prose. Another of Fletcher's plays, *Rule a Wife and Have a Wife,* partially based, as noted earlier, on a Cervantes novella, was not refashioned but still played surprisingly often, at least 388 times between 1659 and 1800. Also popular in North America, it played in New York's New Theatre on 15 December 1806, and again on 26 April 1809, with another performance on 18 November 1812 (*Early American Playbills*).

In England in the nineteenth century, the Spanish War of Independence intensified interest in "things Spanish," and volumes dedicated to the history of Spain and Portugal, as well as soldiers' and travelers' accounts, letters, journals, and other observations, poured from the pens of prominent figures, from Wellington to Byron. While the war and military adventure were the subject of many narratives, there began to appear folkloric sketches of the country, its character, peoples, and "typical" costumes, along with other highly colored accounts that served to rekindle an interest in the literature of the Golden Age.

The first half of the nineteenth century saw the publication of no fewer than a dozen collections of plays, many of which included old favorites of the Restoration and early eighteenth century no longer performed, making these plays available to the reader. Tuke's venerable *The Adventures of Five Hours* was included in *The Ancient British Drama* (3 vols, 1810) and Robert Dodsley's *Select Collection of Old Plays* (12 vols, 1825–7, 1st ed. 1744). Cibber's *She Would And She Would Not* appeared in Elizabeth Inchbald's *The British Theatre; or a Collection of Plays which Are Acted at the Theatres Royal, Drury Lane, Covent Garden and Haymarket* (25 vols, 1808). And Centlivre's *The Wonder, or A Woman Keeps a Secret* was anthologized three times, in The *British Drama. A Collection of the Most Approved Tragedies, Comedies, Operas, and Farces* (2 vols, 1824–6), in Richard Cumberland's *The British Drama: a Collection of the Most Esteemed Dramatic Productions* (14 vols, 1817), and in Inchbald's *The British Theatre*.

These collections give evidence of an abiding interest in Spanish themes and plots, but the plays themselves are at best distant reflections of their sources. Over the course of the nineteenth century, British writers, from Romantics to Victorians, turned their attention increasingly from those earlier adaptations to new translations of original Spanish literature, favoring the prose of Cervantes and the poetry of Calderón.

Not surprisingly, *La vida es sueño* was repeatedly translated, but so was *El mágico prodigioso*, both four times.[37] Lord Holland (Henry Richard Vassall Fox) and Thomas and Fanny Holcroft translated almost a dozen plays of Calderón between them, along with an occasional work by Lope and Solís. In 1805, *The Theatrical Recorder* published two Holcroft translations, *From Bad to Worse* (Calderón's *Peor está que estaba*) and *Father Outwitted* (*El padre engañado*, attributed to Lope). Two years later, Lord Holland brought

---

[37] For nineteenth-century translations from the Spanish, see O'Brien and Pane.

to press three English versions of Calderón plays: *The Fairy Lady* (*La dama duende*), *Keep Your Own Secret* (*Nadie fíe su secreto*), and *One Fool Makes Many* (*Un bobo hace ciento*). Enamored of Calderón, as a "sort of Shakespeare," Shelley translated portions of plays, notably *El mágico prodigioso,* more for the poetry than the plot. Published in *Posthumous Poems* (1824), and edited by Mary Wollstonecraft Shelley, his versions of Calderón, as we shall see, proved to be inspirational to at least one important translator of the nineteenth century.

English interest in Calderón was complemented by the German Romantics, principal among them Augustus Wilhelm Schlegel. In his famous *Lectures on Dramatic Art and Literature* (1809–11), Schlegel brought Calderón to the attention of his countrymen, which has been interpreted by some as an act of "discovery"; however, given the unabated presence of the works – in translation or adaptation – of the Spanish dramatist on the English-speaking stage, it would seem that he had never been lost to the English. Frederick de Armas speculates that since John Black's translation of Schlegel appeared the same year as George Henry Lewes's *The Spanish Drama. Lope de Vega and Calderón* (1846), it is possible that Black's translation could have influenced Lewes, whose ideas of Spanish drama were initially favorable, but were later more critical.[38] Edward Byles Cowell, a contemporary of Lewes and an orientalist at Cambridge University, also became interested in Calderón, although for him, the Spaniard's "hot southern blood" aligned the dramatist with Arabic thinkers and Indian poets. Although Cowell does not devote much attention to *La vida es sueño*, he evidently had read it, as he refers to it being "well translated in the third volume of the 'Monthly Chronicle,'"[39] and stresses the philosophical nature of the work as well as the importance of the central metaphor (de Armas 49–52). As a mentor, Cowell would pass along his interest in Persian and Spanish literatures to Edward Fitzgerald, who produced both a famous adaptation of *The Rubáiyát of Omar Khayyám* and translations of Calderón.

Fitzgerald and Denis Florence MacCarthy, the century's two principal translators, worked between 1853 and 1877. Both favored Calderón, although each approached him in different fashions. Fitzgerald, a friend of Tennyson, wrote very free translations in an attempt to make Calderón interesting to English readers, while MacCarthy, in his five volumes of Calderón plays (eleven *comedias* and three *autos*), tried to keep the meaning and the meter of the original as much as possible, sustaining that the latter was indispen-

---

[38] F. de Armas 44, 59n14. De Armas provides a thorough overview of the reception of Calderón in Victorian England. For a comprehensive treatment of the reception of Calderón in Germany and the Low Countries, see Sullivan, *German Lands.*

[39] Perhaps Cowell was referring to a translation by John Exenford in *The Monthly Magazine* published in 1842, as cited by Pane.

sable for true enjoyment of the works. MacCarthy's attention was first drawn to Calderón by a passage in one of Shelley's essays, and from then on the interpretation of the "Spanish Shakespeare" absorbed his time and directed his talents. The first volume of his translations, containing six plays, appeared in 1853, followed by further installments in 1861, 1867, 1870, and 1873. Calderón was more widely read through Fitzgerald than MacCarthy, however, possibly because according to José de Armas, his versions were more in accord with the taste of the time (154). Although they were meant for readers and not actors, the translations of both Fitzgerald and MacCarthy served to keep Calderón, if not the wealth of Spanish drama, in the public consciousness.

In sharp contrast to the British familiarity with (and periodic contempt for) Spain resulting from the constant contact of the two countries, Americans' knowledge of Spain was remote at best, although the romantic stereotypes of castles and adventure, mixed with the *leyenda negra*, kindled the imagination of many. Significant interest was awakened indirectly, in fact, through allusions to Spain in the poetry of Byron, held to be one of the "exactly four" great living English poets at the time (González-Gerth 259). As well, the affinity Americans felt for the Spanish War of Independence and concern about the French occupation of Spain (1808–13) drew attention to independence efforts of Spain's American colonies, further coloring the dark side of the view that North Americans held of Spain. Because American travel to Spain came slowly, and was not substantial until the latter half of the century, knowledge of the country was limited to maps and accounts of those few who had made the voyage. Principal among these was Washington Irving who, having lived and written in Spain, inspired the American reading public, although the common opinion of Spain was mostly based upon the English notion. While Spain in the Old World was a "far-away land of [...] romantic dreams," Spain in the New World was a land of tyranny, bigotry, and backwardness that fascinated and repelled the nineteenth-century American (González-Gerth 264). Although general interest in Spanish culture was high, American translations of the literature of Spain were few, and were mostly of poetry.

Those few renderings into English of *comedias* that appeared were intended for the reader rather than the theatrical company. In his compendium Elijah Clarence Hills lists forty-nine translations in the US of twenty-five *comedias* between 1800 and 1919: thirty-two translations of twenty-five plays by Calderón; five of five plays by Lope de Vega; five of four plays by Cervantes; two of one play by Moreto and two of one play by Lope de Rueda; and one translation of one play each by Rojas Zorrilla, Solís and Torres Naharro (97).[40]

---

[40] In comparison, contemporary Spanish plays were translated more frequently in the US, with a total of fifty translations of forty-two plays; most popular were the works of Eche-

Although British and American translations in the nineteenth century were primarily of works by Calderón, in the twentieth century translators on both sides of the Atlantic increasingly turned their interest to other major playwrights as well. By the eighth decade, a number of new versions had appeared, most of them done by academics and seemingly destined for students of comparative literature. As one might expect, the works most frequently translated were the canonical *La vida es sueño* and *Fuenteovejuna*, but they did not stand alone. Joining them in collections and anthologies were such works as Tirso's *The Trickster of Seville*, Lope's *Peribáñez* and *Justice without Revenge* (*El castigo sin venganza*), and Calderón's *Devotion to the Cross* (*La devoción de la cruz*), *Secret Vengeance for Secret Insult* (*A secreto agravio, secreta venganza*), and *The Phantom Lady* (*La dama duende*). As for actual stagings, there were occasional university performances, but professional productions were few and far between, in marked contrast with what was happening at the time in Germany and Russia.[41] Calderón's *El alcalde de Zalamea* was mounted in Chicago in 1917,[42] his *Los cabellos de Absalón* was staged at the Phoenix Theatre in London in 1931 in a version by I. Lamdan entitled *The Crown of David*, Lope's *Fuenteovejuna* was put on by a few left-wing theatre groups in the 1930s and, famously, by Joan Littlewood and her troupe at the Theatre Royal, Stratford East, in 1955, and every now and then there was a production of *Life Is a Dream*. But that is almost the entire record.[43]

Why that is so has been the subject of speculation. One important factor, certainly, was the absence of truly actable contemporary translations or adaptations. Another, perhaps, was the notion that Golden Age theatre was about honor and religion, and little else, and therefore could not conceivably appeal to the taste of modern British and American audiences. Possibly, also, as Dawn Smith has suggested, there were lingering effects from the *leyenda negra*, a generalized negative feeling that was aggravated by images coming out of Francoist Spain ("Teatro clásico" 300). Finally, one might postulate that directors and producers in the English-speaking countries had no particular incentive to delve into Spanish theatre, or any other variety of foreign

garay (fourteen translations of eight plays), Benavente (eleven translations of eleven plays), the Alvarez Quinteros (six translations of six plays) and Pérez Galdós (four translations of three plays) (Hills 99).

41   See Sullivan (*German Lands*), Franzbach, Siliunas, Turkevich, Weiner, and Tietz.

42   Speaking of this staging, Nicholson in 1939 notes that it was the only professional production in the US since the beginning of the twentieth century. She quotes the reviewer for the *Chicago Tribune* as saying that "this production is not merely the exhibition of a fine archaism in drama that will appeal to scholars only; it has the native strength and fire of the popular theater" (144).

43   Mention should perhaps be made of *A Bond Honoured*, John Osborne's very free, and considerably truncated, adaptation of Lope's *La fianza satisfecha*, produced by the National Theatre at the Old Vic in London in 1966.

theatre, because, after the mid-century mark, so much interesting work was being done by playwrights in their own lands.

In England, for example, the 1960s and 1970s saw the blossoming of fringe theatre, and both fringe and main stages mounted the works of such fertile and challenging contemporary playwrights as Pinter, Stoppard, Bond, and Hare, works that Greg Giesakam, in a review of Richard Allen Cave's *New British Drama in Performance on the London Stage, 1970–1985*, characterizes as:

> [...] literate, sophisticated, full of nuance and ambiguity and intellectually teasing, but in ways which are resolvable – plays that depart, to a degree, from standard naturalism and contain elements of controlled theatricality but are still broadly susceptible to analyses of the characters' lives and psychologies and employ the classic English style of acting, centered on delivery and character development. (413)

Perhaps the emphasis on character development and the introspective English style of acting prevented directors from thinking about theatre from "Other" cultures, keeping their attention inwardly focused.

Whatever the reasons for the neglect of Spanish theatre throughout much of the twentieth century, the fact is that as the century drew to a close, what had been indifference began to turn into active interest on the part of theatre professionals. And just as the indifference is not easy to explain, neither is the new interest. One factor, at least as regards Great Britain, is that the steady stream of challenging new plays by Pinter and his contemporaries gave signs of drying up,[44] with the result that directors started to look to other cultures for ideas and perspectives. Helping to encourage this turn outward, as Smith suggests, was the United Kingdom's entry into the European Economic Community, for membership in the EEC resulted in more attention to Britain's continental neighbors and greater possibilities for travel to those countries. One increasingly popular destination for travelers, not just those from Great Britain but from the United States as well, was Spain, which, free at last of the stigma attached to Francoism, could now be regarded with fresh eyes.

However one explains it, there is no doubt that as the twenty-first century approached, professional theatre companies once again began to take a genuine interest in the *Comedia*, commissioning new translations and searching for ways to stage classical plays that would respect the ideas and

---

[44] Playwright David Edgar wrote in 1991 that "from 1970 to 1985 new plays were about 12% of the regional main house repertoire. In the past five years the proportion has dropped to 7%. There has been a shift of writerly energy from theatre to the novel and film. [...] For the first time since 1956 there is a whole generation of talent and young British directors who affect little or no attachment to the production of new work" (quoted in Wandor 4).

values embedded in them while at the same time making them accessible and relevant to spectators of today. The critical year in the rediscovery of Spanish classical drama by professional companies in the English-speaking world was, as one might suppose, 1981. That year marked the tercentenary of the death of Calderón, and the event was memorialized on both sides of the Atlantic. Leading the way was the Intar theatre of New York with its June staging of *Life Is a Dream*, in a very free adaptation made by the production's director, Maria Irene Fornes. The production revealed some of the traps that lie in wait for those who would attempt to trim the ideology of older works in order to make them appeal to modern sensibilities. Although Mel Gussow, the reviewer for the *New York Times*, was respectful, and took pains to praise the work as "a seventeenth century classic with modern overtones," he objected strenuously to the liberties that Fornes had taken with the text that had resulted in a completely different ending.

A more adventurous choice of play, and a more consequential production, was the staging of *The Mayor of Zalamea* by the National Theatre – now the Royal National Theatre – in July of 1981. That work, which was performed in a new, specially commissioned verse adaptation by the well-known poet and playwright Adrian Mitchell and directed by Michael Bogdanov, was widely acclaimed. Michael Billington in the *Guardian*, for example, praised Bogdanov's "on-rushing, bare-stage production," and described Calderón's play as a "fast, exciting, incident-packed drama" with "plenty of moral complexity." "If there is a problem with the play today," he continued, putting his finger directly on an issue that would raise itself in so many turn-of-the-century productions, "it is making a modern British audience [and North American, he might have added] accept the premium the Spanish place on honour and virginity."

Later in the fall of 1981, the Milwaukee Repertory Theater made an even more daring choice than the National Theatre when it mounted a production of *Secret Injury, Secret Revenge* (*A secreto agravio, secreta venganza*) as its contribution to the observation of the Calderón tercentenary. Employing an adaptation by Amlin Gray, and directed by René Buch, the work achieved a surprising success, partly because Buch faced head on the tests that it presents for American spectators and actors. The chief difficulty, of course, has to do once again with the demands of honor, here presented in even more alienating fashion than in *The Mayor of Zalamea*. Buch's solution to the challenge, as revealed in a subsequent interview, was to show the code as functioning like "any tyrannical absolute. The values of the individual are in conflict with the values of the system" (Giles 42).

In the fall of 1983 *Life's a Dream* received another professional staging, this one by the Royal Shakespeare Company at The Other Place in Stratford-upon-Avon. The production was greeted with rapture by a host of critics. The normally severe Nicholas de Jongh in the *Guardian*, for example, called the

work "astounding, a complete revelation," while the ever astute Michael Billington wrote in the same paper that *Life's a Dream* is "a powerful humanist
work that argues man must triumph over both fate and the chaotic flux of
existence and accept moral responsibility." Voicing a sentiment that would be
heard many times in the future, he added that "it is as relevant today as when
it was written."

The excellent adaptation used for the production resulted from a collaboration between Adrian Mitchell and the play's director, John Barton, and,
not surprisingly, it was to be employed in a number of other stagings in the
future. Critiquing one of those, Jackie Fletcher wrote in the on-line *British
Theatre Guide* that:

> It used to be said of John Barton that he chewed razor-blades for breakfast.
> While this might refer to his directorial style, as an ancient Cambridge
> academic and associate director of the RSC, Barton knows his stuff when
> it comes to the drama of the period. Mitchell, always a most lyrical poet
> in terms of language, was an apt co-translator. This is a very fine text, the
> language flows like honey; it caresses your ears and effortlessly seduces
> you into listening and wanting more.

Mitchell, working as he had before from a literal version supplied by
Gwenda Pandolfi, was also the translator/adaptor of the next important
production of the 1980s, Lope's *Fuente Ovejuna*. Chosen by the National
Theatre for its 1988–9 season, it too, like *Life Is a Dream*, proved to be a
revelation. Part of the reason was the exceptionally dynamic direction of
Declan Donnellan, which was recognized by an Olivier Award for Special
Achievement. Another part was the power of Mitchell's words, employed
here, as in *The Mayor of Zalamea* and *Life's a Dream*, in the service of what
Dawn Smith has called his "radical populist ideology" ("Teatro clásico" 304).
And, of course, part of the reason was the inherent quality of Lope's play,
a magnificent work that has the capacity to appeal to modern sensibility
more easily than others because of its less problematic presentation of the
honor theme. The reaction of the critic for the *Evening Standard* to work,
production, and adaptation was typical of the critical reception at the time.
"*Fuente Ovejuna*," he wrote, "is a great play by a great writer, and in Declan
Donnellan's directorial debut at the National Theatre it has been graced by a
production of monumental qualities. [...] This inspiring play, in a robust new
version by Adrian Mitchell, affirms the power of love over brutality [...]."
Audiences at the National Theatre during the 1988–9 season were apparently in agreement with the critics, because they voted *Fuente Ovejuna* their
favorite production of the year.

Curiously, the very positive reception accorded the National Theatre's
staging of *Fuente Ovejuna* in 1988–9 does not seem to have led to further

professional productions in Great Britain in subsequent years. In the United States, however, there were several, including one presented by the highly regarded Berkeley Repertory Theatre in the fall of 1990 and another by the National Asian American Theatre Company in New York City in 2002. This last production was particularly noteworthy for its transcultural implications, for it was presented by a company staffed by Asian-American actors, directors, designers, and technicians. The production utilized a translation/adaptation by Mia Katigbak and was directed by David Herskovits who, according to Una Chaudhuri, the critic of the *Village Voice*, created a "performance style that [recalled] without reproducing, forms of folk theater, children's theater, even puppetry." The result was a staging that was both highly entertaining and thought-provoking, encouraging the audience to find contemporary relevance in Lope's classic work.[45]

While *Fuente Ovejuna* was proving its enduring viability in the productions just noted, *La vida es sueño*, as mentioned earlier, continued to demonstrate that it had an appeal for companies in the English-speaking world that could not be matched by any other work of the Golden Age. In the final years of the twentieth century it was produced numerous times by professional groups both in the United States and in Great Britain, utilizing a variety of directorial approaches and a nearly equal variety of translations. In the US, in addition to several stagings in New York City, there were productions in Cambridge, Philadelphia, Denver, Hartford, Chicago, and Stockbridge, Massachusetts. And, in the UK, in addition to a number of productions in London, there were others in Leeds and Edinburgh. Many of these productions deserve comment, but because of constraints of space we will note here just a few.

One that deserves particular mention is the presentation of Calderón's masterpiece by the American Repertory Theatre in Cambridge, Massachusetts, in 1989. The translation used in this instance was that of Edwin Honig, and the direction was by Anne Bogart, whose production was highly stylized, with restricted movement, angular gestures, and a minimal set. Her conception was generally lauded, with critics such as Kevin Kelly in the *Boston Globe* and David Pasto in *Theatre Journal* once again noting the contemporary relevance of the themes of the play.

Bogart may have brought a modern sensibility to her staging of *Life Is a Dream*, but her approach could not be described as particularly daring. Daring, however, is precisely the word for the conception of the Catalan director Calixto Bieito, first realized in a production of John Clifford's fluid adaptation that was mounted by the Royal Lyceum Theatre Company for the

---

[45] As we write this, we have just learned that the Stratford Shakespeare Festival in Stratford, Ontario will mount a production of *Fuente Ovejuna* in its 2008 season, utilizing a new translation by Laurence Boswell, and directed by Boswell.

Edinburgh Festival in 1998. That production later traveled to both London and New York, and was subsequently incorporated into a version in the original Spanish seen in Barcelona, Madrid, and Almagro. The action of the play took place in and around a circular cinder-track, over which hung a giant tilted mirror in which the spectators could see reflections both of the actors, dressed in modern clothes, and of themselves. What was truly revolutionary about the production, however, was not the manner in which the stage was set and the actors costumed, but its graphic violence and sexuality. As might be expected, the staging provoked mixed reactions in the various venues where it played, but the critics were, by and large, fascinated. Michael Billington in the *Guardian,* for example, found the production to be "sensational," while Ben Brantley in the *New York Times* pronounced it "vivid," "engrossing," and "transfixing." All, once again, commented on the modernity of the work.

It would be wrong to suggest here that only the most canonical Spanish works were being offered to English-speaking audiences in the final decades of the twentieth century, and the early 1990s in particular were notable as a time of considerable expansion of the repertory. Spearheading that effort was the small, but prestigious, Gate Theatre in London. Indeed, between 1990 and 1992 the Gate presented no fewer than seven British premières – four plays by Lope de Vega, two by Tirso de Molina, and one by Calderón. Those works are as follows: in the spring of 1990, Lope's *Punishment without Revenge (El castigo sin venganza)*; in late fall of 1990, Tirso's *Don Gil of the Green Britches (Don Gil de las calzas verdes)*; in the fall of 1991, Lope's *The Gentleman from Olmedo (El caballero de Olmedo)*, Calderón's *Three Judgments in One (Las tres justicias en una)*, and Tirso's *Damned for Despair (El condenado por desconfiado)*; and, finally, in the winter of 1992, Lope's *Madness in Valencia (Los locos de Valencia)* and his *The Great Pretenders (Lo fingido verdadero)*. The whole group of plays was deservedly recognized by an Olivier Award for Special Achievement in 1992. Clearly, much of the credit was due to Laurence Boswell who was Associate Director of the Gate in the early 1990s, and who several years later held the same position at the RSC where, in 2004, he was primarily responsible for the extremely successful season of Spanish plays.

We shall shortly turn to that season, which constituted another important phase in the discovery of Golden Age plays by professional companies in the English-speaking world. In the meantime, we must cite a few other less canonical works that found their way to the stage as the century drew to a close. One of these was Calderón's *Schism in England (La cisma de Ingalaterra)*, which, in John Clifford's translation, was produced by the National Theatre during its 1987, 1988, and 1989 seasons. Another was *The Doctor of Honour (El médico de su honra)*, presented in another translation by John Clifford by the celebrated Cheek by Jowl company in 1989. Still another was *The Last Days of Don Juan*, Nick Dear's title for his adaptation of *El burlador de Sevilla*, a play that, rather surprisingly, has had difficulty securing its proper place in the English-speaking world. Mounted by the Royal Shakespeare Company in the Swan Theatre in Stratford-upon-Avon in 1990, and directed by Danny Boyle, the production apparently failed to argue convincingly for the merits of Tirso's play. And, finally, we should mention *The Painter of Dishonour* (*El pintor de su deshonra*), put on by the Royal Shakespeare Company at The Other Place in Stratford, in 1995. Translated by David Johnston and Laurence Boswell, and directed by Boswell, it was a production that did indeed do honor to the work on which it was based.[46]

The arrival of the new millennium in 2000 brought an interesting new development in the modern staging of *comedias* in the English-speaking world. Whereas previously the works presented had been of the more serious sort – tragicomedies, histories, melodramas – now comedies themselves began to be discovered, as they had been during the Restoration, and this happened initially in the United States. The person most responsible for this expansion of the repertory in North America is, without a doubt, Dakin Matthews, who undertook to provide a series of translations notable for their wit, their fluidity, and their fidelity to the metrical schemes of the original texts. Most of these were later brought to vivid life on the stage under the direction of Anne McNaughten.

The first of Matthews's translations was of Alarcón's *The Walls Have Ears* (*Las paredes oyen*), but the first to be professionally staged was, apparently, the same author's *The Truth Can't Be Trusted, or The Liar*, from *La verdad sospechosa*. Mounted in February 2000, by the Antaeus Company in North Hollywood, a company of which Matthews was co-founder, the staging was said to be a "delight" by ShowMag.com, an on-line entertainment magazine, with the translation, the cast, and the direction by McNaughten all singled out for praise. Several weeks later the production played at the Chamizal Siglo de Oro Drama Festival in El Paso, Texas, where it was similarly well received.

In the fall of that same year, another professional company, Writers' Theatre of Glencoe, Illinois, presented another of Matthews's translations, *Spite for Spite*, from Moreto's *El desdén con el desdén*, in a staging directed by Michael Halberstam that was showered with encomiums by the critics for both local and national publications. Rupert Christiansen in *The Chicago Tribune* called the play "a gem," and Hedy Weiss in the *Sun Times* raved about Matthews's "sparklingly witty, blithely contemporary translation," Halberstam's "meticulous staging," and the "splendid" acting of the "effervescent cast."

Three and a half years later, another company in North Hollywood, Andak, founded by Matthews and McNaughten, also presented *Spite for*

---

[46] See Fischer, "Historicizing."

*Spite*, and that production, subsequently seen at the Chamizal Festival, generated similar enthusiasm, with Rob Kendt in the *Los Angeles Times* calling the play "a screwball confection as light as it is tasty." In the meantime, in January 2002, Antaeus had introduced *The Proof of the Promise* (*La prueba de las promesas*), the third of Matthews's translations of Alarcón. Like the Matthews/McNaughten productions of *The Liar* and *Spite for Spite*, it too subsequently played at the Chamizal Festival.

At about the same time that Antaeus, Andak, and the Writers' Theatre were making a persuasive case for the comedies of Alarcón and Moreto, the Pearl Theatre in New York was making its own case for Calderón's *La dama duende* in the eloquent translation of Edwin Honig entitled *The Phantom Lady*. Although Calderón's play, utilizing the same translation, had been presented by SoHo Rep in 1989, it failed then to garner much attention. When Pearl's production opened in December, 2001, however, the critics applauded enthusiastically, and audiences flocked to attend. Interestingly, the reviewers focused on what they regarded as the work's subversive aspects. Thus, David Lohrey on CurtainUp.com wrote that "the playwright succeeds in undermining oppressive social conventions," while in the *New York Times*, D. J. R. Bruckner commented that "the play's free-thinking, skeptical mockery of social customs and its celebration of women who ignore them are so modern that it is difficult to believe that it was written by a Spanish courtier before 1630."

Interestingly, professional companies in Great Britain were somewhat slower than companies in the United States to discover the delights of the Golden Age comedies. All that was to change in 2004, however, when the Royal Shakespeare Company included productions in English of Lope's *El perro del hortelano* and Sor Juana's *Los empeños de una casa* in its season of Spanish *comedias* at the Swan Theatre in Stratford-upon-Avon. Although stagings of the other two plays that made up the season – English versions of Tirso's *La venganza de Tamar* (*Tamar's Revenge*)[47] and Cervantes's *Pedro de Urdemalas* – were not, with some exceptions, well regarded by the critics, *The Dog in the Manger* and *House of Desires*, as the two comedies were called, absolutely bowled the reviewers over. Thus, for Michael Billington in the *Guardian*, Laurence Boswell's production of Lope's play in David Johnston's translation amounted to a "dazzling evening," while Susannah Clapp in the *Observer* found it nothing short of "glorious." As for *House of Desires*, while Billington had reservations about the play itself, he highly approved

---

[47] An earlier translation of Tirso's play by Paul Whitworth, *The Rape of Tamar*, was staged at the Lyric Hammersmith Studio Theatre in London in 1992. The production, directed by Whitworth, who also played the role of King David, was apparently well received.

of Catherine Boyle's "sparky translation," Nancy Meckler's "exuberant" and "festive" production, and the "fine" ensemble that brought it to life, including a "knockout performance" by Simon Trinder as Castaño, the *gracioso*.

The fact that professional companies were discovering the fun to be had with Spanish romantic comedies in the new millennium does not mean that they were neglecting the more serious plays. Productions of *Life Is a Dream*, for example, continued to abound, with stagings in such far-flung places as Ashland, Oregon; Costa Mesa, California; Oklahoma City; Chicago; Atlanta; New York City; London; and Sydney, Australia. *The Mayor of Zalamea* was produced twice more, once by the Southend Shakespeare Company in London, in a new adaptation by Jean Black, and once by the Everyman Theatre in Liverpool, which used Adrian Mitchell's adaptation. The latter production, directed by Gemma Bodinetz, was particularly well received. The review of "Nariz Azul" on bbc.co.uk began with the declaration that "[t]his is quite simply a play that has everything," and continued with praise for the adaptation, the direction, and the "superb" teamwork of the cast. In *The Independent* of London, Lynne Walker was equally enthusiastic, calling attention to the "fascinating clashes in class, code, and creed," the "astute" direction, the "brilliant" work of Mitchell, and the "engaging and characterful performances."

Gratifyingly, two of Lope's best plays, *The Gentleman from Olmedo* and *Peribáñez*, were also given renewed attention in the last few years. The former, as mentioned earlier, had been presented by the Gate Theatre in 1991. Utilizing the same translation, that of David Johnston, the Watermill Theatre in Newbury, England, reintroduced it in 2004. Lyn Gardner in the *Guardian* called the production "very much a class act," praising in particular John-ston's translation, which she called "splendid," and the direction by Jonathan Munby, which she said allowed "the streaks of light and dark, laughter and desolation [to be] played to perfection."

As for *Peribáñez*, although it had been put on by the Marlowe Society in England in 1997, its first fully professional staging took place at the Young Vic in 2003. Employing a new prose translation by Tanya Ronder and directed in modern dress by Rufus Norris, the production was, by and large, received with enthusiasm, despite – or perhaps because of – the fact that, like Intar's staging of *Life Is a Dream* in 1981 and some others that we have discussed, it gave a less than accurate impression of the original work. The modifica-tions made were, once again, in the interest of softening the presentation of the honor theme, as Susan Fischer has shown in a recent article ("Staging Lope"). Thus, Casilda's expression of approval of her husband's act of venge-ance at the end of the play was completely eliminated, and the bloody deed itself was shown as if executed in a fit of psychopathic jealousy rather than as the result of a calculated defense of matrimonial honor. Interestingly, not all who saw the performances were convinced that the changes made were for the better. James Fenton, for example, wrote in the *Guardian* that "I felt on reflection that director and translator had been over-afraid of contemporary moral squeamishness," that "a certain amount of moral clean-up had taken place. Making the text playable is one thing. Making it entirely acceptable is another."

An indication that interest in Spanish Golden Age theatre is now spreading beyond the shores of the British Isles and North America is the fact that in the summer of 2006, Company B in Sydney, Australia, also undertook to stage Ronder's translation of *Peribáñez*. Directed by Neil Armfield, the production, like that of the Young Vic, received excellent reviews. Aleksei Wechter, for example, writing for *SydneyStageOnline*, summed up his reactions as follows: "Vega's writing, like Shakespeare, remains relevant today as the themes explored are universal and the story is engaging. Add to this Company B's contemporary production values, an exceptionally skilled cast and crew and you're in for a treat."

Finally, we should mention two very recent professional productions. The first is Andak's staging of Tirso's *El burlador* in Dakin Matthews's rhyming verse translation, which he has entitled *Don Juan, The Trickster of Seville*. The production, directed by Anne McNaughten, was first presented at the NewPlace Studio Theatre in North Hollywood in January 2006, and two months later it was presented again at the Chamizal Festival in El Paso. The other production is Washington Women in Theater's staging of *Friendship Betrayed*, Catherine Larson's prose translation of María de Zayas's *La traición en la amistad*. The performances, which were directed by Karen Berman, took place at the Warehouse Theater in Washington, D. C., in the summer of 2006, and again in October, in connection with a conference sponsored jointly by the Association for Hispanic Classical Theater and the Asociación de Escritoras de España y las Américas (now named Grupo de Estudios sobre la Mujer en España y las Américas).

Looking back, two important and simultaneous developments facilitated the reemergence of the Spanish *Comedia* in English in the early 1980s. First of all, companies began increasingly to look beyond Shakespeare for classical theatre productions, as witnessed by a series of small-scale stagings of contemporaries of the Bard. Second, in commemoration of the three hundredth anniversary of the death of Calderón, translations were mounted by important companies both in the US and in Great Britain. After 1990, the *Comedia* entered the terrain of both popular and experimental theatre, with productions of plays beyond the usual two or three, some rarely if ever seen even in Spain. Translators and adapters turned their talents to versions destined for performance as opposed to textual study.

Dawn Smith's observation in 1995 was indeed prescient: "[H]a habido un gran cambio de actitud: la comedia áurea española ya no es una simple curiosidad para cultos, sino que aporta algo nuevo y apasionante al panorama teatral británico de hoy" ("There has been a great change in attitude: the Golden Age Spanish *Comedia* is no longer simply a curiosity for intellectuals; rather it brings something new and exciting to the panorama of British theatre of today") (309). Nonetheless, the *Comedia* is still an exception in the lineup of any professional theatre's classical repertoire. Whereas Molière is sure to show up, a Spanish work is still a relative rarity on the British stage and even more so on the American stage. In addition to the general challenge of relevance and actuality of any four-hundred-year-old play, modern producers still face the particular challenge presented by the exoticism of the Spanish code of honor present in so many *comedias*. Honor is, as Anthony Giles observes, "the aspect that most critics, including Spanish ones, have objected to. [...] If Golden Age drama is regarded as embarrassing and anachronistic even by Spaniards, it is hardly likely to be a welcome addition to the American repertoire" (42).

Don Marcus, the artistic co-director of the Ark Theatre in New York, confessed in an interview that before the Ark's 1985 production of *Life Is a Dream*, he could not remember having read the play: "Maybe I didn't do my assignment that week in college" (Giles 15). Apparently he was not alone. If most reading lists include, in all probability, the two standard *comedias* and a handful of others at most, missing class for one week can obliterate the genre altogether. Despite the efforts of translators to increase the repertoire of English-speaking theatre companies, the *Comedia* is still a *rara avis*. The sheer vastness of the number of plays on the one hand, and the zero-sum nature of the classical theatrical canon on the other, means that although more plays are translated and "discovered," they are not necessarily studied or read, much less anthologized.

What is it about a classical Spanish play that might captivate a translator, director, actor, or spectator? The plot presented the original appeal for Restoration playwrights and their audiences, and it would be disingenuous to suppose that plots are not still primary among the attractions of Spanish theatre for today's, but themes can also be a powerful draw. In some cases a drama might be in touch with a prevailing ideology or taste, despite or perhaps because of its concomitant timelessness or universality. Dawn Smith observes that what attracted Adrian Mitchell to the *Comedia* was what he saw as a common theme running thoughout: popular resistance to oppression; it is no surprise that Mitchell's translations have been of works by Lope and Calderón that exemplify this. Furthermore, as noted earlier, his versions reflect his own radical populist ideology, itself current in Great Britain of the 1980s ("Teatro" 304). The National Theatre production of *Fuente Ovejuna*, directed by Declan Donnellan, was praised by Richard Eyre as "one of the most thoroughly truthful productions of a classical play that I have ever seen. It was entirely true to itself, to its period, to its inherent meaning, while at the same time being in the present tense" (Smith, "Teatro" 305n11). Clearly,

Mitchell met the challenge of communicating the actuality and relevance of Lope's work in this appealing staging.

Repeated modern productions testify to the draw of *Life Is a Dream*, despite the fact that it had not been one of the most appreciated of Calderón's plays until the nineteenth century. What makes the play so appealing to modern audiences is not the paciness of the "Spanish plot." As one reviewer commented, "*Life is a Dream* embraces most of the plot and character permutations of Renaissance drama, but the text has such dignity, the metaphysical pity is so appealing, that one has to take it all seriously" (Fletcher). Rare in a production review, the focus on the language of the performance points to a fundamental question, the *sine qua non* of production – the playtext.

Certainly the success of recent English-language productions of the *Comedia* must be due in part to the increasing number of playable translations and adaptations aimed at performance, not at literal or close translation, versions of the originals capable of attracting and engaging modern audiences. Penned by poets and veterans of the theatre with a keen sense of stagecraft and poetry in their own right, these translations or adaptations attempt to make the work livelier, more animated, and more vigorous, in order to attract and involve the interest of modern audiences.

Clearly, the nature and purpose of the translations themselves become essential. There is still a distinction evident between more "literal" and academic translations destined for anthologies or critical editions, and translations/adaptations made for performance, that is, between reader-oriented and performance-oriented texts.[48] "On the page," as David Ritchie comments, "a play is fixed, permanent, spatially arranged, and access to it is conceptual; on the stage a play is fluid, ephemeral, primarily temporally arranged and access to it is physical" (quoted in Santoyo 97). Some modern theorists of translation, such as Susan Bassnett, suggest that a direct and "faithful" translation of a play should not necessarily be undertaken with performance as a prime factor; instead, the translator must function within the linguistic structures of the text itself: "For after all, it is only within the written that the performable can be encoded and there are infinite performance decodings possible in any playtext. The written text [. . .] is the raw material on which the translator has to work and it is with the written text, rather than with a hypothetical performance, that the translator must begin" (102).

Nevertheless, as Bassnett observes, the "co-operative translation [...] produces probably the best results [for performance]. It involves the collaboration of at least two people on the making of the TL text – either an SL and a

---

48 A case in point is G. Minter's translation of *Don Gil of the Green Breeches* [parallel text edition meant for academics and comparatists] and the version contained in *Two Plays: Damned for Despair, Don Gil of the Green Breeches*, translated and adapted by Laurence Boswell, Jonathan Thacker, and Deirdre McKenna, an adaptation made for performance.

TL native speaker, or someone with knowledge of the SL who works together with the director and/or actors who are to present the work" (91). This method mirrors the collaboration that is the essence of theatrical production, although it would be difficult to imagine any translation, no matter its initial aim, that would not be "worked on" by the company that brings it to life on the stage. For a production to be an unqualified success, such as Donnellan's *Fuente Ovejuna*, it must ring true to the ear of the English-speaking audience, due in large part to the excellence of the translation. In stark contrast to this production, the Royal Shakespeare Company's *The Last Days of Don Juan* in 1990 used Nick Dear's prose translation/adaptation, which some reviewers characterized as needing the hand of an English-language editor, and which Smith described as "bastante sosa" ("fairly bland") vacillating "torpemente entre el lenguaje del siglo XVII y el actual" ("awkwardly between seventeenth-century and present-day language") ("Teatro" 305).

Any translation, whether destined to remain "on the page" or "on the stage," whether penned by poets and veterans of the theatre with a keen sense of stagecraft and poetry, or by academics with a profound knowledge of and respect for the language of the source text, will inevitably be different from the original and must lose some of its essence. Choices must be made: whether to highlight the polymetry or the plot in a translation, whether to attempt a recreation of the original or to contemporize for the modern audience.

But in truth, few performance reviews mention the quality of the translation of the play they evaluate, unless it is by a well-known writer. This is surprising, given that playtexts are by definition and of necessity based on language, and the choices made by the translator will provide keys to the expression and interpretation of any performance. The varying approaches to translation yield vastly differing results that cannot be divorced from the productions that employ them. While the performance script must spark interest in a modern audience, if it deviates too much from the original, does it cease to be a *comedia*? Is there a hierarchy of fidelity, with literal translation on a higher rung than adaptation? A literal translation can communicate the nuances and complexities of the original, but not always in a way that can be spoken trippingly on the tongue. On the other hand, an adaptation made from a literal translation can elide those same nuances and complexities, making it difficult for the director or performers to appreciate and communicate them to the audience at all. Happily, a director working in close consultation with a translator, or even in some cases, a director who has been the translator, can bring extraordinary insights to light.

The paradox of the translation of the *Comedia* into English is that it must serve two masters: textual scholarship and performance. For a performance to be successful, the literary scholar must first make the text known and understood, and it is then up to the translator to convey it in a form that speaks to the contemporary generation of readers or spectators. Michael McGaha has articulated the qualities of the ideal translator of the *Comedia*: he or she should have absolute control of both languages as well as practical experience in the theatre, and should be both a poet and an excellent literary critic. While most who approach the task can claim several of these qualifications, few can claim them all. When performances of the *Comedia* in English are successful, typically they are the last in a series of stages, involving several different hands. First, the literary scholar fixes the text and makes it known to and understood by the literal translator, who provides a basis for the adapter, who then conveys it in a form that speaks to the contemporary generation of readers or spectators. It is ultimately the public – however limited – that will decide if the play becomes popular. For those scholars who lament the general ignorance of both critics and public alike, the question of translation versus adaptation seems at once crucial and beside the point. We doubt that Lope would think twice about it.

# TRANSLATING AND ADAPTING THE *COMEDIA*

# Translating *Comedias* into English Verse for Modern Audiences

First of all, a brief disclaimer. There are a number of things about which I can claim to be moderately knowledgeable; unfortunately, Spanish language and literature are not two of them. So everything I say here must be taken with that caveat. I wish it were not so; I believe the theatre of the Golden Age deserves a more knowledgeable translator than I am, certainly one with greater fluency than I have in either classical or modern Spanish. Nonetheless, I have undertaken to translate plays from this period, not so much out of a confidence in my own abilities, as out of a recognition that almost no one else was doing what cried out to be done: to offer playable English scripts to American theatres for production. Yet the question remains: who am I to be doing this? And this brings me to the two areas where I am knowledgeable, which I hope will mitigate, though never entirely excuse, my obvious weaknesses.

As an English professor, specializing in Shakespeare and dramatic literature, I am fairly knowledgeable about the general state and conventions of sixteenth- and seventeenth-century theatre – in the British Isles and elsewhere. With a second specialization in language and rhetoric, I am fairly knowledgeable about early modern syntax and early modern rhetorical principles and practices, which were fairly standard across the continent in the sixteenth and seventeenth centuries. And with a third specialization in prosody, I have a pretty good grasp of English verse form, especially of dramatic verse form, which is a narrower and very specific type of poetry.

Second, as an actor, playwright, and director, I have a pretty good understanding of characterization (especially as it is suggested by language); of the practical dynamics of dramatic structure (basically, "actability" – what makes a play actually work or not work on stage); and of, for lack of a better word, "speakability" (what kind of stage language meets the sometimes contrary demands of stylishness and naturalness that classical verse plays for modern audiences often make on the actors).

The initial question, of course, is how one should translate verse from one language to another. I started, as it were, backwards. Since playability was my prime interest and English was to be the language of performance, my first rule was that the verse must work on the stage for English speakers and listeners. Therefore, whatever verse forms I came up with had to assist rather then hinder communication between actor and audience. I felt they needed not only to sound natural to the ear, but also to sound appropriate to the character, the situation, and the overall dramaturgical and poetic experience of the play.

So there was the initial dilemma, the dilemma all cross-cultural translators face: how to be faithful to an "exotic" original and at the same time deliver it to the audience in as familiar a fashion as possible. Not that I believe that audiences do not sometimes prefer exoticism, or that one should dilute or suppress the exoticism of every original in favor of familiarity and palatability. Rather, my point is twofold: (1) Spanish audiences of the Siglo de Oro did not experience *comedias* as particularly exotic – unless of course the subject matter was exotic; and since my chief goal is to recreate that experience for an English-speaking audience, familiarity should normally trump exoticism; and (2) most plays are meant to feel like immediate experiences, yet paradoxically that effect is achieved by the mediation of theatrical conventions. So conventions – and verse is, after all, a convention – are adopted or erected not to make the playgoing experience more difficult, but more manageable: to facilitate it. Sometimes a play erects its own conventions, or at least some of them, on the fly – as in, for example, "When I step off this platform or when the light shifts into a bluer spectrum, I am reliving a memory." But most audiences, ancient and modern alike, enter a theatre already aware and accepting, at some level, of a whole gamut of shared conventions – artifices, as it were, or shortcuts or frames – by means of which they allow themselves to experience a "play" as somehow "real."

So here are some of the questions I asked myself about verse:

First, should I translate the play into English rhyming verse? To this, my answer was, from the beginning, yes.

Second, should the audience always experience the play as verse? Believe it or not, this is a distinct question, and the answer is not immediately obvious.

Take the question of assonance, for example, so common in the *romance* runs in *comedias*.[1] English, with its embarrassing and confusing multiplicity of vowel sounds – compared to the scarcity and purity of vowel sounds in Spanish – is so unsuited to extended assonating as perhaps to make the effort self-defeating. If, for example, I were to translate a *romance* run into purely

---

[1]   My discussion of Spanish verse forms throughout this essay is based on the thorough and concise analysis found in Martel and Alpern's *Diez Comedias* (xxv–xxix).

syllabic verse, and if by some miracle I could assonate the even-numbered lines, not many members of the audience would even hear the verse, being denied the two nearly essential markers of verse-recognition for the English ear: meter and rhyme. Or if they did, since the English ear is not particularly keen at counting syllables on the fly, it would have to be done by: (1) artificially intoning the language (as is common for many contemporary oral presenters of "free verse"), which would probably destroy any illusion of characterization or dramatic reality; or (2) stopping at the end of virtually every line to mark the line length; and/or (3) so severely limiting word choice for the even-numbered line-ends (to achieve actual assonance) that monotony of sound and phrase length would soon defeat any possible aesthetic experience of the language as verse.

Or, for another example, take the common experience today of listening to a Shakespeare play. I realize this sounds like heresy, but only occasionally – and then almost always because of rhyme – does the audience actually hear the play as verse. Because of the dense imagery or elevated rhetoric or archaic syntax or exotic word order (or the occasionally sounded "-èd"), they may think they hear the "blank verse," when what they are mostly hearing is the "poetry" – and even then it is sometimes only because they've been told it is "poetry." The vast majority of listeners will not actually hear the "verse." And, of course, most audiences will leave *Merry Wives* or *Much Ado* convinced they've heard nothing *but* verse, when in fact they have heard very little.

This is not simply due to the prosodic unsophistication of the average audience member; it is due instead to the peculiarities and subtleties of Shakespeare's blank verse in all but the earliest plays. His ongoing experiments testing the boundaries of meter resulted in a very flexible kind of verse – one that, I think, works emotionally and subliminally on the audience, rather than obviously. (I would offer as examples of "obvious verse" Shakespeare's own early rhyming verse experiments in *The Comedy of Errors* or *Love's Labor's Lost*, or, more recently, the magisterial rhyming translations of Molière by Richard Wilbur.) To put it another way, I believe it is possible that English dramatic verse – by which I mean the artificial configuration of stresses in a line (meter) and occasionally of lines into stanzas (verse form), and the artificial replication of sounds in and across lines (rhyme or alliteration or assonance) – may be part of the audience's experience of a play without being at every moment part of their conscious experience of the play *as* verse.

My conclusion, after a fair amount of thought and practice was that, yes, the audience should experience the play as verse – but that I would try to control that experience in such a way that the verse did not become too distancing, too obvious, or too monotonous.

The "distancing" I was trying to avoid was both "archaism" and "artificiality." In other words, I would try to make my verse sound "contemporary" – since for the original audience it *was* contemporary – and "natural" – unless of course the Spanish was itself meant to sound "artificial." The major reason for doing this was that this was to be, after all, *dramatic* verse and therefore must at some level be believable as conversation with others (dialogue) or with oneself (soliloquy). And, as I felt it would be a mistake to limit oneself to seventeenth-century diction or syntax, similarly I felt it would be a mistake to limit oneself in verse form. I was trying to translate into the native tongue and prosodic conventions of my listeners, not into the native tongue and prosodic conventions of their seventeenth-century English or American counterparts.

The "obviousness" I was trying to avoid was an over-reliance on strict meters and strict rhymes that would call too much attention to the verse as *verse*, when what I wanted the audience to attend to was the dramatic language – whether dialogue or soliloquy – as *versed speech*. A factor in this decision was the recognition that for Siglo de Oro audiences, all stage speech was versed, whereas for modern audiences, very little is. Thus, any play that presents itself in verse will sound, to the modern ear, automatically highly artificial – *unless* that verse has a naturalness and subtlety about it that minimizes the obvious artificiality.

The "monotony" I was hoping to avoid is that lying in ambush for any writer of English dramatic verse who is determined to write in rhyme. In heavily inflected languages like Spanish, rhyme is an almost natural phenomenon because of the similarity of endings in so many declensions and conjugations. (Assonance is likewise much easier to accomplish.) In a minimally inflected language like English, with its dizzying multiplicity of vowel sounds and virtual absence of noun declensions and paucity of verb conjugations, rhyme is much harder to come by naturally – unless one favors a heavily Latinate vocabulary, which will inevitably become numbing itself, no matter how clever the rhymes are.

Third, given my commitment to write in rhyming verse and to have the audience experience the play – at some level – as verse, what kind of verse should I attempt?

This question further resolved itself, for me, into two parts: (1) what kind of English rhyming verse would best avoid the traps of artificiality, obviousness, and monotony; and (2) what relation should there be between the English verse and the Spanish verse?

My answer to the first question was swift: if I were to write in rhyme, I would choose generally not to write in strict meter – that, is in the accentual-syllabic meter that is the mainstay of traditional English verse, the meter that counts both stresses and syllables, and follows predictable patterns of stress alternation. These patterns may be challenged, in the best poet's hands, by the counterpointing rhythms of reversals and substitutions, but the patterns remain strong and predictable nonetheless. Nor would I write in the purely syllabic verse favored by the Siglo de Oro writers; the English ear, I felt, simply cannot hear syllabic verse as verse; it wants meter and rhythm. So I would choose instead the looser (and older) accentual verse, in which only the stresses are counted, with the number of unstresses accompanying the stresses being more or less at the discretion of the versifier. (This is a venerable verse form from Old and Middle English, though it generally includes – as my version does not – a midline break in a four-foot line and strong alliteration on the stressed syllables.)

One of the main reasons for minimizing the strict, especially iambic, meter was that so much of the *Comedia* is written in octosyllabic lines, for which a four-foot English line would be an obvious equivalent. But that very line – iambic tetrameter – has an unfortunate tendency to drop into doggerel very quickly, especially when the rhymes become chiming and predictable. The looser, swinging rhythm of an accentual four-foot line, especially when the rhymes are not pounded home, reduces the tendency toward trotting monotony. An added advantage of the accentual verse form is that, if so desired, one may transform it at any moment – in any individual line or over a run of lines – into an accentual-syllabic form simply by limiting the unstressed syllables to one per stress. Another, perhaps more obvious, reason for not requiring strict meters in the English translation – especially of the shorter stanzas – is that the octosyllabic line, the most common one in the *comedias*, is itself not strictly metrical; there is no strong repeating rhythm, just the required number of syllables.

My answer to the second part of the question – the relationship between the Spanish and the English verse forms – was complex.

(1) As much as possible, the polymetry of the original should be honored, if not replicated. In other words, as a general rule, when the meter and/or rhyme scheme of the original changes, so should the meter and/or rhyme scheme of the translation, and for the same reasons. (This of course assumes both a more or less line-for-line correspondence between the original and the translation and an ability to identify the reason for the change.)

(2) The stanzaic forms and line lengths should echo as much as possible the stanzaic forms and line lengths of the original. In a perfect world, the stanzaic *effect* of the translation should capture the stanzaic *effect* of the original as well – that is, when the original uses a strict form, like the sonnet or the *décima*, the translation should both adhere to that form *and* achieve the same effect of concentration and formality as the original. Or, to take another example, the final clinch rhyme of a quatrain should be as effective in English as in Spanish. But when the original uses a loose form like the *romance* – popular, for example, for extended narrations – then a similarly loose form in English, one appropriate for storytelling, should also be used.

(3) When the original has no obvious parallel in English – like the *romance*

– then the English verse form should be as flexible as the original. And ideally, all *romance* verses should be translated into the same English verse form.

(4) On the rare occasions that the Spanish uses something like blank verse or rhyming couplets, the equivalent English forms should be used.

(5) Then, in order to avoid the possible monotony of these various rhyming verse forms – even with as flexible a meter as purely accentual verse – I decided to make a more generous use than the Spanish writers did of enjambment (run-on lines) and caesuras (mid-line breaks). The effect, in most places, was to downplay the rhyming by varying the phrase lengths and burying a substantial number of rhymes in the middle of syntactical units rather than at the ends, where the ear would pick them up more easily.

(6) I took the further liberty, especially in the comic verse, of using the mid-word rhyme: in other words, I allowed myself occasionally to rhyme hyphenated half-words at the ends of lines. (And I took the even further liberty at times of hyphenating them in questionable ways to achieve the rhyme.)

(7) The result of all these choices is what I have since categorized as "stealth rhyme." The effect is that while virtually the entire play is indeed rhymed, for long runs of lines the audience may be aware of the rhyming only subliminally. But when I want the rhymes to be heard clearly – usually to clinch a point or construct an aphorism, or to highlight one of the more formal stanzas, either for comic or serious effect – I will make the meter approach the more recognizable accentual-syllabic and place the rhymes at the ends of phrases where they can be heard to chime. Thus the "rhyming verse moments" will stand out, as it were, against the background, not of prose but of other, less obvious "stealth rhymes" – like the gold threads woven into a tapestry or the gold leaf in an already colorfully illuminated manuscript.

Well, on to the verse forms themselves – or as I have written for the Acting Edition of Alarcón's *La prueba de las promesas* (*The Proof of the Promise*): "The proof of the pudding is in the eating; / The proof of the promise is in the keeping."[2]

---

    2   I used multiple editions of the Spanish texts when working on my translations. For ease of citation, the Spanish texts reproduced in this article are drawn from the following sources: Ruiz de Alarcón, Juan. All plays. Electronic texts on the AHCT website (http://www.comedias. org/textlist.html); Moreto, Agustín. *El desdén con el desdén*. Electronic text on the AHCT website; Tirso de Molina. *El burlador de Sevilla*. Electronic text on the AHCT website; *El burlador de Sevilla*. Ed. James A. Parr (when noted).

## The *Redondilla*

A *redondilla* is a four-line stanza of octosyllabic lines rhyming *abba*; it often makes up fifty percent of a *comedia*'s verses. To render it in English, I have generally used an *abba* quatrain of accentual tetrameters. When the content or style of the quatrain – or the string of quatrains – in Spanish struck me as formal or aphoristic or particularly poetic, or when it was appropriate to the character or the situation, I have kept the meter fairly iambic by restricting the unstressed odd syllables to one per foot. For comic or narrative or more conversational *redondillas*, I have allowed myself greater flexibility in the number of unstressed syllables in the line. For example, from *El burlador* (or *Don Juan, The Trickster of Seville* in my translation):

| | |
|---|---|
| How did you get in this mess with her? | ¿Cómo estás de aquesta suerte? |
| Tell me quickly, what did you do? | Dime presto lo que ha sido. |
| By God, I ought to run you through, | ¡Desobediente, atrevido! |
| you brazen, disobedient cur! (57–60) | Estoy por darte la muerte. (57–60) |

With the traditional elision and expansion, the Spanish is a regular octosyllabic *redondilla*. The English has a perfectly iambic third line; but the other three, through reversals and additional unstressed syllables, are looser, less regular. The translation is, like the original, end-stopped; but it is also loose, including a swapping of the third and fourth lines – both to achieve the rhyme and to place the emphasis on the strong word "cur." It may be worth noting that with end-stopped *redondillas* like this one, it is sometimes possible to turn the translated quatrain inside out and achieve virtually the same effect. Thus:

Tell me quickly, what did you do?
How did you get in this mess with her?
You brazen, disobedient cur!
By God, I ought to run you through.

I would categorize this *redondilla* as a pretty fair sample of the commonest type of translation I use in my versions.

A second *redondilla* example, again from my *Don Juan*, shows two different things: first, that the accentual tetrameters can be transformed into almost perfect iambics when necessary or appropriate; and second, that run-ons, instead of end-stopped lines, can be used to create different effects; the run-ons in the first stanza can take a pair of English *redondillas* – and quite poetic ones at that – and mold them into a two-stanza profession of faith in which the rhymes are hidden in the first stanza and grow increasingly chiming in the second purposely to create the same climactic build that appears in the Spanish:

Tisbea, give us an order, part
those rosy lips and issue your
commands to those that so adore
you with the idolatry of the heart,
 that they will fly at your desire,
cross hill and plain, unquestioningly,
to dig the earth or plow the sea,
or cleave the wind or tread on fire.
(645–52)

Di lo que mandas, Tisbea,
que por labios de clavel
no lo habrás mandado a aquél
que idolatrarte desea,
 apenas, cuando al momento
sin reservar en llano o sierra,
surque el mar, tale la tierra,
pise el fuego, el aire, el viento.
(645–52)

## The *Romance* and the *Romancillo*

The *romance* and the *romancillo*, because they are not stanzaic and are assonated rather than rhymed, present a different challenge to the English translator – especially since they account for so much of the typical *comedia* – typically thirty to sixty percent of the total. These octosyllabic and hexa-syllabic forms that assonate on the even-numbered lines – for long runs of sometimes two hundred lines or more – have no obvious English equivalent. Traditional blank verse will probably not do because pentameters would be too long for either, and because unrhymed metrical or accentual verse of any length would fail to display the virtuosity of these long runs of assonance. But assonance is almost unhearable by the English ear and perhaps unachiev-able by the English poet without damaging the aesthetic experience – or at least I found it so.

My current practice is to use either loose or strict ballad form – tetram-eter quatrains rhyming on the even-numbered lines (*abcb*) and, for tighter rhyming, on the odd-numbered lines as well (*abab)*. Here is an example of each, one loose and one tight, both from *The Walls Have Ears*:

What good are all these lame excuses,
These fabrications and these flights
Of fancy – when the simple truth
Alone your filthy tongue indicts?
It didn't bother you at all
To speak of me so maliciously,
And now you're bothered that someone else
Reported your insults back to me?
(1742–9)

¿Qué sirven falsas excusas,
qué quimeras, qué invenciones,
donde la misma verdad,
acusa tu lengua torpe?
Hablas tú tan mal de mí
sin que contigo te enojes,
¿y enójaste con quien pudo
contarme tus sinrazones?
(1742–9)

A man who's freshly come to Court
An heir new-made, a neophyte,
A ship just venturing from port,
A fledgling on his maiden flight,
A man who in the eyes of the King,

Hombre que a la corte viene
recién heredado y mozo
– pájaro que estrena el viento
nave que se arroja al golfo –
que a los ojos de su rey

| | |
|---|---|
| And in the eyes of the people, too, | y a los populares ojos, |
| Dare not seem weak in anything, | ni debe mostrar flaqueza |
| Nor yet can hide himself from view, | ni puede esconder el rostro, |
| A man unused to sail, depends | ha de regir sus acciones |
| On guides experienced at sea, | por los expertos pilotos, |
| Who care for him like his own friends, | obligados, por parientes; |
| Are bound to him like family [...] | por amigos, cuidadosos [...] |
| (808–19) | (808–19) |

But I am not religious in this practice. In my second translation, of *La verdad sospechosa* (*The Truth Can't Be Trusted or, The Liar*), I used heroic couplets (*AA BB CC*, etc.) for Don García's first big lie (the fictional "dinner on the Manzanares" [665–748]), tight ballads (*abab*) for his second big lie (being caught in "Sancha's" bedroom [1524–1711]), and loose ballads (*abcb*) for his third big lie (the "duel" with Don Juan de Sosa [2718–73]).

| | |
|---|---|
| There in a thicket, deep and dark, amid | Entre las opacas sombras |
| The high and overshadowing elms was hid | y opacidades espesas |
| A secret clearing, black as the face of night, | que el soto formaba de olmos |
| In which there stood a table, clean and bright | y la noche de tinieblas, |
| [...]                                    (665–8) | se ocultaba una cuadrada, |
| | limpia y olorosa mesa [...] |
| | (665–70) |

| | |
|---|---|
| There lives in Salamanca, sir, | En Salamanca, señor, |
| A gentleman of noble fame | hay un caballero noble, |
| And family. His forebears were | de quien es la alcuña Herrera |
| Herreras, Don Pedro is his name. | y don Pedro el propio nombre. |
| Heaven has given him a daughter, | A éste dio el cielo otro cielo |
| A second heaven, with suns for eyes | por hija, pues, con dos soles |
| And cheeks as rosy as the water | sus dos purpúreas mejillas |
| On the horizon at sunrise. | hacen claros horizontes. |
| (1524–31) | (1524–31) |

| | |
|---|---|
| In the early evening, at St. Blaise, | A las siete de la tarde |
| Promptly at seven o'clock, he wrote, | me escribió que me aguardaba |
| Don Juan de Sosa will wait for me, | en San Blas don Juan de Sosa |
| To discuss a matter of some note. | para un caso de importancia. |
| Because it was a duel, I said | Callé, por ser desafío, |
| Nothing. A man would only speak | que quiere, el que no lo calla, |
| If he wanted to be stopped or helped – | que le estorben o le ayuden, |
| Two things that only a coward would seek! | cobardes acciones ambas. |
| (2718–25) | (2718–25) |

The gradual degradation of form was meant to capture the increasing frenzy of García's lying.

More recently, I have stayed with the loose and tight ballad forms, preferring the tight – and moving closer to pure iambics – when the speech seemed
more formal. There was one instance, for example, in *La verdad sospechosa*
where Alarcón swapped assonating vowels in the middle of a run (at line
1524 in my translation); the previous conversation was in *e–o* assonance, and
then shifted to *o–e* for the lying soliloquy. At that point, to mark the change,
I shifted from loose to strict ballad rhyme.

And at times, when it was possible and appropriate, I have carried the
same rhyme beyond a single quatrain, creating a little more of the continuous
effect of the *romance*. At other times, though it was not common Spanish
practice, I have used a couplet to close a long *romance* run, especially when
the number of lines was not divisible by four and I had two leftover lines to
deal with. The experience of such closing couplets is not unfamiliar to the
English-speaking theatre-going audience.

## The Quintilla

The *quintilla* is a five-line octosyllabic stanza rhyming a variety of ways, but
only rarely ending with a couplet. Thus *aabba* or *ababa* or *abaab* or *abbab* are
all common, while *abbaa* and *ababb* are rare. (There are, in fact, some of the
rare couplets in the passages cited below.) The *quintilla* is not a particularly
frequent verse form. In *El burlador* it occurs in three runs, totaling only 135
of the play's 2,870 lines, or about five percent. In the four other plays I have
translated, it accounts for about seven percent in *La prueba de las promesas*,
five percent in *La verdad sospechosa*, three percent in *El desdén con el desdén*
(*Spite for Spite*), and does not even occur in *Las paredes oyen*.

I have used a five-line accentual tetrameter to translate the *quintilla*,
favoring the iambic in those cases where I found the poet treating it as a
somewhat stricter form than the *redondilla*. In my early efforts, I did not
necessarily follow the exact rhyming sequences of the original; indeed, I
occasionally allowed myself the rare couplet at the end when I felt it was
appropriate. In my later efforts, I have been more rigorous in following the
poet's original sequences and in avoiding the couplets.

For an example of mostly iambic – and highly rhetorical – *quintillas*, I
offer this from my *Don Juan*:

| | |
|---|---|
| As sure as there are fish in the sea | Como es verdad que en los vientos |
| as sure as there are birds in the air, | hay aves, en el mar peces, |
| as all creation everywhere | que participan a veces |
| of all four elements must be | de todos cuatro elementos; |
| composed, as there is loyalty | como en la gloria hay contentos, |
|    in friends and treachery in foes, |    lealtad en el buen amigo, |

| as happiness is sure to those | traición en el enemigo, |
| who come to glory, as sure as night | en la noche oscuridad, |
| is black, as sure as day is light, | y en el día claridad, |
| so sure the truth I here disclose. | y así es verdad lo que digo. |
| (345–54) | (345–54) |

But the Siglo de Oro poets are not always so formal with their *quintillas*; often they use them in conversational passages – like *redondillas* – even splitting lines between characters. In those cases I have tended to be more colloquial and loose in my translation, as, for example, in this exchange at the wedding feast in Dos Hermanas from *El burlador:*

GASENO.    Hey! lunch is served inside, let's go!
        Perhaps you'd like to take a mo-
        ment's rest, your excellency?
        (*DON JUAN takes the bride's hand.*)
DON JUAN.   Why try to hide it?
AMINTA.         It belongs to me.
GASENO.    Start up the music, a song there, ho!
DON JUAN.   (*To CATALINÓN*) Did you say something?
CATALINÓN.        Just worried 'bout how
        these rubes could give me an ugly death.
DON JUAN.   Her hands, her eyes, her sugar breath,
        they set me aflame – I'm on fire now!
CATALINÓN.  Go on, just brand the poor little cow
        and put her out to pasture with the other three!
DON JUAN.   Let's go inside – they're watching me.
BATRICIO.   A nobleman where I get wed –
        what rotten luck!
GASENO.        Sing up!
BATRICIO.         I'm dead.
CATALINÓN.  They'll sing and then they'll weep, you'll see.
        (1813–28)

Compare with the following from Parr, with changes from other texts:

GASENO.    Ea, vamos a almorzar,
        porque pueda descansar
        un rato su señoría.
        (*Tómale don JUAN la mano a la novia.*)
JUAN.      ¿Por qué la escondéis?
AMINTA.        Es mía.
GASENO.    Ea, volved a cantar.
JUAN.      ¿Qué dices tú?
CATALINÓN.        ¿Yo? Que temo
        muerte vil de esos villanos.

JUAN.                Buenos ojos, blancas manos,
                     en ello me abraso y quemo.
CATALINÓN.           Almagrar y echar a extremo;
                     con ésta cuatro serán.
JUAN.                Ven, que mirándome están.
BATRICIO.            ¿En mis bodas caballero?
                     ¡Mal agüero!
GASENO.                              Cantad.
BATRICIO.                                      Muero.
CATALINÓN.           Canten, que ellos llorarán.
                                     (1783–97)

There are a number of things about this passage that can give the reader
further clues to my translating methods. First, since in the case of *El burlador*
there are two quite different versions, each with some claim to primacy, I have
felt free occasionally to conflate versions of the Spanish – cherry-picking,
as it were, what I thought were the most playable elements of each. (The
result, unfortunately, is a lack of coordination between my lineation and that
of either copytext.) Some texts, for example, read Aminta's first response as
"No es mía"; others read "Es mía." Either makes sense, I think. I could just
as easily have written, and in an acting version, I could very well give the
actors the additional choice of:

JUAN.          Why hide it?
AMINTA.                                  It doesn't belong to me.

In one version, Aminta is more self-assured and in control of her fate ("I
can do what I want with my hand"); in the other, she is more the good little
wife who accepts the fact that she belongs to her husband ("It's not mine to
give any more").

Second, because translating into rhyme is a strenuous exercise, sometimes compromises need to be made. In this case, I found it necessary to
add a phrase not in the Spanish ("her sugar breath") to meet the challenging
demands of the *quintilla* rhyme scheme. This will happen often, especially
in the more complex schemes; and what is demanded of the translator is that
it not happen randomly or unnecessarily, and that the added words be either
neutral or natural to the context. (In this case, I was fortunate to find an
appropriately amorous phrase from *The Merchant of Venice*.)

Third, sometimes the tetrameter can be pushed to the limits – especially
for comic effect in English – by the addition of extra unstressed syllables,
but the actor must be particularly sensitive to this. Catalinón's exasperated
surrender ("Almagrar y echar a extremo; / con ésta cuatro serán") I have
expanded and reworked into: "Go on, just brand the poor little cow / and put
her out to pasture with the other three!" The second line thus not only rewords

the joke while retaining the essential meaning ("With her, there'll be four"), but also requires careful stressing so that it remains a very loose tetrameter ("and PUT her – or put HER – out to PASTure with the O-ther THREE!") instead of expanding into a lame hexameter ("and PUT her OUT to PASTure WITH the O-ther THREE!") And doing this, interestingly enough, reverses the prosody of the original – which has a neat eight syllables in the punch line, but requires quite a bit of elision in the set-up line to keep it octosyllabic. Of such compromises are translations made.

## The Tercet

The tercet, roughly equivalent to Dante's *terza rima,* though not a frequent verse form in the plays I have translated, is one of the most challenging. It is composed of running stanzas of three eleven-syllable lines; yet the rhyme scheme bridges stanzas, the middle rhyme of each tercet becoming the first and third of the next, until the passage is finished with an alternately rhyming quatrain. To translate it, I have used mostly iambic pentameters rhyming *ABA, BCB,* etc.

Tirso does not use it in *El burlador.* In *Las paredes oyen,* Alarcón never uses it; in *La verdad sospechosa,* only once (2976–3048); in *La prueba de las promesas,* he again uses it only once (1859–925) – both times for serious conversations among men. Moreto uses it similarly for male conversations in *El desdén con el desdén* (1986–2067).

I found this form to be one of the hardest to translate because the rhymes are woven braid-like through the entire passage. Here's a brief sample:

| | |
|---|---|
| Señor, what's this? What kind of man are you, | Señor, ¿qué es esto? ¿Qué desigualdades |
| To show such unbecoming fickleness | muestras en tus pasiones, siendo indinas |
| Of passion, such vacillation as you do? | de un heróico varón las variedades? |
| First you're inflamed by Blanca's blessed loveliness, and then you douse the fire | Yo te vi ya abrasar por las divinas partes de Blanca, y ya tu amor bañado |
| Of love in Lethe's cool forgetfulness, | del Lete en las corrientes cristalinas; |
| And now, just when our great and noble Sire | y agora, cuando en el feliz estado |
| Has made you Councillor of Castille, approving you in everything you could desire, | de excelso presidente de Castilla el rey con justo acuerdo te ha ocupado |
| Just when I thought that this last sliver of | con que entendí que la postrera astilla |
| The dart from Cupid's bow was finally clear – | de la flecha amorosa despidieras, |
| Ambition leaves no time for tender love – | pues la ambición no sabe consentilla, |
| I find your former suff'rings reappear, | hallo que convalecen tus primeras |

| | |
|---|---|
| And marvel how your ashes – once so cool – | penas, y miro tus cenizas frías |
| Burst into flames that singe the highest sphere. | llamas brotar que abrasan las esferas. |
| (1859–73) | (1861–75) |

## The Longer Stanzaic Forms

The sestet (*sextilla*, lyric strophe), octave (*octava*, rhyme royal), *décima*, and sonnet all appear in the five plays I have translated; and all – being stricter forms than the ones so far examined – seem to require a more formal approach in translation, both in prosody and in tone.

Alarcón, perhaps the least lyrical of the three poets I have worked with thus far, uses them the least – except for the *décima*, which he uses to great effect, I think, for love letters, wooings, and conversations about love in *Las paredes oyen*. In Act II (1398–1577), for example, the reading of Mendo's ambiguous and somewhat stilted love letter (two *décimas* long) is followed by conversations between Lucrecia and Ana and then Celia and Ana that continue quite cleverly and sometimes colloquially in *décimas* for another hundred and fifty lines, as the disillusioned Ana, with Celia's prodding, takes the first critical steps in the transfer of her affections from Mendo to Juan.

The formality of the octave, or rhyme royal, is used in *El burlador* to emphasize (the appropriately named) Octavio's immaturity and pompousness. After an almost Shakespearean run of essentially blank verse (*endecasílabos sueltos* closed with a couplet) that opens Act II, an outraged Octavio enters spouting formal *octavas*, forcing the King to respond equally formally (1094–1125), though we know from the previous exchange he is in no mood for polite conversation.

The sestet is essentially a lyric form, mixing long and short lines in an *aBaBcC* scheme. It is used for the most poetic passages – which (as Shakespeare notes) could also be the most feigning – such as Mendo's wooing of Ana in *Las paredes* (446–523). More seriously, Tirso uses it in *El burlador* for a shift of tone and to great emotional effect in the extended seaside lamentings of Isabela and Tisbea in Act III:

| | |
|---|---|
| ISABELLA. Why do you complain, | ISABELA. ¿Por qué del mar te quejas |
|   sweet fishergirl, so prettily against the sea? |   tan tiernamente, hermosa pescadora? |
| TISBEA. A thousand times complain! | TISBEA. Al mar formo mil quejas. |
|   If you see something in its cruelty |   Dichosa vos, que en su tormento agora |
|   to laugh at, more blest you! |   de él os estáis riendo! |
| ISAB. Against the sea I was complaining too! | ISAB. También quejas del mar estoy |
| |   haciendo. |
| Where are you from? |   ¿De dónde sois? |
| TISBEA.      From where | TISBEA.      De aquellas |
|   the wind has whipped the fishers' huts and |   cabañas que miráis del viento heridas, |
|     made | |

| | |
|---|---|
| such desolation there | tan victorioso entre ellas, |
| that you can see their humble walls decayed, | cuyas pobres paredes, desparcidas, |
| and in their ruins, hoards | van en pedazos graves, |
| of birds build nests among the shattered | dándole mil graznidos a las aves. |
| boards. | |
| (2198–2209) | (2198–2209) |

The sonnet – octet/sestet as in the Italian form – is, as Lope notes, best for reflection – especially a crucial reflection made before a change of heart as in Moreto's *El desdén con el desdén*, when Diana assesses the alteration of her affections in Act III:

| | |
|---|---|
| My heart in flames? I can't believe it's true. | ¿Fuego en mi corazón? No, no lo creo; |
| What can there be in a marble heart for fire | siendo de mármol. ¿En mi pecho helado |
| To feed on? In a breast of ice? Thou liar, | pudo encenderse? No, miente el cuidado; |
| Coward. Yet can I doubt what's clear to view? | pero, ¿cómo lo dudo si lo veo? |
| The only conquest I aspired to | Yo deseé vencer, por mi trofeo, |
| Was over cold disdain. Yet higher and higher | un desdén; pues si es quien me ha abrasado |
| He fans the flames of love. The gates of desire | fuego de amor, ¿qué mucho que haya entrado |
| Once opened, who knows what things may enter through? | donde abrieron las puertas al deseo? |
| I never saw the danger, I'm to blame. | De este peligro no advertí el indicio, |
| I set a fire against my neighbor's walls | pues para echar el fuego en otra casa |
| And saw the sparks from it set mine aflame. | yo le encendí, y en la mía hizo su oficio. |
| Then wonder not, my soul, what thee befalls. | No admire, pues, mi pecho lo que pasa; |
| Since he who builds a bonfire in the street, | que quien quiere encender un edificio |
| Is usually the first to feel the heat. | suele ser el primero que se abrasa |
| (2553–66) | (2553–66) |

However, even the sonnet is not immune to ironic treatment, as in *The Walls Have Ears*, when Juan's aching lament of his unsatisfied hunger for Ana's love is finished by Beltrán's comic coda, echoing the rhymes of the sestet, on his own inability to get a decent meal in Juan's service (317–33). Or for another example, at the end of Act II of *The Proof of the Promise*, after Lucía articulates what women look for in a lover, Tristán responds with a humorous sonnet of his own, sarcastically rejecting her explanation (1831–58).

## The Songs

A number of songs appear in the five plays I have translated – the most in *El desdén* and *El burlador*; and in both cases, the playwrights have integrated them beautifully into the story. As a general rule, I try to mimic the verse form of the originals, most often with simple quatrains of alternating tetrameter/trimeter lines, rhyming on the even numbered lines. Some songs, however, are more complex – like the *seguidillas* in the Muleteers' "Song of Viveros Inn" in the second act of *The Walls Have Ears* (1902–20). The translation of songs is controlled as well by other factors than rhythm and sense; the melody requires that certain notes and their accompanying syllables be sustainable, so "quantity" – or length of syllable – becomes an added concern.

## Some Conclusions

Granted that my experience with Siglo de Oro *comedias* has been limited, yet I still think there are lessons to be drawn from my attempts to translate them into English.

First, I think I was right (and lucky) intuitively to insist on rhyming verse in the translation – even though at the time I had no right to do so and, more frighteningly, no reason to think it was even possible. I am more convinced than ever that verse and rhyme are at the heart of the *Comedia* experience, and that it is not only possible but necessary for translators to take that rhyming verse seriously and to try to capture both its form and its effect in any translation.

Furthermore, there is a difference between "verse" and "poetry," and a play in verse is not all in poetry. Certain verse forms – primarily the *redondilla* and the *romance*, even with their rhymes and assonances – can lend themselves to an easy, relaxed, at times even colloquial stage speech that can sound completely natural in English and is only slightly elevated above prose. Other more rigorous verse forms – like complex inter-rhymed stanzas – require a more poetic treatment, especially if, in the Spanish original, the tone and diction are also elevated.

However, at least in the plays I translated, the "poetic" sections, those whose elevated diction, richer figures of speech, and sometimes more complex prosody demand similar effects in English, are more often than not likely to be parodic or of questionable veracity. In other words, more often than not, when characters shift into "poetry" they are likely to be literally lapsing into lies. For every *serious* "purple passage" – like the description of Lisbon in *El burlador* – there are as many or more poetical feignings, like the elaborate narrative lies that Pedro manufactures to fool the King and Octavio, both of which are elaborately introduced poetical *romance* runs after simpler *redondillas* (125–51; 279–314). Octavio's response and Don Pedro's final assurance to Octavio (cited above) are set in rather elegant *décimas*: Octavio's are overwrought and foolish and Pedro's, elegant and deceiving. And Juan's occasionally beautiful wooings – which also require poetic translation – are of course simply lies. García's fabrications in *La verdad* are probably the most poetic elements of that play. Mendo's lies and love letters in *Las paredes* are similarly only "poetic" maneuvers to win a lady, as is Carlos's elegant but lying praise of Cintia in *El desdén*. (Admittedly, I chose five plays relatively untouched by the excesses of *culteranismo*; still I think it is safe to say that these poets' serious use of the more elegant poetic forms and more elevated poetic diction is minimal. More often than not they are used for comic or ironic effect.)

Finally, while the exact tone and effect of each verse form, and the allied effect of switching between them in the course of a scene, may not be as narrowly identifiable as Lope would have us believe in his "New Art of Writing Plays," nonetheless it is undeniable that translating these plays without paying close attention to their verse forms and without making a real effort to reproduce them – or at least something like their effect upon the audience – is to do these great *comedias*, and these poets, and our modern audiences, a real disservice.

# Translating the Polymetric *Comedia* for Performance (with Special Reference to Lope de Vega's Sonnets)

## VICTOR DIXON

At this time, when performers and public alike are increasingly aware of and receptive to the immense diversity of theatre, historically and geographically, when both increasingly value *difference*, it seems opportune to reexamine, with a view to their translation and presentation today, the distinctive nature of the plays produced by seventeenth-century Spain, comparatively few of which have been seen as yet on the English-speaking stage.

The huge quantity of those plays, and the high quality of many, were determined very largely by the demands of an extremely varied audience drawn from the whole of society, from all but its lowest, least lettered ranks to its loftiest and most cultured. Its royalty, nobility, and clergy, moreover, as well as attending the public theatres and often themselves commissioning plays, saw command performances at court. As with cinema and television today, that audience expected a constant stream of new works, especially three-act *comedias*, so that all imaginable subjects had to be grist to the playwrights' mill, including many never thought suitable for dramatization before. It wanted, like all audiences, to be told an engaging story (which meant, broadly, a unified action). But Spaniards expected so far as possible to see a whole one enacted, not merely a crisis whose antecedents and aftermath were narrated or foreseen. In defiance (when need be) of the other unities, this usually meant shifts of place and/or time. By emptying the stage, bringing on other characters and assisting the imagination with references in their lines, such shifts were easily effected, given the minimalist scenic conventions in the *corrales*.

Those theatres' structure meant also that the public were close to the performers, involved but never expecting more than momentarily to suspend their disbelief, aware indeed, like the actors, that the play was simply play. Its truthfulness lay rather in the fact that it represented human experience as complex and diverse. The story was usually light-hearted, but sometimes sombre, and often both. In the darkest tragedies, for instance, they (and the specialist actors) expected substantial roles for one or more clowns. All knew, though, that as a "mirror of life" their drama afforded, despite a veneer of contemporary reference, a convention-bound, stylized, unrealistic image. Another, obvious aspect of this unrealism was that (as in other kinds of early modern drama, but with far fewer exceptions) the authors wrote their *comedias* entirely in verse. In a late sixteenth-century treatise in dialogue form, the fact that Classical dramatists had done likewise seemed to the principal speaker an astonishing folly on their part, in that while "proposing to imitate, they utterly destroy the very sinews of imitation, which is based on verisimilitude, and metrical discourse has no semblance at all of truth";[1] another speaker, however, defended verse as productive of greater *deleyte* ("artistic pleasure"), and the playwrights and their public clearly agreed with the latter (López Pinciano 1: 205–7; 2: 221–2, 286–8).

In most of these respects the theatre of Spain's Golden Age was similar to that of Elizabethan and Jacobean England, which should counsel translators and directors against a tendency to impose a more naturalistic, post-Stanislavskian style on productions of it today. But the unique feature of the *Comedia* that I wish to emphasize here is that its verse was polymetric. It exploited a range of poetic forms of kaleidoscopic diversity, inherited from a rich medieval and Renaissance tradition – narrative, lyrical, and rhetorical. As Morley observed, "the extraordinary variety of meters employed in the *comedia* surpassed anything known in any other drama of the world" (283). That diversity was characteristic of Spanish verse of its time, and in drama had been anticipated in part throughout the sixteenth century, but its incorporation into the formula of the *Comedia* must be attributed to Lope de Vega. He clearly recognized its potential in the theatre, not least because it could temper unreality with a measure of verisimilitude, and that in this it had Classical credentials. Of the well-known eight lines of advice on the matter in his *Arte nuevo de hacer comedias (The New Art of Writing Plays)*, the first two (305–6) are the most significant: "Fit the verse-forms wisely to the matters with which you are dealing" (Rozas 191). In a treatise that constantly echoes Horace's insistence on "decorum" (appropriateness), they undoubtedly recall a passage in his *Ars Poetica* (lines 73–98).

Lope's precepts, and more especially his extensive practice, had however much deeper implications for Golden Age dramaturgy. As Vern Williamsen has said, the polymetric system worked "as an informative signal, either intuitive or deliberate, in the progress of the work as it moved from the poet's pen to the participating public on either a conscious or subliminal level" (127). Or, as I put it myself some years ago in the introduction to my edition of Lope's *El perro del hortelano (The Dog in the Manger)*: "The Golden-Age drama-

---

[1]   All such translations from Spanish, throughout this study, are by its author.

tists have at their disposal a very wide range of metres, any of which at any moment they may chose to employ, to generate the pace, mood and style they have in mind for a particular 'beat', very much as a composer may change tempo or key from one passage to the next" (53).[2] More recently Juan Leyva, analyzing as an example Lope's *Las bizarrías de Belisa (The Gallantries of Belisa)*, has sought to show that by his use of different metres "the dramatist indicates to the director and the actors not only what is to be said, but how, and with what movements it should be highlighted" (112). More recently still, Mary Malcolm Gaylord has argued persuasively that "in Golden Age plays, not only words and grammatical structures but the particular metric forms in which they are uttered are called on to add to dramatic speech the persuasive energy that Austin calls illocutionary force (force intentionally invested in an act of speech)" (78). By exploiting polymetry in these ways (and also by incorporating songs and dances, with – as Umpierre in particular has shown – a similar range of dramatic functions), they produced a drama closer than most to other stylized kinds of theatre, like (to give only Western examples) operas, operettas, and the musicals that now fill so high a proportion of the theatres in our large cities, in all of which we expect, within an overarching continuity, a considerable variation of structures, speeds, and styles.

To over-simplify, the *Comedia* is characterized by a high proportion (rarely less than seventy-five percent) of rapidly moving narration, dialogue, and action, usually in traditional Spanish octosyllabic metres – *redondillas*, *quintillas* or *romances*.[3] But the playwrights interspersed passages in other verse-forms, especially *décimas* (octosyllabic too, but of more recent invention) or various forms of Italian origin, with lines of eleven syllables (sometimes mixed with others of seven). Many of these passages were set-pieces, and were frequently signalled as such, by "Listen" or some such phrase. Self-consciously delivered by the actors, they were probably often applauded by the spectators.

Again it was Lope who led the way. He at least, almost always, underlined his shifts of time or place by beginning in a different metrical form the new *cuadro* thus created,[4] but within it he frequently chose to change to one or more other forms. He must have been conscious of those choices and have felt them to be appropriate (though no doubt they were sometimes

[2]   I added that perhaps the editors of *comedias* should label successive sections with their metre-names, as the equivalent of tempo-indications or key-signatures, and that practice has since been followed by myself and a number of others.

[3]   Broadly speaking, the earliest *comedias* were dominated by *redondillas* or *quintillas*, but use of the latter had diminished by about 1600, and the former were gradually replaced by *romances* as the poets' principal "work-horse" or "default mode."

[4]   *Cuadros* has become the commonest scholarly word for these building-blocks of the *Comedia*, though personally I prefer the contemporary *(s)cenas* or *salidas*, or indeed "scenes," as we term the same units in Shakespeare.

a matter of instinct or routine), and in performance they must have affected the impact of his plays on their hearers, whether or not they could count his syllables or register his rhymes, as internal references show that some did. In an analysis of six of his plays, I have argued that study of their metrical structure (whether we perform them in the mind's eye, or on the boards) provides important keys to their interpretation ("The Study").[5] I stressed for instance that he invariably used the Italianate metres as an instrument of emphasis, but in a wide range of different ways, that many of his songs and dances crucially reinforce leading ideas, and that one of the reasons why *El castigo sin venganza (Retribution, not Revenge?)* can be regarded as his greatest work is that it displays his consummate mastery of polymetric technique.[6]

Other dramatists of course exploited polymetry in individual ways. Like Lope, they would often resort to unusual forms, and choose specific ones for monologues or soliloquies meant to stand out as set-pieces. I will give a few examples from well-known plays. In Act I of Guillén de Castro's *Las mocedades del Cid (The Youthful Deeds of the Cid)*, Diego Laínez is given a soliloquy in seven *décimas* (lines 358–427), and Rodrigo one that begins with three eight-line Italianate stanzas, each ending: "el padre de Jimena" ("Jimena's father") (518–41). In Act II, a dialogue between Rodrigo and Jimena consists of nineteen stanzas of a very "old-fashioned" type: a *redondilla* plus a *quintilla* whose third line is a half-length *pie quebrado* (1038–1208). Tirso de Molina begins *El condenado por desconfiado (Damned for Despair)* with three successive soliloquies: one by Paulo in thirteen six-line *liras*, one by Pedrisco in twelve *quintillas*, and another by Paulo in eight *octavas* (1–200). For Paulo's later, mysterious encounters with a shepherd-boy Tirso uses: in Act II, 126 *romances*, but in Act III a less common popular form, six-syllable *endechas* (1471–1616, 2616–77). Somewhat similarly, in Act I of *El burlador de Sevilla (The Trickster of Seville)* he gives the fisher-girl Tisbea a 142-line soliloquy in seven-syllable *romancillos*. The concluding *cuadro* of his *Don Gil de las calzas verdes (The Real Don Gil)* starts with a soliloquy by Martín in four *octavas*, all of which end with the apt proverbial phrase "que nunca falta un Gil que me persiga" ("I'm never without a Gil to pester me") (3063–94). His *Marta la piadosa (Pious Martha)* begins with Marta and her sister Lucía, both in love with Felipe, soliloquizing in a sonnet apiece on their despair at his having killed their brother (1–28).

---

[5] I disagreed in a few respects with the nevertheless fundamental, pioneering study by Diego Marín. For factual data on Lope's metrical practice, all scholars rely on the work by Morley and Bruerton.

[6] It uses no less than thirteen distinct metrical forms, and includes eight more or less formal monologues not unlike *opera seria* arias, as well as nine soliloquies – especially five by the Duke in the final act, the first of which progresses through three different forms. (By "monologues" I mean throughout this study speeches addressed to others; by "soliloquies" those spoken "aside" or by characters alone on stage.)

Calderón (and those who followed) increasingly used fewer verse-forms, and rather as a structural device to separate scenes than to colour particular passages or in isolated set-pieces. But his *La cisma de Inglaterra* (*Henry VIII and the English Schism*) contains in Act I a monologue in fourteen *octavas*, in Act II a gloss in *décimas* on a four-line song, and in Act III a whole *cuadro* in a very unusual combination of octosyllables and *pie quebrado* (333–444, 1111–54, 2280–421). In *La vida es sueño* (*Life Is a Dream*) he uses *décimas*, in Act I and at the end of Act II, for Segimundo's famous soliloquies (103–72, 2148–87). To be sure, the seven *décimas* of the first soliloquy are followed by ten for dialogue, and the four of the second are preceded by thirteen; but he isolates five *décimas*, near the end of *No hay burlas con el amor* (*Love Is No Laughing Matter*), in a monologue evidently meant not as merely decorative but to underline the theme of his play, since each concludes with its title (2905–54).[7] In Act II of *La dama duende* (*The Phantom Lady*) he ends a *cuadro* with a sonnet (called a "discurso") by Don Juan, and another in reply by Doña Beatriz (1899–1916).[8] Finally, his most celebrated sonnets are those in which Don Fernando philosophizes on flowers and Fénix on stars in the second act of *El príncipe constante* (*The Constant Prince*) (1652–65, 1686–99). Each is recited by the one to the other, and so stands out very clearly from their duologue in *quintillas*.

The importance of polymetry in Golden Age plays can be most readily illustrated, however, by the sonnets in those of Lope. He was one of the world's most accomplished and prolific poets in that exacting form. Some 1,600 of his sonnets have survived,[9] and the best are among the finest poems in Spanish. But very many were written as integral parts of plays; of his over three hundred unquestionably authentic *comedias*, as shown by Morley and Bruerton's analyses (42–73, 272–406), nearly eighty-four percent include at least one sonnet. He used them in many ways (in performances to onstage hearers, in arguments, as letters, and so forth), but the first of his specific remarks on verse-forms in his *Arte nuevo*, "el soneto está bien en los que aguardan" ("The sonnet's fine for those who stand and wait") (Rozas 191), implies awareness of their particular suitability for soliloquies.[10] A sonnet-

---

[7]    Vern Williamsen once quoted three translations of this, of which only his own used a similar form ("The Critic" 150–2). He commented (140) that by thus making it more clearly a set-piece he risked its being cut in performance, but surely only an insensitive director would omit any version of the lines.

[8]    Margaret Rich Greer has cogently argued that this pair of sonnets, rather than being mere rhetorical decoration, "is close to the thematic as well as the textual center of the play" (87).

[9]    In 1936 Otto Jörder listed 1,587, and more have been discovered since.

[10]    For comments on Lope's "unique sense of stagecraft" in this respect, see the pioneering study by Dunn (213). On the emotive power of soliloquies in general, Lope said a few lines earlier: "Colour the soliloquies in such a way that the actor may wholly transform himself, and being himself transported, transport the hearer" (Rozas 190).

soliloquy can allow its speaker ("aside," but more succinctly than Hamlet) to grapple subjectively with often conflicting emotions and motives, and succeed in thinking clearly about them (or revealingly fail), before reengaging with the objective action; but it may also serve the dramatist to reinforce patterns of imagery and allusion, or to clarify and emphasize central ideas.

I discussed in detail in 1973 what I called the "love-duet" that ends Act II of *El castigo sin venganza* ("*El castigo*"). In the sonnet-soliloquy that initiates it (lines 1797–810), the passive, introverted Federico apostrophizes his attraction to his father's bride, Casandra. What in Act I he thought an "impossible" fantasy he could harmlessly entertain has since become, with her encouragement, a neurotic obsession. In the quatrains it is still an "imposible pensamiento" ("impossible fancy"), barbarous and insane, as heroic but potentially fatal as the flight of Icarus; in the tercets he concedes that it must be hopeless, uniquely "imposible eternamente" ("impossible for all eternity"). But now Casandra enters, not seeing and unseen by him, with a soliloquy of her own (1811–55). Its more dynamic *quintillas* underline her vindictive determination to provoke the seemingly static but climactic gloss in thirteen stanzas on "Sin mí, sin vos y sin Dios" ("A stranger to myself, to you, to God"), in which he will confess his utter capitulation (1916–75). Each of these three "arias" is what Peter Dunn called a "moment of truth" (212); all "flow from" but also "grow back into" the action of the play.

*Fuente Ovejuna* too contains a single sonnet. In the final act the villagers have murdered the overlord who had oppressed them, and the Catholic Monarchs' Judge has arrived to question them, of course under torture. Lope's spectators knew – and today's, in my view, should be made aware in advance – that the play's true climax is to be that all, rather than spare themselves, will say only that "Fuente Ovejuna did it." But Lope, maintaining suspense by inserting a brief "sub-plot" scene, now produces a master-stroke. Unpredictably, Laurencia appears and speaks a sonnet-soliloquy (2161–74). No longer a hater of men, an abducted bride, or a virago bent on revenge, she reflects almost philosophically in the quatrains that love causes one to care only for the well-being of its object. This is the statement of a theme, which is to be followed by three variations. In the tercets she tells of her fears for her husband's safety. Appearing, he rejects her pleas to flee, out of loyalty to herself and his kith and kin. Then both bear witness to the solidarity of those we hear suffering just off-stage.[11] The sonnet, as Bruce Wardropper said, "imposes a tone of immense seriousness on the dramatic moment"; it creates "a deliberate pause, toward the end of the action, for the purpose of

---

11 Lope will end this superbly constructed *cuadro* with a moment of comic relief, when the heroic bumpkin Mengo over-indulges in wine, followed by a sentimental exchange between the rustic couple, and immediately replace the latter on stage (with no change of metre) by the Catholic Monarchs, their counterparts at the other extreme of the social structure.

summing up the ideological content of the drama" (163): that the selfishness personified by the overlord and his henchmen must be replaced, as all the other characters know or learn, by the altruistic love they display in manifold ways.

The two sonnet-soliloquies in the final act of *El villano en su rincón* (*The Countryman and the King*) serve similarly to clarify an essentially similar message. The first (2306–19) is given to the classically minded King. Once irked by and still intent on rebuking Juan Labrador's *Beatus ille* self-sufficiency, he has come himself not only to admire the rustic and his philosophy (like Alexander faced by Diogenes, he has just said [2261–77]), but to appreciate the diversity of mankind (as shown by a monologue based on an observation by Philemon [2222–53]). He now paraphrases in the quatrains a pair by Epictetus, contrasting the stress endured by a man immersed in affairs with the contentment of another who lives at peace. Indirectly inviting sympathy for himself and admitting envy of Juan, in the tercets he too echoes Horace's epode, but also returns to his monologue's theme – "¡O vida de los hombres diferente!" ("How different are the lives of men, how various!") – with the implication that all contribute to the well-being of a society.[12] The second sonnet, in the final *cuadro* (2706–19), is spoken by Juan's daughter Lisarda. She shares with the marshal Otón a passion that defies the difference of rank between them, and their eventual union will be another of the play's illustrations that mutual love can lead to harmony despite disparity.[13] But of course such harmonization is always precarious; as Lope has had her say before: "Amor [...] canta con trabajos" ("Love sings, but suffers hardships" – though also, punningly – "Love sings, but has its low notes") (1165–6). To stress that point – and maintain suspense – he now has her pray, apostrophizing inconstant Fortune, that her rise will not lead to a fall.

In *La dama boba* (*The Dumb Belle*), by contrast, Lope places two sonnets in the middle of the *cuadro* that constitutes over eighty percent of Act I. The first (lines 525–38), recited at a kind of academy hosted by the bluestocking Nise, and then discussed in nine of the *redondillas* that frame them both, is idealistic – a claim by its author that his pure love, transcending both the elemental fire of earthly passions and that of the sun in the firmament, reaches the Neoplatonic Idea of love, a fire in the minds of angels. The second, shortly after (635–48), is in sharp contrast materialistic – a soliloquy in which her poor suitor Laurencio decides (again in Neoplatonic terms)

---

[12]  Lope had found in a compendium of Greek *Sententiae* both the observation by Philemon and the pair by Epictetus, but mistakenly read Isocrates as the source of the latter (Dixon, "*Beatus*" 294–6, and "*El villano*" 14–15, 18–19).

[13]  Others are the marriage between her brother and the poor peasant-girl Costanza and that between the King's sister and his "cuñado," which anticipated the Franco-Spanish dynastic union of 1615.

that of a lover's three *desiderata*, virtue, beauty, and profit, he would not get with her the third, the basest but the one he needs, and so must court instead Finea, her richer though apparently ineducable sister. In fact Finea, wooed by him, will acquire such learning, wisdom, and wit that she can outsmart all the other characters in order to marry him, and so exemplify the time-honoured notion that love can elevate and enlighten. Our first sonnet, one critic was able therefore to claim, is "the most concise statement of the play's meaning" (Holloway 238). But others, led by Robert ter Horst, stressing the irony that the educator's motives seem wholly mercenary throughout – as the girls' father has asserted in a passage in *octavas* (245–68), all men seek in marriage what they think they lack most – have pointed out that this theme is complemented, more satirically, by the second.

Finally, *El perro del hortelano* contains no fewer than nine sonnets. Two in Act I (551–64, 757–70), though supposedly different drafts of a letter, are covert declarations of love. The rest are all soliloquies in which the speakers, taking stock of their situations, try more or less successfully to decide on future action. In the first, for instance, at the end of the initial, dynamically expository *cuadro* (325–38), the Countess Diana reveals to the spectators her attraction to her secretary Teodoro, confronts the conflict it creates in herself between love and social rank from which the whole action will spring, and even unwittingly hints at how it will eventually be resolved. Together, as one critic has put it, they "signal and sustain, in staccato fashion, the basic points of the action" (González-Cruz 541). But all elucidate too what the play has to say about love: how it is constrained by social pressures, but also complicated by other feelings, and whether or not it can be "cured."[14]

I have sought to demonstrate how by their exploitation of the resources of polymetry the *poetas* who wrote *comedias* contrived to lend their works variety, complexity, clarity, and depth. To leave such artistry out of account in their translation and production today is clearly to misrepresent their distinctive nature, to detract from their expressiveness, and frequently to obscure or oversimplify what they have to say. Ideally, therefore, everyone involved in their performance should be fully able not only to understand the original texts in their historical and cultural context, but to appreciate the effects produced by the various verse-forms and the frequent changes therein. In practice, of course, this can hardly ever be the case, but total unawareness should also be out of the question. In particular, the creator of a version to be presented to a director should never be a writer forced by having little or no Spanish to rely on a so-called literal translation, unless its maker is a bilin-

---

[14] The cures the characters successively contemplate are those in Ovid's *Remedia amoris*, specific echoes of which appear in Marcela's sonnet in Act II (lines 1794–1807) and Teodoro's in Act III (2562–75); see Vega Carpio, *El perro* 28–34 and 56–8.

gual Golden Age specialist and provides him in addition with very copious annotations, not least on the use and effect of the original verse-forms.

A review of some fifty English versions produced in the last half-century yields a great deal of disappointment in this respect. Far too many have been in prose, in defiance of a principle that to me seems axiomatic: when authors elect to communicate with their public in verse, poetically, a prose rendering of their work must inevitably do violence to its nature. No matter how earnestly some have sought to produce "poetic prose," and to mirror their originals' variations of register, mood, and pace, their versions, even if well performed, must always have sounded flatter, more naturalistic, and less stylized than they should. On the other hand, those who have opted for verse have had consciously to contend with the enormous problems posed by the differences between the two languages, in respect not only of – for instance – their sources, sound, syntax, and relative succinctness but also – what most concerns us here – of their methods of versification. Those differences "in the conventions of rhyme, meter and rhythm that exist between English and Spanish poetry" have been extremely well set out recently by Michael Kidd, but while he is critical, as I shall be below, of some of the translators who have tried to overcome them, he fails in my view to justify his own decision to "abandon form altogether" in pursuit of content and resort to prose (50).

In particular, every line of Golden Age poetry consisted of a precise number of syllables (with obligatory stresses), but in English verse, based on feet, they have rarely been counted so strictly. English has no close equivalent to the *romance* verse-form, with its assonating vowel or vowels at the end of alternate lines, and such assonances are so readily available in Spanish that any poetaster can pen them almost as easily as the prose they can resemble. The rest of a *comedia*'s lines almost always end with a perfect rhyme; *esdrújulos* (words that carry the accent on the antepenultimate syllable) and totally unrhymed *sueltos* are rare. In English, such rhymes are far harder to find, and run the risk of sounding contrived. Not a few translators, neverthe-less, have sought to mirror the polymetry of the *Comedia*, either by using a range of verse-forms of their own, or more commendably by replacing the original ones by more or less close equivalents, though with different degrees of skill.[15] Some versions, set out on the page as poetry, on the stage could only sound like prose, so excessively irregular in rhythm or length are their lines, or so imperceptible their enjambements. Attempts to use rhyme as heavily as did the Golden Age *poetas* have induced some translators to resort to similarly inaudible eye-rhymes or false rhymes, others to sound over-clever

---

[15] The most impressively exact but also eminently performable have been George W. Brandt, in his translation of Calderón's *auto The Great Stage of the World*, and Philip Osment (with the collaboration of two Golden Age specialists) in his of Cervantes's *Pedro, the Great Pretender* for the Royal Shakespeare Company's Spanish season in 2004–5.

or inopportunely comic, and several to over-paraphrase or employ an order of words too remote from modern speech.

One series of versions, for both positive and negative reasons, offers particular food for thought: those which Adrian Mitchell, with all-too-rare honesty, published as "adaptations" of two plays by Lope and three by Calderón. The highly acclaimed production at the English National Theatre in 1981 of his *The Mayor of Zalamea* seemed to herald a new epoch in the history of the *Comedia* on the British stage. A racy but reasonably faithful translation, in roughly octosyllabic verse, matched Calderón's metrical changes and imitated his forms. His *romances* were rendered without assonance or rhyme, but his other three – *redondillas, quintillas,* and *silvas* (type 4) – in accord with the rhyme-schemes of each. By contrast *Life's a Dream*, seriously marred by too much adaptation, and especially by substantial additions to its subplot, contained many passages in pentameters (attributable presumably to collaboration with John Barton), and its shorter lines were of varying length. Some lines were unrhymed, others had rhymes in alternate lines, and others rhymed in pairs, but overall the metrical changes were rarely Calderón's. In his *El castigo sin venganza*, strangely retitled as *Lost in a Mirror* but happily only a little adapted, Mitchell responded to Lope's far wider range of forms by varying his own very often, but again with limited correspondence between his changes and Lope's. Federico's soliloquy, for instance, became an almost regular Shakespearean sonnet, but twelve lines almost as long at the start of Casandra's blurred the contrasts of character and pace. Mitchell's *Fuente Ovejuna*, far more heavily and misleadingly adapted, in verse that seemed less audible as such, was by contrast disappointing. Most disturbingly, Laurencia's sonnet was eliminated entirely, and the first twenty-four lines of her dialogue with Frondoso reduced to only four.[16] In point of fact the production in 1988–9, again at the National Theatre, marked another significant step towards the *Comedia*'s reception in Britain; the direction and adaptation won loud applause from the public and from the critics. But only one of the several reviewers I read remarked on the missing sonnet; did they know how much they were missing? A remarkable feature, nevertheless, of all but the first of these versions (and of Mitchell's *The Great Theatre of the World*) was that he often turned short passages into songs, and added a number of his own.[17] Some might be thought out of place in their contexts,

---

[16] Surprisingly Mitchell, in an interview later, described the *cuadro* in question as "one of the best torture scenes in the whole history of theatre" and "one of the reasons why" he chose the play, and indeed that in placing the torture off-stage "Lope knew what he was doing" (Ferrán Graves 179).

[17] In *Life's a Dream* he added a song by Clarín in the first *cuadro*, and one by Rosaura at the end of Act II, reprised and echoed in Act III. In *Lost in a Mirror* he turned nine passages into songs; in *Fuente Ovejuna* three, as well as giving the peasant women a battle song. Similarly,

but the innovation is one that future translators might bear in mind (provided the singers know that their words must always be clear).

Other translators have chosen to render the *Comedia* primarily (though not entirely) in blank verse, most notably James Lloyd in his edition and translation of Lope's *Peribáñez*, and above all the late Kenneth Muir, in collaboration with Ann Mackenzie, in their admirable translations of eight by Calderón.[18] In my two versions of plays by Lope (*The Dog in the Manger* and *Fuente Ovejuna*) I decided to do the same, convinced that performers and spectators accustomed to our own classic verse drama would most readily accept the *Comedia* in that more familiar metre. Well aware, having acted in Spanish in a number of Golden Age plays, that pentameters by nature can sound much less pacy than octosyllables, I avoided the obvious error of using more words than the author, attempted to echo his changes of speed, mood, and style, and expected (since I planned to direct the productions) to be able to get student actors to vary their delivery in the appropriate ways. In *The Dog in the Manger*, however, I thought it essential to render all the nine sonnets as sonnets, though I adopted the Shakespearean rhyme-scheme as less challenging than the Petrarchan (which James Lloyd nevertheless employed with great skill in his *Peribáñez*). In *Fuente Ovejuna* I did likewise, but resorted to rhymes and assonances for the peasants' forays into verse, and for *romances* in narrative passages used an unrhymed ballad metre. I judge now that my pentameters were somewhat too regular and too insistent in their rhythms, and that I could have essayed (and in future would) rather more variation.[19]

Of course, in translating for the English-speaking stage today, many other questions arise that I lack the space to go into fully here. In my view, for instance, we should not cut, add, or adapt for performance without demonstrable justification. Our vocabulary, to match the authors' own range, should be copious but as far as possible timeless, neither archaic nor modern-vernacular, let alone crude. We should never "dumb down," never underestimate our

in *The Great Theatre of the World* a song added at the start was later reprised, a Dance of Death was performed in an intermission, and a large number of passages were sung.

[18] Their similar, bilingual *Jealousy the Greatest Monster* is to be published shortly at Oxford by Oxbow Press. Significantly, I think, Muir stated in 1992 that although in their *The Schism in England* they had kept to blank verse for the monologue in Act I that I mentioned above, he then believed that "we ought to have retained the stanza form, so that the passage would have been a kind of spoken aria" (109).

[19] An interesting procedure proposed and exemplified by Cynthia Rodríguez-Badendyck in her translation of Lope's *El mayordomo de la duquesa de Amalfi* (*The Duchess of Amalfi's Steward*) was to mirror the metrical changes by composing lines of English verse with three, four, or five stresses. I personally could not accept, however, her total abandonment of rhyme, particularly in respect of that play's three sonnets, though her versions of each do consist of fourteen long lines. By contrast, in Edwards's renderings of them (*Three Spanish Golden Age Plays* 30, 62, 75) the similarly unrhymed lines are very irregular in length, and in no case number fourteen.

audiences' capacity to make their own translations, in the sense of perceiving modern analogies for situations or concepts (though, for example, seventeenth-century Spaniards' supposed obsession with *honor* would be less of an obstacle to empathy if that ambiguous word were often rendered, not inaccurately, either by "self-respect" or "integrity" or by "reputation," "image," or "good name").[20] Enriching allusions should not be omitted for fear that some in our audience may not fully understand them, but can sometimes be clarified briefly; untranslatable jokes or obscure quotations can be replaced by others equivalent. Above all it is a challenge, but not an impossibility, to be both accurate and actable; we should test our lines, as we write them and later, by performing them, at least to ourselves. But we ought too to be available to collaborate with directors, designers, and actors, and respond to their queries, doubts, and ideas. I am tempted to go on, but must conclude by stating again my central contention here: that a significant part of our task must be to discover ways to reflect the polymetry that makes Spanish Golden Age plays a unique kind of theatre.

---

[20] Compare Melveena McKendrick's shrewd advice in "Communicating the Past" on discussing with students this problem and others like it.

# Lope de Vega in English:
# The Historicised Imagination

## DAVID JOHNSTON

### Translation and the Original

As the colophon to its Spanish Golden Age season, the Royal Shakespeare Company was invited to bring *The Dog in the Manger*, *House of Desires*, *Tamar's Revenge*, and *Pedro, the Great Pretender* to Madrid's Teatro Español for the 2004 Festival de Otoño. It was not an invitation that Laurence Boswell, who had designed the season and directed Lope's *The Dog in the Manger*, the play chosen to open the eight-performance run in Madrid, accepted without trepidation. After all, this was to maraud into the lion's den, so to speak, to bring English-language versions of these Golden Age plays home to the birthplace of the *Comedia*, to an historical theatre situated less than a mile from Lope's home and Cervantes's final resting-place.

In the midst of its preparations, the Company began to discuss the issue of surtitles. The question was to prove surprisingly vexed. On one side, academic advisors counselled caution, urging the Company to revert to the original Spanish as the basis for what Madrid audiences would read. This, they argued, would alleviate those differences between source and target texts that inevitably open up in any translation process, thereby mollifying any potential unease or even resentment on the part of the receiving audience. On the other side, another group, mainly the translators, insisted that the surtitles should be condensed translations of the new versions, partly to reflect what was happening on stage, partly to emphasise that these are versions that give English-language expression to these classical plays, while simultaneously belonging to themselves.[1]

---

[1]  In the event, the surtitles were written from the translations. On the opening night of *The Dog in the Manger*, for example, an expectant Madrid audience read Tristán's opening "What a bollocks!" rendered as "¡Qué chapuza!" It brought spontaneous applause.

The polemic was instructive, focussing as it did on competing visions of translation, on different ways of considering the source text. On one hand was the view of the philologist, always returning to the fixity of the text, examining its "interanimation of words," in I. A. Richards's phrase, as the defining feature of what was considered an unchanging literary status (Richards 16–17). The translation exists, in this view, in thrall to the original, a pane of glass that offers as close an unmediated access as possible to the original.[2] Surtitles based on Lope's Spanish would therefore provide spectators with the means of mapping their imagination back to the original play, which, in that experience, would remain located within its culture and within its moment. On the other hand, the translators were concerned with engineering the collapse of such separations, so that the plays could be experienced as much in terms of their difference as of any perceived equivalence. Both theatre and translation are, of course, necessarily outward-looking. Theatre practitioners and translators are no less concerned than philologists with "interanimation," but in theatre event and translation process alike such interanimation occurs most completely not on the page, but in the liminal spaces that are opened up between stage and auditorium, between cultures, and between historical moments.

The success of the RSC Golden Age season may well consolidate a developing direction in *Comedia* studies, one that has already made itself felt in relation to the theatre of Shakespeare. The implications of the "foreign Shakespeare" (Kennedy) take us far beyond the "uniqueness"/"universality" debate between Reichenberger and the ever-eloquent Eric Bentley. Just as we have come to consider the notion of a universal Shakespeare as a construct laden with overtones of cultural ownership, recognising increasingly that the most vivid and telling productions of his work are often created in those interstices generated, often at random, between different cultures and between different times, so now we need to be more alive to the possibilities of a Lope without his language. In other words, there will not be a single English Lope, but a series of Lopes brought alive, not through the privilege of a perceived universality, a concept impossible to sustain philosophically or culturally, but through the multiple bilateral negotiations of individual translators deeply influenced by their different locations in time and space.

If we accept this, then we must conceptualise the relationship between the original text and the act of translation as an act of extension, indeed of completion. It is not an act of completion, however, that should be viewed as a teleology. Indeed, in its crucial ability both to safeguard the past and to project that past into the present moment of performance, translation is, by definition, post-teleological writing. And because that moment of

---

2   The original metaphor belongs to Gogol.

performance is always in the here and now of any given audience, the act of completion that both translation and staging bring to a playtext is constantly superseded by the next iteration. Translation, in that way, posits an infinity of possible extensions and completions. If performance can only be conjugated in the present tense, then translation takes us inevitably into that part of the subjunctive mood governed by contingency.

## Translation and Time

Kierkegaard, following on from Hegel, noted that we live forwards, although we understand backwards. Meaning is retroactive, and while clearly the past and past texts contained possibilities for meaning that are irretrievably lost to us, the translation of past texts into present contexts helps us to discern the ways in which our perspective may illuminate or awaken other possibilities in what, although it has gone before us, is still nonetheless ours. Translation derives from and enables a dialogical relationship between past and present, between dead author and living translator, in a way that throws the instability of the past into sharp relief. The events of the past, its movements and ideas, are in constant flux as the ever-changing present casts them in new light, endows them with fresh perspectives. If we accept this profound instability of the past – or how we imagine the past – we also have to consider that the full range of meanings of any text are dispersed across time and space, constantly projecting themselves into the future in potentially endless extensions and completions.

To some extent, this has been implicit, for example, in the various political ends that *Fuenteovejuna* has famously served in performance, from Bolshevik Russia to the Republican cause in García Lorca's Spain and Joan Littlewood's England. It is, of course, in the nature of theatre that different performance styles and stagings may supply or append different ideological readings to any text. It is at this point that some may cry foul, harking back to perceived notions of authorial intention or original context. But it is important to remember that any play exists in and across a number of different temporal dimensions. There is the moment in which it is written, which of course may or may not be the moment in which it is set. This separation will, however, usually be bridged in the perspectives on time that the play offers, and this telescoping is no less crucial in the process of translation – an issue to which we shall return in connection with Lope's *The Gentleman from Olmedo*. Beyond this dimension is the moment in which the play, or the play in translation, is performed, the rigorous historical present; and overarching both of these dimensions is the play's reputation, the aura it has accumulated across time. This is what gives the play its purchase, the reason why practitioners and audiences return repeatedly to it across time.

It was undoubtedly the auratic quality of plays like Lope's *The Dog in the Manger*, arguably one of the finest comedies written in the Spanish language, that prompted the RSC's nervous surtitle debate. Of course, translators are as drawn – and unsettled – as anyone else by the auratic quality of a play. But translation is not centrally concerned with the preservation of aura, and, no matter how unsettled the translator, if there is a surfeit of reverence in the translation process, then the product of such a process may not work as a piece of new writing. The default process of creative literary translation is not set in the search for equivalence, but in the exploration of the boundaries between one language and another, one context and another. In this way, translation invests in the creation of a new object, an object that, at its most irreverent, is neither of here or there, of now or then. It is an object, like the theatre event itself, that encourages journey, excites cultural and linguistic exogamy, and through its hybridity lifts our gaze outwards from our cultural matrix, whatever its configuration.[3]

The translator, therefore, like the theatre director, confronts a simultaneous series of temporal engagements. This is the baseline for what are the problematics of, and the creative opportunities presented by, the translation of a play written in the past. If we think historically about the play, we will inevitably see that its existence in time is an itinerary between past and present rather than a simple location, an enclosed site (Clifford 11). The dynamics of this location – the play's simultaneous pastness and presentness – energise the re-creative processes of translation and staging, offering translator and director alike the opportunity to contrive a series of encounters and engagements, translations in their own way, that enable the play to be experienced as both historical artefact and culturally alive. A play written in the past is both a source of and a target for temporal agency. When it comes to preparing historical plays for performance, awareness of that temporal agency is paramount, because it allows the translator to galavanise and, in the case of an author like Lope, historicise the conditions of reception.

## Translation and the Other

George Steiner (1988) places the "hermeneutic motion" at the heart of the translation process as a necessary counterbalance to monadic separatism (Chapter 3). Hermeneutics is a structuring principle of translation, both in terms of the contexts that the translator activates within the boundaries of the new text, and in the ways that these imported perspectives trigger the ability of spectators, in the here and now, to reactivate in the new text the

---

[3] The surtitles debate shows how a cultural matrix need not necessarily be geographically or historically defined; it may also be located professionally.

original play's political, social, and ethical strategies, and linguistic methods. Unlike the historian and the New Historicist critic, therefore, translators must necessarily incorporate a heightened and explicit sense of their own situatedness in the present into their working practice. Unlike many critical writers, translators cannot simply decontextualise themselves. Instead, in the translation process, they move backwards and forwards between scrutiny of the original play's affects, on one hand, and how those affects impact upon and may be re-created in their own (and, by extension, their audience's) historical experience.

In that way, the new object, the translated historical play, inscribes itself into a different way of thinking about the past, transcending the bifurcation between past and present that is apparent in many aspects of our key historiographical discourses, where self-decontextualising writers represent themselves as somehow aloof from the historical processes of their own cultures (Bal 1). A play translated from this position, from the translator's invisibility in time, will produce a museum piece, of interest perhaps to scholars in the way that cartographers pore over maps of familiar territory, but it will not grant access to the play's living pastness, to its status as an artefact that is simultaneously other and ours.[4] It is a stance that ignores the real reason why we are – or should be – interested in artefacts from the past. Surely it is because these provide a point of encounter, a stimulus that triggers the hermeneutic motion that allows us to journey between past writing and present thinking, deepening in the process our knowledge and experience of both (Snell-Hornby 26). This point of macro-encounter is engineered, throughout the translation process, by a series of micro-encounters that, in terms of audience experience, render porous the divides between past and present. It is not fanciful, in this regard, to see the translator as a shaman, in the sense that he or she opens a conduit between the present and the past that emphasises the aliveness of both now and then. It is impossible, of course, to raise the dead, but translation offers us the possibility of reviving dead authors temporarily – always temporarily – through the rituals of performance and acts of radical re-creation (Johnston, "Translation").

The translator who seeks to historicise the imagination and the experience of his or her audience is, consciously or not, working in the Heideggerian tradition of a number of contemporary writers, such as Hans Ulrich Gumbrecht, who are crucially concerned with understanding what it means for something to be present to us in terms of the range of impacts which that act (rather than state) of presence may have upon both our bodies and the space that we occupy. The translator of Lope de Vega must therefore ask what it means for Lope to be present, always mindful of the fact that the

---

4   The phrase "invisibility in time" offers an extension of Laurence Venuti's very useful discussion of the ethical and literary implications of the "translator's invisibility."

circumstances and conditions of reception of that presence will be as various as there are places and times of performance. But however that presence is elaborated, it should be predicated upon complexity, eschewing both the characteristic aloofness from the present, to which we have already referred, and a more postmodern subjection to the mechanisms and processes of the immediate. In this latter regard, while we recognise that the tendency to see history as clay in our hands may lead to insightful remouldings, we should also perhaps be wary of the deceptive synchronism – Clotaldo in pinstripe suit, for example – that insidiously erodes the human complexity of the past and undermines the right of the past artefact to belong to itself. Naïve avant-gardism and crass subjectivism forget that we are made of the past; the past is that which we are. And this radically circumscribes our capacity as transla-tors and creative artists to transform it. There is no model that conceptualises these limits; there is only the testing ground of rehearsal and the crucible of performance (Johnston, "Securing").

## Translation and the Spectator

What we are talking about here is a quality of theatre. There are, of course, instances where translational methods rooted in aloofness and subjection have led to satisfactory productions. But just as any translated text offers important opportunities for intercultural activity, equally in the case of a translated historical play, there will always be the sense that an opportunity for intertemporal enrichment has been missed. What translation can achieve most effectively in the case of Lope and his fellow Golden Age dramatists is the re-creation of the same sort of hybridity that characterises our own expe-rience of past and present. I have always conceived of my own translations of Lope's plays as hybrid texts that move between and over different historical moments, simultaneously locating and uprooting the historical imagination of the spectator so that the translated text is experienced not as historically fixed, but as a threshold text, moving backwards and forwards, inviting a dialogism that is reflective of our own existential dialogism between past and present.

It would of course be theatrically naïve to reject such hybridity in favour of an alleged textual coherence. Recent work in the area of cognition and reception has clarified our notion of the way that spectators blend in and out of the fictional world created through performance – sometimes annoy-ingly because of external distraction, at other times in order to reflect upon issues arising from the fiction portrayed on stage (Fauconnier and Turner passim). An obvious example of the latter form of blending-out is when we exit the suspension of disbelief to reflect upon the individual performances or the lighting design. It is an example that reminds us that it is the intensity that spectators experience in the blend itself that most wholly influences their view of the overall quality of the production. In other words, the theatrical experience is a more holistic one than simple immersion in fiction; it is assured by the rooted doubleness of spectator perception and cognition in both fiction and theatre event. In the case of the historicised Lope, a similar blend may be assured through the hybridity that allows the play to be both other and contemporary. In this way, such hybridity creates a richer night out in the theatre. It challenges more, exciting comparisons and contrasts, and it does exactly what theatre does best: to use the familiar as an optic for journeying into the unfamiliar. By blurring the borders between times, the translated historical play allows the spectator to engage with – and to participate in – the flow of history itself. The Lope play retains its status as a product of seventeenth-century Spanish dramatic culture, but it also asserts its right to be considered as a cultural contestant in our present. What the translator does is to re-create for his or her audience the simultaneous interplay of the work's historical contexts, drawing together the various temporal dimensions that together configure the play's existence in history.

The conditions of contingency and liminality in which the translation process takes place are ever-changing. Lope's theatre will accrue fresh meanings and generate new potentials for performance as it migrates through time and space. In some ways all we can do is to try and hold on to its coat tails as it does so. It would be otiose to attempt to prescribe specific strategies for the translation of Lope's theatre. Indeed, it is the way in which contingency operates throughout the translation process that explains why translations tend to date so quickly, and why published versions should enjoy only a short shelf life. Multiple translations of any one play are, in this regard, absolutely necessary. As one who has written two different versions of both García Lorca's *Blood Wedding* and Lope's *The Gentleman from Olmedo*, I am conscious how the values of a translation lie in its difference from another translation, in the way that some of the value of a particular performance of a play lies in the way that performance asserts itself against other performances.

## Translator Intervention in *El caballero de Olmedo*

It is time now to illustrate these issues of theory through practical examples. These are offered entirely as descriptive accounts of tactics adopted in order to achieve the strategic results set out in the aforegoing argument, and are not being touted as somehow superior solutions. These are simply means that were found to an end.

In 2004 Jonathan Munby, an acclaimed director who has worked extensively with the RSC, approached me to write a translation of a Lope play for the Watermill Theatre (also known as the West Berkshire Playhouse), well known for its innovative Shakespeare productions at the hands of Ed Hall. Finally, we decided that we would revisit *The Gentleman from Olmedo*, of which I had originally written a version as part of the London Gate Theatre's award-winning Spanish Golden Age Season between 1991 and 1993 (Johnston, *Two Plays*). What we wanted to emphasise in this new production was the European ballad tradition to which the play belongs, its story-telling qualities, and in order to clarify its strong narrative line – Lope de Vega is the most economical of story-liners – it became clear that a number of narrative issues needed to be written forwards. Leaving aside the issue of audience prescience of Alonso's death, without which the earlier comedy remains little more than a sketch of manners, the principal dramatic action that required to be reactivated was the implicit contrast that the play establishes between the then and now of Lope's own audience. As a variation on the implicit ontology of the honour code (through which retributive justice, in this case administered traditionally by the King, functions restoratively for the audience), the emotional impact of the play is sustained along the fault line of loss. It is partly a sense of loss prompted by a death foretold. But this broadens into a more deeply rooted disquiet that the dreams of the old order are dead, that modernity has brought with it a collapse of forms and standards.

This may not be a new perception, but it is one that was particularly vivid throughout Europe in the first decades of the seventeenth century. The temporal doubleness, as Lope's audience blended in and out of awarenesses of then and now, is of course mirrored by the cognitive responses of a contemporary audience to the dual temporal framework of watching a seventeenth-century play in twenty-first century England. It is a dramatic action that prompts a profiling of the self, and the circumstances in which the self finds itself, through contact with temporal otherness. But there is also a key moment in the play when the sense of loss implicit in this is brought home with extraordinary dramatic force. It is in the act of murder itself, specifically in the fact that this is a gunshot murder carried out by a servant. There is no sense of honour here, either accorded to the victim of the deed or that may accrue to the moral perpetrator. The sound of that gunshot, no matter how it was fabricated on stage, was designed to be shocking, heralding as it did a modernity of brutality, where the violence of firearms prefigured a new and terrifying egalitarianism.

This requires careful negotiation in any performance of the play in translation. Surely the aim of the translator in this particular case is to allow his or her audience to feel the same sense of shock, so that the grief for things lost may be given some sort of name. Moreover, there are possible overtones here of Indiana Jones in the Kasbah, where our modern hero's shooting of his whirling dervish assailant is presented as modern techno-pragmatism in the face of medieval ritual. A number of potential solutions present themselves, from acting style and scenography, to translator intervention in the script itself. In the final analysis, the Watermill version opted for the insertion of the simple exhortation from Fernando, uttered immediately before the fateful shooting: "But you will challenge him, won't you?" This was designed partly to set audience expectations, to heighten their sense of a flouting of values, and partly to continue the process of individuation between Fernando and Rodrigo that is present but never fully developed in Lope's original. By using the epithet "Gentleman" for the eponymous hero, rather than "Knight," favoured by Jill Booty, a perfectly possible rendering of the original "caballero," this new version sought to fuse chivalric and civic value systems so that, finally, what our contemporary audience was witnessing was an onslaught on civilised values.

## Translator Reordering in *El caballero de Olmedo*

This is one example of how translation may function as a mode that permits an audience to grasp the relationships between past contexts and past practices on one hand, and between this holistic understanding of the past and our experience of the present on the other (Pym 17). Of course, Alonso's murder was embedded in another context, one that extended the private into the political realm. The rivalry between Rodrigo and Alonso is a function not merely of the proverbial rivalry between neighbouring towns, Olmedo and Medina, but it also reflects the nervousness of a kingdom divided against itself, with the hidden presence of the enemy within. This is a context that would have been understood by Alonso's audience as an abiding feature of national history, and without it the pervasive sense of hostility to the figure of the outsider may be interpreted as sheer personal prejudice. Such a relegation would reduce our sense of the human and political complexity of that distant circumstance, at a time when our own biopolitics are no less complex and no less in need of similar consideration.

That Medina and Olmedo were loyal to different factions goes some way towards explaining why the King should exhibit his favour to Alonso, even at the risk of causing offence in Medina. There is much at stake in the political manoeuvring that forms the backdrop to this nexus of relationships. What is at work is the complex interplay between notions of loyalty and betrayal, key political terms in the feudal Castile in which the play is set, and which were still in debate in Lope's Spain. The difficulty is that the scene between the King and the Constable, in which these politics are adumbrated, is highly problematic in English, in that it seems to add absolutely nothing to the play. The famous effeminacy of the King could well provide a playing style to goad the scene along, but that is still to leave Lope's subtext of pervasive rivalry, envy, and politicking virtually invisible. The quotation that follows sets out the new scene that, in the Watermill production, supplemented the problematic encounter between King and Constable. In it the Queen replaces the Constable (in part to allow for a more balanced debate, in part for company reasons). The discussion about political sectarianism now provides a context for the decree regarding Jews and Moors, and it develops a number of the original play's key metaphors and images in its attempt to create a genuine (but not intrusive) synchronicity between this Castilian fear of the enemy within and our own contemporary circumstances:

| | |
|---|---|
| COURTIER. | Your Majesty. The Queen is here. |
| KING. | My lady, this is not the time. |
| QUEEN. | Sire, there are things we must consider |
| | before we set out to Medina. |
| | It is one of your most loyal towns. |
| KING. | Which is why we are going there. |
| QUEEN. | But you still intend to honour |
| | Don Alonso de Manrique? |
| KING. | He is a man of strength. And valour. |
| | He stands with the Crown of Castile. |
| | He attended my sister's wedding. |
| QUEEN. | There were a thousand nobles there! |
| KING. | He stood out! |
| QUEEN. | A face in the crowd! |
| | Whose family lives in Olmedo! |
| | And Olmedo is a hotbed |
| | of dissent. Full of Navarre's spies. |
| KING. | Are you saying that he's a spy? |
| | I think he's proven his valour. |
| QUEEN. | What *is* matters less than what seems. |
| | In a kingdom that's divided, |
| | perception is all that matters. |
| KING. | To honour a man from Olmedo |
| | will help to heal those divisions. |
| QUEEN. | Sire, is it wise to honour the stag |
| | in the home of the hounds? |
| KING. | I see. |
| | You think we should run with the hounds? |
| QUEEN. | I think you should humour the hounds, |
| | or at least not cause them offence |
| | by flaunting a pup from Olmedo |
| | in the place where they are top dogs. |
| KING. | Dogs will always be dogs, my lady. |
| | By honouring Alonso, |
| | we send a message to Olmedo. |
| QUEEN. | By honouring Alonso, |
| | the Crown will create more division. |

|         | Sire, take care. Castile's enemies |
|---------|------------------------------------|
|         | are all around, like a shadow |
|         | that turns with us as the sun turns. |
|         | The hawks are waiting in that shadow. |
|         | We must give them no scope to pounce. |
| KING.   | Castile's enemies are known to all. |
|         | I have signed a decree of observance |
|         | with regard to those Moors and Jews |
|         | who wish to dwell within Castile... |
|         | We have decreed that wherever |
|         | Moors and Jews live with Christians, |
|         | in this our Kingdom of Castile, |
|         | the Moors shall wear a green hood, |
|         | the Jews a tabard of red, |
|         | so that all Christians may know them. |
| QUEEN.  | The decree's wise. As far as it goes. |
|         | But other enemies dwell within. |
| KING.   | We are tired of this debate. |
| QUEEN.  | I have said all that I can say. |
|         | It's time we left for Medina. (Trans. Johnston)[5] |

Notoriously difficult too is the play's final scene when the King adminis-
ters justice in barely two lines of dialogue. The pointing up of the political
background now allows for these words to be extended in a way that rounds
out the issues brought forward in the debate between King and Queen.

| KING.   | Take them away, far from our sight, |
|---------|-------------------------------------|
|         | and tomorrow morning early |
|         | in the public square of this town, |
|         | let them be hanged. Take the bodies, |
|         | quarter them and then bury them, |
|         | in unmarked, unconsecrated graves, |
|         | somewhere on the road to Olmedo. |
|         | And we shall watch justice done |
|         | before we depart ... loyal ... Medina.[6] |

---

[5]   See the appendix after this essay for a comparison of this and the following passage as
they appeared in the published English version (1992) and Lope's original text.

[6]   For typical press reaction, see Shuttleworth's review, from which the following quotation
is taken: "Taking his inspiration from a folk song and setting his action some three centuries
back, the playwright uses a Spain in flux to examine notions of the old and the new, what is
gained and lost by adhering to each competing code or attitude. Tellingly, his King of Castile
seems to embody a wisdom which draws on the best of both worlds."

## Translation and Language: *El perro del hortelano*

The intellectual habits of philologists may well persist, as they continue to map translated texts onto the language of the original. The examples set out above are concerned to show how the dramatic actions contained within Lope's language may be developed, at times reordered, so that the play itself – which after all, is the thing – achieves its impact in performance, impressing itself on new audiences as a voice from elsewhere and long ago that, somehow, contrives to be accessible and relevant.

If Lope de Vega is to survive as a translated writer, above all we have to ensure his relevance. Relevance, of course, is an abused term. But in the context of performance, relevance is crucial, not in the way that a sociologist of literature would understand it, but in terms of the complicity between stage and auditorium. The spectator will stay in the blend only if he or she has affective or cognitive reasons to do so. The language of a play is one of the principal ways in which we are enticed into complicity, with a series of dramatic actions communicated through the stylistic arrangements of stage language. Literary translation is about finding a discourse for the other. But that discourse, to put it bluntly, has to be understood; in other words, we must be able to map stage language onto whatever template we employ for processing naturally occurring language. This is one of the principal reasons why Shakespeare is growing more distant from contemporary audiences. It is not just that his language is intrinsically difficult; more precisely, there has been a significant shift between the way we process language now and the template of the Elizabethan spectator. The shift has, of course, been less marked in the case of the Spanish Golden Age, but the fact remains that intralingual versions of the Spanish classics are still routinely commissioned for performance, and many Spanish actors still struggle unproductively with polymetric verse forms.[7] In that regard, English-language translations, for example, can release new potentials for performance in exactly the same way that Shakespeare has found an afterlife beyond English. For that to happen, to achieve the translational strategy of an historical artefact that is culturally alive, we should remember that Lope's stage language in English is also a source of temporal agency and transmission. If Lope is to be relevant, in

---

[7] Characteristic was the view of Adolfo Marsillach who, on assuming directorship of the Compañía Nacional de Teatro Clásico, frequently talked of his desire to create a special school where young actors could be taught the intricacies of delivering verse. See, for example, my "Spain's New Golden Age." An excellent example of a fine intralingual version of *El perro del hortelano* is Emilio Hernández's "versión libertina," produced in Madrid's Centro Cultural de la Villa, in 2003 (Lope de Vega, *Es de Lope*).

the sense set out here, he will, first and foremost, be relevant through the language that the translator provides for him.[8]

This, of course, takes us back to the issue of the surtitles, and the different Lopes imagined and projected by the two opposing sides of the debate. In translation, to attempt to freeze Lope's language, inhibits our capacity, in the words of Michel de Certeau, referring to museum-bound art, "to wonder what made it possible, to seek, in passing over its landscape, traces of the move-ment that formed it; to discover within it histories supposedly laid to rest" (198). In terms of the doubleness of spectator experience that lies at the heart of the theatrical experience, this reminds us that we cannot consider Lope's stage language as somehow transcendent. Certainly whatever language the translator supplies for him will have to attend to his historical (and, of course, cultural and artistic) otherness, but it must also, surely, elucidate that strange-ness for a new audience. This historical hybridity, where language is both past and present, maps itself easily onto the central tension of Lope's stage language (see note 7), where formal arrangement and rich stylisation strike resonant chords with more naturally occurring utterances, creating in transla-tion a linguistic environment that is both other and accessible.

A single final example will demonstrate one possible way of achieving the synchronic historicism that is a prime goal of this translation method. Embedded within the overarching purpose of making the language perform-able, which, in broad terms, is achieved by maintaining the collusion between speakability and significance, this example, taken from *The Dog in the Manger*, sets out a new reading of the phonetics, punctuation, and both kinetic and kinesic patterns of the original. In a play that is as linguistically self-aware as this one, it is important that formally organised speech complements the more racy dialogue of characters like Tristán. In this play, formally organised language coalesces into sonnet form at nine key moments – mainly when characters are speaking in soliloquy from the heart of their being. In other words, these are opportunities for Lope to allow his actors to appeal most

---

8    There has been some debate as to the translation – or not – of the *Comedia*'s polymetric forms. To dictate that translations into English should mimic the same polymetrics is essen-tialist. Some translations may re-create them, others not, but as with all translations, fitness for purpose will prove the final arbiter. The tradition of verse theatre is much more limited in English. Moreover, rhyme in English, which is by and large created through word-pairings, which may inflect meaning to the rhyme, tends to create different effects than the more seman-tically neutral rhymes frequently generated by suffixes in Spanish. English rhyme in that way tends to be more self-aware, so that it is very often best employed to comic effect. We tend to experience Lope's stage language in terms of the tension between strictly organised forms and the energy of what those forms express. The default form that I have used in my translations of Lope has been the eight-beat line, partly to capture something of that tension without incur-ring in some of the stylistic excesses of English-language verse, partly to ensure the narrative rhythm of the drama.

directly to the audience's emotions. This is language strictly controlled, but it speaks no less, in this play, of spiralling emotions. In this particular sonnet, Diana has just physically struck Teodoro, drawing blood from his nose. She keeps the handkerchief with which he has staunched the blood, an action whose fetishistic implications are not lost on anyone. In recompense she has offered him a handsome sum of money, provoking the following exchange between Tristán and Teodoro:

| | |
|---|---|
| TRISTAN. It's good work if you can get it. Being hit. | TRISTÁN. Bien puedes tomar al precio otros cuatro bofetones. |
| TEODORO. For handkerchiefs, she said. And then she kept the bloodied one. | TEODORO. Dice que son para lienzos, y llevó el mío con sangre. |
| TRISTAN. It's proof your nose is a virgin. She's had her wicked way with it. Now she's paying for the pleasure. You should make her pay. Through the nose. | TRISTÁN. Pagó la sangre, y te ha hecho doncella por las narices. |
| (Johnston, *Dog* 91) | TEODORO. No anda mal agora el perro, pues después que muerde, halaga. |
| | (Kossoff, *Perro* 175) |

This is further indication that there is much more to Diana, sexually at least, than meets the eye. This is expressed forcefully in Teodoro's sonnet, immediately preceding this exchange:

| | |
|---|---|
| If this isn't love, what name can we give it? | Si aquesto no es amor, ¿qué nombre quieres, |
| Such madness is surely part of love's excess, | Amor, que tengan desatinos tales? |
| and if this passion's the way such ladies live it, | Si así quieren mujeres principales, |
| then they're furies, and that, a furious caress. | furias las llamo yo, que no mujeres. |
| Their honour puts them on a different plane, | Si la grandeza excusa los placeres |
| while lesser lovers may give and take, | que iguales pueden ser en desiguales, |
| and where there's simple joy, instead gives pain, | ¿por qué, enemiga, de crueldad te vales, |
| and brings sweet destruction in love's wake. | y por matar a quien adoras, mueres? |
| Her hand has the power to strike and to beat, | ¡Oh mano poderosa de matarme! |
| but the power of love has a scope much wider, | ¡Quién te besara entonces, mano hermosa, |
| and punishment from such a hand tasted sweet | agradecido al dulce castigarme! |
| when I felt that fire raging, deep inside her. | No te esperaba yo tan rigurosa, |
| A fire and a rage beyond all normal measure, | pero si me castigas por tocarme, |
| so that when she struck me, we both felt pleasure. (88) | tú sola hallaste gusto en ser celosa. |
| | (170–1) |

The change to the Shakespearean sonnet form makes sense in the context of an RSC production. But the form also lends itself to elucidation, so that each quatrain develops one particular thought, building up to the clinching rhyme in the couplet. Hence this sonnet is constructed thus: first quatrain, love and madness; second quatrain, passion and the prohibitions of rank; third quatrain, power and passion as one; couplet, the sado-masochism lurking in this. Lope, of course, wrote with his own groundlings very much in mind, and this particular sonnet depends on its communication of sex as the great class leveller in order to achieve its real effect in the theatre. In this way, it works as a dramatic action and a poetic soliloquy, while endeavouring to develop a stage-language that is both other and accessible.[9]

We should be realistic. In terms of the number of memorable professional productions of Lope de Vega plays in the English-speaking world, Melveena McKendrick's complaint that "the dramatic genius of sixteenth and seventeenth-century Spain is virtually unrecognized outside the circle of Hispanic Studies" still resonates today (*Theatre* 270). There is an incipient sense, however, that this is beginning to change, in the English-speaking world at least. But if we wish to see Lope where he belongs, which is on the stage, rather than being accorded that empty accolade of "genius," which we so often apply to those foreign writers we think we should know, but don't, then we have to think long and hard about how we set about creating an afterlife for Lope in English.

As a matter of routine, programme notes assure us that Lope still has much to say to us today. Of course he does. But we have to resist the tendency to lay him out as a body for forensic examination, lying inert under the probings of philologists and New Historicist critics. If Lope is to speak, he has to be heard, and the ability to be heard, to communicate, is a quality that is no less contingent than it is intrinsic. Lope always knew how to find audiences when he was alive. The ultimate act of betrayal, surely, is to deny him those audiences today.

---

[9]   Victor Dixon's sonnet is translated with a different purpose in mind, although interestingly he also uses the Shakespearean sonnet (Dixon, *Dog* 86).

# Appendix

Johnston, *The Gentleman from Olmedo.*
  Absolute, 1992 (129–30)

KING. Good Alvaro, this is not the time.
CONSTABLE. Sire, these are just routine
  affairs that need merely your approval.
KING. Tell me what they are, but be brief.
CONSTABLE. The Order of Alcantara,
  may now change its red cross to green.
  Your request, sire, has been granted by
  His Holiness the Pope.
KING. We are grateful for his favour.
CONSTABLE. There are two more decrees
  to sign, both important in their own way.
  With regard to those Moors and Jews
  who wish to dwell within Castile …
KING. I am familiar with the writ and
  desire to see it enforced as a token of
  my respect, for the Dominican Order.
  We have decreed that wherever Moors
  and Jews should dwell with Christians,
  in this my kingdom of Castile, the
  Moors should wear a green hood and
  the Jews a tabard of bright red.
  Thus shall all good Christians know
  them and avoid their unclean presence.
CONSTABLE. With regard to Don Alonso,
  also called the Caballero of
  Olmedo, Your Majesty has
  conferred upon him the right to
  wear the cross of Santiago.
KING. He first came to my attention
  at the wedding of my sister,
  here in Valladolid, a man
  of good name and reputation.
CONSTABLE. I have heard, sire, that he
  intends to do you honour once again.
  He will ride in the fiesta
  tomorrow in Medina.
KING. He does well to pursue these arts,
  I hold great things in store for him,
  honours in both estate and rank.

Lope de Vega, *El caballero de Olmedo.*
  Castalia, 1983 (106–10)

REY. No me traigáis al partir
  negocios que despachar.
CONDESTABLE. Contienen sólo firmar;
  no has de ocuparte en oír.
REY. Decid con mucha presteza.
CONDESTABLE. ¿Han de entrar?
REY.                                Ahora no.
CONDESTABLE. Su santidad concedió
  lo que pidió vuestra alteza
  por Alcántara, señor.
REY. Que mudase le pedí
  el hábito porque ansí
  pienso que estará mejor.
CONDESTABLE. Era aquel traje muy feo.
REY. Cruz verde pueden traer.
  Mucho debo agradecer
  al pontífice el deseo
  que de nuestro aumento muestra,
  con que irán siempre adelante
  estas cosas del infante,
  en cuanto es de parte nuestra.
CONDESTABLE. Éstas son dos provisiones,
  y entrambas notables son.
REY. ¿Qué contienen?
CONDESTABLE.                      La razón
  de diferencia que pones
  entre los moros y hebreos
  que en Castilla han de vivir.
REY. Quiero con esto cumplir,
  Condestable, los deseos
  de fray Vicente Ferrer,
  que lo ha deseado tanto.
CONDESTABLE. Es un hombre docto y santo.
REY. Resolví con él ayer
  que en cualquiera reino mío
  donde mezclados están,
  a manera de gabán
  traiga un tabardo el judío
  con una señal en él,
  y un verde capuz el moro;
  tenga el cristiano el decoro
  que es justo; apártese dél;
  que con esto tendrán miedo
  lo que su nobleza infaman.

CONDESTABLE. A don Alonso, que llaman
el caballero de Olmedo
hace vuestra alteza aquí
merced de un hábito.
REY. Es hombre
de notable fama y nombre.
En esta villa le vi
cuando se casó mi hermana.
CONDESTABLE. Pues pienso que determina,
por servirte, ir a Medina
a las fiestas de mañana.
REY. Decidle que fama emprenda
en el arte militar,
porque yo le pienso honrar
con la primera encomienda.

| Johnston, *The Gentleman from Olmedo*. | Lope de Vega, *El caballero de Olmedo*. |
|---|---|
| Absolute, 1992 (159) | Castalia, 1983 (163) |

KING.                    Arrest them,
take them away, far from my sight,
and tomorrow morning early
in the public square, cut off their heads.
We will see that justice is done
before we depart from Medina.

REY.                    Prendedlos,
y en un teatro, mañana,
cortad sus infames cuellos.
Fin de la trágica historia
del caballero de Olmedo.

# Found in Translation:
## María de Zayas's *Friendship Betrayed* and the English-Speaking Stage

### CATHERINE LARSON

> The craft of the translator is [...] deeply ambivalent. It
> is exercised in a radical tension between impulses to
> facsimile and impulses to appropriate recreation.
>
> (Steiner, *After Babel* 246)

What is lost, and what is gained, in translation? Is the expressive cliché *traduttore, traditore*, so ironically relevant in the case of my translation of a play whose title is *La traición en la amistad*, the most accurate representation of the act – my act – of translation?[1] This essay examines several interrelated aspects of the translation and staging of María de Zayas's *La traición en la amistad* for the English-speaking stage. The first treats the topic of translation (art, craft, science) itself, from literal issues of vocabulary choice to metaphoric "translations" of a culture far removed from that of twenty-first-century United States and Mexican audiences. My experiences with "betrayal" in the course of reconstructing Zayas's comedy are explored via their connections to the field of translation studies. This analysis also focuses on the translator, as well as the text, examining how my decisions in creating a translation and working with an acting company forever changed the way I look at the theatre. Performance is understood differently now; the ways in which the translated words on the page came alive in production illustrate the

---

[1] In his recent memoir *If This Be Treason: Translation and Its Dyscontents*, Gregory Rabassa plays with the concept of the translator as traitor, reminding us of Segismundo's comment about the rebel soldier: "The treason done, the traitor is no longer needed" (3). Willis Barnstone takes the metaphor even further, concluding that the translator's ultimate task is to betray: "Now we know the good meaning of *traduttore, traditore*. The translator must be a traitor to the letter in order to be loyal to the meaning, art, and spirit of the source text" (260).

distance between academic understandings of the theatre and those of theatre practitioners. At the heart of this new understanding lies the play created by María de Zayas, now forever altered by the newly created translation, a text that simultaneously is and is no longer hers.

As part of a project focused perhaps more on the written text than on the performance text, I translated Zayas's comedy as my principal contribution to the 1999 bilingual edition of the play that Valerie Hegstrom edited. In planning the book, we had discussed our projected audience and the type of text we wanted to create. We decided to cast the net wide, hoping that the book would be appreciated by academic and lay scholars and used in graduate- and undergraduate-level classrooms in the fields of Hispanic literary studies, theatre studies, and gender studies. This decision led us to plan a text containing a great many notes on mythological allusions, conventions of Golden Age theatre, etc. In our discussions, however, I do not recall that we spent much time imagining the play (in Spanish or in English) translated into performance for the stage. Despite our profound love for the theatre and our growing interest in the performance of early modern theatre and performance studies in general, it would be fair to state that, like most academics in the field, we tended to view the text as written artifact.[2] In retrospect, such an admission seems strange, especially considering our years of attending the Siglo de Oro theatre festivals in El Paso, Texas and Almagro, Spain, as well as the offerings of Spain's Compañía Nacional de Teatro Clásico.

It was mid-project, rather than at its inception, when I really started to think about *Friendship Betrayed* as a text for performance. This reconsideration of the dramatic text led me to make several decisions. I started reading Zayas's words with performance in mind, and I became increasingly aware of instances when I thought that the prose might be too long or awkward,[3] when explanations in the notes might guide a future performer as well as a future reader, when allusions needed clarification, as well as when a scene seemed to beg to be performed onstage. Indeed, as I uncovered the written text, I discovered its brilliance (with few exceptions) as a performance text, which

2   Jonathan Thacker comments on this issue in "'Puedo yo con sola la vista oír leyendo': Reading, Seeing, and Hearing the *Comedia*": "The traditional barrier between the academy and the stage remains largely intact" (151). Michael McGaha suggests that having theatrical experience (or, lacking that, collaborating with a theatre professional) is one of the three qualities essential for translating the *Comedia*: "Es precisamente esta preparación la que más suele faltar en los traductores académicos, y a esto se debe que tantas traducciones sean irrepresentables" (80) ("It is precisely this preparation which tends to be lacking in academic translators, and this is the reason that so many translations are unplayable").

3   Jeffrey M. Green observes, "Translation also entails editing of a sort. Very often, as one translates, one comes upon writing that appears awkward in the original." Green asserts that a translator's decision to reproduce or fix this type of awkwardness depends on whether or not he or she believes it was intentional (25–6).

is especially astonishing given the marginalized role of female dramatists in those times. Yet it is clear that Zayas understood the formulas that were making her era a Golden Age of the theatre: she had talent, and she penned a play that could have functioned well on the stage. Working with the verbal signs she created enabled me to think about the nonverbal signs and structures of the performance and to imagine the play as fully realized onstage.[4]

Critics from the field of translation studies, often translators themselves, have focused a great deal of attention on the salient issues in any translation. Willis Barnstone posits three main areas of consideration in the practice of translation:

1. Register, or translation level
   A) literalism
   B) middle ground
   C) license
2. Structure, or degree of source text in translation
   A) retaining structure of source text in target text
   B) naturalizing structure of source text in target text
   C) abandonment of original structure and creation of new one
3. Authorship, or dominant voice
   A) retaining voice of source language author in target language
   B) yielding voice of source language author to translator's voice in
       target language. (25)

Jean-Michel Déprats asserts that translators should address three major questions: "*theatricality* (are these translations meant to be read, or performed on stage?), *historicity of the language* (should the translation be deliberately archaic or modern?), and *the question of verse* (should the translation be in metered verse, free verse or prose?)" (12).[5] As I have noted above, a recognition of the text's inherent theatricality became increasingly significant to me during the process of creating the translation. I address the historicity of the language later in this essay, and the question of verse is discussed below. If

---

4   For more on this topic, consult Sophia Totzeva. In addition, see the text vs performance relationship examined in Carlson.

5   Green adds yet another – but similar – set of criteria for approaching the act of translation:
   1. *Accuracy* in rendering the literal meaning of the original.
   2. *Correctness* in the use of the target language (corresponding to correctness of use of the source language).
   3. *Aesthetic criteria* such as the sonority of the translation, the structure of clauses and sentences, and felicity in word choice.
   4. *Expressive criteria*: does the translation have the same emotional tenor as the original?
       (54)

I were to evaluate my efforts from the perspective of Barnstone's model, I would suggest that I straddled the space between literalism and the middle ground in terms of register, retained the voice of the source language author, and abandoned the structure of the source text in the translation to English. It could be argued that my translation was more broadly than narrowly faithful to the sense and spirit of the source, but I strayed little from her phrasing and lexicon, and I consciously attempted to keep the voice of Zayas as intact as possible in deference to the author (Barnstone 26–8). The site of greatest divergence from the original text was clearly in the area of structure.

Vern G. Williamsen tackles the issue of structure in translation head on:

> One of the most interesting problems for me to deal with has been the polymetric versification of the Spanish originals. [...] Comedia translators have tended to adopt one of three solutions to the problem: 1) ignore the verse and translate the work into prose; 2) accept the fact that English is not easily susceptible to rhymed verse and opt for a standard of English blank verse; or 3) make an attempt, although clumsy at times, to reflect the Spanish style. Those who follow the first procedure rarely attempt to justify it in any way, claiming that English prose is a proper form for representing Spanish verse since the structural meaning of the latter can never be properly rendered for the benefit of an English audience. (139)[6]

Whether or not one agrees with the assertion that the structural meaning of Spanish verse "can never be properly rendered," Williamsen has effectively captured the key issues of the structural debate in translation. The most significant decision I made was the most difficult. After weighing the advantages and disadvantages of all approaches, I determined to create a prose translation, although in several key places I tried to recreate both the form and sense of Zayas's poetic language – such as the passages sung by the men Gerardo has hired to court Marcia[7] – or to intercalate brief examples of poetry into the prose with the goal of providing poetic echoes of the original

---

6   Victor F. Dixon, on the other hand, states, "The most difficult and debatable question that the translator of Spanish Golden Age plays must face is undoubtedly that of form. The Comedia is an epic and lyric drama, steeped in diverse poetic tradition, and dependent for much of its impact on the power of verse. To render it in prose is to my mind therefore unthinkable, an abdication" ("Translating Spanish Plays" 99–100).

7   ¿Por qué, divina Marcia,          Why, divine, Marcia, do you flee from my sight
    de mis ojos te ausentas,          And leave me dejected and in this sad plight?
    y en tanto desconsuelo            If you are not a lion, nor an unfeeling beast,
    triste sin ti me dejas?           Maybe you will suffer for my pain at least.
    Si leona no eres,                                    (72–3)
    si no eres tigre fiera,
    duélete, desdén mío,
    de mis rabiosas penas.

text. In a few places, however, I believed that a poetic rendering was the only option. The most successful example of such a moment appears in Marcia's famous sonnet defining love and its effects, which begins the second act of the play:

| | |
|---|---|
| Amar el día, aborrecer el día, | Love the day, but also hate it, |
| llamar la noche y despreciarla luego, | Call out for the night only to despise it later, |
| temer el fuego y acercarse al fuego, | Fear the fire and draw closer to it, |
| tener a un tiempo pena y alegría; | Feel at the same moment both pain and joy, |
| estar juntos valor y cobardía | Bring together valor and cowardice, |
| el desprecio cruel y el blando ruego | cruel disdain and sweet entreaty, |
| temor valiente y entendimiento ciego | brave fear and blind understanding, |
| atada la razón, libre osadía; | reason bound up, daring left free, |
| buscar lugar donde aliviar los males, | Seek a place to diminish misfortune |
| y no querer del mal hacer mudanza; | and then refuse to make that misfortune change, |
| desear sin saber que se desea; | Desire, without knowing that you dare to desire, |
| tener el gusto y el disgusto iguales | Join pleasure and displeasure in equal measure, |
| y todo el bien librado en esta esperanza; | and liberate all good in this hope, |
| si aqueste no es amor, ¡no sé qué sea! | If that is not love, I do not know what is! |

(86–7)

The translation of the sonnet attempts to capture the contrasts, repetitions, internal rhyme, and visual and auditory images of Zayas's poetry, and even its layout on the page reminds the reader of the original, written in verse. Certainly, it could be argued, prose is capable of evoking poetry – its rhythm, the musicality of its language, its visual imagery. Nonetheless, I am cognizant of what was lost in my decision to create a translation that was principally in prose form, even with the addition of occasional poetic moments. I will leave it to others to judge the effectiveness of my choice for the wide audience my co-creator and I envisioned.

Zayas probably never saw her play performed on a public stage, and it has only been very recently that interest in this play, and in women writers in general, has led to productions of the text. In February and March 2003, director David Pasto staged *Friendship Betrayed* for audiences in Oklahoma, Texas, and Mexico with a group of actors from Oklahoma City University. Because the translation had won its Franklin G. Smith Translation Prize, the Association for Hispanic Classical Theater sent me to Oklahoma City to consult with the company a few weeks before the première. When this group of young actors started the project, most of them had limited knowledge of Spanish, so even the pronunciation of names was challenging for them. In addition, they found it essential to learn about the cultural, historical, and theatrical contexts of the play. In working even briefly with the group, I experienced a profound appreciation of their talent and professionalism. This cast of undergraduate students came to comprehend the *Comedia* and to understand the characters they portrayed, finding extraordinary ways of translating what they had learned in the movement from page to stage – and I came to understand and appreciate the play even better by virtue of seeing them in action. Those of us who have little direct experience with the nuts and bolts of the theatre would be well served by involving ourselves more directly with performance.[8]

Pasto's creativity and directorial innovations taught me a great deal about the nature of the theatre. His most polemical decision was to convert Fenisa and Belisa's altercation at the conclusion of the play, which Zayas created as a cat fight, into a sword fight. Although the use of swords was not literally specified in the text, the action did, he believed, capture the spirit of Zayas's spunky female heroines and, via the obvious symbolism of the sword, make evident their equality with the male characters of the play. Barbara Lopez-Mayhew observes, "The director justified the duel by literally interpreting Zayas's message to women 'to take arms'" (179). Pasto's choice caused a stir among those in the audience who knew the play, although it appeared to delight others – as a moment of exciting theatre, as a sexually charged encounter, or as an "in-your-face" celebration of women in a play from seventeenth-century Spain.[9]

The director's interpretation of the fight scene, which was faithful to the spirit of the original text but clearly not a literal rendering of it, led me to a self-conscious questioning of my translation of Zayas's text. Had I fully understood the implications of the many decisions I had made consciously, not to mention those I had only intuitively assimilated in the act of translation?[10] To what extent had I taken Zayas's words, carefully edited by Valerie

---

[8]   At the time I wrote and submitted this essay, I had not yet seen the production of a professional company, Washington Women in Theater, performing the translation (July and October 2006). The group's director, Karen Berman, created a fast-paced, sexually vibrant comedy, in which love in all of its permutations is explored on stage.

[9]   Arguing that the El Paso staging generally corresponded to the original text, Lopez-Mayhew also notes the anachronism inherent in Pasto's decision to use eighteenth-century-style costumes, especially for the male characters, to establish their characterization as weaker than the women (178–80). Additionally, Lopez-Mayhew's essay compares the El Paso performance with the 2003 Almagro adaptation of the play by director Mariano de Paco Serrano. See also Laura L. Vidler's discussion of cultural communication in recent stagings of Alarcón and Tirso for English-speaking audiences. Vidler observes, "Through various elements of translation, as well as staging techniques, the productions at once remain faithful to and depart from the 'letter of the source text' and successfully bring the culture of the Spanish *comedia* to America" (71).

[10]   Barnstone neatly summarizes the question: "In literature the question is *how* to translate. And how to do it well is of course the rub, which leads to the traditional and overwhelming

Hegstrom, as too authoritative to touch – or had I gone too far, creating an adaptation that overly privileged my voice? Had I shown sufficient respect in my interpretation of Zayas's work? Umberto Eco speaks to these concerns:

> It seems that to respect what the author said means to remain faithful to the original text. I understand how outdated such an expression can sound, when so many translation theories stress the principle according to which, in the translating process, the impact a translation has upon its own cultural milieu is more important than an impossible equivalence with the original. But the concept of faithfulness depends on the belief that translation is a form of interpretation and that [...] translators must aim at rendering, not necessarily the intention of the author (who may have been dead for millennia), but the intention of the text [...]. (4–5)

But is the intention of the text, especially a text created centuries before, truly available for the translator's rendering? I join those who affirm that the translator is simply one reader among many, one whose job is to offer an interpretation that will deliver that text to multiple other readers – as well as to the spectators, the "readers" of the staged text – because they cannot access the original text as it was written.[11] Numerous other literary critics and translators echo these thoughts, most notably Barnstone: "Translation theory and literary theory come together in the act common to them both. reading. Reading is an act of interpretation, which is itself an act of translation (an intralingual translation from graphic sign to mind)" (7).

This perspective, which underscores the ways information is exchanged, has a number of advocates. In *After Babel*, Steiner examines the act of translation from the perspective of all acts of communication: "Translation is formally and pragmatically implicit in *every* act of communication, in the emission and reception of each and every mode of meaning, be it in the widest semiotic sense or in more specifically verbal exchanges. To understand is to decipher. To hear significance is to translate" (xii). Steiner sees a multi-layered process in which the act of literary creation is a translation of

enigma of faithful and free translation. With equal ardor and intelligence, there are those who argue, and indeed demand, utter fidelity in translation, while others, the majority, propose that one should no more ask for a slavish reproduction of the original text into its interlingual incarnation than expect that the practice of writing and reading will be a transference of the world into a perfect and unimaginative mimesis. Finally, there are those who offer a curse on both houses, saying that good translation is itself impossible anyway. This refutation is metaphorized in the argument that translation is like looking at the wrong side of the tapestry" (23–4).

11 Williamsen observes that "[b]ecause any translation necessarily reflects the individual critical reactions of the individual translators, the only proper judges of a translated text are those to whom the original is not accessible. No translated Comedia text will completely satisfy any critic-reader other than the translator himself [*sic*] and those whose only reaction to the text is informed by that translation" ("Critic" 137).

experience(s); subsequent translation of that product between two languages provides yet another layer. Or, as Jean Boase-Beier and Michael Holman put it: "[l]ooked at [...] as a transfer of material between media, it is possible to view painting, sculpture or writing as a translation of a mental idea into a visual, concrete image and, going back one stage further, to view the process of forming mental images as a translation from perception of external reality to conceptual knowledge" (2).

The related issues of creativity and authority in translation have received a great deal of scrutiny. Boase-Beier and Holman summarize the critical debate as follows. "The relationship between the creative achievement of the writer and the creativity of the translator is one of the central concerns of literary translation studies" (7). "But," they argue, although translation is often perceived as derivative, "much recent work in both literary criticism and translation studies has challenged the notion of the authoritative original" (2).[12] There are a number of reasons why: "[o]ne is the way in which all texts assimilate, borrow, imitate and rewrite other material. [...] [o]riginal writing, too, is rewriting" (2). Zayas, of course, was also transforming and adapting – i.e., translating – writers who had preceded her, from the models whose general style she emulated to specific lexical elements such as her "borrowing" from Tirso de Molina's *El burlador de Sevilla* (*The Trickster of Seville*), seen in, for example, Marcia's "Bien dijo quien decía / mal haya la mujer que en hombres fía," further transformed in Fenisa's comical retort, "Mal haya la que sólo un hombre quiere, / que tener uno solo es cobardía."[13] This would support Steiner's position regarding the multiple layers of transformation that occur before recipients of an image could interpret it.

In discussions of faithfulness, creativity, and authority, debates over lexical choice, often revealing deeply held beliefs, occasionally frame the discussion in black-and-white terms. Boase-Beier and Holman address reasons why some translations may be viewed as flawed: "a translation will be perceived as 'wrong' by a particular reader if it does not fit the image that the reader prefers to associate with the original text. This judgment usually comes about at a moment in the text which jars, which draws us away from our immersion in the fictional or poetic world created by the work, and makes us realize we are reading a work created of words" (5).

---

[12] Barnstone adds to the debate: "In literary translation the source author and the translator commonly set up a dialogical relationship, instigated for chronological reasons by the translator, and then parent and child struggle for primacy" (8). Moreover, the Bible, "available to the vast majority of its readers worldwide only in translation, but rarely regarded as anything other than an original work in the particular language of the individual reader in question," offers a perfect example of the issues at stake (Boase-Beier and Holman 3).

[13] See my own "Gender, Reading, and Intertextuality," as well as studies by Matthew D. Stroud ("Love, Friendship, and Deceit") and Constance Wilkins ("Subversion through Comedy?") for more detailed discussions of the relationship between Zayas and Tirso.

The image of words that jar speaks directly to a decision that I made consciously in translating *Friendship Betrayed*. In my attempt to interpret Zayas's words in a form that could be understood and appreciated by twenty-first-century audiences, I had used contractions throughout the translation, aiming at the kind of casual dialogue that would occur naturally among young people of the same age. Later, however, I reversed that decision, taking the stance that the prose looked *too* casual and that the translation had lost the "feel" of seventeenth-century theatre. In response, I changed instances of "can't" and "doesn't" to "cannot" and "does not" (e.g., "Enough of that, Don Juan; do not take me for a fool," 105), and "let's go"[14] became "let us leave." My evolving decision on this issue of linguistic convention was the result of weighing my goal of avoiding stiffness by employing more easily accessible language against the goal of respecting the era in which the text was originally written. Ultimately, I came down on the side of reflecting, via the banned contraction, the more formal discourse of the seventeenth-century Spanish upper classes.

This small decision on the part of the translator is indicative of the attempt to keep the text from jarring, to keep it as faithful as possible to the spirit of the original. Nonetheless, translators find themselves in the ambivalent space between faithful rendition and playable text. Rabassa describes his translation of Calderón's *Los cabellos de Absalón* (which he entitles *David's Crown*) in similar terms: "I had to be wary of making [Calderón] too Shakespearean on the one hand but also seeing to it that he didn't sound like Arthur Miller on the other. Here again, I let nature, my nature, take its course, seeking the logical and avoiding the outlandish" (184).[15] Rabassa understands the tensions inherent in translation, including the conflict between intuitive decision and conscious choice. And whether or not a decision is consciously made, the issue at hand is cultural resonance. As Green suggests:

> The feeling that something important has been lost in translation depends on the critical reader's ability to find and identify it. In any event, something essential is always lost in a translation simply because it is written in a different language. Some details may be effective in the source language but pale in the target language, while others must go into the translation though they weren't present in the original. [...] What really gets lost in translation, however, is the cultural resonance of the words used.
>
> (149–50)

---

14 I will add that for a while, I had even toyed with language along the lines of "We're out of here," which I rejected as being far too colloquial.

15 Susan L. Fischer's analysis of the staging of Lope's *El perro del hortelano* (*The Dog in the Manger*) in English translation cites Déprats on this point: "Should accuracy and metaphoric richness be sacrificed in favor of an oral style, a spoken language?" (n.p., cited in Fischer, "Some are Born Great" 12).

Dealing with the transmission of cultural resonance was something that quite literally opened my eyes. In my previous readings of the play, I had briefly noted how Zayas used the convention of love entering through the eyes, but it was through the action of translating her words that I really came to understand her employment of the metaphor. Marcia's first words in the play speak to Zayas's insistence on drawing attention to the connections between sight and blindness, the eyes, and love in seven direct references:

> As I was saying, I saw Liseo in the park the other day, and he was more charming, more handsome, and more gallant than Narcissus [the perfect mythological allusion] himself. When he laid his eyes on me ["*Puso los ojos en mí*"], they delivered that special poison that they say you drink in through your sight. My eyes were the doors that let him enter; with incredible daring and a complete lack of respect, he came right on in. He followed me and found out where I live, and he tied to my nobility a blind bond ["*el ciego lazo*"] that only death can take away. He lovingly sought me out, making his eyes a compendium of the thousand gifts of his soul. (37)

Zayas continues her emphasis on the connections between sight and love throughout the play, for example, having Fenisa fall instantly in love with Liseo the moment she sees his image in the small portrait that Marcia carries with her constantly [Marcia. "Why so quiet all of a sudden? Tell me honestly, how could I possibly lose by surrendering myself to eyes so incredible [...]" (41)]. The eyes are dangerous [Liseo to Fenisa. "Are you not tired of killing me, since your beautiful eyes are capable of committing murder?" (117)], and in yet another commonplace, they are tied to jealousy [Don Juan. "If I have upset you, my Belisa, then kill me ... with your eyes, because I am their slave," (103) to which Belisa replies, "Just stop and look at how inconstant you are and how I have every right to kill you."(103). Don Juan later retorts, "your beautiful eyes belong to Don Juan and only Don Juan" (104)]. The translation, addressing these and numerous other references to the eyes, focused my attention on Zayas's textual strategies, her stylistic emphases, and her understanding of the esthetic and philosophical conventions of her day. Attempting to capture those cultural resonances, I saw more clearly elements that, in previous readings of the play, had been placed in the margins. I found something in the process of translation.

The words "lost in translation" will, no doubt, continue to inform translation studies. I prefer, however, to focus less on what is lost in the transfer of information between texts than on what is found when one undertakes the task of reconstructing a literary text in a different language. What did I find in translation? First, I came to appreciate the playwright's abilities differently, simply because I was working at the microscopic level with every word. I gained a better understanding of the nature of performance and of the possibilities inherent in the theatrical translations that occur every night onstage. I more deeply understood the subtleties and complexities of the translator's profession, its *ars poetica*, its theorists, the conflicting ways of looking at translation: a focus on constraints and freedom, a discussion of ethics. Green notes:

> For the translator, each job presents new and unexpected problems, and in solving them one learns more about the languages one works with, one improves reading and writing skills, and the context of one's work teaches one a new vocabulary of words and concepts. Translators must master the significance of detail and nuance. They must find the patience to choose the right words and place them in the right order. However, the deepest lesson of translation is the courage to live with uncertainty. When you try to tie down the meaning of words in texts and transmit them intact, you see how little there is to grasp and how slippery are the criteria for success. Nonetheless you proceed. (5)

Indeed, learning how to live with uncertainty may well be the greatest "find" of all.

Between the time I translated *Friendship Betrayed* and now, I have read a fair amount about translation and translation studies, and I have discovered some ambiguities and quirkiness. The field is extraordinarily diverse. Volumes have been written describing various theories of and approaches to translation, including those of literary history ("translation from Dryden to Derrida") or translation specifically for the stage ("performance revisited"), as well as analyses of oral interpretation vs the written text ("guides and native informants"). Some essays treat the issue of censorship, and some look at translation as a social science ("performative linguistics: doing things with words") or as metaphors for larger issues ("intercultural connections and transactions"), while still others expound upon the political or ideological function of translation ("translation and power").

I have also found a high degree of metadiscourse on the topic, with practitioners of the art dissecting their decision-making, probably because making decisions lies at the heart of their task: every sentence is, in essence, nothing more than a compendium of the translator's lexical and syntactic choices.[16] I found that translators, much more often than not, seem to write about what they do in the first person. Perhaps because they may believe that their own voice has been lost in the act of interpreting the words of others, translators' discussions of their art and craft frequently reveal their egos: their personal motivations for selecting their career or for approaching their job in a specific

---

[16] In *What Is Translation?* Douglas Robinson takes on eleven different writers' contributions to translation studies in eleven chapters of metacritique.

way, analyses of the economics of the profession.[17] Rabassa's *If This Be Treason: Translation and Its Dyscontents* is, quite literally, a memoir. More than once, I heard a hint of resentment in translators' complaints about the ways in which their work is criticized by those who devalue the translator's role in the communicative process or who blame the sins of the original text on the translation. Yet, other writers evince a more joyful approach to the profession, as seen in the first words of David Gitlitz's essay on the topic: "Empiezo con una confesión: soy adicto a la traducción de comedias" ("Let me begin with a confession. I'm addicted to translating Golden Age plays") (45). These studies are flamboyantly self-reflexive, with nothing lost in the translation of their experience. And if the confessions of these translators – with my voice included among them – appear to echo the old-time words, "I once was lost, but now I'm found," so be it. Now I see.

---

[17] Alan K. G. Paterson writes, "¡Qué sorpresa la mía! Como Lazarillo al darse cuenta de que era escritor, me doy yo cuenta de que soy traductor" (113). ("What a surprise! Like Lazarillo upon realizing that he was a writer, I realize that I'm a translator").

# Transformation and Fluidity in the Translation of Classical Texts for Performance: The Case of Cervantes's *Entremeses*

## DAWN L. SMITH

As Jorge Luis Borges reminds us in "Pierre Menard, autor del Quijote," no text remains exactly as it was written; every new generation of readers understands that text from a different perspective, changing and enriching the way it is interpreted. For the translator of a literary text, particularly from an earlier century, Borges's essay is also relevant. There are now many English translations of *Don Quijote*, from the first one by Thomas Shelton (1612–20) to the recent version by Edith Grossman (2003). None of them is – nor can aspire to be – a faithful reproduction of the original text. Each reflects the personality of its translator, insofar as he or she is required to make subjective decisions about style, vocabulary, and allusions – decisions taken with the reader in mind and, in the case of translations for the stage, with a view to making the text resound with an English-speaking audience.[1] Each translation also reflects the time and place of its origin, however indirectly; a British translator brings a different perspective and vocabulary than does a translator from the United States; even current events or the prevailing climate of opinion may have an influence. As a recent reviewer aptly observed, "translations march to the beat of the times in which they are made" (Duffy D5).

This essay explores ways in which translation for performance is shaped by a variety of ambient influences. It draws, primarily, on my own experience of translating Cervantes's *Ocho entremeses (Eight Interludes)* more than ten years ago and reviews the principles that guided that translation. In retrospect the project is placed in a context that includes the reception history of Cervantes's *Entremeses*, in Spanish and English, as well as changing attitudes on both sides of the Atlantic towards the performance of Spanish

---

[1] Paradoxically, a modern translation tends to make the source of the text more intelligible to its target audience, whereas native speakers may have difficulty understanding it because the language has become archaic.

classical drama in English. The essay concludes with a comparison of two versions of passages selected from *La guarda cuidadosa* (*Sir Vigilant*), which suggest how translation constantly adjusts to the changing sensibilities of the public.

It is well known that the eight plays and their accompanying *entremeses* that Cervantes published in 1615 were never staged during his lifetime. The edition is even titled *Ocho comedias y ocho entremeses, nunca representados* (*Eight Plays and Eight Interludes, Never Performed*). In the "Prólogo al lector" Cervantes tells us that when he was unable to find a theatre manager willing to stage his plays, he sold them to a bookseller. More than a century passed before another edition was published, in 1749. By this time, however, under the influence of the Bourbon court and new "enlightened" ideas, there were many critics who scorned Golden Age drama for its failure to adhere to classical models. Cervantes's plays were also condemned, and at least one critic expressed the belief that these "grotesque" plays were not really by Cervantes, but had been published in his name (Smith, *Interludes* 168). It was not until 1816 that the *Entremeses* were published in a separate edition and thereafter acquired a life and reputation of their own.

Evidence of early performances is hard to find. In 1932, Federico García Lorca's company of student actors, La Barraca, performed *La guarda cuidadosa* and *La cueva de Salamanca* (*The Magic Cave of Salamanca*) to a rural audience. Since then the *Entremeses* have been frequently performed in Spain (usually in groups of two or three, or occasionally with short plays by other playwrights, such as Molière).[2] I am not aware of an attempt to perform any of the *Entremeses* in conjunction with Cervantes's *comedias*.[3]

It took even longer for the *Ocho entremeses* to reach the English stage. This may have been because there were few translations available,[4] but also because Cervantes was primarily known as the author of *Don Quijote*, not as a writer of plays (with the possible exception of *La Numancia*). Moreover, there was little interest in the Spanish classical theatre as a whole in Britain (outside university Spanish departments), let alone in their potential for performance.[5] The influential theatre historian and critic Peter Arnott wrote

---

[2] For performances of Cervantes's plays during the period 1939–91, see Muñoz Carabantes. A notable production of three of the *Entremeses* was mounted in 1996 by José Luis Gómez and Rosario Ruiz Rodgers at the Teatro de la Abadía in Madrid.

[3] A further difficulty arises from the fact that Cervantes gives no indication as to how the two were intended to be paired (Smith, *Interludes* xxxiii).

[4] Two earlier translations of all of Cervantes's *Ocho entremeses* were published by S. Griswold Morley in 1948 and Edwin Honig in 1964. There are a number of individual translations, published separately (e.g., Walter Starkie's version of *The Jealous Old Man* in *Eight Spanish Plays of the Golden Age* and *The Vigilant Sentinel*, translated by Angel Flores).

[5] An exception was the 1966 adaptation by John Osborne of Lope de Vega's *La fianza satisfecha* (as *A Bond Honoured*), performed by the National Theatre.

in 1981 that: "Perhaps the lack of interest in the Spanish theatre is due to the fact that it was, historically, a dead end: it had no repercussions, no wider influence, on the European scene" (197).[6]

In Britain in the 1970s there was still some indifference to foreign plays, a relic, perhaps, of the isolationism of the Second World War. There was also confusion about the nature of translation. The standard English translations of plays by Chekhov and Ibsen available in that period, for example, reveal the prevailing attitude towards translating classical texts: the primary aim was to make them readable, not performable.

A parallel exists between the state of Golden Age drama in English translation and that of Golden Age theatre in performance in Spain during the same period. The two decades following the death of Franco saw the birth of the Compañía Nacional de Teatro Clásico in Madrid (1986) and the founding of the annual Almagro Festival (1985). After many years of relative neglect and without a sustaining tradition of performance, the struggle to revive national classical theatre was difficult and often frustrating. It would take some years before Spanish directors were able to shake off a tentative approach to Golden Age plays and find fresh, confident ways of performing them. Meanwhile, there was little to attract the attention of British directors and convince them that Spanish classical theatre was worth staging in English.

The uncertainties about performance of Golden Age drama began to change in the 1980s and 1990s, and this soon encouraged more translation of texts into English for the purpose of performance. In the US the annual Chamizal Siglo de Oro Drama Festival in El Paso, Texas (founded in 1975) brought together professional and amateur acting companies from the US, Spain, Portugal, and Latin America to perform Golden Age plays. After 1980, an annual Spanish Golden Age Theater Symposium (originally organized by the University of Texas at El Paso) was offered concurrently with the Festival. It provided a unique opportunity for scholars and students to see live performances of Golden Age theatre and to hold discussions with the directors and actors involved. The plays began to take on a new dimension: the concept of them as texts for reading only was transformed by the experience of seeing them performed. This had an immediate influence on the nature of the papers presented at the Symposium and, eventually, on the work of Hispanists at large. A further significant outcome was the founding of the Association for Hispanic Classical Theater, which began with the aim of compiling a research collection of videotapes of plays in performance. It would later expand its activities to include organizing conferences (including

---

6    This attitude was further supported by the infamous "Leyenda Negra," rooted in Elizabethan propaganda against the Spain of Felipe II, which subtly persisted until Spain entered the European Economic Community (and, later, the European Union). See Smith, "El teatro clásico español."

the annual El Paso Symposium) and promoting the translation of Golden Age plays for performance.[7]

In October of 1987 an international conference was held in Calgary, Canada, organized by Louise and Peter Fothergill-Payne. It brought together a group of specialists in the field of English and Spanish sixteenth- and seventeenth-century drama for the purpose of studying parallels between the two traditions (Fothergill-Payne). The conference included participants from Canada, the US, Great Britain, Israel, and Germany.

Meanwhile, in Britain the attitude towards Spanish classical theatre also started to change during the 1980s (Smith, "El teatro clásico"). The National Theatre (now The Royal National Theatre) staged successful English versions of plays by Calderón and Lope de Vega: *El alcalde de Zalamea* (*The Mayor of Zalamea*) (1981) and *Fuenteovejuna* (1989). The Royal Shakespeare Company also staged versions of *La vida es sueño* (*Life's a Dream*) (1983) and *El burlador de Sevilla* (*The Trickster of Seville*) (1990/1). At the same time, the small independent Gate Theatre (founded at the beginning of the 1980s with the aim of staging the best of world theatre) ran an ambitious program of seven Golden Age plays between 1990 and 1993. The most successful of these was a fine version of Tirso's *El condenado por desconfiado* (*Damned for Despair*), directed by Stephen Daldry.[8] In 1992, another small, independent company mounted an exciting production of Tirso's *La venganza de Tamar* (*The Rape of Tamar*) at the Lyric Theatre, Hammersmith.[9]

It was against this background of increasing interest in the staging and translation of Golden Age drama on both sides of the Atlantic that I undertook my translations of Cervantes's *Entremeses*. The initial impetus was in 1979 when a university colleague was looking for a short playtext for use in his drama class. This led to a translation of *El retablo de las maravillas* (*The Marvellous Puppet Show*), which was performed by students in a programme that also included two short plays by Bertolt Brecht. Watching the text come to life on stage was a revelation, particularly as the students involved in the project had no acting experience and yet managed to portray the clumsy, bamboozled characters to hilarious effect. Their gradual, often unconscious, involvement as actors in the performance found a striking parallel in the plot of the play itself (further convincing me that Cervantes always intended his plays for the stage).[10]

---

[7]  See the website for the AHCT: <www.comedias.org>.

[8]  In 1991, the Gate Theatre received a prestigious Olivier Award for its entire season devoted to Golden Age plays.

[9]  Paul Whitworth directed and also translated the text.

[10]  Arguments in the debate over this issue are found in Spadaccini and Talens (64–70); and Reed (189); see also my review of Reed. In Cervantes's time texts were habitually read aloud by a group of readers, so the differences between a text to be read and a text to be performed would not have been as great as they are perceived today.

From this modest beginning the project evolved over the next fifteen years to include all eight *Entremeses*. They were published by Everyman in London in 1996. As I state in the Introduction:

> I […] hope that my version will make readers aware that these pieces are not just intended to be read, but also to be performed. With this in mind, I have attempted to produce a text that can be staged today without compromising the integrity of the original. (xxxix)

While designed to break with the tendency to produce pedantic translations to be read rather than performed, this edition nevertheless aimed to provide a parallel text that would capture all the nuances of the original in equivalent terms. It also provided explanatory notes and an informative, critical introduction, designed to give readers a full picture of the historical, literary, and linguistic context of the plays. I hoped that by offering a rich compendium of background information along with a lively version of the text, this approach would appeal to potential stage directors.[11]

Above all, the text had to *sound* right when spoken aloud, not least because this was so evidently a priority for Cervantes himself. We constantly tested it orally, with friends, students, even family members, tuning and refining each passage. Rhythm was of paramount importance. Although Cervantes wrote six of the *Entremeses* in prose, the natural musicality of his language and the rhythms of his sentence structure demand a similar treatment in English.[12]

Unlike the challenge facing the translator of a *comedia*, translating the two *Entremeses* written entirely in verse (*El Rufián viudo llamado Trampagos* [*The Widowed Pimp*] and *La elección de los alcaldes de Daganzo* [*The Election of the Magistrates of Daganzo*]) proved relatively easy because the comic nature of the pieces relies on the subversion of the poetic voice. Both *Entremeses* are written in hendecasyllables, a meter that closely resembles the pattern of spoken English. For songs, I followed the Spanish text in using octosyllables or passages of six syllables. I did not, however, adhere strictly to the original rhyming patterns since, as generally acknowledged, these rarely work in English translation.[13] Instead, I allowed consonantal rhymes to occur irregularly throughout the texts and, occasionally, in couplets (Smith, "El envés" 517).

---

11 The text of two or more of these *Interludes* was used in performance in Nova Scotia, Canada (Acadia University, 1998), New York (Oddbods Company, 1999), and as the English simultaneous audio version in Washington, D. C. (Gala Hispanic Theater, 2002).

12 A detailed presentation of my approach to translating the *Entremeses* is found in "El envés del tapiz" and "El reto de las maravillas."

13 For a useful discussion of the problems of translating Golden Age playtexts, see essays by Victor Dixon, Gwynne Edwards, Ann L. Mackenzie and Alan K. G. Paterson in *Traducir a los clásicos*.

A translator never works in isolation. She depends constantly on the advice and opinion of others as a way of testing and checking the text, both for its accuracy and for its effect. It is also essential to work closely with a Spanish native speaker. I owe a huge debt of gratitude to María Luz Valencia, who worked untiringly with me throughout the project, vetting every draft and discussing alternative versions until we were each satisfied that the final choice captured the meaning, tone, and weight appropriate to both languages.

Cervantes's *Entremeses* draw deeply on the social and historical events marking Spain at the end of the sixteenth century and the beginning of the seventeenth century. They are also rooted in the turbulent events of Cervantes's own life. All this finds expression in the comic mode in Cervantes's brilliant use of language, his veiled allusions and associations and sometimes wicked play on double meanings. The translator must be aware of all these factors and try to evoke responses in the modern reader/spectator through a range of equivalent images and associations. This means changing some allusions, looking for parallels that will resonate with today's public and elicit a laugh where Cervantes intended one. Most difficult of all, perhaps, is knowing whether one has found all the hidden meanings in the original, particularly if an allusion is not overt – just the merest hint that is left to the reader/listener to complete. The translator must be careful, not just to convey the hidden meaning, but also not to overstate it, leaving it instead as ambiguous as in the original (Smith, "El envés" 514).

The act of translation is a highly subjective one, involving arbitrary choices. María and I decided to tilt our version towards the British reader/spectator, partly because the volume was published in London, but also because our own cultural and linguistic backgrounds were more attuned to British idioms and, especially, to British humour.[14]

Whereas the translation of a classical text that is destined only to be read is likely to survive unchallenged for many years (for example, the famous Scott-Moncrieff translation of Proust's *À la recherche du temps perdu* still stands as a classic in its own right despite the recent appearance of a new English version), a dramatic text destined for performance is subject to modification by directors and actors charged with staging it for a modern audience. When liberties are taken in staging a Shakespeare play, the English-speaking public is able to react, favourably or otherwise, based on its knowledge of the original. A translation of a foreign text, on the other hand, risks serving merely as a "pre-text" for a script that expresses more of the director's view of the play than the ideas of the original author. The public remains unaware of what has happened because it is unfamiliar with the source.

In Britain, however, much has changed in the theatre since the first major

---

[14] Hence the decision to translate the title *La guarda cuidadosa* as *Sir Vigilant*, which we felt more aptly conveyed the irony of the piece than a more literal translation.

productions of Spanish Golden Age plays were staged in London and Stratford-upon-Avon in the 1980s. More and more Spanish plays have been translated and performed in a variety of theatres, both in London and elsewhere in Britain. While political changes in Europe brought Spain out of its isolation and into full participation in the new European Union, Britain was also becoming more open to foreign plays. A vigorous new generation of translators also appeared who were able to transform the nature of translation for the stage, establishing it as a respected art that stands on its own. These translators include well-known playwrights Michael Frayn and Christopher Hampton, directors Timberlake Wertenbaker and Jeremy Sams, and Ranjit Bolt (described by one reviewer as "translator as star").[15]

All these factors helped pave the way for the Royal Shakespeare Company's successful summer season of Spanish Golden Age Plays in 2004, which presented *The Dog in the Manger* (Lope de Vega), *House of Desires* (Sor Juana Inés de la Cruz), *Tamar's Revenge* (Tirso de Molina), and *Pedro, the Great Pretender* (Miguel de Cervantes).[16] For the present study, the inclusion of the Cervantes play in the season is significant, not only because *Pedro de Urdemalas* is a complex play, seldom performed even in Spain, but also because the language is especially challenging for the translator. Philip Osment bravely chose to follow the verse forms as well as the rhymes. This makes for a lively text for reading, although the restrictions his choice inevitably imposes sometimes distract the reader (rather like watching a man walking a tightrope and wondering whether he will fall!). They were even more problematic for the actors, as director Laurence Boswell admits in the interview with Kathleen Mountjoy: "I think that Philip's so concerned with the metrical structure only, with rhyme, that [in retrospect] I would go again and ask him to put more meat on it, as I feel it's a bit pallid [...]" (186–7).

No doubt the experience of working as script consultant with the RSC during their Golden Age season, and of seeing the Cervantes text take shape on the stage, encouraged Mountjoy to tackle the *Entremeses* herself the following season. As a doctoral student at Oxford, she set up a Playwriting and Dramaturgy Society, whose first project was to translate and perform three of the *Entremeses*: *El retablo de las maravillas*, *El viejo celoso* (*The Jealous Old Man*) and *La guarda cuidadosa*. These were first performed in Oxford and, later, at the Edinburgh Fringe Festival (Thacker, "Sex, Treachery" 185–99). The group's performance-based approach to translation is demonstrated in an excerpt from the Mountjoy version of *La guarda cuidadosa*,

---

15 Their translations include versions of plays by Molière, Chekhov, Ibsen, and Goldoni. Their observations are published in *Platform Papers*.

16 See Kathleen Mountjoy's interview with RSC Associate Director Laurence Boswell. These productions (except for *Tamar's Revenge*) were transferred to London during the winter season for a further successful run.

preceded by the original text and compared with the corresponding passage from my own translation.

### *La guarda cuidadosa* (Miguel de Cervantes, first published 1615)

| | |
|---|---|
| SOLDADO. | ¿Qué me quieres, sombra vana? |
| SACRISTAN. | No soy sombra vana, sino cuerpo macizo. |
| SOLDADO. | Pues, con todo eso, por la fuerza de mi desgracia, te conjuro que me digas quién eres y qué es lo que buscas por esta calle. |
| SACRISTAN. | A eso te respondo, por la fuerza de mi dicha, que soy Lorenzo Pasillas, sota-sacristán desta parroquia, y busco en esta calle lo que hallo, y tú buscas y no hallas. |
| SOLDADO. | ¿Buscas por ventura a Cristinica, la fregona desta casa? |
| SACRISTAN. | *Tu dixisti*. |
| SOLDADO. | Pues ven acá, sota-sacristán de Satanás. |
| SACRISTAN. | Pues voy allá, caballo de Ginebra. |
| SOLDADO. | Bueno: sota y caballo; no falta sino el rey para tomar las manos. Ven acá, digo otra vez. ¿Y tú no sabes, Pasillas, que pasado te vea yo con un chuzo, que Cristinica es prenda mía? |
| SACRISTAN. | ¿Y tú no sabes, pulpo vestido, que esa prenda la tengo yo rematada, que está por sus cabales y por mía? |
| SOLDADO. | ¡Vive Dios, que te dé mil cuchilladas, y que te haga la cabeza pedazos! |
| SACRISTAN. | Con las que le cuelgan desas calzas, y con los dese vestido se podrá entretener, sin que se meta con los de mi cabeza. |
| SOLDADO. | ¿Has hablado alguna vez a Cristina? |
| SACRISTAN. | Cuando quiero. |
| SOLDADO. | ¿Qué dádivas le has hecho? |
| SACRISTAN. | Muchas. |
| SOLDADO. | ¿Cuántas y cuáles? |
| SACRISTAN. | Dile una destas cajas de carne de membrillo, muy grande, llena de cercenaduras de hostias, blancas como la misma nieve, y de añadidura cuatro cabos de velas de cera, asimismo blancas como un armiño. |
| SOLDADO. | ¿Qué más le has dado? |
| SACRISTAN. | En un billete envueltos, cien mil deseos de servirla. |
| SOLDADO. | Y ella ¿cómo te ha correspondido? |
| SACRISTAN. | Con darme esperanzas propincuas de que ha de ser mi esposa. |
| SOLDADO. | Luego ¿no eres de epístola? |
| SACRISTAN. | Ni aun de completas. Motilón soy, y puedo casarme cada y cuando me viniere en voluntad; y presto lo veredes. |
| SOLDADO. | Ven acá, motilón arrastrado; respóndeme a esto que preguntarte quiero. Si esta muchacha ha correspondido tan altamente, lo cual yo no creo, a la miseria de tus |

dádivas, ¿cómo corresponderá a la grandeza de las mías?
Que el otro día le envié un billete amoroso, escrito por lo
menos en un revés de un memorial que di a su Majestad,
significándole mis servicios y mis necesidades presentes
(que no cae en mengua el soldado que dice que es pobre),
el cual memorial salió decretado y remitido al limosnero
mayor; y sin atender a que sin duda alguna me podía valer
cuatro o seis reales, con liberalidad increíble, y con desen-
fado notable, escribí en el revés dél, como he dicho, mi
billete; y sé que de mis manos pecadoras llegó a las suyas
casi santas. (Spadaccini 171–4)

## Version A
*Sir Vigilant* (translated by Dawn Smith, 1996)

SOLDIER. Why do you follow me, man, like a lost soul?

SEXTON. I'm no lost soul. I'm solid flesh and blood.

SOLDIER. That may be so. Still, my misfortune compels me to ask who you are and what business you have in this street?

SEXTON. My good fortune compels me to reply that my name is Lorenzo Pasillas. I'm under-sexton and jack-of-all-trades in this parish. My business in this street is the same as yours, but I have better prospects than you.

SOLDIER. So, you're looking for Cristi-nica, the kitchen maid who lives in this house?

SEXTON. If you say so.

SOLDIER. Well, come over here, you devil's jackass.

SEXTON. At your service, you renegade knave.

SOLDIER. Stand a little closer.
Me and you ... what a crew!
Knave and Jack ... what a pack!
Give us a king and we'd have a full house!

## Version B
*The Watchdog* (translated by Kathleen Mountjoy et al., 2005)[17]

SOLDIER. Following me around like a lost soul what are you, my shadow?

SEXTON. I'm no shadow, but I'm here in the flesh.

SOLDIER. Well, sir, the bad luck I have had in the past forces me to conjure you to tell me who you are, and what business you have in this street.

SEXTON. I have the good luck to inform you that I am Gordon Gherkin, the assistant warden of this parish, and I seek what I shall find in this street, though you may seek all day without finding anything.

SOLDIER. Stop talking in riddles man! Are you seeking peradventure, Cristina, the kitchen maid of this house?

SEXTON. *Tu dixisti.*

SOLDIER. Put 'em up, Satan's bell-ringer!

SEXTON. Come and get it, heathen joker!

SOLDIER. If I'm the joker, I'm the joker who holds her heart. I'll club you till you fold. Don't you know, Mr Uh... Gherkin, that the girl's hand is mine?

17  I am very grateful to Kathleen for her generosity in providing this text and her helpful comments on the project.

I told you to come here, Pasillas
my friend, so I can run you through
with my pikestaff. Don't you know
that Cristinica is mine?

SEXTON. Don't you know, scarecrow,
that I've already bid on that piece
of baggage? What's more, my price
is right!

SOLDIER. God's blood! I swear I'll run
you through and through, I'll leave
your head full of holes.

SEXTON. Never mind my head. Look to
the holes in your own breeches!

SOLDIER. Have you ever spoken to
Cristina?

SEXTON. I speak to her whenever I
please.

SOLDIER. What gifts have you bestowed
on her?

SEXTON. Heaps of them.

SOLDIER. How many? Tell me what they
were.

SEXTON. I gave her a quince jelly-box
filled with snowy white wafers
left over from the Mass. To these
I added four wax candle stubs
– whiter than ermine they were,
too.

SOLDIER. What else have you given her?

SEXTON. A letter promising to serve her
in a thousand different ways.

SOLDIER. How has she answered you?

SEXTON. I have reason to believe that
she will soon become my wife.

SOLDIER. So you haven't yet taken your
vow of celibacy?

SEXTON. Far from it! I may be a bit thin
on top, but I can marry whenever I
please. You'll see soon enough.

SOLDIER. Just a minute, you hairless
wretch. Answer me this: if the
wench truly welcomes your atten-
tions – which I doubt, considering
how paltry your gifts are – how do
you think she'll reward my gener-

---

SEXTON. What would you know, a
lecherous old card like you? I've
already won that little Queen of the
kitchen.

SOLDIER. Damn you, you trumped up
upstart! I've said I'll club your head
into pulp and I swear by the King
I will!

SEXTON. I'm trumped up! I'll deal you
what you deserve!

SOLDIER. Have you spoken to Cristina?

SEXTON. I speak to her … whenever I
want.

SOLDIER. Have you given her anything?

SEXTON. Lots.

SOLDIER. What? When?

SEXTON. I gave her a jam jar of the
purest, whitest hosts left over from
the Mass and also a few of our
leftover candles, white as ermine.

SOLDIER. What else have you given her?

SEXTON. I gave her one of these **prayer
cards** (emphasis DLS), with my
thousand desires to serve her
written on the back.

SOLDIER. And how the devil did she
respond to that?

SEXTON. I feel she's led me to believe
she will do me the honour of
becoming my wife.

SOLDIER. (*lifting the sexton's habit with
his rifle butt*) What? You've not
taken your vows of celibacy yet?

SEXTON. I haven't completely lost the
habit. I can marry when and whom
I please. You'll soon find out.

SOLDIER. Come here, you balding
under-sexton. Answer me this: How
can the girl have answered you so
favourably, which I don't believe
she has, given how piddling your
gifts are? Especially when you

osity? Only the other day I sent
her a letter, professing my love,
written on the back of a petition to
His Majesty, no less, with a list of
my past services and present needs.
(As a soldier I'm not ashamed to
admit I'm poor.) My petition was
approved and sent to the Royal
almsgiver for prompt attention. So
you see, I didn't give a thought to
the value of that piece of paper.
Instead, with a nonchalance and
generosity that astound even me, I
scribbled my note on the back of it.
> This done, my sullied heart can
> better rest,
> For by her saintly hand the
> note's possessed.
> (Smith, *Interludes* 61–2)

consider how large my gifts will be
in comparison. Why, just the other
day I sent her a love letter written
on the back of a communiqué that
I had sent directly to the King
himself, reminding His Majesty of
my past services and my present
needs. **I care not how I've served
my country, but how my country
can serve me** (emphasis DLS).
I'm not above admitting that I'm a
little financially embarrassed at the
moment. My petition **has recently
been returned to me stamped
"pending" by the Department of
"InDueCourse"** (emphasis DLS).
So, you can see how highly I rank
my love, if I'm prepared to extol
her virtues on the back of such an
important document.

Cervantes's text is loaded with allusions that would have resonated with a seventeenth-century audience, but which are lost on today's spectator/reader, in either language. Version A, as already noted, follows the original as closely as possible, using a style that can be easily read aloud or delivered by an actor. Problematic allusions are explained in the accompanying footnotes and hinted at in the text itself ("renegade knave"). Several lines of doggerel verse are inserted, either to make use of the card-playing imagery or to enliven the rhythm of the Soldier's lengthy discourse.[18]

Version B finds ingenious ways of incorporating problematic images (e.g. "heathen joker"), even exaggerating and prolonging the card-playing passage. Some lines are broadly interpreted for enhanced effect (as indicated with boldface): for example, the Soldier's boasting is emphasized with the anachronistic reference to "the Department of InDueCourse." The allusions to the Sexton's sexual abilities are explicitly reinforced through stage business, while the comic element is increased by translating Lorenzo Pasillas as Gordon Gherkin and by mixing modern and archaic language styles ("piddling" and "peradventure"). Mountjoy claims that of the three *Entremeses* that they adapted, this one (which they title *The Watchdog*) evolved furthest from the

---

[18] Angel Flores's 1962 translation omits all ambiguous allusions to cards and heretics. This translation belongs to the period when little was known about Spanish classical literature in the English-speaking world. It appears in a volume of plays by Spanish authors, including Lope de Rueda, Lope de Vega, Calderón, Tirso, Moratín, and Lorca, that was clearly intended to serve as an introduction to the Spanish theatrical tradition and, therefore, to be as uncomplicated as possible.

original. This came about during the period of rehearsals, during which, as she puts it, "we modified the script heavily for the purposes of clarity and comedy; if it wasn't funny, we cut or changed it, and if it was, we kept it."[19]

Mountjoy uses the term "Devised Translation" to describe the ongoing collaboration in rehearsal between Spanish-speakers (familiar with the literal meaning of the lines) and English dramaturges and playwrights "better equipped to render the poetry and provide speakable lines" (Thacker, "Sex, Treachery" 191). This is an obvious improvement on the practice of having a non-Spanish-speaking dramaturge/playwright/poet working from a literal translation prepared by someone fluent in Spanish who has no further influence on the final script, which may mean that the performance aspect dominates and risks distorting the original text.[20]

It may be argued that a performance text is just that: a blueprint for actors and directors, and that the aim of theatre is to put the message over to the audience as clearly as possible, that what may be omitted or changed in the spoken text can be supplemented by stage business and characterization. In the case of the staging of Cervantes's *Entremeses* in English, Mountjoy mentions the problem of how to explain some of the more abstruse allusions to British actors with no previous contact with Spanish literature: "Marrying our more scholarly appreciation of the *Entremeses* with the demands of 'making it funny' is the challenge of dramaturgy, and our Society struggled with this always mismatched pair of goals" (Thacker, "Sex, Treachery" 197). The demands that arise out of performance are grounded in considerations that the literary translator rarely has to confront. A reader can always reread a passage, turn to the footnote, or look elsewhere for further explanation of an obscure reference. The performance text loses its audience if it is not immediately understood, either through language or gesture, or both.

This does not mean that a performance text in translation is necessarily less true to the source than a "literary," or reader's text. Mountjoy's experience with staging the *Entremeses* shows how what has often been regarded as a chasm between the two worlds can be successfully bridged. A collaboration between people who are familiar with the text, on the one hand, and the staging requirements, on the other, stands a good chance of producing a playtext that serves both purposes well. Certainly, the interest of the public in reading the texts of the plays they see performed in the theatres has increased, as shown by the number of these texts available for sale in theatre bookshops.[21]

---

[19] Kathleen Mountjoy to DLS, in an e-mail dated 5 May 2006.

[20] This has been the practice for several of the translated playtexts mentioned in this essay, including Adrian Mitchell's versions of *El alcalde de Zalamea* and *La vida es sueño*.

[21] The playtexts performed by the RSC in its 2004 Spanish Golden Age season were published by Oberon Books. Absolute Classics has published several Golden Age playtexts, including Paul Whitworth's version of Tirso's *La venganza de Tamar* (1999), Adrian Mitchell's

We have come a long way from those early translations of the *Entremeses* that sought, at best, to bring the plays to the attention of English-speaking readers and persuade them that Cervantes was the author of more than just *Don Quijote*. Now it would be unthinkable to undertake their translation without also considering them as texts for performance. There will still be those who prefer to read these texts for themselves (Thacker, "Puedo yo" 160–3); nevertheless, the new emphasis on the performability of the Spanish text in English expands and enriches the scope of the translation.

Translation for performance is a constant process of transformation. Like the theatre that it serves, it must adjust to the evolving sensibilities of audiences. As long as there is an appetite for bringing the best of the world's drama to English-speaking stages, the art of translation will thrive, provided it, too, can flow with the times.

versions of *El alcalde de Zalamea* and *La vida es sueño* (1990) and other plays in versions by Laurence Boswell and David Johnston.

# Translation as Relocation

## BEN GUNTER

In the university and repertory theatres where I work, a crucial step in preparing high-quality performances is harnessing the imaginative energy generated by location. Location, after all, is a prime mover in mapping what Stanislavski calls a play's "given circumstances" (Benedetti 152). Precisely locating a production puts it in a position to profit from American Method techniques of acting and directing, which help the theatre professionals I know communicate and coordinate their best efforts for making shows succeed. Location translates drama off the page and onto the stage.

As a dramaturge passionately committed to seeing the *Comedia* succeed onstage in the United States today, I am challenged by the dramatic possibilities encoded within Golden Age plays' locales. Translating the performance cues that classic Spanish scripts store in their locations – the dramatic depthcharges packed into geographical, political, and social settings – strikes me as a uniquely promising strategy for empowering re-production. Translating location can forge connections between seventeenth-century playwriting conventions and twenty-first-century staging practices, making the stageworthiness of Golden Age dramaturgy visible to US producers, and shrinking the "no translations" blind spot that continues to keep the *Comedia* all too absent from American stages (Weber, "Foreign Drama" 269).

I hope to inspire more stageable translations of Golden Age plays by challenging you, the reader, to think about location in new ways. I will touch here on just three lines of inquiry. First, I will ask you to (re)consider how location functions in the making of classic Spanish drama, using *El burlador de Sevilla (The Trickster of Seville)* as a case in point. Next, I will invite you to examine how strategically relocating a Golden Age script can refresh its impact onstage. Preparing Cervantes's *La elección de los alcaldes de Daganzo (The Election of the Magistrates of Daganzo)* for performance in present-day north Florida will serve as a case study for this stage of the argument.[1]

---

[1] My case study tracks the relocation of an *entremés*, or interlude, into English, but I would argue that relocation can reenergize productions of Golden Age theatre in Spanish, too.

Finally, I will urge you to imagine how practicing translation as a process of rigorous relocation can open opportunities for translators to transmit Spanish theatre's stageworthiness (and not just its stage wording) into English.

## Location as an Active Player in Playmaking, Ripe for Translation

How does location claim its place as a vital participant in the dramatic construction of Golden Age performance texts? This question takes us into territory that, though not totally uncharted, stands definitely off the beaten track in *Comedia* studies. Yet following this line of inquiry is indispensable if one hopes to transplant Golden Age dramaturgy into American theatre practice. The world's first Don Juan play – arguably the most influential playscript in the history of Western theatre (Mandel 21) – provides a persuasive case in point. Transmitting the stageworthiness of *El burlador de Sevilla* clearly requires taking note of the script's dynamically programmed settings.

*El burlador* designedly "lays its scene" (to borrow Shakespeare's words for putting a performance-enriching environment to work in making great theatre) in an after-hours meeting, located *en palacio*. This location proves to be of primary importance; not only does it set the place for Don Juan's first rendezvous, it sets the stakes for the first scene of his first appearance on any stage. Meeting in the palace means that the people onstage are enacting a capital crime – what the dialogue preserved in *Tan largo me lo fiáis* (*What Long Credit You Give Me*) calls "crimen digno de muerte," a crime worthy of death (Fernández 63).

How do translators put this vital performance information into English? They don't. Despite energetic research I have found only one instance where this widely-translated, world-famous text equips English-speaking actors with the slightest hint of the crucial sense of trespass that informs its opening moment. That hint surfaces in the opening lines of Adrienne M. Schizzano and Oscar Mandel's *Playboy of Seville*.

| | |
|---|---|
| ISABELA. | Leave quietly, Duke Octavio. |
| DON JUAN. | I will be light as a feather. |
| ISABELA. | Still – I'm afraid you'll be heard. You know it's a crime to enter the palace at night. (51) |

The production of *El astrólogo fingido* (*The Mock Astrologer*) presented at the Chamizal Siglo de Oro Drama Festival in 2006 (which culturally relocated that *comedia* into Peking Opera), and the production of *No hay burlas con el amor* (*There's No Playing with Love*) presented at Chamizal in 2007 (which re-presented the play as a 1930s American musical) stand as strong persuasions of the performance power that strategic relocation can generate. Susan Jonas lays out a thought-provoking introduction to the delights and dangers of relocation in her discussion of "Transposition" as a "Strategy for Adaptation" in the superlative article "Aiming the Canon at Now."

Nine times out of ten, *El burlador* in English opens without even a glimmering of the complex sense of adventure that its setting writes into its performance score. Location gets lost in translation.[2]

The magnitude of this loss for staging *El burlador* (and, by extension, a wide range of sensitively set *comedias*) in the United States today is enormous. Primed by high-profile repackagings of Don Juan in popular culture (ranging from Ludacris's rap music to Jeremy Leven's movie *Don Juan de Marco*), US actors, directors, and audiences expect every Don Juan story to be all about sex. By setting its opening scene *en palacio*, *El burlador* explicitly sets a more complicated agenda for its action than sexual conquest. Dislocating the inciting event from its setting disastrously compromises its impact, flattening the world of the play into a generic background for booty calls.[3]

Location's role in giving directors broader visions of *El burlador*'s scope, actors deeper roles to play, and audiences higher challenges to rise to is not limited to the play's first scene, nor to events that take place *en palacio*. As the plot develops, so does location's part in making this play playable. Like the precisely positioned sensors that produce an EKG, the cities that Don Juan visits electrify the performance of his story with diagnostic snapshots of a body politic in crisis. Looked at from this angle, location brings home a blackly funny picture of corruption eating away at Spain's political practices, social standards, and moral values.

Naples – the imperial outpost that houses the palace where *El burlador* begins – surfaces repeatedly in Golden Age dramaturgy as a place where moral, social, and political boundaries get redrawn. This is evident in masterpieces ranging from *El condenado por desconfiado (Damned for Despair)*, where Naples precipitates the surprise reversal between saved sinner and damned saint, to *El perro del hortelano (The Dog in the Manger)*, where Naples lures the audience into rooting for a culturally transgressive marriage between countess and commoner, and even encompasses *El pintor de su deshonra (The Painter of His Dishonor)*, where Naples stretches the gender politics of honor past the breaking point. Naples in the early seventeenth century was emblematic of Spain's expensive, exhausting struggle to hold on to an overextended empire; notoriously insubordinate (Fernández 56–7), it played to perfection the role of territory whose very name ("new *polis*")

---

2    The translations that I surveyed before arriving at this conclusion were printed between 1959 and 2006. In addition to Schizzano and Mandel's *Playboy* (the first conflation of *Tan largo* with the *Burlador*), my survey sample includes versions by Campbell, O'Brien, Starkie, Oppenheimer, Walcott, Edwards, Alvarez, Dear, Kidd, and Matthews.

3    There is space to develop this idea with more of the depth it deserves in my dissertation. See the chapter on "Decoding Don Juan's Sex Life" at http://etd.lib.fsu.edu/theses/available/etd-11212005-230512.

challenged the concept of a permanent political order. Opening *El burlador* in Naples prompted audience members to prick up their ears for up-to-date political implications in a *comedia* that is officially set in a fantasy "past."[4] Location provocatively positions this play to get audiences thinking about their nation's political health from the get-go.

When the scene shifts, it moves into even more satirically charged locales, bringing the diagnostic project of the dramaturgy closer to home. The King of Castile's first appearance puts him onstage in conference with his ambassador to Portugal, Don Gonzalo. This Colin Powell figure (soon to become Don Juan's Stone Guest) spins an extravagantly protracted panegyric, painting word-pictures of Lisbon as the eighth wonder of the world. Here, location sharpens performance with the bite of social satire. Between 1580 and 1640, Lisbon – capital of a province that was politically part of the Spanish Empire, but socially quite distinct – acted as a galling counter-example to sore spots in Spain's self-image as the world's most civilized society.

Spain was officially xenophobic, addicted to the idea that it took "purity of blood" to guarantee social superiority (Defourneaux 36–9). In Lisbon, by contrast, Otherness flourished. Jews and *mudéjares* who had been expelled from Castile moved to Lisbon and made that city a living testimonial to prosperity through diversity (Lynch 122–4). Seventeenth-century Spain was economically diabetic, poisoned by the easy money that was pouring in from the New World and running right back out again. Untrammeled by social taboos against usury, Lisbon moneylenders could play this system like bandits, leeching on to the capital that was leaking out of Spain (Kamen 14–15). While social anxieties tended to paralyze early modern Spanish males in poses of ludicrous self-absorption,[5] Lisbon's relative tolerance set its menfolk free to play a fascinating range of identity positions. (As López-Vázquez notes in his watershed edition of *El burlador*, it was in this era that "portugués" came to be "sinónimo de enamorizado o de galante" ("synonymous with ardent or gallant") [213].) Making Lisbon a major player in the mental geography of the play, then, empowered *El burlador de Sevilla* to speak to its audiences in their own here-and-now, subversively unsettling seventeenth-century Spaniards' sense of ethnic, economic, and erotic superiority. Loca-

---

[4] While translations tend to antiquate the time period of *El burlador*, emphasizing Alfonso XI's historicity in their introductory material and even their word choice, the Spanish original's dramaturgy elects to operate in a calculated double time, putting characters from the nation's epic past onstage in the middle of messes that are clearly up-to-date. The performance effect is exhilarating and unsettling – like casting George Washington to oversee the crisis in American identity posed by the Iraq war.

[5] For notions of performing the *hidalgo*, see Covarrubias 590–2 and Defourneaux 40–4.

tion gives the playmaking grounds for mounting a thoroughgoing satire of Spanish social mores.[6]

Location positions *El burlador* to critique Spanish moral values, too. The play's eponymous place name – Seville – brings a host of implications onstage with it. Founded on sandstone so unstable that its architects had to put down pilings before putting up buildings (Covarrubias traces one etymology for the city's name to this feature [936]), Don Juan's hometown mapped a landscape of get-rich-quick morality on to the Spanish psyche (Defourneaux 74–90). By royal decree, all bullion from the New World had to enter Spain through Seville. From Seville, Spanish-owned raw materials were reexported globally. Into Seville, top-dollar finished goods were imported from all over. By the early seventeenth century, Seville had come to epitomize the disdain for domestic industry, the drive for windfall profits, and the misdirection of moral energy that was causing preachers and playwrights to see a Judgment Day headed Spain's way (Elliott 241–61).

As spiritual home to the self-made man, Seville was the perfect setting for upsetting the cult-following that was fast making *valor* – what I would translate as "machismo" today – the most fervently held moral value in Spain. A troubling equation of moral superiority with the ability to carry off a grand gesture at the last minute, *valor* held powerful appeal for an empire in decline. *Valor* excused its devotees from the disciplines of self-examination and self-correction, championing in their stead heroes like "Don Rodrigo en la horca" ("Don Rodrigo on the scaffold"), whose "supreme elegance" in the face of execution inspired eyewitnesses to this hated royal favorite's fall from grace to make him an instant "idol, with people fighting over his relics" and proclaiming the day of his death "the most glorious day in the whole of our century" (Defourneaux 33). *Valor* made a supreme, instantly redeeming virtue out of facing death unfazed. In Seville, Don Juan buys into this morally bankrupt belief. In Seville, and in order to astound the world with his *valor*, his entrepreneurial ethics talk him into keeping a dinner date with the Statue. And in Seville, his faith in *valor* takes him straight to hell (Fernández 92–4). Location drives home the moral lesson of the play.

How much of this richly textured political, social, and moral satire comes through in translation? Precious little. With the exception of radically non-traditional treatments of *El burlador* – translations on the order of Derek Walcott's *Joker of Seville* – every English version of this *comedia* that I have

---

6   Lisbon's impact is deliciously enhanced by the existence of a "Lisbon in Seville," the red-light district where Don Juan's bosom buddy the Marqués de la Mota gets his kicks. The ways in which the dramaturgy multiplies meanings for "Lisboa" – tracing its etymology back to Ulysses and his *Odyssey*, giving it footprints in epic and in Eden, establishing outposts for it in Portugal and in Spain – underscores location's participation in scoring dramatic effects, and argues a multivalent impact for location on performance.

seen seems to regard its locations as interchangeable boilerplate backdrops to seduction, pre-painted and peripheral, minimally distinguishable, fundamentally uninformative performance afterthoughts. Historically, location comes across in translation as dramatic deadweight.

Recent scholarship has begun laying the foundation for more dynamic translation of location, as critics unearth evidence that *comedias* carefully plot not only pivotal locales, but also movement between settings as well. In his elegant bilingual edition of Calderón, for example, A. K. G. Paterson describes a trilogy of carefully situated honor plays: *El médico de su honra (The Surgeon of His Honour)*, *A secreto agravio, secreta venganza (Secret Injury, Secret Revenge)*, and *El pintor de su deshonra*. He notes, "Their respective locations in Andalusia (the frontier with Islam), Lisbon (the Atlantic seaboard that gives onto an overseas empire) and Barcelona–Naples (a Mediterranean orientation) provide reference points in a geocultural map that unfolds from play to play" (17). Similarly, Dawn Smith's luminous translations of Cervantes's *entremeses* – eye-openingly academic and invitingly theatrical at the same time – profit by geographic specificity. Her *Election of the Magistrates of Daganzo* roots itself in an actual historical locus "well known in the time of Cervantes: the case of the feudal lord of Daganzo who refused to approve the appointment of magistrates elected by the town, on grounds that they were incompetent to serve" (*Eight Interludes* 25). If the stageworthiness of Golden Age drama is ever to resurface in English, primed for production with the imaginative vigor that "given circumstances" give a script, if we are ever to remedy the loss of "oomph" in translation that US theatre people are bemoaning when they say they cannot perform *comedias* because they have "no translations," much more of this scholarly reflection on location is urgently needed.

## Relocation as a Tool for Transmitting Stageworthiness

So how do we start unlocking the performance cues that are coded into Spanish scripts' "given circumstances," and then go about re-creating, in dramatically different times, places, and forms of speech, the performance impact that those circumstances were designed to generate? These questions open a second line of inquiry, complete with its own case study: a groundbreaking experience with putting an election satire that Cervantes published in 1615 onstage in north Florida in 2004. During this eye-opening encounter with Golden Age dramaturgy, a team of dramaturges stumbled into a series of relocations-on-the-spot – places where performers found sudden jolts of immediacy as they transported bits of their own hometown into isolated spots from Cervantes's dramatic world. Our attempt to make sense of these oddball blasts of brilliance grew into a quest to field-test the full-scale, systematic,

and strategic use of relocation as a methodology for transmitting performance information across cultural barriers.

The work on *La elección de los alcaldes de Daganzo* began as part of a
dramaturgical workshop entitled "Cervantes on Stage." This workshop was
designed as a four-week immersion excursion for twenty-one middle-school
students who elected to join a summer enrichment program at Quincy Music
Theatre, one scant block from the Gadsden County Courthouse and smack
dab in the middle of the first community in panhandle Florida to be named an
All-America City (1996). In addition to a score of youngsters, participants in
"Cervantes on Stage" included four grownup dramaturges with professional
credits in theatre production and graduate-school training in Spanish, theatre
history, and musical theatre. Together, we embarked on a bold adventure:
getting to know Golden Age theatre by putting it onstage. Product was not the
point; we did not aspire to polished final showings. Process was our passion.
We wanted to work out ways of grasping a script's stageworthiness, and then
identify tools for transmitting that impact across cultural boundaries in terms
that would make sense to twenty-first-century Americans.

Since not one of the young people pursuing this quest was learning any
Spanish at all in school (though they were all living in areas where the
agribusiness boom would go bust without resident populations of Spanish-
speaking "migrants"), we launched our adventure by chasing performance
possibilities through a series of English translations, searching out situations
that could tickle our fancies, invite us to step inside, and equip us to act their
attractions with all our might. We would divide the troupe into teams, read
comparative treatments of crucial scenes out loud, then bring back moments
that screamed "Perform Me!" to the workshop as a whole. After thoroughly
acquainting ourselves with two different Cervantes one-acts (*El retablo de las
maravillas* [*The Marvellous Puppet Show*] and *La elección de los alcaldes
de Daganzo*) in three different English renditions (Morley's, Honig's, and
Smith's), we cast secret ballots to pick one play to prep for staging. *La elección* won the vote by a pregnantly dimpled hanging chad.

When our workshop got down to the practical business of preparing *La
elección* for performance in the US, however, we hit a roadblock – in fact,
a whole series of roadblocks. Cervantes starts his *entremés* with characters
trading insults in a political dogfight that comes out of nowhere. How do you
re-create the sense of starting *in medias res* when the conflict comes at you
*ex nihilo*, with no context to orient your point of attack? The action proceeds
to arc through what must be (judging by how characters react after the fact)
an electrifying array of plot twists: lightning shifts in political alignment,
instant tests of political muscle, and covert coups. These are all developments
that promise magnificent material for performing, but they proved extremely
difficult for us to locate precisely in text. How do you re-present a satire on
political infighting when it is not clear who is in power or what is at stake,

and where? Then Cervantes ends this *entremés* with a kind of *diabolus ex machina*, as a troupe of gypsies invades the private interviews with candidates that Daganzo's power players have set up to settle the election. The result is an aggressively unclosed performance structure that puts a bunch of Outsiders downstage center in the final scene. How do you stage a climax that is designed to throw the world of the play into dynamic flux when that dramatic world's locators are never fixed? With no dramatic markers clearly pointing "this way up," how can you successfully turn a theatrical universe upside down?

Cheek by jowl with these daunting challenges to production, *La elección* offered us tasty inducements to perform it. Sometimes a delicious moment would pop off the page as our troupe of eight- to fourteen-year old *cervantistas* read it, putting enough of the play within our grasp to make trying for the whole enchilada irresistible. As we studied the spots that our theatrical knights errant found most playable – the place where someone recommends a candidate for *alcalde* solely on the basis of his wine-tasting abilities, the spot where lifelong best enemies who have been trying to act grown-up about their differences revert to "you-started-it" wrangling, and the moment where a candidate's stump speech begins to smack suspiciously of "compassionate conservatism" – we began to see an innovative way through the roadblocks standing between us and a fully realizable performance.

Common ground, we found, linked the spots where our actor-dramaturges were striking pay dirt. All their flashes of brilliance sprang from sites in the script where the play's location in Daganzo paralleled our performers' local knowledge of Quincy. Intuitive, sporadic, accidental relocation was helping performers to make richly textured bits of theatre out of places that would otherwise play as one-dimensional clichés. Here's how.

We had introduced Daganzo to "Cervantes on Stage" as a small town in backwoods Spain where big decisions get made – a cultural analog, we came to realize, for Quincy, the All-American micropolis where most of our workshoppers were born. As the seat of local self-government for a whole Whitman's Sampler of rednecks (blue-collar farm workers, middle-class farm owners, and fabulously wealthy folks whose granddaddies invested in "Co-Cola" [as pronounced by the locals]), Quincy was singularly well-equipped to make certain characters from Daganzo come alive for our young actors. Quincy was also perfectly positioned to enrich some of the relationships between Daganzo's characters: intimate local knowledge of Quincy feuds, Quincy taboos, Quincy histories, and Quincy power structures could occasionally make key events in Daganzo read like reenactments of real life for our researchers. Conditions in Quincy could lift lively elements of Cervantes's "given circumstances" in Daganzo off the page, to carry aspects of the play's little-town lampoon of culture-wide weaknesses right into the here and now.

How were performers finding flashes of complexity in one-note character-izations? By taking bits of Quincy back into Daganzo. When *regidor* Alonso Algarroba nominates *labrador* Juan Berrocal for *alcalde*, for example, he can muster only one paper-thin shred of evidence that this nominee deserves a place in public life: Berrocal's extraordinary talent "For top-notch tasting of wines" (Morley, *Interludes* 59). Yet collaborators in "Cervantes on Stage" eagerly competed to act out Algarroba's nomination speech – dialogue that looks flat as a pancake on the page. And they repeatedly filled performances of this speech with a curious mixture of fascination and forbidden fruit that was irresistible to experience and mysterious to explain.

Mysterious, that is, until we dug into location's implications for this dramatic situation. Prohibition lingered in north Florida long after its repeal at the national level, making wine consumption a decisive marker for Gadsden County residents' social and religious status to this day. In Quincy terms (as participants in "Cervantes on Stage" were swift to point out), Berrocal's fitness for public office represented something very different from a one-dimensional gag. Local facts of life in Gadsden County made this character's candidacy rip the lid off a well-aged brew of social and moral anxieties that are alive and active right now. Accidental relocation filled this one-note nomi-nation for a one-joke character with complex layers of conflict, challenge, adventure, and stress for our performers to play.

How were young people finding spurts of surprising glee in relationships between this old play's characters? By taking snippets of Quincy back into specific spots in Daganzo. Take the running war of words between Algarroba and his rival *regidor* Panduro as a case in point. The two *regidores'* relation-ship quickly falls into the pattern of Panduro outsmarting himself, as he tries to outshine Algarroba with big words that backfire on him. Our actors filled one particular skirmish in this predictable conflict with an arresting sense of high-stakes suspense. At the crucial point where Algarroba has a brainstorm about how to settle the election – "just have / Each candidate come in and let good Master / Cloven Hoof, our college man, examine / Them" (Honig, *Inter-ludes* 62) – Panduro outsmarts himself twice in a row. He tries to show off his knowledge of medicine, only to get *examining* doctors (*prota*-médicos) confused with *hernia* doctors (*potra*-médicos); then he falls afoul of the law, where he makes a hash of the title for a "royal prosecutor" (*fiscal*).

Heady humor, this – the kind of wordplay that translators' footnotes like to call "untranslatable." Where were our performers finding grounds for building a vital, immediate relationship into these distant, dusty jokes? In Quincy's local experience of election-day wrangling. To Gadsden County kids, Panduro and Algarroba sounded just like a pair of good ole boys mule-headedly rehashing *Bush vs Gore* on the courthouse steps. By channeling their hometown knowledge of contested election practices into their performances at this point, our young Floridians found a moment of real dramatic gusto in these characters' repetitive rivalry.

How were our collaborators surprising us with little glimpses of a big-picture satire winking through peepholes in their performance? By using Quincy to decode bits and pieces of Daganzo. In the event that comes closest to settling *La elección*'s election, for instance – a surprisingly eloquent address by candidate Pedro de la Rana – I expected to be amused by Cervantes "putting apparently serious comments into the mouths of unlikely characters" (Smith, *Eight Interludes* 27). What took me by surprise, though, was hearing performers bring an electrifying sense of outrage to their readings of Rana's big moment. It was thrilling to hear them handle the rousing conclusion that Rana builds up to, as he caps his conservative platform with the promise to make compassion his official policy.

> Apart from that, I will practice moderation,
> And temper firmness with a gentle hand.
> I will never shame the poor unhappy creature
> Whose crimes I find myself obligated to hear;
> A judge's thoughtless words will often punish
> More than the sentence that a man must serve.
> For power should not diminish courtesy [...].   (Smith 48–9)

Where did Quincy kids come by their insistence that a hideously funny play for power underlay these apparently magnanimous sentiments – that, to quote Dawn Smith, "This is more than a satire of provincial life; it also has a deeper irony that derives from the exposure of racial prejudice" (*Eight Interludes* 26)? Serendipitous relocation was their inspiration.

In Quincy in the summer of 2004, "compassionate conservatism" was a high-profile combatant in a hotly contested argument about how politics should be practiced in the United States. Performers' intensely local positions regarding "compassionate conservatism" charged elements of Rana's oratory with a stirring sense of big issues at war beneath the speech's pacific surface. Our performers played Rana's big ending as local, but not small; the incongruity being lampooned in their performances had nothing to do with a cutesy contrast between modes in a character's self-expression (the Frog who sings), and everything to do with an edgy contest between competing ideals in a nation's identity (the election whose conduct prefigures an empire's destiny).

The more we studied the intuitive, partial, but excitingly potent form of relocation being practiced by our performers, the more impressed we became by location's role in the making of this play. Every success that our actors stumbled into stood at a threshold where location takes the play to a more universal level. Berrocal's local-color qualification for office serves as a stepping stone for the writing to introduce local comedy on a larger scale, opening opportunities for the script to poke fun at a whole string of Spanish towns "famous for their wines" (Morley 59). The local smallness of Algarroba and Panduro's word-wrangling billboards the brilliance of Algarroba's revelation that "councilmen should be examined, too. / Then anyone who's smart enough to pass / Would be awarded a diploma, and / With that he could support himself" (Honig 62).

By making conditions that are local to Daganzo emblematic of what ails the entire Spanish Empire, the scripting underscores the dynamism of location. Cervantes, in fact, makes location the basis for "the inherently subversive world of the Interlude" in which (to quote Dawn Smith) "he places the burden of interpretation on readers and spectators, inviting them to complete the 'meaning' of the play in accordance with whatever context may seem appropriate to them" (*Eight Interludes* 27).

Location acts as a dramaturgical powerhouse because location generates context – the context that performers and spectators need in order to manufacture meaning. Relocation makes interpretations come alive, because relocation (even when practiced accidentally) refreshes, recharges, foregrounds, and reanimates context. If relocation-on-the-spot contains such potential for energizing (re)production, what could relocation accomplish if put into practice systematically, as a methodology for re-producing Spanish drama in English?

## New Strategies for Re-producing Golden Age Plays in the US

To generate a thoroughly successful (re)production, relocation needs to be systematic and strategic (not just accidental and sporadic) – translator-driven, rather than tossed in according to performer taste. Otherwise, relocation runs the risk of falling prey to the perils that dramaturge Susan Jonas catalogues in her essay on "Aiming the Canon at Now: Strategies for Adaptation."

> [I]t can remain merely cosmetic, provide an easy one-to-one correspondence, or a static equation. Moreover, it hardly seems worth the effort if it normalizes the play's otherness. After all, one of the greatest appeals of the theatre is that it takes us on journeys, stretching experience and imagination. (249)

The journey that we went on as we relocated *La elección de los alcaldes de Daganzo* into *Electing a Sheriff in Podunk County, Florida* did not necessarily lead us to radical-sounding text. Indeed, the dialogue we developed for the high point in Algarroba and Panduro's word-war ended up sounding remarkably like Dawn Smith's translation, playing on the resonant dissonance between "impotent" and "important," "persecutor" and "prosecutor" to transmit the delicious confusion between doctors who are *potra-* or *prota-médicos* and lawyers who are *friscal* or *fiscal* into English (see Smith, *Eight Interludes* 45–6). The product of our relocation could look quite conventional.

The process that our relocation journey charted, however, was both radically different from canonical practices described in Golden Age translation literature (Dixon, "Translating" 93–6), and also enormously useful for clarifying the innovative approaches to re-producing Spanish drama in English that directors and dramaturges are just beginning to describe (Johnston, *Stages* 281–94). The "*arte nuevo*" we discovered merits attention, I think, because it is eminently replicable. Its techniques look beyond rural settings, workshop conditions, adolescent actors, and one-act plays, to the fundamentals of reanimating any Golden Age play in the US today. I will focus here on three lessons that we learned, as we used strategic relocation to work out a stageable solution for beginning our performance, a strategic approach to ending our performance, and practical guidelines for keeping the impact of our performance systematically on track through all the plot twists in the play's middle.

Analyzing subtext taught us how to make sense in beginning our performance. Bitter, repeated word wars between Algarroba and Panduro dominate the wording of the opening scene. Taken philologically, these characters stand as irreconcilable (if all but untranslatable) opposites. Approached dramaturgically, however, these characters function as representatives of the same status quo; their sharpest textual combat (that tussle between *potra-alcaldes* and *prota-alcaldes*, which immediately escalates into the pitched battle between *friscal* and *fiscal*) in fact serves to set up their subtlest political collaboration (the campaign to fix the election via the *remedio* and *arbitrio* of holding private interviews with the candidates). Subtextually, Algarroba and Panduro serve the play as matching pillars of an embattled establishment. That is why they join forces to set up the candidate interviews that drive the play's second scene.

Having decoded that subtext, we were in a position to re-create the fundamental structure of the scene – its "skeleton," not just its "skin" – as we strategized a way to relocate the "given circumstance" of Algarroba and Panduro's combative collaboration into the Here and Now. In the summer of 2004, folks in Gadsden County were watching nominating conventions with eagle eyes; for the first time since grandparents were kids, the Gadsden County Sheriff's office was up for grabs in the fall election. When we asked our performers to show us an event where superficial differences between opponents would serve to underscore their fundamental similarities, they gleefully acted out a series of nominating conventions, ostensibly competitive, but hilariously identical in shape.

We constructed a prologue to our performance out of a series of such rallies. Contextualized within these careful exhibitions of conflict, calculatedly staged for public consumption, Algarroba and Panduro's need to articulate opposition while enacting collusion sprang vividly to life. This comic appropriation of a present-day political process gave us a sparkling, performance-stimulating "way in" to the beginning of the play.

By shifting translation's focus away from dialogue (the "skin" of a play) and toward dramatic structure (the "skeleton" that gives the "skin" its fundamental shape), relocation taught us the value of anchoring translation in analysis that is fully dramaturgical (rather than narrowly philological) in scope. Decoding subtext, we learned, empowers performance. The more we pulled subtext into the foreground, the more ownership our American actors brought to their performances, and the more meaning American audiences read into our production.

Foregrounding subtext could make our script sound very different from scholarly translations. Characters' attitudes became audible, and characters' names became active. Thus relocated, the racist undertones in Pedro de la Rana's campaign speech came much nearer to the surface, and Rana himself (the singing Frog) became "Ribbit."

RIBBIT.    If you pick me for sheriff,
                    I will be firm, but fair. (*finding solid ground*)
               I will treat everybody the same –
                    greasers ... I will check you for green cards or visas
                    gold-tooth thugs... I will watch you for dealing the drugs
                    burned-out biker chicks ... no turning tricks at dollar flicks
                    kikes ... don't take whites' cars on hikes
                    wops ... no rolling stops
                    got no home? away you roam!
                    welfare mother? marry some brother!
                    beat your wife? hey, that's life!

Applied to *Comedia* translation generally, the principle of starting the translation process with a thorough analysis of subtext, privileging dramaturgy over philology in the process of decoding performance text, would totally transform US directors' and actors' assessment of Spanish drama's stageworthiness. Imagine a translation of *El burlador* where the potent allusions to cowardice, excrement, street smarts, and regional attitudes that are packed into the name that the playwriting gives to Don Juan's sidekick – Catalinón – get unpacked for actors to play. To date, only one translation that I have been able to locate makes the slightest attempt to transmit information as fundamental to this character's performance as the meaning of his name. Michael Kidd's *Don Juan, Ladykiller of Seville*, tentatively dubbed Don Juan's servant "Chicken(shit)."

Recoding characters' social standings taught us how to find a stageable ending for our performance. Clearly, status is crucial to characters' participation in Cervantes's improvised *elección*. Insiders like Algarroba and Panduro set the agenda, Candidates like Pedro de la Rana compete for a say-so in renegotiating the agenda, and Outsiders (the gypsies) exert no official influence on the agenda. Making performance sense of the play's final scene meant retrofitting the script with legible social markers, privileging the impact of shifts in a character's status over the shape of that character's speech. We needed a way to recode Outsider-ness, so our actors could act (and their audiences could track) status shifts.

Relocation got us there. We asked our eight- to fourteen-year-old *cervantistas* to improvise examples of the silent but legible line that separates Insiders from Outsiders in Quincy. Their favorite example was the Wal-Mart Superstore, where Mexican migrants brought in by busloads to shop will intersect (but never equally intermingle) with cheerleaders and sports luminaries from the high school, dropping in to hang out. Relocating Daganzo's social distinctions to Quincy, we re-presented Cervantes's gypsies as "Mexican migrant chicks," and had them enter singing (to the tune of the *Habanera* from Bizet's *Carmen*):

> We're those Mexican migrant chicks,
> you thought we'd pick a quick crop, then leave the sticks.
> Work kept coming and so did we –
> we've gone from green cards to full-fledged citizenry.

Recoding the gypsies as "Mexican migrants" helped us put onstage the best scholarship we could find about what *los gitanos* (those *diablos*) meant for Cervantes's subversively open-ended finale (Smith, *Eight Interludes* 26–7) – a subversive inversion of the social order, a surprise humanization of the Other, and a delicious displacement of the status quo, seducing even the Pillars of Establishment.

Relocating occupations helped us stage the play's turning points. Literal translation created counterproductive performance cues – false cognates in the performance score. As we approached show time for *Electing a Sheriff*, we ran into a problem: nobody wanted to play Berrocal, because in traditional translation he came across to the Quincy actors as a boozer.[7] Moreover, people balked at reading Algarroba and Panduro, because traditional translation loads their language with (speaking from a Quincy perspective) religious

---

[7] "Boozer" is clearly not the way that other characters in the play assess Berrocal. In the world of the play, Berrocal's palate is seen as awe-inspiring – a talent that seriously advances the public good.

profanity.[8] Relocation led us to solutions that made our *cervantistas* eager to embody these roles in the middle of the play.

To transmit the rich mixture of performance possibilities that Berrocal's gift puts onstage in the Spanish original – part admiration for a palate so marvelously elevated above the pedestrian, part angst about Daganzo's competitiveness in a global economy, part political satire – we strategically relocated this character's occupation to today's America. We translated Juan Berrocal into Jane Colecoke, a taste-tester in Quincy's Coca-Cola bottling plant. This bypassed the anxiety that direct transcription of the character's vocation had created for our actors and their audiences (the anxiety of playing a drunk in an effectively dry county) and re-created the stimulating blend of mores in motion that Berrocal would have embodied for a *corral* audience. Targeting the character's business for re-production by actors and audiences who are clearly rooted in a specific location replaced a false cognate with a truly playable performance text.

To preserve Panduro's emphatic way with words without turning him into the verbal spawn of Satan, we inserted *bleeps* everywhere he salts his statements with religious references. This delighted actors, and tickled audiences' imaginations – exactly the kind of effect Panduro's choice of words was calculated to arouse in the first place. To re-create the "oomph" of Algarroba's faith-based language, we recast it to quote US catchphrases like "so help me God." Thus relocated, interchanges that our actors had found unplayable became showstoppers. Here is a sample, where Algarroba ("Lonnie Snappea" in our relocation) conceives the bright idea of settling the election by interviewing the candidates. Panduro ("Col. Cornpone" in our relocation) provides political cross-fire, while the town's legal expert Pesuña (our "Judge Hangham") takes the final word.

SNAPPEA.       *(light bulb!)* I've got it! Let's round up the candidates and get Judge Hangham to cross-examine them. If anybody knows the ins and outs of Podunk County politics, Judge Hangham knows 'em. She can get the truth, the whole truth, and nothing but the truth out of all four candidates, so help me God. Then we can pick the one we want to win this election.

CORNPONE.    Snappea, that's a get-out-the-vote maneuver worthy of Karl Rove. Wouldn't surprise me to find that the President spends a lot of time examining crosses in the *bleep*ing Oval Office. After all, ole W's got im*pot*ent advisors up

---

8    "Profanity" is diametrically opposed to what the world of the play hears in Algarroba and Panduro's religiously inflected language. The playwriting makes the *regidores'* oaths, in fact, into implements of reconciliation and truce; structurally, the words our actors found offensive are the reverse of stumbling blocks to public virtue.

|  | there in DC, just like Jeb's got im*po*tent sheriffs down here in Florida. |
|---|---|
| SNAPPEA. | Col. Cornpone, you mean "im*por*tant," not "im*po*tent." |
| CORNPONE. | Well, *bleepity-bleep* my *bleep*! I thought Judge Hangham was going to do the cross-up examinations around here. You talk just like a legal persecutor. |
| SNAPPEA. | That's "prosecutor," you nachal-born fool! |

Imagine translation that targets turning points in *El burlador de Sevilla* for production by actors and reception by audiences with this kind of specificity. Historically, translation has yet to make it clear that a revolutionary act takes place at the one place where two of Don Juan's "victims" connect: the pivotal scene where a duchess joins ranks with a fisherwoman, the *Comedia* equivalent of Thelma bonding with Louise (Fernández 48–50, 89–90). Everything about that scene's location – its geographical placement at a porous border, its placement in the plot at a sea-change in Don Juan's fortunes, its jarring juxtaposition of social levels, even its setting in a unique meter – screams "new idea in development." The more literally translators copy this scene's language, however, the more lamentably they obscure the characters' ideological breakthrough. Fidelity to philology adulterates dramaturgy.

### Relocating Translation

Approaching translation as a rigorous, strategic, and systematic process of relocation can teach us new ways to transmit theatre text, because Golden Age classics ranging from Cervantes's election *entremés* to *El burlador de Sevilla* build on location to create performance effects that are absolutely central to their stageworthiness. Grasping this "given circumstance" of Golden Age dramaturgy can teach us to decode subtexts, to recode status adjustments, and to target stage speech to actors and audiences who are precisely located in time and space, in order to recover the performance information that *comedias* build into their "given circumstances." Perhaps the most promising aspect of this *arte nuevo* is its capacity for enriching the performance of character. Relocation sharpens characters' definition, heightens their theatricality, foregrounds their occupations, articulates their allegiances, specifies their social standings, clarifies their attitudes and relationships, and complicates the challenge they pose to dismissal as formulaic or underdeveloped.

In the UK, using character (rather than dialogue) as the basis for translating *comedias* has sparked an impressive resurgence in Golden Age drama's (re)production. Here is how Laurence Boswell, one of the architects of that resurgence, describes his process of preparing classic Spanish scripts for performances in English:

Language is the very surface of a play; as a simple metaphor, it's a kind of wrapping. Faced with a blank sheet of paper, the first time I tried to create a script, I found I could give a character almost any word which would make a kind of sense of the relationship they were in and would kind of relate to the original language. [...] And I thought I couldn't be that imprecise, so I then learnt the whole story and got in touch with the characters, with the rhythm. [...] Then when you go back to the specific moment, the choice of words goes from infinity to two or three, because that character couldn't use that word at that moment. That is how I come at it, like someone who is making a wheel, as it were, trying to look at the hub of the play. (quoted in Johnston, *Stages* 283)

Practicing translation as relocation offers US translators a handle on Boswell's wheel – a concrete way to use "given circumstances" as a tool to get in touch with characters and bring them precisely, vividly, and completely back to life. That's an accomplishment bound to attract eager attention among the theatre people I know.

# DIRECTING AND CONTEXTUALIZING THE *COMEDIA*

# Rehearsing *Spite for Spite*

## MICHAEL HALBERSTAM

In 1998 I was fortunate enough to direct Agustín Moreto's *El desdén con el desdén*, in a world première translation/adaptation by Dakin Matthews entitled *Spite for Spite*. The play was produced by Writers' Theatre, a company I founded in 1993 (and where I still serve as artistic director) on the North Shore of Chicago. Writers' Theatre is dedicated to the word and the artist, deriving all inspiration from the written word and nurturing the process of the artist. I offer here a description of our rehearsal process in bringing *Spite for Spite* from the page to the stage. From a working theatrical practitioner's perspective I will take you through our journey and share some of the challenges we faced along the way in bringing a long-neglected classic to life again.

When approaching the plays of the Spanish Golden Age, we must remember that there are specific dramatic conventions and traditions peculiar to the era. The social mindset of the modern audience exists in a significantly different mental landscape than that of the average Spanish Golden Age ticket buyer. Dakin Matthews's vibrant adaptation of Moreto's text, while preserving the specifics and intents of the source material, must be regarded as a hybrid – archaic in its construct and foundation, but very contemporary in its styling. The adaptation/translation is deliciously scribed with an eye to contemporary American vernacular. Accordingly, we approached Matthews's script as a world première original.

When I first contacted Dakin prior to rehearsals I asked him if there were any conventions that I should be aware of. He replied "No! You're about to invent them all. This has never been produced before." It was at this point I realized that research into the milieu and traditions of Moreto's original, although important, would only get me so far, and that ultimately in rehearsal I would have to deal exclusively with the text at hand. If I became too bogged down in research, I risked staging a museum piece or a lecture, with no emotional relevance for the audience. The process of bringing this classic to fresh relevancy was mostly free of strife and drama because *Spite for Spite* is an extremely well-written and well-constructed play. Consequently, in order to approach it, all I had to do was pay attention to its text and the demands therein.

Love, wife, honor, fidelity, God, revenge, King, marriage! All these words carried a radically different and complex set of suggestions four hundred years ago. Words like "universal" can now carry unfortunate and even sloppy connotations of misogynist, classist, and racist thinking. Who among an enlightened liberal contemporary community would wish to embrace a seventeenth-century idea of religiously confined patriarchal thinking? This is the first challenge any director faces when approaching any period play. So how can this seemingly impossible barrier be overcome?

Despite the radical change of social structure, I ask if the entire spectrum of esoteric and non-socialized emotional experience – primal feeling that forms prior to language and the structure of so-called civilization – has in fact significantly changed since the dawn of time. Is it possible that, like primary colors, there are also primary emotions? As a theatrical practitioner (a sculptor of the human condition if you will, an artist therefore), I believe that in order to access these primal feelings when we encounter them in archaic texts, we must present them in the context of contemporary comprehension. As long as we understand their *original* context we can usually find a modern equivalent. Words like love and death and fear have not changed in their basic primacy. A play that seeks to lift primary emotions into dramatic form through the specific crafting of words upon a page can transcend time and still be meaningful hundreds of years later.

As there are an infinite variety of ways in which directors approach their craft, it is perhaps worthwhile to elucidate some techniques and personal truths that I always strive to carry into the rehearsal hall. In fact, as the creation of theatre is a very personal art, I beg your indulgence while I also offer a few insights into who I am and the way I work. Forgive me if I seem to stray from topic occasionally, but I think it useful to study any production from as specific and individual a viewpoint as possible. After all, a play is a living and organic work of art that exists only in a moment. For a few hours' traffic of an audience's time, actor, playwright, designer, and patron are unified on a singular dramatic meditation. The text serves as mediator for the exchange of truths between the stage and the spectators. When the curtain falls, the art is left to resonate in the memory only.

Prior to founding Writers' Theatre I enjoyed a healthy career as an actor. Although born in the UK I received most of my education in the States. After working as an actor in Chicago for three years, in 1990 I was fortunate enough to be invited to join the acting company at the Stratford Festival in Ontario, Canada. When I returned to Chicago in 1992, determined to create an environment where the artist could be nurtured and the playwright respected, I formed the Writers' Theatre. Through a mutual friend, I was introduced to the owners of a small independent bookstore, located in Glencoe, Illinois, a north suburb of Chicago. In the back of this book-store was a modest-sized empty room around five hundred or so square feet, which had once served as an aerobics gym for the little sports shop that had been the building's previous tenant. This presented the opportunity to create a truly intensive performance environment in which the audience would be inches away from the actors and the front row of seating would be literally onstage. I raised a few thousand dollars and installed a minimalist home-made household dimmer lighting system with instruments made from flood lamps in empty coffee cans painted black. I also obtained fifty yellow, brown, and orange plastic chairs, a four-by-eight platform and a few props. The primary budget line was actor salaries. In collaboration with a friend I adapted three short stories by Chekhov that, when paired with Gogol's *Diary of a Madman*, became Writers' Theatre's inaugural production. We called the evening *Love and Lunacy*. The show was a great success. Within a year, we were able to acquire 250 subscribers and a $30,000 budget. A few seasons later, producing consistently well-received productions, we had a $250,000 budget and almost a thousand subscribers. By the time we produced *Spite for Spite* in September of 2000 we had over two thousand subscribers and an $850,000 budget, and we consistently played to standing room only. Over the preceding seven years we had upgraded our lighting system and at this time we were working with a small but not entirely unsophisticated light board with the capacity to program fifty cues. Our complete set, costume, props, and sound budgets totaled somewhere around five thousand dollars, but the intimacy of the space gave us the opportunity to transform the theatre into a truly encompassing environment. The one constant (both then and now) was paying our actors a living wage. Our union salaries were comparable to the major Chicago venues like the Steppenwolf, and our non-union salaries were often better. This sent a clear message to the Chicago acting pool that they would be our priority, and consequently we were (and are still) able to draw upon a significant and loyal following of artists.

When you experience a show in our bookstore venue you can see the actors sweat; you can practically hear their hearts beating; you notice the dilation of a pupil or the twitch of a facial muscle. The actor is acutely aware of the audience, and the rapport that can exist between the two can make for a unique and dynamic experience. The audience too is under similar scru-tiny. Cellophane-wrapped candy crinklers are pariahs, and sleepers are visible to all. Yet, the involuntary gasps and occasionally passionate vocalizations, from quiet sobbing to hearty laughter, can be an unparalleled thrill. Under these pressure-cooker circumstances, we were keen to find a verse drama that could exploit the space and that the space could embrace.

I would like to say that I chose *Spite for Spite* because of a life-long passion for Spanish Golden Age theatre and that Moreto had been a personal literary hero I was desperate to share with my audience but, alas, I cannot. In fact, prior to reading this play I was largely ignorant of the Spanish Golden Age with the exception of *Life Is a Dream* and had never heard of Moreto. Part of the ritual of choosing a season for Writers' Theatre every year involved several pilgrimages to Chicago's playtext bookstore. I would plant myself in front of the shelving and gather a stock of possibilities to take home and deeply scrutinize. In late winter of 2000, at the height of our search for the following season, I was leaving the store when I glanced through the trade paperback shelf, and my eye caught the name Dakin Matthews. I had just returned from San Diego where my then partner (Scott Parkinson) was playing Mercutio for Dan Sullivan at the Old Globe. This excellent production had been noteworthy in my experience for its fine text work, which had been overseen by that same Mr Matthews. Here he was emblazoned across the spine of an intriguingly titled playtext: *Spite for Spite*. A cursory glance through the cast size and first couple of pages told me that it was possibly producible in our venue and therefore certainly worth a read, so I placed it in the pile and took it home. One morning I picked it up and started to read. I was instantly engaged and tore through it cover to cover. There were shades of Shakespeare in the plot and construct; indeed, Dakin makes frequent use of little quotable Shakespearean snippets. There was a fine story, a challenge for a young cast, and yet a thrillingly contemporary feel to the piece. Most remarkable to me at the end of my first read was the fact that I believed we could meet the exigencies of producing it in our shoebox theatre. I was convinced that I had struck Golden Age gold, and I proceeded to arrange a reading, which went very smoothly and generated a genuine sense of excitement for which I relentlessly hunt while choosing a season. We had been seduced and we prepared to embark upon the journey.

In my experience, translations of any age and genre can be grisly affairs. Any vitality, smoothness of conversational tone or poetry in the writing of the original playwright is often unintentionally and yet absolutely obliterated by arch, camp, or even worse, sedentary and artless plodding prose. Mr Matthews, on the other hand, in his brilliant, sharp, and insightful translation has brought his source material to life. His words sound like real people talking to each other and yet hold within them a theatrical poetic sensibility. Most importantly to my taste, he has created a pleasingly contemporary American voice for his work, which never feels jarring or inappropriate. The immediate and beneficial consequence of this is that the dialogue in his translation falls naturally upon the ear as the conversation of real people in heightened circumstance. In fact, the script reads much better out loud than it does on the page, and, by the way, it reads very well on the page.

We launched into the pre-production process. I engaged a design team, which included set designer Susan Kaip, whose work I had seen at an outdoor Shakespeare Festival in Barat College, just north of Glencoe. To join her I invited Jennifer Keller, a costume designer who I knew could pull off a miracle or two on a limited budget and whose versatility had much served us in the past. Our nationally acclaimed resident lighting designer Rita Pietraszsek took on illumination, and I brought in composers Andre Pluess and Ben Sussman (whose recent work on Mary Zimmerman's *Metamorphoses* and *I Am My Own Wife* on Broadway might be familiar to you).

We met for our first production meeting and began the process by listing the tangible requirements of the script. We had to create a single location that could function for many purposes. That location had to serve as a private place for Diana and Carlos to woo (or not to woo as the case would be), and also as a public area for debate, dancing, and ceremony. It needed to convey the wealth and importance of Diana's family. It also needed places where the characters could observe one another unseen – in other words, hiding places. (I remind you of the size of the venue in bringing this last detail to your attention!) In terms of period, I wanted the play to live in its own time but gently allow for the contemporary feel of Dakin's script.

I have always felt that when staging the classics a slavish adherence to precise authenticity is a pointless exercise. Historical accuracy is a non-existent concept to the seventeenth-century audience and actor. They probably dressed in whatever was fashionable and threw on a dash of historical flavor when necessary. While togas were sometimes used in Shakespeare's *Julius Caesar*, the actors also donned the latest in available pumpkin pants. If the actors had a little money, then as now, keeping in style was important to them.

However, a strictly modern approach would also have drawbacks. If we tried to bring the play into an exclusively contemporary world then we would open ourselves to a host of distractions. I have seen a number of productions mired in a world of cellular telephones and gimmicky updates that ultimately obscure the play. I accordingly informed my designers that I wished them to capture the line and shape of the period but not feel entirely confined by it. If they were to find a contemporary line or two, or wish to deviate in order to find a better shape or look, then they should feel comfortable doing so. In the same way that Dakin's script seduces the audience into a literary experience of days long past with contemporary flavors, a very subtle allowance of modern gestures sprinkled here and there in the design could gently add a subliminal, recognizable doorway for the audience.

The stage shape at our bookstore venue defies conventional description. It certainly follows the grand tradition of what is affectionately known as "store front theatre." For want of a better word, our stage is essentially a wedge. It occupies a square in one corner of the room and is wrapped along two walls by the L of the audience. After paging through research of Spanish architecture from both historical and current context, we came up with a courtyard for the set. Along one wall of the wedge, Susan created a small cloister with an archway and even a little window with a bench in front of it. She draped the walls with greenery. Against the perpendicular wall, she created a small seating area complete with a functional water pool and a statue of Cupid that looked to be strictly for decoration, but at some moment in the play could be discovered to be a fountain with its water source emitting from an appropriately comic location. The corner closest to the corner of the audience L simply held a bench that could be removed should space be needed, but allowed for a seated actor, which could open up the action on the stage and also bring the action into the house. The coloring was a variety of deep clay orange from wall to floor, and the climate it consequently conveyed was rich and moist. The floor was sandy yellow and textured. The audience would ultimately feel as though they were occupying a corner of the courtyard and therefore feel entirely inside the action.

The costumes followed suit. With nine actors to outfit and an inconsequential budget for wigs, significant costume changes were not in the cards. Straying from the appropriate Spanish period, we ended with a hybrid between an English Elizabethan and Jacobean look. It was a little less bulky than accurate period, a little sexier, and from a practical standpoint, we had a good stock available to rent from the University of Illinois at Urbana-Champaign. With a few poet shirts from the late J. Peterman catalog (which gave a lovely hint of modernity), we managed to pull together a world that suggested wealth and power and elegance, and still allowed the characters to move easily. Sexual attractiveness was of vital importance to the look, both for the actors and the audience, as so much of the tension in the play derives from a smoldering repressed sexuality. Pumpkin pants would have been period-accurate but I have never found them to be a particularly attractive look to the contemporary eye (particularly as they necessitate the wearing of tights). We therefore opted for a more Jacobean look with knee-level pants and high socks with boots. Although the ladies' dresses called for large umbrella frames, they would have crowded the tiny stage. However, we held on to the idea of Elizabethan ruffs and collars, which still allowed for an attractive and full bodice. Admittedly some of the ladies' bosoms needed a little theatrical magic in order to attain the desired plumpness (an effect, which I am happy to say, managed to convince a reviewer of the *Wall Street Journal*). Some of our women had contemporary short hair cuts. Our designer came up with hair pieces attached to ingeniously designed lace hair nets, giving the appearance of copious locks. For the men, we opted for short and mostly contemporary styling. Again, this look was in defiance of period, but I find that contemporary lines in hair styling can often help relieve the alienation that audiences initially feel when viewing period costumes.

Some of the greatest hybridization was achieved in the musical score. Again, we aimed for a contemporary flavor and gentle synthesizer presence, but we wanted the shape and tone of the songs and dances to be period in flavor – especially for the dances, which I wanted to feel organic and spontaneous. My choreographer Betsy Hamilton was on the faculty at DePaul University, where I was ending a two-and-a-half-year stint as Shakespeare instructor for the acting conservatory. The dances in *Spite for Spite* I felt were ceremonial, yes, but the dramatic tension of the moment could be greatly enhanced by a flavor of spontaneity. I also wanted character to be infused into the dance, and most of all, when Carlos and Diana dance, I wanted to focus a sense of massively contained sexuality. Again, I instructed my choreographer not to feel confined by period restraints, and she rose magnificently to the occasion. Taking the shape of period dances she created small, choreographed, non-verbal dialogues culminating in a vibrant step dance with a heavy flamenco influence for the Carlos/Diana face-off.

For light, I wanted a rich and warm Mediterranean feel, mostly natural, gently easing into area lighting from time to time if a moment needed to be isolated slightly. Romantic tones were essential, and we decided that the three acts could comprise three successive afternoons, allowing for the inevitable increase of passion as searing and sunny day moves into the blue and silvery evening of moonlight.

Casting was initially easy. Since my first read of the play, I had conceived only one Diana. Karen Janes Woditsch had acted with the company since our first production, the previously mentioned *Love and Lunacy*. I knew that *Spite for Spite* could showcase her prodigious talents with language and the depth of her inner passion. As the chemistry of attraction is a key factor in sustaining the tension of the play, I involved her in finding her Carlos. She happily suggested one of her best friends, Sean Fortunato. The chemistry when they read together was palpable and made for an easy choice. For Polilla I cast Mark Ulrich, an actor with a fine sense of language and a natural and slightly offbeat comic sensibility. Like many of Shakespeare's clowns, Polilla has a wit which drives his relationships and which keeps him in charge of an ever-complicating plot. I plundered my graduation acting classes at DePaul, with whom I had a good rapport and that most vital of all tools, a shared vocabulary. This took care of Bearne, and Don Gaston and little Laura and Fenisa. For Diana's chief lady-in-waiting, Cintia, I wanted a little more maturity, and was fortunate in having the role accepted by Maggie Carney, a comedienne of considerable skill.

Our one radical departure from the text in casting was the change of gender from the Count to a Countess. We operate on a combination of union and non-union contracts. One of the many challenges this brings to the table is that of finding non-union actors of age who are capable of meeting the requirements of the text. We had been unable to locate any potential Counts but had a number of potential Countesses. After a brief consultation with Dakin, he agreed to the change and we hired Joanna Maclay, a former teacher of mine from the University of Illinois and a fine and noble presence. In losing the Baptista/Katherine *Taming of the Shrew* dynamic embodied in a father/daughter pairing, we gained instead the interesting perspective of a daughter rejecting the advice of the mother she does not wish to become. In some ways, the parental chidings became a little more devastating. The text was not at all strained by the choice.

One of the great challenges of performing any text from the hundred years or so surrounding the age of Shakespeare is that comparisons are inevitable. They are also, as Dogberry says in *Much Ado About Nothing*, "odorous." However, there are a few worthy observations that might be of use to the reader. When approaching Shakespeare, directors must have a fairly clear "why?" as to their intent in staging the play. When I directed my first *Hamlet* this summer I wished to avoid Victorian traditions of painting him in romantic and sentimental colors. I wanted the title character to be more recognizably human in the messiness of his emotional interior. I believed that the audience could be drawn to him as much for his foibles as his brilliance. In fact, informed audiences come to see any Shakespeare with a high level of expectations. Artists too come to the table with rigorous standards and traditions waiting to be upheld or re-envisioned. How will Richard III mount his throne? How will the director handle the Witches in *Macbeth*? How will the storm in *The Tempest* be staged so that it doesn't overpower the rest of the play? *Spite for Spite* was thrillingly free of preconceptions from both audience and artist. Consequently the goals in mounting the play were more architectural and archeological. We were there to discover the play and bring it into the light, rather than rediscover it and shine new light upon dusty and perhaps long-hidden corners.

Another significant difference between staging Shakespeare and *Spite for Spite* is the contemporary vernacular of Dakin's verse. No doubt staging Moreto in his native and classical, archaic tongue would offer some of the same challenges that producing Shakespeare frequently does, but the benefit of Dakin's work is that his own skill as a writer has allowed him to create a wholly accessible text. I think it is not an overstatement to claim that a translator must at least grasp the intellectual scope of the source material and its author. Dakin has lived in Moreto's mind very well in this endeavor. I would venture a guess that when trying to translate Shakespeare's canon into other languages it is difficult if not impossible to find a translator who can adequately encompass the breadth of Shakespeare's far reaching sharpness and clarity of perception and imagination. After all, it's not just the words themselves that define the condition, but rather the sound and shape of the words and the way they hold next to each other when spoken out loud. Accordingly the specificity of the text and the entirety of the word itself trigger the emotional transubstantiation between the truth of the actor and the truth of the audience.

Additionally, Shakespeare's text has been so continuously researched, performed, and experimented with over the past four hundred years that a myriad of techniques exist to help the actor mine the truth. There are so many variant editions, essays, and footnotes to help an artist navigate the first steps through a play by Shakespeare. But Dakin's translation/adaptation of *El desdén con el desdén* is, to my knowledge, the only one in English since the nineteenth century.

There are also, of course, guidelines for the actors that hold true for both playwrights. First of all, the verse is heightened. I have always likened the transition of prose to verse in Shakespeare to the transition between speaking and singing in a musical. When words are no longer enough to encompass a feeling, the character must sing. When prose is no longer enough, the character must use verse. The use of verse immediately lifts the actor into a higher state of consciousness, passion, and dramatic tension. Verse must therefore be delivered with deliberate intent while maintaining spontaneity. The actor must think and speak at the same time, while allowing the structure of rhythm to carry the tempo and momentum of the text. Artificial attempts to make the verse sound "naturalistic" by filtering in inappropriate pauses and hesitations will destroy clarity, intensity, and meaning.

If the actor speaks the verse well, and the verse has been well constructed, the audience's ear will soon adjust and spectators will assume that they are hearing normal human rhythms. It is not an accident that Shakespeare employed iambic pentameter, a verse structure that most closely mimics natural human speech rhythms. Any actor used to speaking verse has been trained in the technique of achieving clarity through various methodologies such as breathing through entire thoughts, allowing for energy shifts as the thought changes. The emotion of the line is contained within the verse structure, forcing the actor to be constantly generating new emotions in order to reach the next level of passion. Karen Woditsch, who played Diana, comments: "Two interesting things I found in the performing of it. The rhyming helps the character. There are times when you must hit the rhyme for sense and humour and other times when you do not, but I never found it forced. If you follow the thoughts through to their conclusion, the rhymes take care of themselves, so I learned not to be afraid of the language."

I like to give actors an opportunity to run the play as soon as possible so that they can begin to develop the arc of their character. The arc can be defined as the emotional journey they must make in order to get from the beginning of the play to the final scene. Accordingly, I spend several days on book work in order to appropriately understand the action of each scene and then get the play staged within a week. There was some initial concern that we might be running a little long, and it therefore became important that we should have time to cut, which we would do without jeopardizing structure or sense. An associate recently said to me that he frequently hears people claiming that a play is ten minutes too long. He has decided that he would rather conclude that a play could be ten minutes better. As much as I like this philosophy, I do believe in cuts. By the third week of rehearsals it became clear to me that a few would much benefit the production. Most of the cuts we made were for the purpose of keeping the momentum of the story going, reducing archaic classical allusion, and removing speeches that we felt might be overstating already well-presented arguments.

Our next job was to define the world of the play for the actors. The text gives us the structure of our parameters. This was clearly a society in which formality, structure, and ceremony were of utmost importance. It was therefore going to be necessary for us to find the rules of those ceremonies and the manners of the culture. How should a character of great importance address a character of lesser importance? What was the social etiquette when wooing? When (if ever) should the relationship between the serving woman and Diana be allowed to cross into friendship and the same for Carlos and Polilla? What were the exact mechanics of the dancing ceremony and the festival parade in the third act? We spent much time defining the rituals and what they represented. Although the nuances might not always be immediately apparent to the audience, they had to be specific to the actors. As long as the actors were sure and certain in their functions, the audience would be confident too.

This was also a world in which the fourth wall could be broken. At any given moment a character could step aside from the play and speak directly to the audience without being overheard by the other characters on stage. We had to define how to accomplish this in our very confined environment. Over the three weeks of staging rehearsals we developed a physical vocabulary to encompass this conceit. The execution of the asides was created as a sharp and synchronistic move. The actors in scene (but not able to hear the aside) would cast their gaze or even sometimes their whole being into a moment of furiously active self-reflection. The actors giving the asides would lean towards the audience and bring them into their confidence. In larger group scenes, asides would be accomplished by creating a series of private communications between the non-hearing characters, giving the speaker the opportunity to create the same kind of relationship with the audience. A side effect of this choice, heightened by the intimacy of our environment, allowed our patrons to feel completely drawn into the play. This is no doubt the original intent of asides. There is always a slight feeling of privilege when friends take us into their confidence. It also allows the audience, in a very direct way, to become a player in the production. In order to ensure that this action was consistent and clean, we actually spent a full rehearsal day working through each aside, making them all both technically sharp and psychologically playable.

Our shift from a Count to a Countess allowed for a matriarchal society that, although not accurate to Moreto's world, gave Diana an enhanced sense of power. She did not *need* to get married. Her falling in love with Carlos was not a necessary function of her place. This choice did not unduly burden the play, and was useful in heightening the stakes without detracting from the journey.

One of the hardest conventions to address was Carlos's virtuoso speech to Polilla at the beginning of the play. Moreto's audiences would of course be expecting this convention, looking forward to seeing the actor meet the challenge. Our poor Carlos was utterly terrified initially (as possibly was Moreto's original Carlos). However, we spent a healthy block of time working through the text with him. We could not of course simply accept what Moreto's audiences would have accepted, that a long speech is a convention in such a play. We had to find a psychological need to communicate and to define clearly why he was not inviting his manservant to respond. Fortunately both Matthews and Moreto provided plenty of opportunity for us to do so.

Fortunato states:

> One of the other challenges of the piece was my opening monologue. A couple pages into the play I launch into a twelve- to fifteen-minute monologue that contains a lot of exposition. Luckily, Carlos gets to show a huge range of emotion over the course of it. He goes from cocky ladies' man who has never been entrapped by love to a man whose whole life has been overtaken by his feelings. In reliving his feelings for Diana he gets himself into quite a frenzy. One tricky thing was trying to find a build that lasted for fifteen minutes' worth of monologue. I was fortunate enough to have a scene partner who convinced me that he was really listening to me one hundred percent, every night. Another challenge was that Diana had the whole course of the play to make her transformation while Carlos's happens in one monologue.

Staging presented a number of challenges. The second act is Festival Time, and there were to be nine actors on stage in period costume dancing with each other, and then, in the second scene, the girls in their underwear pretending to dance through the garden as if they were unaware that Carlos was present as Diana attempted to seduce him. In order to accomplish the hiding trick, Carlos and Polilla strolled through the garden while the four women attempted to attract their attention. With never more than six or seven feet between them this was, needless to say, challenging. However, the challenge was met owing to the very versatile nature of the set, which provided several hiding places and two slightly different levels of height. It is always easier to connote greater distance on stage between actors with a variance in levels.

The problems in the third act became those of virtuosity. The final pageant was somewhat truncated by budget, and in a larger space I might have been tempted to add a fair degree of technical support to the scene. There is a scene in which Diana is subjected to being present for the singing and wooing of her ladies-in-waiting by their suitors, fanning the flames of her own increasing desire for Carlos. It would have been nice to have a stage festooned with lanterns and bathed in moonlight, and a complete and handsome change of costume for all. However, in keeping with budget and mission statement, our simple little parade with a dance, a song, and a few ribbons sufficed quite nicely.

By the time the parade was concluded, I suspected that the audience would be more than ready for Diana to yield, and the interest was all in the manner of her dissolution. It is no mean feat for an actress to accomplish, and it is a testament to our leading lady, Karen Woditsch, that she not only managed to hold the interest of the audience but indeed gained an even greater sense of compassion as she slowly capitulated to her natural and erupting desires (or, as Polilla would have it, her fig ripens and falls).

Our only real contextual battle, and perhaps the most complex difference in attitude from Moreto's day to our own, is the apparently callous way in which both Carlos and Diana deliver their final volleys of resistance to each other. Each hoping to push the other into confession of passion, they announce to each other that they are taking other lovers. Diana is almost prepared to marry Bearne rather than admit her love to Carlos. Carlos quite earnestly woos Cintia, and from my read of the text at least, does not let on that his intention is otherwise inclined. The poor dupes, Bearne and Cintia, are brought to hope through the capitulation of loves they never thought possible and are then unceremoniously dropped at the conclusion of the play.

In order to combat this choice, we worked very hard to set up in the earlier scenes that once Bearne has chosen Cintia in the dance, his feelings for her become real and that his love for Diana is a distraction. We applied the same psychology to Cintia. We thus attempted to tell the story that, although they had strong feelings for each other, Cintia and Bearne were momentarily dazzled and seduced by the notion of marrying such powerful partners. We also took great pains to allow the scenes where the falsely wooed lovers are rejected to be tender and gentle, with great care for feelings. I *think* we achieved this. Also I do not believe the choice worked against the spirit and greater authorial intents of the original.

Most professional productions enjoy a week or so of lower-priced performances prior to the arrival of the press during which a production can grow and learn. It is a thrilling part of the process. Preview audiences, however, can be an interesting breed. I suspect that their primary motivation in coming to a preview is the cheaper ticket price, but without reviews and word of mouth as the safety net, they are often a little terrified of the show: "No-one has told me what to think. What if I don't understand?"

During our first two previews I watched the little old ladies in the front row gently slide into a panic as Carlos's speech showed no sign of an early ending. Was this to be the entire evening? (Admittedly, Sean was also a little bumpy and a little thrown off by an old lady in the front row who, despite my pleading pre-show speech only seconds before, proceeded to unwrap the largest candy in America and then rustle the wrapper for a good two minutes following.) By the third preview it became clear that the audience was a little restless with the structure of the play and was not relaxing into its world with the ease we desired. We decided that it might help to tell the audience a few tidbits of information that Moreto's audience would already be armed with prior to curtain: that there would be a virtuoso fifteen-minute monologue, and that the three acts were divided into statement of philosophical argument, action of plot, and resolution of both. At the fourth preview and after this curtain speech they relaxed. We took this one step further a week later and inserted into the program a study guide written by Dakin, giving them some lovely background on the play and its traditions. By the time the show had played for a couple of weeks, the excellent reviews from local and national publications and similar word of mouth had generated a healthy buzz, the audiences were more visibly relaxed, and the pre-show chat became enhancement rather than necessity.

The reviews from *The Wall Street Journal*, *The Chicago Tribune*, and the *Chicago Sun Times* praised the direction, the set design, the costumes, the actors, and especially the translation. The *Sun Times* reviewer wrote: "Now, a sparklingly witty, blithely contemporary translation by Dakin Matthews – a California-based master of many theatrical trades – is bound to give the work a whole new lease on life, just as Richard Wilbur's landmark translations once did for Moreto's French contemporary, Molière."

While revisiting the Writers' Theatre production of *Spite for Spite* has given me great pleasure, I recognize that the virtuosity lies truly with the translator. My muse for the production and for the traditions we discovered was Matthews, and although I raise my glass to Moreto, it was Mathews who gave us a new classic: *Spite for Spite*.

# Directing *Don Juan, The Trickster of Seville*

## ANNE MCNAUGHTON

Every playscript comes with a set of challenges for the director. Some challenges are generic to theatre, some are specific to this text in this particular production. I tend to operate as a director who tries to meet these challenges – or, if you will, to solve these problems – pragmatically.

The recent Andak Stage Company production of *Don Juan, The Trickster of Seville* was no exception, and in this essay I would like to detail what I thought were the challenges, generic and specific, and my attempted solutions. I will not necessarily limit myself to those challenges that are particular to *Comedia* production, however, because in many cases the generic and the specific challenges are so intertwined that solving one is often the key to solving the other. Or, as is sometimes the case, solving one creates problems in the other. In any event, I have divided these directing challenges into two categories: pre-production considerations and the rehearsal process.

Pre-production begins with research, especially in the case of a period work. For a director, an acquaintance with the play's historical context is important not only for an appreciation of the play's thematic concerns, but for an understanding of the psychology of its characters as well; and thereby, I would argue, hangs the success or failure of any production in any period – but more about that later. Such research would include some information about seventeenth-century Spanish literary and language conventions, religious and philosophical concerns and beliefs, superstitions, and the author's biography, to the extent it is perceived to bear on his work. The fact that Tirso de Molina was a Roman Catholic friar – during the period of the Inquisition, no less – is not entirely unconnected to one of the play's primary themes: You play, you pay.

Knowledge of Golden Age theatrical conventions, such as stage configuration and devices, is also important, particularly when it comes to envisioning how a scene may be staged in a less than ideal space. For example, you are going to need something that functions as an "above," and you are going to need a trap, or something that can suggest the action of a trap. If you are ignorant of these configurations and devices, you will not be able to envision what physical action Tirso had in mind when he wrote the scene; and if you are unable to envision that, then inventing an alternative (should you need to, as we did) will be difficult, and possibly even contrary to the intent of the scene. Happily for me, as a director with experience in staging Shakespeare (in a variety of venues, both large and small), the research would show that the basic configuration of the *corral* was similar to that of the Elizabethan stage, so the staging challenges the play presented were not unfamiliar.

As the structural design and devices of the seventeenth-century *corral* were similar to those of the Elizabethan stage, so staging conventions and acting traditions also bore similarities. The unit set had to serve any and all locales and locations: palaces, bedchambers, courtyards, inns, churches, urban streets, country roads, seasides, village greens, and so on. The specific setting of each scene was established with dialogue; transitions between scenes – sometimes wildly different in terms of place and passage of time – demanded a seamless fluidity, cinematic if you will; music and song were often incorporated into the text; and doubling of roles was a common practice. The soliloquy was popular in both traditions, and character depictions were rhetorically based. That is to say, a character's psychology and emotional life (the actor's primary focus) was inextricable from the language that carried it. This last particular is especially important for modern actors and directors to appreciate, as much contemporary actor training sees the language as incidental, even antithetical, to the expression of emotional reality. However that may (or may not) work for contemporary plays, the key to creating an Elizabethan or Golden Age character of emotional immediacy and believability requires the marrying of language and emotion, not the divorcing.

Further research inquiry might include a review of the play's production history, as well as selected scholarly criticism. The interpretive "take" of a particular production or critical work is generally enlightening, and may prove especially helpful in understanding some of the more singular scenes and characters; Tisbea in her soliloquies comes to mind.

After researching the traditions and conventions of Golden Age theatre, the next step in the pre-production process – the design phase – involved our determining how the conventions, now practical staging requirements, could be adapted to our space(s) and resources. First of all, the design for the Andak production of *Don Juan* would have to work on two very different stages. The original venue was our studio-type theatre at NewPlace in North Hollywood; the stage was small (approximately fifteen feet deep by twenty-five feet wide), with extremely limited wing space. The other venue was the Chamizal Memorial Theatre, with a stage area more than three times that of NewPlace. The set would also have to travel between the two theatres; budget considerations dictated that transportation costs be modest; and the entire set, along with the costumes and props, would have to fit into a small pick-up truck and van. The design we came up with worked on both stages, traveled as required, and, most importantly, served the demands of the play.

The set consisted of four units. Upstage was a two-piece platform (six feet wide, three feet deep, two feet high), with steps on its stage left and stage right sides; downstage right and left were two curved-front, pie-shaped units (two feet wide, deep, and high); the fronts of all the units were "tiled" to evoke the sense of a Spanish courtyard. Generally, the upstage unit, though a modest two feet in elevation, allowed for visual variation in staging; it also afforded the actors a place to sit (as did the downstage units) without the necessity of bringing on furniture. More specifically, the upstage platform served for the balcony from which Don Juan must leap in the first scene; for Don Gonzalo's sepulchre; as a throne for Castile; for the bed in Aminta's bedchamber; as a means of establishing different parts of a street within the same scene (Mota and Don Juan in the Little Lisbon scene); and finally, as a way of solving the play's most challenging staging problem – creating the illusion of the Hellmouth.

Even without a trap, which was the case at both NewPlace and Chamizal, the climatic moment of Don Juan's descent into Hell, though made clear through language, must be somehow visually created as well. I think our solution, if not ideal, was effective. The upstage black stage curtains ("blacks") opened, as the two-piece platform was slowly pulled apart (the action accompanied by "hellish" light and sound effects); the Knight Commander "threw" Don Juan between the separated halves of the unit into the arms of waiting "demons." He was then dragged off stage; Don Gonzalo followed, and as he uttered his final lines – "As a man does, so shall he pay!" – the platform pieces were pushed back together and the curtains behind closed.

The necessary austerity of the set design, imposed by budget and logistical considerations, mandated, so to speak, that the costume design attempt to take up the visual aesthetic slack; so we put the bulk of our production budget into the costumes. The extensive experience of our designer, Dean Cameron, in designing and building seventeenth-century period costumes, and his collaboration with us on our four previous Siglo de Oro productions, proved helpful in meeting the substantial challenge of multiple (at least two) costumes for eleven actors and a musician (even Don Juan and Catalinón, who were not double-cast, stood in as guards in one scene). Every other actor played two named roles as well as a variety of servants and/or guards: messengers, wedding guests, Hell servants, demons, and scene changers. Each named role required, of course, a distinctive costume; but what was to be done to distinguish the generic characters and scene changers from the named characters? Capes! Black, hooded capes. The garbing of incidental characters and scene changers in generic capes, a solution suggested by the translator, Dakin Matthews, would solve the practical problem of distinguishing the named, and disguising the incidental; at the same time, the monk's-cowl appearance of the capes would recall the profession of the playwright and the religious themes of the play. (The happy accident of practical solution colliding with concept is one of the more intriguing, even exhilarating, aspects of directing.)

We introduced the cape device at the top of the show, as theatrical conventions are most successful when established early on. The lights came up to discover the assembled company, backs to the audience, in their capes; after singing two phrases of the *Dies irae* (a thematic motif), they turned round to the audience, pushed back the hoods and danced a pavane – the choreography allowing subtle suggestions of character and relationships. The dance segued into the first scene of the play, as Don Juan and the Duchess Isabella, shedding their capes (taken from them by the actors who would later play Tisbea and Aminta), were left alone on stage to speak the play's opening words.

The highly stylized nature of the "cape-dance" signaled the audience that the capes were to be considered a theatrical device. Thus, whenever they appeared in the play proper, as the means of allowing the actors to play their various incidental roles, the previously alerted audience immediately recognized the device and went along with the "deception."

*Don Juan*, like other Golden Age plays, features songs and music. In the four *comedias* I have directed, the songs (as in Shakespeare's plays) are thematic, either in terms of the play generally, or in terms of a particular moment or character; they are not incidental entertainment (even the nursery-rhyme-like repetitiveness of Aminta's wedding song suggests the simple-minded sensibilities of the country folk, and sets up the seduction of the naïve girl and her family). The music, then, must carry the words in a way that will, above all, enhance their meaning. The music composed for the songs in our production (we had the great good fortune to once again engage our longtime collaborator, the composer-guitarist, Carl Smith, an expert in period music, particularly that of seventeenth-century Europe) gave the words visceral life: meaning translated into emotional effect.

Music is also an invaluable tool for establishing the setting and period of a piece. This would apply to any play, but especially to works unfamiliar to the audience in terms of period and culture. Carl informed us that the music of seventeenth-century Spain sounded fairly similar to that of Elizabethan England; so, in the interests of audience orientation, we asked that he take the liberty of giving the authentic sound a little "Spanish flavor."

In addition to helping to establish the play's setting and period, Carl's original score (which he performed live for every performance) facilitated smooth transitions between scenes. Awkward transitions are death to fluid storytelling. Ideally, the music, as a bridge between one scene and its successor, provides a coda for the former and sets the mood for the latter.

Music was also used as underscoring for the aria-like soliloquies of Tisbea and the scenes of Don Juan's calculated romancings. In the case of the soliloquies, I think the musical underscoring, which was appropriate to the dramatic tone of the text, helped the audience appreciate the stylized, less than realistic quality of the "arias." As to Don Juan's scenes of seduction, the underscoring signaled the theatrical (in the sense of non-real, pretending, calculating) nature of his emotional protestations.

Casting is the final, most important, and most challenging phase of the pre-production process. As I mentioned earlier, the play (featuring twenty-one characters plus musicians, guards, servants, etc.) would be done with a cast of eleven actors and one musician. So we would need actors of a variety of ages who could play more than one role, and, in some cases, sing.

Moreover, classical verse plays, such as *Don Juan*, require actors who have a facility with language; finding eleven actors with such ability is not an easy task, even in Los Angeles. Though there are possibly more actors per square mile in Los Angeles than any other city in the country, most are here to pursue careers in film and television; training in classical theatre is not a requirement. But the value of formal training, in voice and speech, and performance of classical works, is an incalculable asset, and something we look for when casting a classical play. Formal training is not an absolute necessity, of course, if an actor is particularly gifted and intelligent – meaning that, in addition to acting talent, he/she has a good strong voice, clear speech, and learns quickly. We have had the good fortune of knowing some such; but, generally speaking, if you can engage trained actors, the whole rehearsal process "hits the ground running."

Then there is the issue of availability. In Los Angeles, good actors are more often than not working on a film or doing television, or doing an Equity production in one of the larger theatres of the regional theatre circuit, either in the Los Angeles area or somewhere out of town. The actors who are available and can commit to a project still often have unpredictable work schedules and limited time, so getting a strong cast usually means that rehearsal hours will have to be, likewise, limited and creatively scheduled. (I have found that scheduling can sometimes require more inventiveness than staging.)

These difficulties notwithstanding, we did have a distinct advantage. As founding members (Dakin was co-founder) of the classical theatre company, The Antaeus Company, Dakin and I have had the opportunity over the last fifteen-plus years to know and work with a good number of accomplished actors – many classically trained and/or experienced. Every actor in our production of *Don Juan*, save one, had worked with us on previous productions or projects. We held one audition to cast the Naples/Castile double (our original choice had to withdraw), but otherwise, the cast was selected by invitation. The resulting ensemble, having worked previously with Dakin and me, and most of them with each other, made the limited rehearsal process possible. It would have been a daunting challenge to attempt to even cast this kind of play through open audition, never mind rehearse such a piece with actors, a dramaturge, and a director who were unacquainted. That delicate, sometimes difficult, period of getting to know how the other members of the ensemble work was bypassed; everyone got on the same bus and hit the highway together.

Our rehearsal process began with a week of what we call "table work." These initial rehearsals, conducted by Dakin, as translator and dramaturge, were devoted primarily to the examination of the play's rhetorical structure and verse forms and how they relate to characterization, both generally and specifically. He explained how the different verse forms are used to create different dramatic tones, how the kind of verse forms a character uses may tell you a great deal about his or her character, as well as his/her mood. As the emotional life of characters in classical plays is revealed through their particular style of rhetoric, so the actors' understanding of how this drama-turgical method works will be of critical importance in understanding the characters they play. The psychological reality of a character – the thing that makes the playwright's text-creature an immediate, believable, human being, the thing the actor must find to make the characterization successful and the process worth the effort – will come only through the acting of the words (a somewhat mysterious phenomenon, I think); but the exploration must begin with understanding the words. If the actor is clear about his or her "objec-tives" and "given circumstances," to use acting jargon, then what remains is to simply make specific sense of the words (What are you saying? Why are you saying it now?) and the character will emerge, à la Pirandello; only, in this case, it is a character in search of an actor. I recall a remark by Stephen Greenblatt, in his *Shakespearean Negotiations*, regarding Shakespeare and other ancient texts. He said that to read works of the past is "to speak with the dead" (1). It may sound somewhat fanciful (I am, after all, a lifetime member of a profession grounded in fancy); still, I would venture to say that acting plays of antique playwrights from times long past goes beyond talking to the dead; it is more akin to channeling the dead. Finally, table work included a discussion of the historical context of the play and the theatrical traditions of the period, a sharing of the information gathered in the research phase of pre-production.

Following the week of table work, our staging rehearsals began. Staging is essentially an exercise in solving problems, both practical and aesthetic. More often than not, they are interrelated; but for the purposes of discussion, I will divide them into two categories. Into the category of practical problems I would place the various challenges presented by the physical space; into the category of aesthetic problems, I would place acting and storytelling challenges.

It was readily apparent that the settings and action of the play were conceived with a larger stage in mind than that of our modest space at NewPlace; the prospect of staging an epic-like play in a "room" was daunting. But some-

times, that which you have difficulty envisioning works in the doing; and so
it was with our North Hollywood *Don Juan*. I have already described the unit
set and how it served particular staging needs, but the need for smooth exits
and entrances was a problem of especial difficulty that had to be addressed;
as I noted earlier, nothing kills the flow of the action like an awkward exit or
entrance. The stage had wing entrances/exits upstage left and right (tight, but
negotiable); downstage, left and right, were two doors, each leading out of the
theatre; one to the lobby, the other to the back side of the theatre. To effect
smooth transitions between scenes, all four of the entrances/exits would have
to be used; but what to do about the doors? Opening and closing doors does
not make for smooth entrances and exits. This is particularly the case if one
scene must follow on the "heels" of the other with only the briefest of musical
interludes to mark the transition; and issues of sight lines and offstage noise
prevented the doors from simply being left open all the time. So how could
we make the doors function like wings? The solution involved "door assignments." Our troupe of heroically cooperative actors, most of whom were
already playing double roles and various incidental characters, agreed to take
on the additional responsibility of opening and closing the doors, depending
on their availability; if an actor was not on stage, he or she, more often that
not, was manning a door. With doors that opened "automatically," entrances
and exits were fluid and unencumbered. One of the actors' joys of touring to
Chamizal, in addition to playing in the generous space, was the elimination
of the "door assignments."

Another major staging challenge that falls into the category of physical
space involved the setting of scenes that required furniture, or other set-
pieces and props that required pre-setting. The set itself provided places for
sitting, and for the placing of objects carried on stage (I avoid "carry-on"
set-pieces if at all possible); but some scenes simply demand extra set-pieces.
Don Juan's dinner with the Knight Commander in Don Juan's rooms at the
inn is an example. It required a table and seating (we opted for stools, as they
could be put atop the table and carried in at the same time); also carried in
on the table were the wine jug and tankards, as well as a lantern (referenced
later in the text). The servants brought the table and its cargo on stage, and set
the scene as they spoke their opening lines; and since the lines had to do with
making dinner preparations for Don Juan's imminent arrival, the set-up of the
scene was not only efficient (the scene was set with no lag time between it
and the one preceding), but made sense. The servants' and Catalinón's frantic
and somewhat extended exit, which leaves Don Juan and the Ghost on stage
alone for the end of the scene, allowed them to clear all the furniture and
props as they flee upon Don Juan's repeated orders to get out. Not only did
the cleared stage – now a non-specific universe – enhance the theatricality
of the Knight Commander's fateful invitation, and Don Juan's first revelation

that he is vulnerable to terror, but, again, allowed a smooth segue from the end of the scene to the beginning of the next.

Also falling into the category of practical staging challenges related to space was the problem of setting Don Gonzalo's sepulchre (we go to the chapel twice) – the logistics of the "Hell Banquet," as we dubbed it, and the descent into Hell. In my discussion of the set design, I described how we created the illusion of a Hellmouth; the "demons" I referred to, those who separated the platform, and those who dragged the dying Don Juan "down" to Hell, were actors in their hooded black capes. Other caped actors set and cleared the sepulchre; and the Hell Banquet, spread on the upstage platform-unit, was set by yet other caped actors. The hooded capes were an effective disguise, and, at the same time (especially when pulled forward to obscure the face, à la the grim reaper), imparted an appropriately ominous sense to the scenes in which they appeared.

We also put the capes to stylistic use in another, less ominous, scene; in this case it was a matter of smoothing a transition (after line 2030) between Don Juan's brief scene with Gaseno and Catalinón, and the seduction of Aminta that follows it. During his brief soliloquy (a lyrical description of the night as a facilitator of desire) that follows the exit of Gaseno and then Catalinón, Don Juan "undressed" – hat, sword and sword-belt, jacket. The discarded items were received by two caped actors, who, at the top of his soliloquy, entered upstage and spread a sheet-like drape on the upstage plat-form to suggest a bed. At the conclusion of his speech, they were gone, and he was seated on the "bed," summoning Aminta. Here, the device not only helped to move the setting from an ante-chamber to a bedchamber, but to effect, as well, a mood transition between the blunt, coarse attitude of Don Juan toward the anticipated deception (shared with the unsympathetic Cata-linón) and the wily gentleness of the deceits he then practices on Aminta. Also, a certain theatrical comment was shared with the audience by having the actors who aided his "undressing" be the same who played his former conquests, Isabella and Tisbea.

Finally, we come to the challenges the text presented in terms of acting and storytelling. The most problematic involved the soliloquies – a conven-tion popular in the *Comedia* and other classic plays, though apparently less interesting to, if even tolerated by, most modern audiences. Perhaps if the soliloquies were set to music, the form would be quite acceptable to the modern spectator familiar with musical comedy, if not opera; in fact, we referred to the soliloquies, particularly those of Tisbea, and Gonzalo's Lisbon speech, as arias. Though we did not, of course, set the words of the mono-logues to music, they were, at certain points, musically underscored as a way of establishing mood and enhancing the imagery.

Nor did we consider the option of simply cutting them, in part or completely, as we believe that if they were not, in some very practical way, important to the theatrical integrity of the play, they wouldn't be there. Not that one, now and again, wouldn't consider a cut here or there; there are instances that sometimes necessitate that long-practiced liberty (length, venue, absolute unintelligibility, etc.); but generally speaking, you bend your energies to understanding the function of a theatrically foreign convention, and then set about making it work for yourselves and your audience.

It occurred to me that the same modern audience that displays an impatience with the classical soliloquy is the same audience that will sit through, even enjoy, the extended monologue of the one man/woman show; so it's not a matter of length. The usually modern subject matter might be more accessible, but I think the experience is acceptable because they can comfortably follow the sense of the narrative. The same cannot be said about many an audience's experience with the classical soliloquy. Though both audience and actors share the problem – ignorance of classical literary forms – the onus of dealing with it falls on the actor. The average modern audience may be unpracticed in recognizing a long rhetorical or emotional arc (the signature characteristic of the elevated style); but if the actors have identified it, and can negotiate it skillfully, most any audience can follow. (Understanding rhetorical structure and its relationship to characterization was a major focus of the pre-staging table work described earlier. If the actor can see how the speech works as an organic entity – how the sense-arcs operate – then she can infuse it with the specificity that will make it not only intelligible, but also engaging.)

Tisbea's speeches were a particular challenge for the actor, in terms of both the form and the characterization. For example, in Tisbea's first speech, the actor had to avoid allowing the short three-stress rhyming lines (assonating in Spanish) of the *romancillo* to fall into a sing-song delivery. Simply being aware of the danger did not, however, guarantee an avoidance of the problem. What did prevent a sing-song cadence was understanding the structure of the speech: the sense-arc(s), if you will. As in the acting of Shakespeare, if the actor simply makes specific sense – rhetorical and emotional – of what he or she is saying, the verse, however simple or complex, will take on the sound and feel of natural speech; the audience will experience the stylized speech as unaffected, and native to the character.

To make specific sense of a speech, the first thing the actor must understand is how the speech works grammatically. Here are two excerpts from Tisbea's first speech that demonstrate what I mean. The examples are very simple, but I think they will illustrate the point:

> **Of all the girls by the seaside**
> who dip their jasmine toes
> in the fleeting waves that kiss
> their feet the color of rose,

**I alone am untouched
by love,** [...]    (375–9)[1]

As one can see, the main point of these first five and a half lines (indeed, the main point of the entire speech) is carried in lines one, five, and the first half of six; the three intervening lines are parenthetical. Apparent as this may be on reading, it is surprising to find how many actors (especially those not trained in the classics) do not know how to vocally "paint" the parenthetical. It is a must-have technical skill (usually involving a subtle manipulation of pitch), because, if you do not vocally note the parenthetical as such, what should be complementary becomes as privileged as the main point, and the sense is blurred or lost; the sense-arc is obscured.

In this example of twelve lines, the main line of thought begins with the first word of the first line of the excerpt, and is picked up again in the last half of the eighth line quoted here; and, again, the intervening lines are parenthetical.

> **Here** where the sunbeams tread
> the lulling surf, and play
> upon the sapphire seas,
> to fright the clouds away,
> and leave in the grainy sand
> sometimes a tiny pearl,
> sometimes just the spark-
> le of their affection, **a girl**
> **can hear the amorous spat**
> **of birds**, as they squeal and squawk,
> and the sweet lovers' quarrel
> of the waves against the rock [...]    (383–92)

In both examples, the intervening lines, while parenthetical, are also richly descriptive, and more than a lovely complement to the exposition. The imagery Tisbea employs in the speech reveals an important aspect of her character – the connection she feels to things wild and free. The actor, then, while making Tisbea's expositional argument clear, must also make the imagery come alive.

Tisbea's "Fire! Fire!" speech (985–1030) presented a different acting challenge. It's fairly clear that the girl is out of her mind with humiliation and rage – over-the-top, teeth-gnashing shame and fury. A believable perform-

---

[1]   All citations of the text are from the Dakin Matthews translation, *Don Juan, The Trickster of Seville*.

ance will require the actor's total surrender to the emotion of a despairing
rage. But how does one play that kind of raw intensity convincingly when the
language is so stylized, and regularly interrupted with the chorus-like excla-
mations: "Fire, fire, fetch water, girls, fetch water"; "Have mercy, love, my
soul is all aflame"? Well, actors have a working maxim: "You can't play an
emotion; you can only play an action." We don't always remember this golden
rule, especially (not surprisingly) when the emotional state of a character is
what the scene is about. The "Fire" speech is a perfect example; the scene is
basically an emotional meltdown. Still, even here, you can't simply play the
emotion and be believably distraught, because the distress will be general and
not specific. What you can play is the specific action of sharing the concrete
details of your shame with those you've laughed at and scorned. Focusing
on creating the images (such as the burning hut) that communicate your loss
precisely is another kind of specific action. Letting the cry of psychic pain,
"Have mercy, love, my soul is all aflame," be expressed as some specific
physical pain is yet another kind of action. If the actor focuses on specific
actions, the emotion will be specific, immediate, and believable.

The primary challenge of Gonzalo's Lisbon speech (721–857) was different
from those presented by Tisbea's: in a word, length. Apparently, in performance the speech is often shortened; we did not choose to do so for two
reasons. First, the lengthy soliloquy, as Dakin informed us at the table work
session (when the actor playing Gonzalo blanched upon turning the fourth
page of the 137-line speech) is a distinctive feature of Golden Age plays; we
really didn't want to cut something that was so characteristic. Secondly, and
this is more fun, theatrically speaking, it's a kind of circus act – Mr. Memory
tames the text beast. The imagery is delightful (and was "painted" with ease
and precision by the actor, Brian George), but the real fun is in watching the
actor lead us through the text without a stumble. When the audience broke
into applause at the end of the speech (which they sometimes did), they were
not applauding the speech per se, lovely as it is, but the skill of the actor. I
would guess that a seventeenth-century audience would have had a similar
reaction.

On the subject of reactions, of critics as well as the "courteous spectator,"
I will conclude my discussion. Overall, the production met with a positive
response from both the general audience and the critics. Audiences, generally speaking, seemed to enjoy the storytelling; but I felt that some were
confused by the style. Less sophisticated audiences, theatrically speaking,
initially seemed unsure about whether or not the play was to be taken as
serious drama or comedy. There is more than a fair amount of comedy in the
early scenes of the play, but the elevated language, the length of the speeches,
the period costuming may have signaled to the theatrically uninitiated: "this
play demands your serious attention." However, by the time Catalinón made
his first speech, most were "on board," though some needed the appearance

of the clown to reassure them that what they were seeing, despite the moralizing, was indeed a – howsoever dark – comedy.

As for the reactions of the professional critics, most could be credited as intelligent, knowledgeable, and fair – whether enthusiastic or taxing. With few exceptions, the newspaper reviews were generally positive; what quarrels there were had to do with casting and interpretive choices. In one instance, a reviewer wrote that she found the actor playing Don Juan to be not "sexy" enough – a legitimate personal opinion, perhaps, but pretty worthless as professional criticism. In several other instances, the criticism was leveled at the interpretation of the King of Castile as a bit of a fool. Unlike the comment about Don Juan's lack of sexiness, whose complete subjectivity made any defense impossible (and uninteresting), this criticism involved interpretive choices that can be defended with textual evidence.

In fact, I think, a close reading of the text reveals that both kings in the piece are fairly clueless characters. The King of Naples, who leaves Don Pedro to sort things out, is completely taken in by the latter's deception – an elaborately poetic speech that completely misrepresents the facts of the situation. No matter how regally the king may speak during his second appearance in his one and only scene, the audience knows he is simultaneously being made a fool of by the Spanish ambassador (an almost perfect example of dramatic irony).

The King of Castile, upon close reading, comes off little better. In his first scene, he is an excellent audience for the Lisbon speech, it must be granted; but his decision to marry Doña Ana off to Don Juan Tenorio – about whom he seems to know little (although clearly Don Juan was originally hustled off to Naples after a sexual scandal in Spain) – initiates a series of marital mismatches and disasters. In his second scene, now aware of Don Juan's tendencies, the king seems to think that marrying Juan off to his victim will solve the problem, but now has to deal with the prior promise to Don Gonzalo and the prior engagement of Don Octavio. His solution to the first is a promotion; his solution to the second is another arranged marriage that creates another set of mismatches and disasters. In his third scene, he is fooled – like everyone else, it must be admitted – and arrests the wrong man. His flowery speech that ends the first act is regal enough, but – again an instance of dramatic irony – the man wearing the crown has pretty clearly shown himself less then perceptive. In his fourth scene, he tries to sort everything out with once again rearranging the various marriages, during which two of his nobles nearly come to blows in his own presence. And in his final scene, when he thinks rather fatuously that he has tied up all the loose ends, one after another complainant – high and low – invades his chamber to demand justice against Don Juan, to which the king's replies alternate between "What are you saying?" and – in Dakin's translation – "Off with his head." Yes, the translation perhaps leans a little heavily on the "Alice in

Wonderland" echo; but by this point can anyone seriously doubt that this king, whose final marriage arrangements are immediately contradicted by the parties onstage, is at least partially, if not predominantly, a character to be more laughed at than bowed to?

# Directing the *Comedia*: Notes on a Process

## ISAAC BENABU

What is it about the directorial process that makes it so difficult to reconstruct? Many directors have given us their reminiscences in writing, and many more have been interviewed about their experiences. Nevertheless, in any academic discussion of the directorial process in theatre, these accounts are at best second-hand evidence recalled in retrospect; generally impressionistic, they are based on memorial reconstruction of a dynamic enterprise that is over by the time it is discussed. They are founded on experience too, of course, but they are selective, and may even be distorted, as anything based on memory is subject to be. In the academy such accounts have value in that they reveal the director's conceptions, but how can we determine if those conceptions were reflected in the practice? Brecht is probably the best example to illustrate the disparity between theory and practice. In a way, I seem to be arguing against my own position in this essay, since most of the points I shall make rely on a "memorial reconstruction" of plays I directed some years ago. But my discussion will assure the reader that the problems addressed here are described after consulting the "bad" (inevitably!) videos made of the performances, as well as adhering always to the playwright's text.

So far, those individual accounts about directing plays referred to above have been unable to describe scientifically the creative process itself. This is why, perhaps, when we research theatre at the university, in much the same way as when we research other academic subjects, the tendency has been to adopt methodologies from other disciplines, such as literature or history, or even psychology. For example, the strategies evolved for reading the literary text have been widely applied to reading a playtext, strategies that can exclude, for example, those emotional and memorial mechanisms of response that only the staged play can elicit.

It is surprising, to say the least, that Theatre Studies, as an academic discipline, have evolved thus far when, to a large extent, basic theatrical processes (the rehearsal is a case in point) have not been observed and described scientifically. Instead, research, again to a large extent, has "straitjacketed" the analysis of theatre into methodologies that are not intrinsic to the subject. For the most part then, Theatre Studies as a discipline have relied on secondary rather than primary material; the library rather than the theatre itself has been the focal point. But there are interesting developments ahead. Borrowing from models derived from the natural and social sciences, from the laboratory and from fieldwork, the theatre can become the focal point in theatrical research, recording how decisions are made on the way to performance.

At this point, I wish to allude to some points raised by Lope de Vega in his *Arte nuevo de hacer comedias* (*The New Art of Writing Plays*) of 1609 – I would prefer "making" plays rather than "writing" them – both because I am discussing the *Comedia* and because they corroborate the notion that the practical is at the epicentre of a playwright's focus. Replying to the academicians who accused him of not knowing the rules of playwrighting, Lope states:

> [...] y cuando he de escribir una comedia
> encierro los preceptos con seis llaves
> [...]
> y escribo por el arte que inventaron
> los que el vulgar aplauso pretendieron,
> porque, como las paga el vulgo, es justo
> hablarle en necio para darle gusto.   (40–1, 45–8)

> ([...] and when I have to write a comedy I lock in the precepts[1] with six keys [...]; and I write in accordance with that art which they devised who aspired to the applause of the crowd; for, since the crowd pays for the comedies, it is fitting to talk foolishly to it to satisfy its taste [Brewster 24–5]).

A very central point in the practice of theatre is stressed here and developed in the treatise, one that I find instructive when directing a play: captivating the audience, for whom theatre is made. The apparent contempt contained in Lope's *necio* conceals an irony addressed to the learned academicians who had criticized the practice of pleasing the audience. He recognizes that spectators, like all consumers, in paying for a ticket, have the right to demand, or rather to receive, what is pleasing to them. In his thinking about theatre, Lope is clearly more to the left than many a postmodern director!

I think it useful to suggest that Lope, Shakespeare, or any of those great dramatists in the age in which the public theatre in Europe was born, would have tested and developed their theatrical skills in the theatre, on the stage itself, and in the course of staging the play; and they would have learnt much

---

[1]   "Precepts" might be more clearly understood today as "theoretical premises."

from the way in which their plays were received by the audience. It is in this spirit that I have undertaken to describe the directorial process in two *comedias* in which I have been involved as director. Of course, what I write here is based on memory, as I have already confessed; but now as then, I have anchored my decisions on the text provided by the playwright, looking for directions in the words that have reached us, because the words, legible as they are, are not intended to be read, but to be deciphered by people experienced in the making of theatre: by actors, by directors, not by readers of literature.

Of the two *comedias* I have directed, the first was Calderón's *The Surgeon of His Honour* (*El médico de su honra*) in 1997, with actors from the Advanced Acting Master's Program at the University of Wisconsin, Milwaukee, for which I used Roy Campbell's verse translation (adapted by reference to the Cruickshank edition of the Spanish text). The play was performed at the 1997 Siglo de Oro Drama Festival at El Paso, Texas. The second was Tirso de Molina's *El burlador de Sevilla* (*The Trickster of Seville*), which I directed in Barcelona with an assortment of mostly professional actors. This play was also presented at the 2000 Siglo de Oro Drama Festival at El Paso, Texas, and subsequently toured a number of cities in Mexico.

## The Surgeon of His Honour

I shall limit myself to studying the play's closing sequence, and attempt to explain how I came upon what I still believe to be Calderón's unwritten yet inscribed stage directions. The last lines in Calderón's play read as follows in Campbell's translation, and in this sequence three characters take part: Don Gutierre, the King and Doña Leonor.

| | |
|---|---|
| GUTIERRE. | What's that you say? |
| KING. | That you should wipe your doors Because there is a bloodstained hand on them. |
| GUTIERRE. | Those who deal in a certain kind of business Are wont to put the sign upon their doors Of what they deal in. I who deal in Honour So place a bloodstained hand upon my door For Honour can be only washed in blood. |
| KING. | Well, give that hand to Leonor. Your worth Deserves her. |
| GUTIERRE. | Yes, I give it. But mark well, Leonor, that this hand is stained with blood. |
| LEONOR. | That does not matter. It means nothing to me And neither can surprise nor frighten me. |
| GUTIERRE. | You see I am the Surgeon of my Honour. |

It is a science I do not forget,
An art I have not lost.
LEONOR.                          Then cure my own
When it's in need of it.
GUTIERRE.                          On that condition
Then, Leonor, I give you this right hand.
Pardon its many errors, my good friends,
For here THE SURGEON OF HIS HONOUR ends.
(81–2)

The original, following Cruickshank's edition, reads thus:

DON GUTIERRE.   ¿Qué decís?
REY.                          Que hagáis borrar
las puertas de vuestra casa;
que hay mano sangrienta en ella.
DON GUTIERRE.   Los que de un oficio tratan,
ponen, señor, a las puertas
un escudo de sus armas:
trato de honor, y así pongo
mi mano en sangre bañada
a la puerta; que el honor
con sangre, señor, se lava.
REY.                          Dádsela, pues, a Leonor,
que yo sé que su alabanza
la merece.
DON GUTIERRE.                          Sí la doy.
Mas mira, que va bañada
en sangre, Leonor.
DOÑA LEONOR.                          No importa;
Que no me admira ni espanta.
DON GUTIERRE.   Mira que médico he sido
de mi honra: no está olvidada
la ciencia.
DOÑA LEONOR.                          Cura con ella
mi vida, en estando mala.
DON GUTIERRE.   Pues con esa condición
te la doy. Con esto acaba
el médico de su honra.
Perdonad sus muchas faltas.   (2930–53)

The first point to remark is that what the director has in his hands is a version of Calderón's play, the result of collation with other editions and not Calderón's manuscript. However, there is no need to feel the perturbation that Stephen Orgel evidently feels in a study somewhat misleadingly entitled *The Authentic Shakespeare*, where he argues that since we do not have

Shakespeare's autograph, every text is the result of speculative readings by its editor. In the case of *The Surgeon of His Honour*, the text we have derives from several seventeenth-century editions contained in *partes* and *sueltas* (collections and individual printings of plays), and more recent editions reflect an honest scholarly approach to the task in hand, some containing a number of more fanciful or subjective readings than others, and they culminate in the critical edition used here. Is this not an honest mode of inquiry in most academic disciplines?

More significant is the fact that the dramatic text is set down according to the conventions for printing plays. This point becomes patently obvious in the closing formula of *The Surgeon*, which, in the printed text appears to form an integral part of Don Gutierre's final lines. However, anyone acquainted with the performance tradition of *comedias* knows full well that it is the actor who, stepping out of character, pronounces the closing formula, and thus pays lip service to the accepted convention for ending plays. So, even if the closing formula, for reasons of versification, follows on the character's words, on the stage there occurs a significant transition or transformation from character to actor, which the text conceals by not marking the pause.

Furthermore, and here the director has to exercise the ability to "read" a theatrical text (Benabu, *Calderón*), there is not a single stage direction in the text given above. Clearly, again, it cannot be that Calderón intended these lines to be merely recited without enactment of some kind, since these are the closing lines of an action that is tragic. These are some of the questions that a director *must* answer in staging this sequence:

1. Why does the King fall silent after the line "Your worth / Deserves her"? What is to be done with him on stage?
2. Where is Doña Leonor during the exchange between the King and Don Gutierre?
3. Does Doña Leonor remain on stage until the end of the play?
4. What is the configuration of characters on the stage?
5. Today, when we are no longer familiar with the closing formula convention, will we omit it altogether, and if we don't, how is the actor to negotiate the transition?

While there are more questions to be asked when directing this play, we have enough material before us to trace the lines of direction – lines, I should add, that were placed there by Calderón himself, lines and words that are contained within the spatial quality of theatrical writing, and that can guide the director.

As obvious as it may sound, a character must possess a determinable identity by the time he/she first appears on the stage. The debate may continue to resound in the halls of academe, but in the theatre this basic question must be resolved by the time the curtain goes up, and preferably much earlier than that! Looking at a character at the end of the play is less problematic than at the start, because all that is known about the character will become more apparent at the close than at the opening, since the picture we have of the character is as complete as it will ever be.

Returning to *The Surgeon*, I shall say of the King that, in the course of production, he seemed, in spite of all the ink spilt (the writer includes himself in this!), to be much more intelligent than the picture of him etched by those moralizing critics who weighed his imprudence. Could it have been the actor who opened this dimension? Possibly, but Calderón provides the keys, if we see the character in the frame of the entire play. Pedro makes mistakes, but then what character doesn't in this play (would it have been a tragedy otherwise?). More important in my eyes is the fact that he demonstrates the much sought-after skills of many modern politicians and people in positions of power (skills already enumerated by Machiavelli): sitting on the fence for as long as possible before acting, measuring his words so as not to commit himself, and using any situation to his advantage. Even with Coquín, when he has often been seen as cruel, what my actor demonstrated on stage was a great sense of dry humour. He intimidated Coquín with the very arms the *gracioso* exercises to take advantage of others: his ability to make others laugh. In this production, the King made the *gracioso* quake with fear, and he made the spectator laugh.

I shall return presently to Pedro in order to discuss his movements in the sequence. But next I turn to Leonor whose victory appears to be a pyrrhic one. She gets her man in the end, but only by exposing her life to considerable risk. But honour is the overriding concern for her as it has been for Gutierre all along. This is why she accepts the bloody hand offered her.

And what of Gutierre? The problem requires some background consideration if we are to explore his role as protagonist, and also because he has become one of Calderón's most controversial characters. Gutierre has to obey the King's command to marry Leonor because, by the restriction he places on his own speech, he cannot tell the King other than through circumlocution why he dare not comply with the royal wish. And the King knows it, of course, for he recognizes in Mencía's death a convenient way of keeping his promise to Leonor. Gutierre tries to counter the King's suggestions by offering a number of hypothetical eventualities that are intended to remind the King of their earlier conversation at the beginning of the third act, and which point to the failure of these measures in the past.

By his own decree, however, Gutierre can find no answer to the King's final and heavily ironic suggestion as to how he should deal with matters, should he find himself in a similar predicament with his new wife. The King's sardonic solution, "Why, [by] bleeding [her]" (81) ("Sangralla" [III.2929]), silences Gutierre as it jolts him into recognizing that, despite his efforts to mask it, the King has pieced together the truth. To pursue further his objections to marry Leonor would be to risk losing the honour for which he has already paid so high a price, the sacrifice of the wife he loved. Honour, in its demand for silence, exacts as high a price now as it did earlier for Mencía in the first act, when it dictated what Gutierre himself describes in the second act as: "For your diet – / Silence" (46) ("la dieta del silencio" [II.1674–5]).

Gutierre, who nurtures his suspicions in silence and acts through it, is bound by silence to the very end. The suffering-in-silence motif, so convincingly developed by Calderón in tragedies like *Las tres justicias en una (Three Judgments in One)* and *El pintor de su deshonra (The Painter of His Dishonour)*, is used here to heighten tragic irony very effectively indeed. And with the tragic recognition that he is condemned to suffer in silence, Gutierre turns away from the King.

A further layer of irony at the end is uncovered by the reverberation of the closing words of the first act, which is where Calderón first suggests a link in the fates of Gutierre and Leonor. Leonor's curse early on, "My grief be yours" (28) ("El mismo dolor sientas que siento" [I.1013–14]), is fulfilled when Gutierre gives her his "bloody" hand in marriage so as to protect the silence that he considers as the only remaining remedy to "cure" his honour. Such is Calderón's skill as a playwright that as the King's ironic "Why, [by] bleeding [her]" rings in Gutierre's ears, Leonor's words at the end of Act I echo, albeit silently, in the audience's: "Since I have lost my name / There's nothing for me but to die" (28) ("Ay de mí! mi honor perdí! / Ay de mí! mi muerte hallé" [I.1019–20]).

The fictional frame drawn at the end of *The Surgeon* points to a bleak universe where human beings are doomed to suffer for unquestionable beliefs forced upon them by the social, or perhaps even by the universal, order. Their innocence, in the biblical sense in which Calderón uses the word (viz. 77/III.2751 in Coquín's speech), also comes into play, a limitation of perspective and perception necessarily imposed by their human condition. The suffering at the end is burdensome indeed! Such an effect is proper to tragedy, and only draws on the real world to the extent that any poetic metaphor does.

This background information will explain more clearly the nature of my decisions in staging the ending, the way in which I saw the characters move in the final sequence. It made sense to me that Leonor should remain upstage since the conversation between the King and Gutierre is not meant for her ears, and though she is on stage, her presence goes unremarked by the interlocutors and she does not participate in the dialogue between the King and Gutierre.

As far as blocking went, I placed the King on a podium on every one of his appearances at the palace. In this scene, therefore, Gutierre approached him having entered from upstage-right (I kept to the design of the *corral* stage, where entrances and exits are through backstage openings). And after the King utters his final words in the play, it made good sense to remove him from the stage. A character whose presence had been so powerful and meaningful in all his appearances could not, in my opinion, stand idly on the stage while Gutierre attempted to dissuade Leonor from accepting his hand.

With the King off the stage, the focus of the action, as supported by the text, fell upon Gutierre and Leonor. His admonitions to Leonor – and there are two – are intended to dissuade her, to intimidate her. This is the only way for Gutierre to avoid carrying out the King's command. In this closing sequence, therefore, Leonor stood stage right, so that Gutierre stood centre stage, as might befit a protagonist at the end of a tragedy (this may not be essential, rather a matter of directing preference). He is the focus of the action at this point, faced as he is by an impasse, and in this production, he was therefore the one to move or turn towards the other characters. As he approached Leonor uttering the intimidating words "Yes, I give it. But mark well, / Leonor, that this hand is stained with blood" (82) ("Sí la doy. / Mas mira, que va bañada / en sangre, Leonor" [III.2942–4]), she was able to face him squarely, and continued to do so as he elaborated a second threat, "You see I am the Surgeon of my Honour. / It is a science I do not forget, / An art I have not lost." (82) ("Mira que médico he sido / de mi honra. No está olvidada / la ciencia" [III.2946–8]), lines that amount to a confession of the deed he has fought so hard to keep secret. Leonor, of course, is all the more resolute to accept this "bloody" hand, come what may, because it is the only way she can redeem a situation of personal dishonour: "Then cure my own / When it's in need of it" (82) ("Cura con ella / mi vida, en estando mala" [III.2948–9]).

My closing remarks on this play concern the transition from character to actor in delivering the closing formula, to which I have alluded above. I felt the tragedy would be all the more poignant if I emphasized Gutierre's isolation at this juncture. Leaving Leonor on the stage would have detracted from this, so with her last rejoinder, she walked proudly off the stage, leaving Gutierre to mumble to himself "On that condition / Then, Leonor, I give you this right hand" (82) ("Pues con esta condición / te la doy" [III.2950–1]), contemplating the hand he made every effort not to proffer, and in total isolation. I had him turn with his back to the audience and look emptily at the spot where Mencía's body had been revealed, the discovery space at the back. At this point the light faded slowly to the sound of a few dying chords. Sensibly or otherwise, my decision was to omit the conventional closing formula.

I shall repeat what I have written elsewhere in order to illustrate why I consider this type of ending so forceful theatrically:

> In the European theatre of the period, the tragic protagonist stands alone at the centre of a world he no longer understands, in which the secure frontiers that contained the medieval fictional hero have been shattered.

God is still officially in the world, but He is invisible. He has withdrawn, so to say, from the *theatrum mundi to* become 'Le dieu caché', as Lucien Goldmann refers to him in his study of the same name on Racinian theatre [...]. Instead we get the picture of man abandoned to his own devices and prey to his conscience; his only option is to trust in divine grace. (Benabu, *Calderón* 84)

This is the decision process undertaken by one director in constructing an ending designed to highlight tragicity. But it is my hope that I have shown that the decisions taken were in line with the text that has come down to us, and that, fanciful as it may sound, I sought to listen to the playwright's voice.

## El burlador de Sevilla

The experience I wish to bring to your notice in the case of Tirso's *El burlador* will be treated more cursorily and is rather different, although it also involves a close reading of the text. Octavio, it will be agreed, is never the most interesting of the characters in any of the Don Juan versions. I was faced with a particular problem. The actor who had auditioned for the part and was very keen to play it had rather effeminate gestures, and he was unable to disguise them on the stage. But his interest in participating was such that I decided to go back to the text to see what possible readings Tirso could offer me.[2]

Certain things are clear to all: Octavio is not presented in a very favourable light. When he first appears it is made clear from the start that he has just awoken, rather late, and his servant Ripio makes fun of him at several takes. His affected declaration of undying love to an absent Isabela, made at the moment when he awakens, prompts Ripio to further mocking: "tu amor / es amor impertinente" (209–10) ("If this is love, these feelings are / more trouble than they're worth" [209–10]), and he explains:

| | |
|---|---|
| ¿Pues no seré majadero, | Then wouldn't I be an idiot, sir – |
| y de solar conocido, | the crown prince of idiocy – |
| si pierdo yo mi sentido | if some girl I loved was in love with me, |
| por quien me quiere y la quiero? | and I still went crazy out of love for her? |
| (I.219–22) | (I.219–22) |

For the audience, all this sequence has an additional dimension. They cannot help but see Octavio in a ridiculous light because they know that Isabela

---

2   All references to the Spanish text of Tirso's play are to the online version prepared by Vern Williamsen. All English renderings are from the Dakin Matthews translation, perhaps less literal than others, but faithful to the sense and spirit of Tirso's text.

was (willingly, perhaps?) seduced by Don Juan in the previous scene. All his exaggerated suffering only serves to emphasize the comedic aspects of the character. And when Ripio, ignorant also of the previous night's revels, urges Octavio to "dar" ("act") on Isabela, his salacious language could imply by way of a jibe that Octavio is impotent:

| | |
|---|---|
| Dando dije, porque al dar | I call it giving, and I tell you, sir, |
| no hay cosa que se le iguale, | There's nothing quite like it – as I hope to live! |
| y si no a Isabela *dale* [my emphasis] | And if Isabel's not willing to give, |
| a ver si sabe *tomar.* [my emphasis] | Then maybe she'll take, if you give it to her. |
| (I.239–42) | (I.239–42) |

In all the four scenes in which he appears in the play, there is little evidence that Octavio should be taken as anything other than a comic character (beware of the Malvolio syndrome!), and it is known that effeminacy on the seventeenth-century stage was often a device for prompting comic reactions from the audience, as the performance of *El lindo don Diego* (*Don Diego the Dandy*) during an earlier Siglo de Oro festival at El Paso so manifestly proved. He is duped by Don Pedro, and abused by Don Juan himself, who takes full advantage (to the audience's pleasure) that Octavio is ignorant of his involvement with Isabela. With Don Diego and the King in Act III, he affects courage when an old man threatens him with a duel. And finally, in the play's closing sequence, he asks the King permission to marry the newly "widowed" Isabela (Don Juan and Isabela never married): "Pues ha enviudado Isabela, / quiero con ella casarme" (III.2947–8) ("Now that Isabella's a widow, sire, / I'd rather marry her instead" [III.2909–10]). Not only is Octavio a cuckold; by the end of the play, he is a consenting cuckold. Although our understanding of effeminacy may have evolved in everyday life, on the stage a man acting like a woman continues to be the object of mirth. My decision to portray Octavio as a fop, I believe, finds support in Tirso's text.

During the post-performance discussion at the Siglo de Oro Festival, my decision to make Octavio effeminate gave rise to some objection, interestingly enough, on the part of two Spanish scholars present who felt personally offended that I had somehow violated Tirso's character. Their words of criticism were so harsh that they reduced the leading actress to tears. I was not about to reveal my reasons for making Octavio effeminate, although I did cite textual support for my interpretation, which I still believe makes my reading of Tirso's text a valid one. I wonder whether they would have objected to the *lindo*'s affectations in Paco Portes's unforgettable rendering of the leading role in Moreto's *El lindo don Diego*.

Clearly, my decision to characterize Octavio in this manner was a personal one. And I realized I was taking a risk, because in some way it was found threatening to an image some Spaniards may have of themselves. It was not the only risk I took in that production. I was privileged to be working with an especially talented leading actress, and it seemed a waste to me to have her play a single female role. So I asked her to play all of the female roles, Isabela, Tisbea and Aminta (Ana never appears onstage, even if her voice is heard within), as if Don Juan, so consumed by his desire to deceive, is unaware that he is always confronting the same woman in different guises. Not only were the different female characters distinguishable by costume and hairstyle, they also spoke in different accents: Isabela in Castilian, Tisbea in Catalan, and Aminta in Andalusian. The risk paid dividends, because it was understood and appreciated by the audience, who is *necio* only when Lope has tongue in cheek!

# Tirso's Tamar Untamed:
## A Lesson of the Royal Shakespeare Company's Production

### JONATHAN THACKER

The second of the four Golden Age plays produced for its 2004 Stratford season by the Royal Shakespeare Company (RSC) was Tirso de Molina's *Tamar's Revenge* (*La venganza de Tamar*).[1] The drama follows the Old Testament story of King David's heir, Amnon, who becomes obsessed with and eventually rapes his half-sister, Tamar, before being murdered in revenge by her brother, the vain and power-hungry Absalom. The RSC's production permitted an all-too-rare opportunity to assess a professional director's and cast's "reading" of a classical Spanish play against interpretations offered by scholars based almost invariably on the play's text. It forced a reconsideration of a number of critical assumptions about Tirso's play, with the fact that it was performed in English, initially to a non-Spanish audience, and at the home of Shakespeare, being factors important to its novelty and freshness.

Before considering in detail the most striking aspect of the RSC's production, that is, the characterization of Tamar herself, it is worth expanding briefly on this point. The last major staging of Tirso's Old Testament play, by the Compañía Nacional de Teatro Clásico (CNTC) in 1997, illustrated some of the difficulties that productions of Golden Age works can face in Spain. Interviews with the play's director, José Carlos Plaza, in advance of its opening nights in Almagro, Madrid, and Barcelona, betrayed his custodial impulse to respect the original tragedy (as he saw it) and resist any attempt to modernize it. The overriding defensive and proprietorial functions of the director and the company are underlined by Plaza's assertion that the play is as good as a Shakespeare work, and his keenness to note that he is rediscovering (perhaps re-displaying) a work not performed since the

---

[1] The play was translated into a very free blank verse by the poet James Fenton, and directed by Simon Usher. It opened in the Swan Theatre, Stratford-upon-Avon, on 28 April 2004, and subsequently toured to Newcastle and Madrid.

seventeenth century (Bravo, Escarré, Galindo). Theatre critics were generally unimpressed with the production. Although the "version" of the playtext, done by José Hierro, tended to be admired for its sensitive cuts and replacing of "frases obsoletas que romperían el clima atemporal" ("obsolete phrases which would destroy the effect of timelessness") (López Sancho), it failed to win audiences over on other counts.[2] The speaking of the verse and the grandiloquent style of acting were both criticized (Pérez de Olaguer, Haro Tecglén) and there ensued a general wringing of hands over the purpose of the CNTC (see especially Ley). Above all, however, critics felt that Plaza had underestimated Tirso's skill in drawing characters, characters that might have spoken to a modern audience, that demanded "una lectura actual" ("an up-to-date reading") (Pérez de Olaguer). The most common complaint was that the playwright's subtlety was abandoned in favour of a loud, simplified style which, *inter alia*, denied characters time for reflection, portrayed Amón's rape of his half-sister on stage, and unjustifiably allowed Tamar to reemerge naked to beg her father for justice. As well as lamenting the lack of an understanding of Amón's and others' psychological development in the pursuit of action (López Sancho, Pérez de Olaguer, Ley, Benach), one or two observers also regretted the missed opportunity that a more perceptive reading of Tamar's ambiguous character might have presented (Haro Tecglén, Ley).[3]

The director of *Tamar's Revenge* for the RSC was free from the pressures associated with staging a Golden Age play at the CNTC: the Spanish verse was translated; the political debate over the role of a publicly funded theatre company was not the issue it had been in Spain; the play was in no sense a lost national treasure to be handled with care and respect. Additionally Simon Usher had at his disposal a group of highly trained and versatile character actors with no preconceptions about Spanish classical drama, and was anyway working within a tradition in which novel reimaginings of old plays are accepted, indeed expected. The result was a "reading" for the stage of *La venganza de Tamar* that prioritized character and investigated emotional expression and repression (and their sources) within a claustrophobic ruling family, with universal (and thus modern) implications. Usher, with the liberty granted by another (English Shakespearean) tradition, provided a version of Tirso's play that, while generally misunderstood by British critics for whom the work was all but unknown, "nos gana por goleada en nuestro campo" ("gave us a beating on our home ground") in the metaphor of Almudena Guzmán, writing in the wake of the Madrid performances.

---

[2]   I have chosen throughout to offer my own translations. (I would have liked to use Fenton's translation of *Tamar*, but it was too free for my purposes.)

[3]   There is a summary of the critical reception of Plaza's *La venganza de Tamar* in García Lorenzo (27–31).

Although he read academic studies on Tirso and his work, Usher approached *La venganza de Tamar* from outside another limiting tradition, this time the scholarly one. As Ruano de la Haza has recently argued, scholars have been wont (taking a false lead from A. A. Parker, perhaps) to play down the importance of characterization, and the existence of "real" characters, in Golden Age drama:

> Está claro que si tanto críticos como actores y directores están en general convencidos de la inutilidad de extraer y mostrar la humanidad que puedan poseer los personajes del teatro clásico español será inevitable que ese teatro degenere en abstracciones, intelectualismos o que se convierta en un sermón o en una función de circo y sea adaptado, desguazado, podado, transformado, convertido en extraño, grotesco, una extensión de la España de pandereta: Segismundo de torero, Peribáñez de cantaor flamenco, Marta la piadosa de sevillana. (240)

> (It is clear that if critics as much as actors and directors are in general convinced of the futility of extracting and demonstrating the humanity that the characters in Spanish classical theatre can possess, this theatre will inevitably degenerate into abstractions of purely intellectual interest, or will be converted into a sermon or a circus performance and will be adapted, broken up, pruned, transformed, changed into something strange and grotesque, an extension of the Spain of stereotypes: with Segismundo as bullfighter, Peribáñez as flamenco singer, pious Martha as *sevillana*.)

Usher's character work on Tirso's play does, by contrast, extract and demonstrate the humanity of the playwright's creations, and in the case of Tamar, produces unexpected and disturbing results. In his review of the production for *Comedia Performance*, Christopher Weimer confirms that:

> [Usher's] conception of some characters was far from conventional. Katherine Kelly's Tamar was no naïve maiden even before the rape: her song in the garden and her flirtation with the unknown intruder were decidedly seductive, and it was difficult not to be disturbed by her obvious pleasure when kissing Amnon during the erotic game he proposes to cure his lovesickness. (236)

Weimer's surprise is understandable. In their interpretations of the play, in spite of its title, scholars have generally concentrated on examining the characters of Amón, David and, to a lesser extent, Absalón, at the expense of Tamar, who is the other major figure in both the Biblical narrative and Tirso's drama. As we shall see, Tamar attracts attention in passing and at times for the importance of her dramatic function, but a detailed analysis of her *character* and its development has been slow to emerge. The bold interpretation of this figure by Simon Usher and his principal actress, Katherine Kelly, in the RSC's production, forces a serious reconsideration of her.

We shall begin by looking at some of these brief scholarly readings, which have created the "conventional" image of Tamar, before re-exploring the play-text in the light of the RSC's production. In 1950 in a wide-ranging article on Tirso's Old Testament plays, J. C. J. Metford, while assessing the figures of Amón and David as "among Tirso's greatest creations" (158), reckoned that Tamar "is nevertheless drawn with great sympathy and given a witty and engaging personality" (157). In her *preámbulo* to the play, Blanca de los Ríos criticizes Tirso for his inconsistency in drawing Tamar's character which, "queda algo borrosa oscilando entre la doncella dulce y atractiva, la no muy ardiente prometida de Joab y la burlada deseosa de venganza" (360) ("remains rather blurred, switching between the lovely, attractive girl, Joab's less-than-ardent *fiancée*, and the victim thirsting for revenge"). Margaret Wilson describes her as "well rounded out from the flat biblical sketch," initially possessing "warmth and gaiety [which are] turned into cynicism and sour wit" (111). In his influential 1969 edition of the play,[4] Alan Paterson explains how he sees that, "[f]rom her first entry, there is a restlessness and sense of oppression akin to Amón's; in her imagery of love as a consuming fire or appetite, her inner mood is picked out [...] the spirit of the coquette is suggested; darkness relaxes the strict observance of decorum!" (18). This perceptive view of Tamar's characterization in the early part of the play is consonant with Simon Usher's production, as we shall see, but for Paterson this coquettishness gives way by the wedding scene at the end of Act I, a public event of course, to her "ruthless and immediate" (18) action in demanding the death of the insolent masked guest. Thus in her participation in the play-within-the-play of Act II it is only "*unwittingly* [that] she offers herself as the person on whom a genuine passion can feed" (17, my emphasis). Paterson goes on to see Tamar's character as symmetrical to Amón's in that she takes over his role as aggressor in her malicious and hateful vengeance. McKendrick too has Tamar as "unsuspecting" as Amón lures her into his play, concluding that "[t]he sinister discrepancy between Tamar's understanding of the situation and the obsessed Amón's intentions in this play within the play is dramatically very potent" (119).

In his bilingual edition of the play, John Lyon also gives just a brief assessment of the princess's character. In the garden scene she shows "mildly flirtatious annoyance" (29) at Amón disguised as the gardener's boy. Of the play-within-the-play he writes that Tamar moves from "flippant amusement to perplexity, to suspicion and finally to horrified realization of the situation" (28). Later:

---

[4]  All quotations are taken from Paterson's edition and given by act and line number.

[o]n dimly perceiving that she is the true object of Amnon's love, Tamar shows scant charity for her brother's plight. Faced with the possibility of losing her lover, Joab, she abandons Amnon to his fate. After the rape she develops a passion for vengeance which knows no bounds. Tirso portrays this, not as a natural demand for justice for the violence done to her, but as a deep, brooding obsession which corrupts and destroys all natural feeling in the character. (24)

Everett Hesse, probably the work's most prolific critic, believes in the sincerity of Tamar's protestations of affection for her melancholic brother at the beginning of the play-within-the-play (II.497–500).[5] He also notes her enthusiasm (and imprudence) when playing the role of the Ammonite princess in Amón's charade (37) in which, however, there is no "true love" (41). It is only through Amón's cunning that an "unwary Tamar" (46) agrees to act her part, and she "*guilelessly* encourages him to express his sexual desires" (47, my emphasis).

Raymond Conlon's article on Amón's psychology explores the prince's attraction to and violent rejection of Tamar whom he rapes in order to "hurt his parent," David (48). He characterizes Amón's reluctance to consider marriage to his half-sister Tamar after the rape (a possibility under Jewish law in spite of their consanguinity) as vindictive.[6] Tamar's character is only touched upon but Conlon does read her words "¿Dónde iré sin honra, ingrato, / ni quién me querrá acoger" (III.42–3) ("Where can I go to without honour, wretch, and who will take me in?"), as an "entreaty to marry her" (49), which suggests that, in his view, Tamar's fear of dishonour outweighs her now impossible love for Joab and any hatred for Amón.

In her description of a rare dramatic portrayal of Tamar, Dawn Smith writes of the actress (Jules Melvin) who played the part at the Lyric, Hammersmith in 1992:[7]

Melvin was indeed electrifying: her portrayal of an impish, spoiled child who becomes a blazing, vengeful woman was completely convincing. The audience was riveted by her cat-like sensuality: such perfect matching of actor and role made one appreciate the strength of Tirso's conception of the character. (40)

---

[5]   Hesse's *Tirso's Art in* La venganza de Tamar: *Tragedy of Sex and Violence* is actually a collection of overlapping essays that are frequently descriptive and reveal some misunderstandings about the play, but also provide a number of useful insights gleaned from close textual reading.

[6]   In the Biblical source, II Samuel 13, Tamar proposes that Amón ask David for her hand before he carries out the rape.

[7]   This production, entitled *The Rape of Tamar*, was done in an English translation by Paul Whitworth.

Even more useful is the contrast with the US revival, under the same director (Paul Whitworth), which happily Smith was also able to see. Here, although "Susan Patterson [Tamar] was physically and psychologically able to portray the character of Tamar *before* the rape, she failed to make a plausible transition to a vengeful, deadly woman *after* the rape" (40, emphasis in original). The failure was reflected in some uncomprehending press reviews.

Marcia Welles, in a psychoanalytical reading of the work published in 1995, attempts to explain the relative silence – which we have noted – surrounding the figure of Tamar in the original Biblical source, in Tirso's play, in Calderón's *Los cabellos de Absalón* (*Absalom's Hair*), and in critics' responses to her. Rather than seeing Tamar emerge, as Welles would have it, into "subject-hood" (353) during the tragedy, unmasking "a crisis of masculinity" (362) among the leading male characters, there is an anxious tendency, she argues, to play down or contain the character's disruptive energy. Appealing to a primitive staging of the play, in which the rape takes place off-stage, between Acts II and III, Welles asserts that the "sexual crime against Tamar, private and intimate, is effaced" (343), that her damaged body is not shown, and that as a victim she is "aestheticized. Her body is kept distant from the audience" (344). (The rape, incidentally, was graphically enacted on-stage in Usher's RSC production, as it was in the CNTC's production in which Tamar's naked and bloody body was displayed.) To describe Tamar as coquettish, as Paterson does, can be read, argues Welles, as a patriarchally sponsored critical attempt (unconscious, no doubt) to tame Tamar's later fear-inducing violence. Thus, "[m]uch in [Paterson's] analysis (especially the reading for proleptic allusions in act 1 to developments in act 3) reveals an aspect of the ideology of rape, according to which the victim is held responsible – at least in part – for the violation" (352).

Nevertheless, earlier in her article, Welles had written that "[t]he elaboration of desire as a process (rather than as a given) invokes the dynamics of the incest dread, which explains why *La venganza de Tamar* is so erotically charged" (347). Here the critic is referring to the subtle first-act development of Amón's incestuous desire, absent from Calderón's *Los cabellos de Absalón*. This eroticism, difficult to ignore in the play, requires exploration especially as it is a predominant feature of Usher's production of the play. This RSC's *Tamar* does not limit the erotic impulses to the love-sick Amón (as Welles does and as Lorca does in his *romance*, "Thamar y Amnón").[8] It may be that Usher's depiction of a sensual, erotically charged Tamar will be seen as

---

8  The story also featured in the popular ballad tradition that contains at least one example of a poem in which Tamar's response to Amón's declaration of love is ambivalent. The final line of the ballad is given to Tamar and reads: "Si de mi amor estás malo, no te levantes de esta cama" (Bénichou 113) ("If you are ill for love of me, do not arise from this bed"). I am grateful to Jack Sage for this reference.

politically incorrect if we follow Welles's feminist reading: even to suggest
that Tamar should have fed the desire of Amón is, it would seem, to open up
the possibility (comforting to patriarchy) that his half-sister has some share
in the responsibility for Amón's later sexual violence against her. However,
if Tamar felt some degree of sexual desire for her half-brother, this does not
mean that she is to any extent responsible for his raping her. Surely scholars'
recognition of her flirtatious behaviour towards a socially inferior "gardener"
in the heat and darkness of the *seraglio* should not be interpreted as a male
desire to absolve or reduce Amón's monstrosity. Such a view implies that
the play's reader or audience cannot separate female sexual desire, or even
arousal, from an individual's responsibility for his own reprobate actions.
Indeed, I would argue that to turn Tamar into a child who has never thought
about or experienced sexual feelings not only undermines Tirso's characterization of her through her love song in Act I (I.353–80 and 441–54), but
makes the passion which she shows in her later vengeance impossible to
stage (as the US production of the play in 1994 apparently revealed). Tamar's
"sensuality" (as when played in the Lyric version in 1992) is essential to the
play's success on stage. It also allows for an interpretation of the tragedy that
does not deny the continued thematic importance of sin, justice, and mercy,
but which simultaneously returns us to the eternal human complexity of the
story. Its appeal to a modern director, a Golden Age audience, and its status
as an Old Testament story argue for just such an interpretation.

In order to explore further the characterization of Tamar and its implications, we shall re-examine the text of three key moments in which she is
involved, all from the first two acts, in the light of the 2004 production from
the Swan. These moments are Amón's falling for the woman he later realizes
is Tamar in the garden, the wedding at the end of Act I, and the "Ammonite
princess" play-within-the-play of Act II.

Destroying the sanctity of the walled garden is the first of the four clear
violations committed by Amón during the play, establishing him as a disruptive, selfish but passionate character.[9] The space in this *locus amoenus* is an
exclusively female one, reserved for David's wives and other women. His
invasion is of their most intimate place, where in this case, Dina and Tamar
find a rare freedom to talk of love. Although Dina brings up the subject of
Joab (I.302), Tamar never mentions him by name in the scene, but talks
and sings of love, and then an absent lover, in general terms: "Pues traes
instrumento, canta, / que en los jardines amenos/ ansí Amor su mal espanta"
(I.320–3) ("As you have your instrument, sing, for in pleasant gardens/ Love
is soothed with music"). As de los Ríos noted in calling Tamar "la no muy

---

[9]    The others are the disruption of the wedding, the rape, and the forcing of Tamar (as a
shepherdess) to uncover her face.

ardiente prometida de Joab" ("Joab's less-than-ardent *fiancée*"), the relationship between the apparent lovers is undeveloped, naturally very formal, and
possibly rather one-sided.[10] Joab is not of royal blood and is David's indispensable general, but is unlike Tamar in every respect. He *may* be the focus of
Tamar's "Ligero pensamiento" ("Thought so light") song in the garden scene,
but above all the princess's words establish her clear yearning for physical
love. The heat, symbolizing unassuaged passion, the darkness and isolation
allowing freedom from normal palace etiquette, and the music that intensi-
fies Tamar's emotions (I.417–21) combine to create an atmosphere of pained
longing. Tamar sends her amorous thoughts in the form of a green bird to her
lover to drink at his fountain. Whether or not one takes the song to have erotic
overtones – and there are strong hints that it does – Tamar concentrates on the
satisfaction of her desire in the song's refrain, "pajarito que vas a la fuente,
/ bebe y vente" (I.365–6, 379–80 and 453–4) ("Little bird who flies to the
spring, drink and come back"). The consumption of food is associated with,
or symbolizes, satisfaction of sexual appetites throughout the play, perhaps
most obviously in the rape scene where Amón dismisses his servants with
the words: "a solas quiero comer / manjares que el alma espera" (II.1081–2)
("I want to eat alone dishes for which the soul has longed").[11] By the song's
third verse Tamar admits to being jealous of her own bird/thought and the
fruits of love that he could be enjoying:

> celosa estoy que goces
> de mi adorado ausente
> la vista, con que aplacas
> la ardiente sed de verle.
> Si acaso de sus labios
> el dulce néctar bebes
> que labran sus palabras,
> y hurtalle algunas puedes [...]    (I.445–52)

> (I am jealous that you are enjoying the sight of my absent lover, and
> are able to quench your burning thirst to see him. If you chance to
> drink the sweet nectar from his lips made by the words he speaks and
> are able to steal some [...].)

10 In his programme notes to the RSC production, translator James Fenton also hesitates
over this relationship, writing only that Tamar "appears to be in love" with Joab. The production emphasized the text's association of Joab with David, where the latter represents military
prowess, order, and authority. There is no spark of passion between Tamar and the safe Joab,
so different from Amón.
11 Other examples occur at I.485–86; II.673–77; II.699–700; III.1–20; and III.953–62.

The even partial satisfaction of physical desire is externalized by Tamar in the form of a bird that can fly on the breeze over the garden wall to the world of men and war. That she should admit to and then feel jealous of her own desires is an indication of the degree to which her role as David's daughter represses her, preventing her from expressing her sexuality. Despite her elevated status, her unspecific yearning is a feeling with which most members of any audience, male or female, will recognize as belonging to a youthful emotional awakening.

Although in James Fenton's translation Tamar's song is not explicitly erotic (22–4), the scene itself in the RSC production is highly charged with eroticism. The two women enter blindfolded, while the lighting remains bright and bathes even the audience (as would have been the case in the *corral*), and wearing very short skirts and revealing leather bra tops. They breathe deeply and loudly and are clearly perspiring in the intense night-time heat. They both seem on the point of sexual arousal, perhaps as a result of their conversation about men and love. In their poses and movements, for example, the intimate grasping of Tamar by Dina (Emma Pallant) and their cross-legged sitting, they show that they are in a place that guarantees them absolute privacy. There is no fear of disturbance or anxiety about appearance, and there exists an equality between them discernible in Tirso's text. Tamar's song is languorously delivered, and she continues to hum its tune as Amón speaks his asides making their voices mingle, and subtly suggesting a union. The groping about in the dark – the actors cannot see in this scene and need to have the two "servants," who remain on stage throughout the play, guide them and prevent them falling into the audience – suggests vulnerability, while the blindfolds also remind us of the god of Love and his vagaries. *Amor* is invoked by both Tamar and Amón during the play.

This is a Tamar who is very young and perhaps newly aware of her sexuality. Amón's subsequent horror at realizing he loves his sister may be in part explicable by the fact that she has turned into a woman while he has been at war. His intervention here interrupts the women's talk of love, but keeps alive the erotic subtext as he kisses Tamar's hand (a recurrent theme as scholars have noted) and jokes about providing sexual services for the old king's other "wives." Now in company, however lowly, Dina and Tamar have to return to their social roles, and although they banter with the "gardener" briefly, Tamar closes the interlude with a high-handed (but dramatically ironic) threat to have the man thrown out, "Yo haré que os echen de casa" (I.546 and cf. III.79–86) ("I shall have you thrown out of the palace"). There is no hint, of course, in the text or Usher's production that Tamar and Amón know exactly who each other are at this stage, but their awakenings to sexual stimuli have been simultaneous and subtly linked on stage. Although the scene brings a new twist to falling in love *de oídas* (by hearsay), the *Comedia* convention is that the audience expects two young lovers who meet in a comparable way to consummate their love.[12]

By the end of the first act, when Amón attends and disrupts the wedding of Elisa and Josefo, there is more than a hint in Usher's production that Tamar "knows" at some level the identity of her importunate lover, or is, at least, attracted to the figure sexually. Amón's blindness has given way to a mask that disguises his identity from her, but this sharp and witty girl could well be expected to recognize behind it one of the few men she knows well. He admits only that he was the "gardener" and that he is now a "noble amante" (I.823). As we have seen, the scene tends to have been read as Tamar's flat and proper rejection of the masked man, backed up by her apparently unambiguous order to have him killed, but the Swan stage bore witness to another possibility. Amón's continued verbal erotic assault on Tamar picks up on the mood of the previous night, the desire for union, "puesto que la noche obscura / también voluntades casa, / hecho tálamo un jardín" (I.773–5) ("since the dark night weds wills too, turning a garden into a marriage bed"). The wedding with its own inevitable sexual consummation offers a backdrop of the imminent prize of the fruits of romantic engagement, to which Tamar has referred in the first speech of the scene (I.739–43). Tamar again does not recoil at the first hints of lovers' talk, although if she were committed to Joab, one might expect her to. She allows Amón to convert her literal words to the language of love (especially her use of "castigo" [I.799]), and, crucially in Usher's production, she allows her body, kneeling behind a kind of low altar (made of the same benches on which she will later be raped, and Amón be killed) to respond to Amón's insistent and intimate touch. The scene neatly encapsulates Usher's interpretation of Tamar as a sensuous woman, aroused by the ardour and lawlessness of a lover who shares her passionate yearning. The delayed violence of her response "dalde muerte, o dadme nombre / de desdichada" (I.838–9) ("put him to death, or call me cursed") reflects only her confusion at her lover's boldness and her own acquiescence.

When Tamar finally brings the wedding to a chaotic conclusion with this demand that the masked man be killed, he has already escaped to safety. In the Swan production he has exited before she reacts, as if a dream is over and she has returned to reason; in Tirso's play the stage direction reads "Bésala, y vase" ("He kisses her, and departs") before her first exclamation (I.833), at least hinting at the possibility that at some level Tamar wants to let Amón escape.

The young royals' next intimate scene is the play-within-the-play of Act II, a tour de force on stage. Here the textual evidence suggesting a *mutual* attrac-

---

[12] Tirso also engages here with the precedent set by Gil Vicente in his *Tragicomedia de Don Duardos*, just as he does in his comedy, *La huerta de Juan Fernández* (*The Garden of Juan Fernández*).

tion is much more obvious, and put together, creates a good case for Usher's reading of the scene and the relationship. Some time has passed since the wedding, and Tamar has no doubt dwelt upon the passionate masked guest. After David's welcome home and his discovery of Amón's life-threatening melancholy, Tamar is the last of the family to leave Amón's quarters. She responds to his call instantly with "Príncipe mío" (II.490), and goes on to assure her "gallardo hermano" (II.495) ("handsome brother") that she will climb mountains to return his health to him. The term *gallardo* is an interesting one. One would perhaps expect *querido* or an equivalent to stress her sisterly love for him. Instead she draws attention to his physical bearing.

Tamar proceeds to demand that Amón stop speaking in riddles and declare his illness, "Dime ya tu mal. ¡Acaba!" (II.525) ("Tell me what the trouble is. Stop this!"). Her subsequent speeches make perfect sense if one judges that she has already guessed that his passion is for her and that she is excited by it, even willing to reciprocate it. Tamar, like Casandra in Act II of Lope's *El castigo sin venganza* (*Punishment without Revenge*), is physically attracted by a man who would draw her into an incestuous relationship, but cannot be the one to break the taboo, to broach the subject.[13] She repeatedly encourages him to express his desires knowing that he is talking of love (with his hand-kissing at II.517, a vivid reminder of the garden scene and the wedding): "Si de una hermana no fías / tu secreto, ¿qué he de hacer?" (II.537–8) ("If you won't trust your secret to a sister, what can I do?"); "Si hablando no me lo enseñas, / mal tu enfermedad sabré" (II.545–6) ("If you won't tell me in words, I can hardly know what your affliction is"); "Si, como hay similitud / entre los nombres, le hubiera / en las personas, yo hiciera / milagros en tu salud" (II.565–8) ("If there were a likeness, as there is between our names, between our persons, I would perform miracles for your health"). These last words especially are difficult to interpret except as a thinly veiled invitation to Amón to declare himself openly and be reciprocated. The miracle that would ensue would be the breaking of the incest taboo. The frustration for the passionate Tamar is that Amón then launches into yet another deception – his invention of the Ammonite princess – and misses the chance for reciprocity, and the unmediated expression of a mutual passion.

Lyon's view that Tamar in this scene moves from "flippant amusement to perplexity, to suspicion and finally to horrified realization of the situation" (28), and other scholars' claims that Tamar is "unwitting" or "unwary" or "guileless" or "unsuspecting" simply do not correspond with the passionate princess to whom we have been so deftly introduced. When Amón asks her to be a surrogate lover, he repeats and mixes the images with which we the audience and Tamar herself are familiar, "serás fuente artificial, / que alivia al

---

13  See especially II.479–501.

enfermo el mal, / sin beber mientras que corre" (II.714–16) ("you will be an artificial spring, which soothes the patient's affliction, without his touching the water that flows"). Again (and throughout this speech [II.669–716]) the eroticism is just below the surface with the idea that Tamar can heal his sickness and partly satisfy him without his actually consuming her. Tamar's lines of acquiescence go beyond what would be expected, "tu gusto ejecuta luego, / que en mí tu dama hallarás, / quizá más correspondiente / que la que ansí te abrasó" (II.719–22) ("do what you wish now, for you will find in me your lady, and one perhaps more willing than she who scorched you thus"), and she will act his lady for the rest of the year (II.728). She invites him to become her lover in reality, a blatant hint that Amón misses in his utter failure to believe that the love is possible, or else his need for the love to be forbidden. For the lovers' tryst Amón predictably recreates the garden scene (II.758) at night, and with the passionate hand kisses (II.785), another reminder for Tamar that his love is real and for her.

As Amón's passion threatens to overcome him, Tamar resets the distance between them using the double identities that they both now have (II.793–800). If Tamar has fallen for her passionate half-brother, with a "persona" so similar to her own, she is certainly not interested in the immediate consummation that he is, which would deprive her of her virginity. When subsequently defending her actions to Joab she explains that, "Es mi hermano; sé el poder / del ciego amor que le quema" (II.904–5) ("He is my brother; I know the strength of the blind love that burns him"), and appears to be talking about her incestuous desire for him (his kind of love) rather than her unproven or safe love for Joab. The difference in Tamar's attitude to the staid Joab and the passionate Amón is brought out in Usher's production at II.873 when the princess prevents Joab from departing to warn the king of the siblings' apparent love. Having responded with enthusiasm and earnestness to her brother, shivering as she feels the blood/fire coursing through his veins (II.516) and encouraging him to declare himself, then kissing him passionately, she refuses to look at Joab as she defends herself in a matter-of-fact argument addressed to a spot somewhere beyond the auditorium. Her body language belittles him as she appears to scorn his intrusion into a scene he cannot understand.

Judging by text-based scholars' reactions to date to the figure of Tamar in Tirso's play, a reading of the princess's character that emphasizes her sensuality and suggests a passionate attraction to Amón is likely to be polemical. (Weimer's review suggests as much.) It does raise interesting problems and questions and not only about the breaking of the incest taboo. Is it really likely that Tamar would reciprocate her brother's passion for her? The answer perhaps lies in the royals' similarity – an argument used sophistically by Amón to justify his love in a sonnet (II.1009–22). Both young individuals are awoken from repression of sensual feelings to the world of passion and physical desire at the same time and in a moment of blindness. Even if their loves turn out to be expressed differently, the possibility of correspondence is certainly justifiable. How do we explain Tamar's urging of Joab to ask for her hand in marriage? Here David's general is Tamar's secure love, the one she knows her rational self should pursue. Joab is constantly associated with her father and the legitimate etiquette of the court. However, Joab can provide Tamar with the protection for her honour that she requires even if she admits to herself her attraction for Amón. And should Tamar not seek a marriage with Amón, a point played down by Tirso despite its presence in the Old Testament source and Calderón's version of the story? One can argue that Tamar does bring up this possible legitimate resolution of their relationship (III.42–5), but one does not need to in order to accept that she may be attracted to Amón's unceremonious and physical expression of passion for her. Their feelings may appear to be in harmony without any expectation that either character should seek a social legitimization of their love. The attraction, indeed, especially for Amón, has been in breaking rules.[14]

Above all, however, I would argue that Tirso does not provide his audience with an unproblematic drama. The result of the rape at the end of Act II does narrow the work's focus to the well-explored themes of the ability of David and Tamar and Absalón to show mercy or punish sin justly. We also see in action, and are forewarned of, the consequences of the corrupting influence of the thirst for power. However, the play's longest-running and most pervasive theme relates to the relationship between Amón and Tamar.[15] These two characters experience a first love that breaks a taboo and is therefore all the more concentrated and highly charged. As in many relationships between men and women, however, what seems like correspondence is based on mutual incomprehension and a romanticization or transformation of the notion of love in the lovers' minds. That Tirso should make a tragic story of this element reveals an extraordinary sensitivity to the subtleties of human love, a remarkable imaginative faculty in the elaboration of the source material, and above all a clear sense of the messy interrelatedness of existence on the human plane. That Tirso's dramatic vision should be interpreted so vividly through translation, within a different culture, raises important questions for future directors of Golden Age theatre in Spain.

14 The two references by Tamar to a love that is "sazonado" ("seasoned") (I.743 and II.1078) may also be a hint that she does see a future as Amón's wife. The first is used when she is blessing the married couple at the wedding, the second when trying to make Amón think before acting dishonourably towards her.

15 Scholars have tended to value Calderón's *Los cabellos de Absalón* more highly than *La venganza de Tamar* perhaps because the main themes are clearer and less ambiguous. See, for example, Metford (154), Sloman (100), and Ruiz Ramón (199).

# The Loss of Context and the Traps of Gender in Sor Juana's *Los empeños de una casa* / *House of Desires*

## CATHERINE BOYLE

### The Generation of Meaning in Performance

The question that preoccupies me here regarding the performance of *Los empeños de una casa* / *House of Desires* has its roots in a pervasive situating of Sor Juana within a specific field of meaning that has the potential to close off some of the most radically gendered resonances in her writing.[1] The attraction of Sor Juana for the Royal Shakespeare Company (RSC) for their Spanish Golden Age Season in 2004 was manifold: on one level, the play was a "find"; it had added value by virtue of its being written by a Mexican nun; and it was a bold, outspoken comedy that leaned in its playfulness more towards Molière than its immediate antecedents of Calderón de la Barca and Lope de Vega. It was apparent to the creative team from the first reading that the author was playing some interesting games with the codes of honour that were manifestly central to all the plays.

During the season, one well-respected broadsheet asked me to write an article that would tell the life of Sor Juana, and that would be accompanied by the translations of her love poems by Joan Larkin and Jaime Manrique. The interest in the poetry was not in presenting her work, nor was it in these particularly daring translations (which seek to bring out the sexual word play of the originals); it was, rather, in the perceived lewdness of the poems, rendered extra-titillating by the fact of their being written by a cloistered nun. It takes no leap of the imagination to see where that particular journalistic interest was coming from, and it is not surprising that this was not the only occasion on which this approach was adopted; the marketability of "obscene"

---

[1]  Throughout the essay I will make a distinction between *Los empeños de una casa*, Sor Juana's original text, and *House of Desires*, my translation, which will only be referred to with specific reference to the RSC production.

poems is, obviously, much greater than the reflections of an academic. In the context of the re-enactment, the revitalising, of Sor Juana's writing in a modern context, we come face to face with a core problematic of theatre translation, and one that cannot be answered purely through linguistic solutions: the question of how the source culture is situated in the target culture. What space can be found for it? How will the source culture be heard? How will it sell? In this respect, the request for the sexy nun poems plays an interesting – and coherent – role. Immediately, the text and the event are situated in a series of manoeuvres that are dictated by the types of appropriation at play. The question, then, is how the readings of meanings generated by the original are filtered through the readings of the director, the interpretations of the cast, and the reception by audiences.

The performance of *House of Desires* brought Sor Juana out of the cloisters, from obscurity in the UK into a public space open to a broad public. Her voice, which had been heard and studied exclusively in the academy, was put to the test in a commercial cultural context in which the broader implications of her writing – read within the academy in a series of considered and scholarly formulations – are tested. In this sense, the play is made to live in ways that it did not when it was written: performed for a general public and opened into unpredictable reception and open readings at all levels. That is to say, subject to myriad reactions; read against dominant narratives and engrained gender relations; spurious interest in sexuality and her ability to write in such erotic ways; wonder and suspicion around her intelligence and her acerbic insights into gender relations.

In the words of Patrice Pavis,

> [t]he theatre translation is a hermeneutic act: in order to find out what the source text means, I have to bombard it with questions from the target language's point of view: positioned here where I am, in the final situation of reception, and within the bounds of this other language, the target language, what do you mean to me or to us? (*Crossroads* 138)

It is from this "bombarding with questions" that the translator starts to arrive at multiple meanings embedded in the text, which are open to interpretation, and will be subjected to a series of hermeneutic acts from first reading through to reception. The process of translation – this hermeneutic act of interpreting the text – is inevitably and unsatisfactorily reduced to a series of decisions and words that cannot hold the whole spectrum of the results of the interpretative and analytical act. Pavis sees the work of the translator as being that of effecting, in the first instance, "a *macrotextual* translation" (*Crossroads* 139) – the analysis of the broader systems and structures of the work involving the translation of the linguistic microstructures: "theatre translation is not a simple linguistic question: it has too much to do with stylistics, culture, fiction, to avoid these macrostructures" (140). The source text is being pulled towards us, separated from its source and origin, and, in this move, it is "concretized," "made visible" (140), and even, and paradoxically, made more accessible and easier to understand than the original. (Certainly, linguistically, this was true for *House of Desires* and was an active part of what was sought by the director.)

One of the aspects of the hermeneutic act of translating Sor Juana is that, from the point of view of the academic and analyst, translation will inevitably throw up many more questions than it is possible to resolve in a performance text. Some of these may be resolved in the performance where, following Pavis, the "surrounding culture focuses attention and determines the way characters (as carriers of fiction) and actors (who belong to a theatrical tradition) express themselves" (142). Yet, these become forces that may work counter to each other. What happens, for example, when the actions of the characters collide with not only the theatre traditions but also the self-perception of the actors? More specifically, what happens when the male characters are forced into positions of idiocy (one of the tropes of the play) that male actors find difficult to contemplate, and attempt to resolve by a further level of parody that – perhaps not consciously – undermines the gender analysis at play?

In terms of *House of Desires*, I want to use these considerations to reflect upon the gender implications of the dramatic space in which Sor Juana sets the play. In the instance of this production, the director and the set designer shared my vision of a play into which Sor Juana writes herself – not in the easy autobiographical terms of Leonor's speeches, or of spurious conjecture about her life at court, but rather, seeing the play as an articulation of specific female spaces, and eliding an initial convent atmosphere of distant sounds (keys turning, doors opening and closing, silence interrupted by muffled sounds) with an image of the conceptualisation of the performance. The performance is framed by an image of Sor Juana writing at her desk, breathing life into the characters, moving them into place as pawns in her imagination, thus bringing immediately to the fore one of the key meanings of the word *empeños* (which include trials, pawns) in the title, and foregrounding the sense of the lack of real agency of the characters, who are puppets to abstracted codes that will guide them to an inevitable end: reconciliation with the codes that dictate their destiny. The play is constructed so that the space is gendered throughout. For a large part of the first act we hear only female voices. This is ruptured by the violent entry from the street of Leonor being forced into the house as part of Doña Ana's brother's plot to kidnap her, trap her in his house, where he will woo her and separate her from her lover, Don Carlos, with whom she is in the process of eloping. The sound of the male voice is startling and disruptive, and soon takes over the space, and this alternation of the male and female voices, one disrupting the

other, emerges at other points in the play. Yet, although the male actors have
to come to terms with portraying exaggerated representations of caricatured
base male instinct and stupidity, the space will return to their dominion.

One of the challenges of cultural transmission lies in many ways in what
Barthes calls the citations in any given text: "the citations which go to make
up a text are anonymous, untraceable, and yet already read: they are quotations without inverted commas" (160). The move away from the source text
disrupts the recognition of what is known within the source in untraceable
ways – cultural resonance, sayings, allusions to historical moments, jokes,
word plays, memory. The hermeneutic act of translation is the process by
which we retrieve as far as we can the citations, the untraceable, and make it
visible so that it can inform the transferral of meaning to the target culture.
The target text inevitably sets up a new set of affiliations through its language
and context, which will then be subject to "the hermeneutic competence" of
the audience (Pavis, *Crossroads* 142). What we receive through this series
of manoeuvres is the residue of meaning, from which we reconstruct a new
set of citations, affiliations, and meanings. In terms of *House of Desires*, the
residue I see is both the forceful gendering of space, and impotence in the
face of successive loss of context – particularly of the male enclosed in a
house where women seem to be in control – both of which are readable and
traceable, but only through the hermeneutic act, through the force of cultural
understanding.


## Wounded Speech

In *Los empeños de una casa* Sor Juana articulates and performs a complex
gendered space, what it is to be, in Judith Butler's formulation, "injured by
language" (1). That is, what it is to be created and determined by dominant
codes, and to have them enforced through myriad repressive impulses. If Sor
Juana, at the time of writing *Los empeños de una casa*, occupies a privileged
space for linguistic expression, she will also always insist that her speech has
brought her persecution. In the play she echoes this in numerous instances
of the wounding power of language: Leonor is brought into parlous "fame"
by speech; her father Don Rodrigo speaks at length of and is driven single-
mindedly by the dire consequences of not heeding the power of reputation
and gossip; social limits are created to contain licentious behaviour.

Reading *Los empeños de una casa* in the context of Sor Juana's other
writing, and in the specific context of performance, it is clear that there is an
averting of the gaze away from the potentially significant content to a more
ironic, comic quality that shields the force of her assertions. Only in her *Spiritual Self Defence* (1681), in which she dismisses her confessor for what we
can confidently call "injurious speech," in her metaphysical poem *Primero*

*sueño* (1685), and in the *Response* (1690), in which, veiled as a sister nun, Sor Filotea, she addresses to the Bishop of Puebla a virtuoso defence of women's right to life of the mind, did Sor Juana sustain a constant level of discourse that expressed fully her powerful intellectual self. In, for example, her response to a gentleman from Peru who sent her clay vessels and verses in which he exhorted her to mould herself into a man, Sor Juana responds with a mixture of rhetorical humility, real irony, and some truthful insights into her state. Resonant of the *Response*, she talks of her stammering and stuttering, of her lack of ability, and of the pretension of responding to so great a figure. She ironically challenges and praises him, but also explains her lack of corporeal state:

> I have no knowledge of these things,
> except that I came to this place
> so that, if true that I am a female,
> none substantiates that state.   (Peden 141)

In these lines she states what she will in the *Response* and in *Los empeños de una casa*: that her "depository," her sanctuary, takes the shape of a space where the defining utterance "woman" will not force her to live the state of wife or virgin, and therefore serve man as such. At the same time, the utterance "man" is linked subtly and inextricably to violence, for even if she were to follow his advice and to attend to his counsel, she fears that "no strength on earth can 'en-Tarquin'" ("entarquinar"). This verb, which she will use on a number of occasions in her work, including in *Los empeños de una casa*, means sexual violence against a woman's honesty, creating the affiliation in the poem with abuse, violence against women. In her hymn to Saint Catherine she writes of the violence enacted upon the saint, whose voice, nevertheless, endures:

> Illumination shed by truth
> will never by mere shouts be drowned;
> persistently, its echo rings,
> above all obstacles resounds.   (Peden 189)

A voice that will persist beyond the noise and prattle that surrounds it, as seen and testified through comparison and testing against the men of her time:

> No man, whatever his renown,
> accomplished such a victory,
> and we know that God, through her,
> honoured femininity.   (Peden 191)

This, of course, becomes an immodest reference to her own learning, another performance of self.

In *Excitable Speech,* Judith Butler explores the question of what it means to be "injured by language":

> The problem of injurious speech raises the question of which words wound, which representations offend, suggesting that we focus on those parts of language that are uttered and explicit. And yet, linguistic injury appears to be the effect not only of the words by which one is addressed, but the mode of address itself, a mode – a disposition or conventional bearing – that interpellates and constitutes a subject. (2)

This resonates profoundly with the ways in which Sor Juana situates her understanding of how the human subject is constituted socially, named, and interpellated. This naming is to be found in the force of the words in the circumstances in which they are uttered: the site and impact of their performance. The paradox is that this also creates

> [...] a certain possibility for social existence initiated into a temporal life of language that exceeds the prior purposes that animate that call. Thus the injurious address may appear to fix or paralyse the one it hails, but it may also produce an unexpected and enabling response. If to be addressed is to be interpellated, then the offensive call runs the risk of inaugurating a subject in speech who comes to use language to counter the offensive call. (Butler 2)

Sor Juana knew that language both wounded and gave the opportunity for being brought into social – in her case intellectual – existence. If we are reminded in her *Response* that she has suffered persecution, that she has been sorely wounded by the words of the Bishop of Puebla in the guise of Sor Filotea, then it is this wounding that will also compel her to write her virtuoso defence of women's right to a life of the mind – a space beyond their constitution by recognised norms. Yet, as we know, she also prefaces her future silence. If she is isolated in her convent cell, she will call herself into social existence through her words, and use them to claim a place in a natural history of learning and intellectual enterprise through her linguistic conjuring of a tradition to which she belongs – both male and female – "sin que a uno u otro se incline" ("not to either state inclined") (Peden 141).

What is important here is the insistent force of performance, and the projection of the injured voice. She forces the recognition that the space from which she writes is constructed for the injurious naming of women, contextualising woman within well-defined boundaries – the home, the convent, houses of correction for fallen women. Power will reside elsewhere, in the male, and be performed in utterances and linguistic injuring that barely veils the swift recourse to violence. If, in *Los empeños de una casa*, she provides us with a camped-up version of a cloak-and-dagger comedy, where "being-is-playing-a-role" (Sontag 109), she also embeds a tale of violence through utterance and action. While she uses the safe contexts of the comedy – the court, the inevitably reconciled lovers – she also allows us to glimpse the violent circumstances or actions that shadow them. These elements, of course, are constant in this genre, but the important point is that she writes from the site of injury by speech, and in that sense, the genre is feminised. In this process she tests the playing out of the concept of honour, questioning two key ideas: firstly, whether honour as an abstraction is fully mastered, and, secondly, how honour, as injurious speech, maintains its power; in Judith Butler's words: "For the threat to work, it requires certain kinds of circumstances, and it requires a venue of power by which its performative effect might be materialized" (12).

### An Instance of the Loss of Context of the "Venue of Power"

What we see in *Los empeños de una casa*, as Albert G. Salceda shows us, are the vestiges of the *galanteos de palacio* (palace gallantries) that set up the structures for the marriage market of the court, where the medieval chastity belt has been replaced by the ignominy suffered by those who infringe sexual codes, and the "indelible stain" (Salceda xxv) of allowing the "depository of man's honour and mother of their children" to be a maiden or widow with the hint of *liviandad* (loose behaviour). The quotation concludes:

> Claro es que la disciplina palaciana, como cuantas en el mundo han sido, se relajó y burló en ocasiones, cuyo número impide conocer su lograda clandestinidad; pero no debió de ser grande, cuando lo era tanto el de posibles denunciadores y, sobre todo, denunciadoras, y cuando la crueldad de las consecuencias del decir ajeno inspiraba tan general y saludable terror al qué dirán. La mayor parte de los escándalos de Corte llegados en rememoración histórica hasta nosotros se nos antojan hoy, cuando más, chismes de bar elegante, de tinelo o de portería; y el origen de casi todos no es haber sido entonces fácil el amor de las damas, sino difícil el amor propio de sus galanes. (Salceda xxvi)

> Palace discipline, like those all over the world, was relaxed and mocked on occasion, the number of which impedes our understanding of its well-managed clandestinity; but it could not have been so great, when it was the object of so many accusers – and above all of female accusers – and when the cruelty of the consequences of other people's words inspired such general and salutary terror of what other people might say. The greater number of court scandals that have come down to us in memory seem

today, at most, like the gossip of elegant bars, servants' quarters, or of porters' gates; and the origin of almost all of the scandals seems to have been not the easy morals of the women in love but the difficult self-love of their suitors. (My translation)

It is this "difficult self-love" that Sor Juana, in keeping with this understanding of the *galanteos de palacio*, displays in *Los empeños de una casa*, the residues of which cause problems in *House of Desires*. She suggests a moment of disintegration around notions of honour and courtly comportment, and seeks to interrogate key utterances, the constitution of which have femininity at its heart. These, then, become echoes in the rest of the noise, and the challenge is not to silence them, not to re-enact and masculinise her drama. The most powerful concept of honour, which she will reveal in glimpses as a violence-inducing game, is dislocated momentarily from its prime locus to a house dominated by women. It is this loss of context, the loss of the venue of power, which destabilises.

In the third act of *Los empeños de una casa* Don Juan, the smitten but abandoned lover of Doña Ana, considers his position. How can he balance the demands of honourable conduct and the need to avenge dishonour – even if only suspected – that decorum also demands? The dramatic challenge in translating and performing Don Juan's speech is that it edges very close to meaninglessness; it defies the impulse to clarify meaning. The challenge here is to resist meaning, and to allow the language to perform a "wounding" of the concept of honour, and of the inability of males to master intellectually a concept of their own creation.

The speech starts well enough:

| | |
|---|---|
| Con la llave del jardín, | With the key to the garden |
| que dejó en mi poder Celia | – which Celia left in my possession |
| para ir a lograr mis dichas, | as the means to pursue my happiness – |
| quiero averiguar mis penas. | I shall discover the source of my grief. |
| (Sor Juana Inés de la Cruz 130) | (Boyle 81) |

So, Don Juan starts out with a semblance of command, of action, decision, direction – into the garden of the house in which he and the other characters are trapped until all is revealed and reconciled, or lost. Yet, immediately he is thrown into doubt: the force of his decision is disrupted by his awareness of the need to discover/uncover the source of his woes. The evidence of his eyes is the proof that he has been dishonoured, but he is still ridden with doubt, which has impeded the journey towards a proper response. His honour has certainly been offended, and he has not assured revenge, thus making dishonour certain.

¡Qué mal dije averiguar,
pues a la que es evidencia
no se puede llamar duda!
Pluguiera a Dios estuvieran
Mis celos y mis agravios
En estado de sospechas.
(Sor Juana 130)

Yet, how wrong to say discover,
for how can clear evidence
now be called doubt?
I only wish to God
that my grievance and jealousy
were still mere suspicions.
(Boyle 81)

This is a line of thought that pushes him into (unaccustomed?) analysis, as he asks: "¿cómo piensa mi honor?" ("what is my honour to do?"). Honour is abstracted as a separate entity that must be heeded carefully as the sure guide of actions and decorum; his self is as nothing if the social demands of honour are not followed to what he imagines as its letter. The character is led relentlessly by Sor Juana into baroque games of wit and ingenuity, which he cannot master. The pace and tone of the speech becomes more agitated – how can he manage the difference between "certidumbre falsa" ("false certainty") and "duda verdadera" ("true doubt")? And, if the codes of honour are harmed by mere suspicion, then woe betide the man who does not judge suspicion to be a true measure of grievance, and thus of the need for revenge. And yet, man, lesser than but bound by the codes of honour, remains unconvinced, still besotted, and lost in the quagmire of the subtle managing of honour in terms of what other people see and will say; where the terror of other people's views will collide with the "difficult love" of the suitor:

Que como al honor le agravia
solamente la sospecha,
hará cierta su deshonra
quien la juzga incierta.
Pues si es así, ¿cómo yo
imagino que hay quien pueda
ofenderme, si aun en duda
no consiento que me ofendan?
(Sor Juana 131)

For, since honour is sullied
by mere suspicion,
he who doubts the evidence of the truth
faces dishonour for sure.
But, if that's the case, how can I
imagine that I can be offended,
when though my mind is full of doubt
it refuses to contemplate that offence?
(Boyle 82)

The constant slippage in terminology erases the possible subtleties of meaning in the understanding of the concept, and he is finally tempted into thinking that if he has not permitted the offence, then he will not be offended. Sor Juana places him in a context in which the impetus towards action is thwarted by the need to question the basic impulses on which he operates. His language is "wounded" and in that wounding his ability to act is diminished. What will he do? He will wait, and hope that his honour will "stoke the flames of my revenge" (Boyle 82). The dominant discourses demand that he should act against Doña Ana's new lover and should lead him inexorably to that end – but his agency in it is merely an illusion that Sor Juana turns into a parody of action and meaning. This is what becomes difficult to translate into performance, for the wounding turns into a wounding of masculinity itself, which is paraded as oafish, incapable of mastering clear thought, subject to the codes of appearance and decorum, with real agency only allowed within these confines. Performing this is the performance of a revelatory experience, and of an uncomfortable masculinity.

In *House of Desires* the male actors sought to command this uncomfortable masculinity by sending it up, at times diverting the audience's gaze from the serious underpinning of their actions. However, for the play to move back towards its source there must be a sense in which the wounding of self through careless actions and their translation into the gossip, words, and injurious speech of others is real. Yet, at the same time, it is the case that the male characters – as opposed to the male actors – cannot escape from Sor Juana's gender trap, for she performs a savage wounding of masculinity and of a moment in the disintegration of codes on which it performs its difficult self-love. And she writes it from a position in which, at least during that period, she has used her flight from injured speech to assert a commanding voice.

VIEWING AND REVIEWING THE *COMEDIA*

# Tirso's *Burlador de Sevilla* as Playtext in English

## JAMES A. PARR

I wish to express at the outset my admiration for those who have set their hand to rendering this problematical Spanish text into English.[1] The *Burlador* presents many problems, both in the original Spanish and, even more so, in any attempt to find equivalences for its linguistic registers and metrical schemes in a rather differently structured language. There is probably no need to elaborate on the differences in form and manner of expression that separate the two languages in question. Anyone who knows both will be aware of most of them.

In order to limit the scope of the undertaking, it has seemed prudent to refer to only two translations. The choice of these two had to be somewhat arbitrary, and it has come down to those to which I have been most recently exposed. It was my good fortune to have my own edition of the *Burlador* used as a playtext by an amateur (but otherwise highly professional) company in Oxnard, California, known as Teatro de las Américas. The performances took place at the Petit Playhouse on Heritage Square in Oxnard between 25 February and 26 March 2006. To make the play accessible to a monolingual English-speaking audience also, the company decided to project supertitles above the stage, and the version they chose for this purpose was Gwynne Edwards's *The Trickster of Seville and the Stone Guest*. This turned out to be a felicitous solution for all concerned, but, watching the performance, while also keeping track of the supertitles to the extent possible, it struck me that there were interesting discrepancies between what I was hearing from the actors and seeing projected in the space above them.

One reason that occurred to me immediately was that Edwards was obviously following an edition prepared by Américo Castro, having no other recourse, for all practical purposes, at the time he prepared his version, around 1986. (Indeed, he reproduces one of Castro's editions on facing pages of his

[1]   Karen Pérez was my dutiful research assistant for this project, and her work was ably directed in my absence over the summer by Dr Shannon Polchow. I am very grateful to both. Any errors are my own.

translation, and that is the Spanish text I quote here.) The text the actors were using, however, follows the *princeps*, eschewing contamination from *Tan largo me lo fiáis (What Long Credit You Give Me!)*, since my edition is based on Luis Vázquez's of 1989, and since Vázquez – responding to Alfredo Rodríguez López-Vázquez's synthetic anomaly of 1987 for Reichenberger – made certain that he toed the line with respect to fidelity to the *princeps*. I suspect that few if any others in the audience that night found anything awry in the otherwise seamless meshing of performance text and supertitles. To paraphrase Pope, a little learning can be a troubling and distracting thing.

Another reason is that Edwards simply goes astray on occasion. Yet another is that he does not offer a literal translation of Castro's somewhat synthetic text, but calls his version instead a "free adaptation" (xl). So in assessing his contribution, we shall have to be guided less by his faithfulness to the letter of a Spanish original than by his ability to capture the sense and sensibility of that original. Edwards further enlivens things by attempting to maintain not only the syntax of prose but also the rhythm of iambic pentameter – a self-imposed challenge and a fascinating one, certainly. I am especially interested to see in what ways his free adaptation exercises that self-assumed freedom in regard to characterization, tone, and urgency.

The other version to be examined is Dakin Matthews's privately printed *Don Juan, The Trickster of Seville*, which is primarily in rhyming verse. This is an authentic playtext, in the sense that it has been performed twice by the Andak Stage Company, first in North Hollywood and once again at the Chamizal festivities, both in early 2006. The need to maintain rhyme leads here to some clever solutions. An example from early in Act II reads as follows:

DON JUAN.    When I left Naples, on the order of
             the king – whose word, Octavio,
             is law – alas, I had to go
             away without showing my love
             to you with a proper good-bye.
OCTAVIO.     For that, my friend, I give you ab-
             solution. Since we're both in fab-
             ulous Seville now – you and I!    (1157–64)

Internal rhyme is transformed into end rhyme in "absolution" and "fabu-lous." The two words themselves do not rhyme, obviously, but there are segments of those words that do (ab- and fab-). In the flow of speech of a normal performance, it seems very doubtful that the audience would note anything out of the ordinary. In fact, this ingenious solution would probably be perceived as an integral part of the *abba* pattern of the *redondillas* in the original, which it attempts quite successfully to capture. It bears mention that this passage is also something of a "free adaptation" in the manner proposed by Gwynne Edwards. It is instructive to note what Edwards does with the passage:

DON JUAN.     Octavio, my apologies! I left
              Naples with what must seem unseemly haste.
              The King's orders, you understand, so blame
              Him for my not taking my leave of you.
              He sent for me quite unexpectedly.
              I couldn't disobey but neither could
              I say goodbye to you. You will forgive
              My disrespect now won't you?
OCTAVIO.                                    There's no need
              To forgive when now we renew our friendship
              In Seville.   (II.112–21)

Matthews is a bit more lyrical, I suppose, while Edwards's rendering might be thought prosaic in comparison. That difference should not surprise, given the media in which the two translators have chosen to work. Does one capture better than the other what is being said and the way it is being expressed in the original Spanish? Answers to that will doubtless vary according to one's taste in these matters. In my estimation, both capture sense and sentiment quite well. Where taste comes into play is in the preference for the consonantal end rhymes of the Spanish (captured by Matthews) versus the elaborations of Edwards and the metrical beat of his prose.

Let us look now at a few instances of their treatment of passages in Act I, with an eye toward ways in which the translation affects characterization, the urgency of the action, and whether it changes the tone of the passage. The very first words of the text are Isabela's comment to her male companion, with whom she has apparently just concluded an erotic encounter:

ISABELA.     Duque Octavio, por aquí
             podrás salir más seguro.   (I.1–2)

Edwards renders it thus:

ISABELA.     Quickly, Octavio, follow me through here
             And you'll escape unseen by anyone.   (I.1–2)

Matthews offers:

ISABELLA.    Here, duke Octavio, you
             Can slip out safely here, now!   (1–2)

Both versions introduce a sense of urgency not found in the Spanish, with their respective "quickly" / "you'll escape" and "here" / "now!" Both would seem to be attempts to improve upon the original by creating heightened dramatic tension, transforming a seemingly casual – perhaps even languid – remark (given the preceding activity), into an anticipation of the tension that will be introduced momentarily, when it becomes clear that the man in question is not Octavio. In Edwards's free adaptation, Isabela generously offers to serve as guide, another aspect not found in the original. By an exclamation mark at the end (which would find oral expression through intonation), Matthews achieves the desired effect more economically than Edwards. The point I would reiterate, however, is that there is, as yet, no perceptible sense of urgency in the original Spanish.

A moment later, Isabela expresses a wish to have more light. Her companion is not pleased. Following Edwards:

ISABELA.                          Then let me bring
                    A light.
D. JUAN.                    But why on earth do you need a light?
ISABELA.          So that my soul can in the sight of you
                    Find confirmation of my happiness.
D. JUAN.          You bring a light, I swear I'll put it out!
ISABELA.          Heaven help me! Tell me truthfully! Who are you?
D. JUAN.          I'll tell you who I am: a man who's nameless.   (I.9–15)

In the Spanish, Isabela says simply "Quiero sacar una luz" (I.9–10). Edwards introduces causation with his "then," making her wish derive from the previous statement by Don Juan. Then the straightforward response, "Pues, ¿para qué?" (I.10), is intensified by adding "why on earth …?" Juan's next response is embellished in like manner by adding "I swear" plus an exclamation mark at the end. The Spanish is again a simple direct statement: "Mataréte la luz yo" (I.13). Finally, the famous "¿Quién soy? Un hombre sin nombre" (I.15) is transformed into an arrogant display of perpendicular pronouns in his "I'll tell you who I am [...]." This strategy might be called "helping the playwright with his half-hearted attempts at characterization." All of the above instances, but particularly this last one, may be seen as attempts to improve upon the original. A corollary consideration is, of course, the fact that the translator has adopted a metrical scheme that calls for iambic pentameter lines of a certain length, therefore necessitating some "filler" words.

Matthews's version is somewhat more faithful, in my estimation:

ISABELLA.                          I want to light
                    a light.
DON JUAN.                    Whatever for, my sweet?
ISABELLA.          To make my heart's delight complete
                    by sharing these joys with my sight.

| DON JUAN. | I'll smother that light, if you do so! |
| ISABELLA. | Oh God! Who are you? |
| DON JUAN. | Who am I? |
| | A man without a name.  (9–15) |

Shortly, Don Juan will say "Detente: dame, duquesa, la mano" (I.17–18). Edwards proposes: "Oh, don't play hard to get! Give me your hand!" (I.18). Surely, the time for playing hard to get has long passed, but this could serve as an additional note of characterization, highlighting again his presumptuousness. Exclamation marks have been added in the English version. Matthews also adds emphasis: "Wait, Duchess – no! / Give me your hand, give it to me!" (17–18). The exclamation marks in both cases are tantamount to director's notes, indicating that the line(s) should be uttered with more than usual emphasis. Isabela's response, "No me detengas, villano […]" (I.19), which Edwards translates as "I order you to set me free at once!" (I.19), further enhances characterization in English, suggesting a more forceful Isabela, someone who is now asserting herself and taking control. Matthews's version suggests pique rather than power: "Don't touch me, you monster of villainy!" (19). It too makes rather a stronger statement than is found in the Spanish. Isabel's comment strikes me (in the Spanish original, that is) as a huffy and somewhat haughty name-calling that has more to do with class than with villainy. She is saying that he is beneath her, and, by implication, beneath contempt. He has behaved like a lower-class person, a *villano*, the sort of man she would not likely tolerate in her presence, and it goes without saying that she would never, ever allow such a person to touch her.

To the King of Naples' inquiry, Don Juan responds with another oft-quoted line: "¿Quién ha de ser? / Un hombre y una mujer" (I.22–3). Edwards offers: "Who do you think it is? / A man and a woman. Do you need more proof?" (I.22–3). Matthews proposes: "Who should we be? A man and a woman – obviously!" (22–23). There can be no doubt that Matthews comes closer to the original. Edwards adds to the sarcasm implicit in the Spanish ("¿Quién ha de ser?") a further note of impertinence, indeed defiance, with his gratuitous "Do you need more proof?" The predominantly flat characterization of Tirso's original has become already, less than twenty-five lines into the play, a fairly well-rounded portrayal. This might be seen as artful, even masterful, on Edwards's part, or it might be viewed as tampering with the text.

The king's next comment is an aside, "Esto en prudencia consiste," followed by his order to the guards: "Ah, de mi guarda! / Prendé a este hombre" (I.24–6). Edwards gives us: "[*Aside*] I think that prudence might be called for here. / Attend here quickly! Guards! Arrest this man / immediately" (I.24–6). As in previous passages, lexical items that serve to speed up the action loom large. Neither "quickly" nor "immediately" is in the Spanish version, and neither is really necessary, since one can safely assume that an order from the king will indeed be attended to quickly and immediately. Again, Matthews is closer to the mark: "(*Aside*) A little tact might be just the thing. / Where is my guard? Arrest that man, / and hold him there" (24–6). As is often the case with Edwards, Matthews adds four words not needed to convey meaning ("and hold him there") in order, in this instance, to fill the top portion of a run-on line.

The king's charge to the Spanish ambassador, Don Juan's uncle, is an interesting one – and one that can cause problems for the translator. It reads:

> REY.          Don Pedro Tenorio, a vos
>                    esta prisión os encargo.
>                    Siendo corto, andad vos largo;
>                    mirad quién son estos dos. (I.29–32)

Indeed, Edwards goes astray with the third of the four lines, which is obviously the most problematical, and, as usual, he adds a sense of urgency not apparent in the original:

> KING.         Don Pedro, I command you see to it
>                    That this arrest is made with utmost speed.
>                    Force might be needed; use it if you must.
>                    Attempt to identify the guilty pair. (I.29–32)

Compare this with Matthews:

> NAPLES.                                      To you
>                    Don Pedro Tenorio, I give the case
>                    of this prisoner. You have more space
>                    to maneuver in than I have. Do
>                    what you can. Find out who these two are.    (29–33)

There is nothing here about doing things "with utmost speed," and the rendering of "Siendo corto, andad vos largo" is an elegant approximation. The sense of that line would seem to be "I can only touch on this now, but you look into it more deeply." "You have more space / to maneuver in than I have" is a nice solution. As far as I can determine, however, Edwards's notion that the phrase has something to do with the possibility of using force has no merit.

In the off-stage action described in hyperbolic detail by Don Pedro, the Spanish ambassador and uncle of Don Juan, there is a description of the latter's leap into the garden, which, in Spanish takes place off a balcony: "viendo vecina la muerte / por el balcón de la huerta / se arroja desesperado" (I.133–5), but in Edwards's version, the hasty exit is by way of a window: "But conscious then, no doubt, that death was close / At hand, he made a dash for it, and threw / Himself into the garden from a window" (I.133–5). Matthews has him leap from the balcony, as in the Spanish. The change of balcony to window is fairly inconsequential, but it is part of an ongoing pattern of such changes by Edwards. The cumulative effect of these changes is to create a rather different story and also to change aspects of its tone and tenor.

Don Pedro's equally creative description continues:

> Siguióle con diligencia
> tu gente; cuando salieron
> por esa vecina puerta,
> le hallaron agonizando
> como enroscada culebra.   (I.136–40)

Matthews proposes:

> Your people followed immediately,
> but when they went out by this gate,
> they found him half-dead on the ground,
> coiled up like a snake and writhing.   (136–9)

This seems fine, except for the change of door to gate. Edwards offers:

> The guards went after him as best they could,
> Rushed quickly down the stairs, made their way out
> Into the garden by some other door,
> And found him lying there, rolling about
> And twisting like a serpent facing death.   (I.136–40)

Both capture the sense of the description, particularly the meaning of "agonizando" ("half-dead" and "facing death"). Despite the added urgency in both English versions ("rushed quickly" and "followed immediately"), it is noteworthy that Edwards here translates "puerta" as "door," while Matthews is the one who uncharacteristically takes a liberty.

The description continues:

> Levantóse, y al decir
> los soldados: "¡muera, muera!",
> bañado de sangre el rostro,
> con tan heroica presteza
> se fue, que quedé confuso.   (I.141–5)

Not unexpectedly, Edwards paints the scene in more vivid colors:

> Then suddenly, he's up and on his feet;
> Your men are closing in to make the kill;
> His face is just a mask of blood, occasioned
> By the fall, when, all at once, inspired by
> Some superhuman agency, he's gone.   (I.141–5)

Compare this with Matthews's version:

> But suddenly, the villain bound-
> ed up as the soldiers neared him shout-
> ing "Kill him, Kill him," and his face
> bathed in bloody gore, and with
> heroic speed, the man went rac-
> ing off, and left behind confusion.   (140–5)

Clearly, both translators accelerate the pace of things, each in his own way. Both English versions are more vivid and dramatic than the original. Edwards substitutes "superhuman agency" for "heroica presteza," thus reinforcing the link with diabolical forces already suggested in the ophidian imagery, studied in detail by Aurora Egido. Edwards ignores completely the note of confusion at the end of the passage in Spanish, while Matthews makes the personal impersonal ("quedé confuso" becomes "left behind confusion").

There are some problematical passages just ahead that merit our attention. One is Ripio's rather racy description of his favorite kind of woman, from which he draws a "pointed" conclusion that he applies to Octavio's situation with Isabella:

> RIPIO.                    Pues, ¿es quienquiera
> una lavandriz mujer,
> lavando y fregatrizando,
> defendiendo y ofendiendo,
> los paños suyos tendiendo,
> regalando y remendando?
> Dando dije, porque al dar
> no hay cosa que le iguale,
> y si no a Isabela dale,
> a ver si sabe tomar.   (I.233–42)

Edwards slips in a few end rhymes along the way in his own display of "energy and steam":

> RIPIO.                    It's plain audacity
> To call a washer-woman a nobody.
> I tell you, master, she's superbly clean;

> She's always full of energy and steam,
> Eager to put her linen on display,
> Anxious to give her all in every way.
> Her generosity's a precious gift,
> There's nothing else can ever equal it.
> The moral is give it to Isabel.
> If she rejects it she can go to Hell.   (I.233–42)

The sense is communicated, although the last line is dissonant by virtue of its overstatement. The idea is to see how well she responds to the "giving," not to suggest that she be totally set aside. "Eager to put her linen on display" is effective, but the conceit of deriving "dando" from the previous "remendando" is lost in translation, as we say. Matthews is somewhat more explicit, just in case anyone should be obtuse to erotic innuendo:

RIPIO.          I'll take a washerwoman any day –
                taunting and teasing when she talks,
                lathering up and scrubbing away,
                ready to give and quick to repay,
                as she spreads her linens on the rocks.
                I call it giving, and I tell you, sir,
                there's nothing quite like it – as I hope to live!
                And if Isabel's not willing to give,
                then maybe she'll take, if you give it to her.   (234–42)

"As she spreads her linens on the rocks" could be innocent – something a washerwoman of that day might have been expected to do – or it could be a highly suggestive double-entendre ("rocks" is slang for testicles). Matthews's obvious mastery of the idiom leads one to the latter conclusion. Whether the play on words would come across in the flow of speech and action on stage seems debatable, however. It may be something to be savored when reading his text silently, as closet drama. The last two lines of the passage capture perfectly the sense of the original, as well as the give and take of translation.

Then there is a complicated verse in which Don Juan plays with the difference between "mar" and "amar." His interlocutor is Tisbea, and he is referring to his recent brush with death by drowning in the sea:

D. JUAN.          Y en vuestro divino oriente
                renazco, y no hay que espantar,
                pues veis que hay de amar a mar
                una letra solamente. (I.593–6)

Edwards:         And so in the light of your lovely dawn
                 I swear I'm born again and fear nothing.
                 To tell the truth, from ocean to devotion
                 The distance must be reckoned very small.   (I.593–6)

Matthews:        [...] and now I rise in your eastern sky,
                 reborn. Don't be afraid, sweetheart;
                 from die to live was the hardest part,
                 from live to love's just an o for an i.   (593–6)

Both go slightly astray, I believe, in their rendering of "y no hay que espantar," the meaning of which is more on the order of "and that's not so surprising," but, be that as it may, the two equivalencies they find for Don Juan's play on words are quite ingenious and more than satisfactory.

A bit farther along in Act I, Catalinón offers one his several cautionary notes, which is met with his master's characteristic response:

CATALINON.   Los que fingís y engañáis
             las mujeres de esa suerte
             lo pagaréis con la muerte.
D. JUAN.     ¡Qué largo me lo fiáis!
             Catalinón con razón
             te llaman.
CATALINON.            Tus pareceres
             sigue, que en burlar mujeres
             quiero ser Catalinón.   (I.901–8)

There are obvious possibilities here for running aground. Edwards navigates these shoals as follows:

CATALINON.   What sort of man is it that takes advantage
             Of these poor women? But you'll pay the price
             For it one day. I hope you'll rot in Hell!
D. JUAN.     Plenty of time for me to pay that debt!
             Whoever gave you your name was right.
             Catalinón, he's always got the runs!
CATALINON.   You run your way. In matters of deceiving
             Honest women, I prefer to run away.   (I.901–8)

The wish that his master "rot in Hell" is decidedly out of character, unless it were to be expressed as an aside. Even then, it would ring false, it seems to me. The linking of *catalina* (whence, perhaps, Catalinón) with excrement derives from a note in Castro's edition, but the elaboration of the meaning to include diarrhea is Edwards's own. Of course, "runs" might also, by a stretch of the imagination, suggest cowardice, or running away, and it is in precisely that sense that the character himself will use it in the next exchange: "[...] que en burlar mujeres / quiero ser Catalinón." The name can suggest either possibility, and Edwards is quite aware of that fact.

Matthews's version is more succinct and less problematical but, at the same time, less satisfactory:

CATALINÓN.  People who cheat and lie like you
                     with women, and trick them all that way,
                     when death comes callin', they'll have to pay!
DON JUAN.   But there's so much time till the bills come due!
                     So scaredy-cat, I see, is the on-
                     ly name for you!
CATALINÓN.                              Do what you please,
                     when it comes to cheating women like these,
                     I'm happy being Catalinón.   (901–8)

Three details before concluding: (1) the stage directions to Act II include "don Diego Tenorio, de barba." Edwards has him merely "bearded." Matthews gets it right, "an old man," although it could well be a false beard designed to give the appearance of age; (2) farther along in Act II, Don Juan, addressing Mota, speaks of "cierto nido que dejé / en güevos para los dos" (II.212–13), which clearly suggests a joint venture, with further implications for homoerotic bonding. Edwards makes it all seem rather solitary by saying "There's a little love-nest I'd like to find. / A little plot I'd like to hatch" (II.211–12). Matthews is no better: "I've got a coup- / le of eggs myself, just about right / for hatching; I want to check the nest"; (1255–7) and (3) there is Catalinón's hyperbolic assertion that, to demonstrate his loyalty, he is now prepared to commit sexual violence on anything or anyone his master may designate:

CATALINON.  Digo que de aquí adelante
                     lo que me mandas haré,
                     y a tu lado forzaré
                     un tigre y un elefante.
                     Guárdese de mí un prior,
                     que si me mandas que calle
                     y le fuerce, he de forzalle
                     sin réplica, mi señor. (II.330–7)

Edwards tames this bestiality and irreverence beyond recognition:

CATALINON.  I promise, master. Seen and never heard
                     I'll be! Obedient to your every word,
                     That's me! At your side my loyalty
                     Will force an elephant or fierce tiger

> To its knees. And as for any blabbing preacher,
> He'd best look out! Give me the order, sir,
> To shut him up, I'll do it silently,
> To good effect, and not a word I'll speak.   (II.330–7)

Matthews is on target:

> CATALINÓN.  All right, from this time on I'll keep
> my trap shut, sir, and if you want
> to bugger a tiger or an elephant
> I'm at your side – without a peep.
> Or if some abbot fights to preserve
> his honor, and you tell me to shut
> my mouth and hold him down, I'll put
> him down – 'cause, master, I live to serve.   (1369–76)

This brief foray into two translations has not taken us very far into either text, but it may be sufficient to indicate how each can be expected to proceed with the remainder of the original. It further suggests that both have produced viable playtexts – their stated intentions – although both are rather different from Tirso's (and even Castro's) version. Matthews has worked valiantly and well to maintain something of the rhythm and rhyme, including the polymetry, that are so characteristic of Golden Age plays. He is especially good at capturing *redondillas*, even reproducing successfully their *abba* rhyme scheme, as we have seen in two or three examples. Some will have noticed that Roy Campbell's version has not been mentioned. I have ignored it – although I used it years ago, *faute de mieux*, as a classroom text for a course in literature in translation – for reasons stated succinctly but eloquently by Gwynne Edwards: "Campbell's translation is unreadable and unactable" (xxxviii).

What is much to be desired at this point in time is a translation based on the uncompromising critical edition of Luis Vázquez, which represents a considerable advance in critical rigor over the old standby of Américo Castro. As indicated earlier, my own editions (one in Spain, one in the US) are based on the text established by Luis Vázquez. If there is still interest in fidelity to the original, someone must take this necessary step. Other editions, including Castro's, borrow in greater or lesser degree from *Tan largo me lo fiáis*, which Vázquez has ably demonstrated to be an impoverished *refundición* of Tirso's masterpiece, clearly by another hand – but certainly not that of Calderón, to whom it is attributed on the cover page. Both Edwards and Matthews follow a version of Castro, Edwards because he had no viable option at that time, whereas Matthews was not acquainted with my edition, as he has indicated in a private e-mail.

Although my intention when I began this project was to determine which of the two offered a better playtext, I realize now that this is not possible.

It may well be that Edwards's is better for British actors – and he indicates that he has them very much in mind when preparing his version – while Matthews's is better overall. There are subtleties that the first is able to express in one passage, but the other may elucidate something elsewhere that the first has missed or ignored. On balance, Matthews aligns his version much more closely with the Spanish, in every way. Neither indicates the proper number of asides, however. I had also planned to use the Vázquez/Parr editions as my point of reference, but it soon became clear that this would not be fair to either translator, for both have followed some version by, or inspired by, Castro. All I can do in that regard is to urge that someone do a translation based on an edition that is as faithful as possible to the *princeps*. My remarks here might be taken as a modest addendum to Isaac Benabu's very fine essay on reading the opening of the *Burlador*, published in the *Bulletin of the Comediantes* near the end of my tenure as editor. Barbara Mujica's study in that same issue has also provided insight and motivation.

Finally, we have seen that changes made to accommodate the metrical pattern or rhyme scheme chosen by a given translator can affect such aspects as characterization, immediacy of the action, and tone. Some of these changes may make for a more stage-worthy product, particularly for today's audience, whose attention span seems to have diminished considerably; but one has to ask at times whether it is justified to take certain liberties with the Spanish text. This is especially so when we find ourselves with an out-of-character Catalinón who would damn his master to hell – to his face, no less; or a recurring and unjustified emphasis on urgency; or simply a failure to render what is in the Spanish text, as when Don Juan confides in Mota that he has reserved a little nest for the two of them, or when Catalinón's hyperbolic attempt to impress Don Juan with his new-found loyalty, replete with outrageous assertions, is diminished beyond recognition.

I trust that others may see merit in this sort of close reading and that they may be moved to take it to the next level. So I shall end, not with Cervantes's tapestry simile but with his own closing words from 1605, "translated" into proper Italian: *Forse altri canterà con miglior plettro.*

# Anne McNaughton's *Don Juan*:
# A Rogue for All Seasons

## A. ROBERT LAUER

Any translation suggests an act of violence, transfer, or change. Dictionary definitions of the term "translation," suggesting changes of form, medium, or use, do not aid in ascertaining with any degree of certainty whether a translation is either wrong or inaccurate. The problem is confounded when the object or text being translated is imperfect in its original form or, allegedly, simply a version – or at best some sort of hybrid – of a lost archetype whose paternity itself is merely putative. When the translated text is dramatic, there is an additional change or transfer from the playtext (the text that undergoes the act of translation from one language to another) to the performance text (the text that is subsequently decoded and interpreted by innumerable agents) (Rozik 13, 15). When the translated text is the progenitor of other texts (other Don Juan types in the case of *El burlador de Sevilla*), additional problems ensue. Should the Ur-Text[1] be altered to suit the tastes of a modern theatre audience? Or should the original form – poetry in this case – be retained precisely to try to preserve a whiff of the "unvisitable past […] where they do things differently," as Jonathan Miller would state? (*Afterlife* 44). If the first choice is made, the translated text would be further removed (i.e., transferred) not only from its original language or lexicon but also from its pristine form of expression; if the latter is chosen, the text's structure might be preserved but, inevitably, the original lexicon would be altered. Subsequently, regard-

---

[1]   I am using the term Ur-Text to refer to the original or pristine text upon which the initial act of violence of a translation is first inflicted. In the case of the Don Juan play, which exists in at least two different versions, *¿Tan largo me lo fiáis?* (*What Long Credit You Give Me*) and *El burlador de Sevilla*, the term Ur-Text refers to the lost archetype (as used in textual criticism) or to the "conflated" text that editors like Alfredo Rodríguez López-Vázquez and translators like Dakin Matthews have attempted to make apparent. Once this Ur-Text is defined or made manifest (as a working script or playtext), no further violence of the "shock and awe" variety should be visited upon it.

less of whatever choices are made, a translated text would always reflect a departure, a divergence, or a repositioning from an original order of stasis.

Having said this, one may judge that a dramatic text has been well translated, not only into another language but also into another medium, if the following four points are observed:

(1) The translation shows an apparent proximity to the form and content of the play.

(2) The translation remains true to the spirit of the work, even if inevitable changes are made.

(3) The Ur-Text is respected both in its script form (as playtext) and spectacular manifestations (the performance text/s).

(4) A vision of congruency and intelligibility is discerned, even if the work is the product of a director's creative interpretation.

With the above four points in mind, one would state that Dakin Matthews's *Don Juan, The Trickster of Seville* is an excellent translation in rhyming verse of *El burlador de Sevilla*, the play long attributed to the Mercedarian friar Gabriel Téllez, more commonly known as Tirso de Molina.[2] My reasons follow. Having consulted the two versions of the Don Juan myth, *¿Tan largo me lo fiáis?* and *El burlador de Sevilla*, Dakin Matthews chose to create "a kind of stage-oriented conflation," as he calls it in the introduction to his translation (3). If one considers that both works have their strong and weak points, this decision seems wise to me. The translator also chose to do a rhyming instead of a blank verse or prose translation, knowing full well that rhyming verse was essential to the drama of the Spanish Golden Age. On these two grounds alone Dakin Matthews's translation would have been a good and judicious rendition. What makes it particularly notable, however, is that he has framed the work using the original Spanish polymetric form. After all, a multi-stanzaic system of versification in Spanish classical drama is what makes this theatre unique among national theatres by its allowance for built-in changes in tone. A perfect example of an alternating tonal change occurs in Act II, lines 1485–1562, in the exchanges between Don Juan and the Marqués de la Mota (in *redondilla* form with an *abba* rhyme), thrice interrupted by a musical refrain in another rhyme (*cc*). Herein, the portentous lines "He who must wait for his lady fair / lives in hope and dies in despair" in effect become a leitmotif that culminates in the attempt on Doña Ana de Ulloa's honor, an act that would have brought Mota to despair and imminent

---

2    The attribution of this work to Andrés de Claramonte, as well as the debate with respect to the alleged priority of either *¿Tan largo me lo fiáis?* or *El burlador de Sevilla* are critical issues beyond the scope of this essay. Albert E. Sloman makes, in my estimation, a reasonable exposition and, perhaps, a resolution of these two hotly debated issues.

death. Moreover, an unrhymed translation of this particular play would not have been as effective, for much of its vigor depends not only on cognitive but also on aural seduction. In effect, Dakin Matthews's work is not merely an English translation of a hybrid Spanish work. It is also an adaptation of the original Spanish form to a newly translated English content. Hence, this rendition gives both readers and spectators a formally and tonally proximate work in English of a classical Spanish text that, being a "stage-oriented conflation," might actually be closer to the elusive Ur-Text than either *¿Tan largo me lo fiáis?* or *El burlador de Sevilla*.

This remarkable sense of structural proximity also finds its equivalent with respect to content, or what I would call being true to the spirit of the work. I shall point out only two examples. In the description of sundry prostitutes in Act II, Don Juan inquires about one of them, Constanza, while the Marqués de la Mota makes certain linguistic observations in his reply:

[DON JUAN.] ¿Constanza?
MOTA.                              Es lástima vella
                              lampiña de frente y ceja.
                              Llámale el portugués vieja,
                              y ella imagina que bella.
DON JUAN.    Sí, que velha en portugués
                              suena vieja en castellano.   (II.1219–24)

Dakin Matthews's rendition of these hilariously somber lines is as follows:

DON JUAN.    How's Constance?
MOTA.                              Pathetic. First went
                              the hair, the eyebrows. Some Portagee
                              called her a real classic, and she
                              took what he said as a compliment.
DON JUAN.    It must have been his accent; she
                              thought he called her classy ...   (II.1216–20)

The purist might object to some aspects of this translation. To some extent, however, the English rendition surpasses the Spanish original. The pun on vieja/velha/bella (classic/classy) is remarkably close in both languages and refreshingly ingenious in English (as the pun in Spanish and Portuguese would be). To that extent this would be an excellent translation. To actually explain why Constance might have heard something different ("It must have been his accent") is pedagogically brilliant and perhaps necessary for an English audience. But to refer to the Portuguese as a Portagee, even without textual backing, is in this case an example of the English surpassing the original in spirit, for Don Juan will indeed disdain what will be associated with Portugal and the Portuguese, including, of course, the Spanish ambassador to the Dual

Kingdom, Don Gonzalo de Ulloa, whom he kills, and Ulloa's daughter, Doña Ana, whom he attempts to rape.

Another example of sheer translation genius occurs when a lady drops a note from a window, which Don Juan receives: "A mí el papel ha llegado / por la estafeta del viento" (II.1309–10). This is rendered as "And this note has been sent me – how? – / by air mail, special delivery?" (II.1302–3). As in the previous example, the translation is proximate (accurate) in lexicon. Moreover, the English rendition is actually superior to the Spanish original – and funnier. In both cases one senses that Don Juan is being ironic and laughing at his good fortune. But "estafeta del viento" ("wind mail" [my translation]), while purportedly funny on account of the ingenious and figurative wording used by Don Juan in Spanish, is outstandingly witty in English precisely for its literalness, for one does have air mail nowadays. The surplus phrase, "special delivery?", while unnecessary, reiterates and clinches the meaning of the first referent, in case a reader or spectator might be too shy to accept the actual – and hilarious – literalness of the first concept. By not changing the lexicon (that is, by not making an abrupt change or alteration in the translation from one language to another), the English adds a sense of awe and surprise, perhaps no different from what a Baroque subject might have experienced in an age that so highly valued *admiratio*. In these two cases we have both a sense of remarkable proximity to an original text as well as a feeling of remaining true to the spirit of the text, whether by a change of tone ("Portagee") or by a surplus referent ("special delivery?").

In addition to showing an apparent proximity to the form and content of the playtext and remaining true to the spirit of the work, even if inevitable cosmetic or structural changes are made, a performance text should respect its progenitor and offer a congruent and intelligible vision of it, even if this vision is ingenious and highly creative. To do this, of course, a director must understand the play she chooses to stage. Updating an early work radically by changing its context and appearance is not only confusing but also a cop-out. One goes to the theatre (as one goes to church) not to see what is already visible before one in the everyday world, but to experience the Holy, or what Peter Brook calls "the Invisible-Made-Visible" (*The Empty Space* 47). For me personally, a modernization or adaptation of any dramatic text is, in addition, an insult to any audience and a condescending display of arrogance, *superbia*, the ultimate sin. It is an overvaluing of the *hic et nunc*, a childish pre-Oedipal display of "anxiety of influence." One would do well to remember, with T. S. Eliot, via Peter Brook, that "We don't inhabit the metropolis of history. We're in the suburbs" (*The Empty Space* 44).

When translating a classic work like *El burlador de Sevilla* from playtext to performance text, as Anne McNaughton did when she staged Dakin Matthews's *Don Juan, The Trickster of Seville* at the NewPlace Studio Theatre in North Hollywood on 4 February 2006, there should have been only two ideological challenges: (1) Did the director understand the play; and if so, did she respect it in its transition from script to show, even if changes might have occurred in the process? and (2) Was her presentation cogent and intelligible? Needless to say, a presentation is cogent and intelligible only if the director comprehends the play.

In the case of Don Juan, of course, a universal myth has been created around this figure, and it is apparent that critics, readers, and spectators disagree about its essence or meaning. Ann Davis lists between six hundred and two thousand versions of the Don Juan story (160). In addition, there are several canonical versions of the myth that influence the way Tirso de Molina's drama is staged. Moreover, although there are multiple Don Juan figures (whether named Don Juan Tenorio, Dom Juan, Don Giovanni, Don John, John Tanner, John Tucker, or even Jeanne), in effect there are only two universal Don Juan types: the one that chooses Thanatos and is damned, and the one that chooses Eros and is saved. Tirso's Don Juan belongs to the first type.[3]

The biggest challenge for any director doing *El burlador de Sevilla* is to avoid being led astray by other Don Juan types (especially by the braggart and popular Don Giovanni) or falling into the trap of an authorial intentional fallacy. Tirso de Molina's Don Juan is a fluid and slippery "vaginal" character in the service of the Semiotic Other. As such, he must be shown as eternally young and perhaps slightly effeminate. He is evil incarnate; still, he must retain a human form and be shown as vulnerable on occasion. If he is shown as older or overly virile, as in the 1987 Gustavo Pérez Puig Radio Televisión Española (RTE) version, in which Javier Escrivá, the late actor playing Don Juan, was fifty-seven years old, the character will be unable to arouse pity or sympathy. But if he is shown as too young and vulnerable, as in the case of Johnny Depp in *Don Juan DeMarco*, he will overwhelm one with schmaltz. Mark Doerr, the actor who played the role of Don Juan in Anne McNaughton's

---

[3]    Additional contemporary (i.e., Golden Age) Spanish versions of this type would be *¿Tan largo me lo fiáis?* and Alonso de Córdoba's *La venganza en el sepulcro* (*Vengeance in the Sepulchre*). Some well-known European versions that follow this first mode are Molière's *Dom Juan*, Shadwell's *The Libertine*, DaPonte/Mozart's *Don Giovanni* and, in the US, the Early American *Don Juan: or, The Libertine Destroyed*, a work wherein Don Juan is merely an outlaw brought to justice by Don Antonio, the late Governor of Seville.

Other Baroque versions, starting with Antonio de Zamora's *No hay plazo que no se cumpla, ni deuda que no se pague, y convidado de piedra* (*All Accounts Must be Settled, All Debts Paid, and The Stone Guest*), paved the way to the second modality of the Don Juan figure that culminated in Spain with José Zorrilla's *Don Juan Tenorio* and in the UK with Lord Byron's *Don Juan*, and Shaw's *Man and Superman*.

It makes no difference if in sundry renditions Don Juan becomes a woman, as in Roger Vadim's *Don Juan ou Si Don Juan était une femme ...* (*Don Juan or If Don Juan Were a Woman*), or a mental patient, as in Jeremy Leven's *Don Juan DeMarco*. Jeanne belongs to the first modality; Don Juan DeMarco to the second.

production, was simply sterling. Although the trickster of Seville's deceitful nature and violent personality were apparent from the beginning of the work, he never lost his youthful charm and mellifluous voice, qualities that would help him seduce Tisbea and Aminta successfully.

The second problem that can confuse any director is to try to surmise what the authorial intention was, especially when *El burlador de Sevilla* has been classified as a tragedy, a comedy, a religious play, and an eschatological drama. It is also an error to imagine that this work must be theologically sound because it was allegedly written by a priest. It would be better to forget who wrote the play and remain faithful to the playtext, using, perhaps, a functional model like the one suggested by Étienne Souriau to determine what is the gist of the drama in purely actantial terms.

A dramatic functional model in the style of Étienne Souriau (83–112) would give one the following. The protagonist or Thematic Force of *Don Juan, The Trickster of Seville* is Don Juan Tenorio. He is a slippery dramatic actant, a protean figure, a trickster, whose Object of Desire is to dishonor people – both men and women – so as to make them damaged goods as far as marriage is concerned. In a figurative sense, their dishonor would be tantamount to a kind of civil death in a patriarchal society that values purity and legitimacy. Hence, he tricks four women into giving away their honor to him; in so doing, the women's protectors are either killed (Don Gonzalo), put in jeopardy (Don Octavio and the Marqués de la Mota), or aggrieved (Batricio, Gaseno). Since the dishonored women are merely mediatory signifiers in a more comprehensive and systematic attempt to offend other significant patriarchal actants (noblemen, Old Christians, kinsmen, kings, and, ultimately, God as transcendental signifier – the true Opponent of this work), it stands to reason that some critics have detected in Don Juan a homosexual element (Marañón 640). Don Juan is not a productive entity; he bears no children. He is an enemy of the patriarchy and all that it entails: essentially, marriage and heterosexual continuity. He is not in the service of Eros, a productive activity, but Thanatos, a black hole, a dead end. He does not make love. He is merely simulation, porn, "more real than the real" (Baudrillard 154), a simulacrum, a *trompe l'oeil* in the service of death. It is not accidental that he deceives by giving something other than the expected "perros muertos" or "scams" (II.1251). He likes to "bugger" people (men, especially, at least symbolically). In effect, his ultimate wish is to "bugger" the dead, and God.[4]

Catalinón, of course, is a deceptive Helper, for he appears to be in the service of Don Juan – the iconic representative of the Semiotic Other – while in effect he is in the service of the Symbolic One, as his numerous moral

---

[4] It is not accidental that the term "bugger," although connoting anal intercourse (used here in a figurative sense), is also related to heterodoxy, especially the Albigensian heresy, a remnant of Manichaeism (*Compact Edition OED*).

warnings demonstrate. In the Manichean struggle between the Semiotic and the Symbolic realms, the second sphere of cognition uses the statue of Don Gonzalo as its own Helper, who in effect admonishes Don Juan to accept life (marriage to Duchess Isabella) and the trappings of the patriarchy (becoming Count of Lebrija) or death (an act that would force Don Juan to accept the statue's invitation to dinner, which in effect is a choice for the chthonic forces). Needless to say, in the poetic versions that inform the Don Juan myth, the *galán* who accepts the skull or dead man's invitation to dinner ends up dead ("Camiñaba Don Galán," quoted in Baquero 1: 5–6). Mythically, to eat with the dead is a desire for death, as the Persephone myth demonstrates. Anthropologist Arnold van Gennep reminds us of one of the taboos regarding journeys to the land of the dead in legend: "one must not eat with the dead, drink or eat anything produced in their country, allow oneself to be touched or embraced by them, accept gifts from them" (165). Don Juan, of course, does all of the above, including the perfectly logical gesture (for him, lover of death that he is) of extending his hand to the dead, instead of to the living (Duchess Isabella, whom he was to marry that Tuesday).

Once the protagonist chooses his fate, the monarch Alfonso XI, as maximum mortal representative of the Symbolic Order, determines the outcome of the Object(s) of Desire. If Don Juan wished to take honor away from the men and women with whom he came into contact earlier, the King, as Judge, upon the former's demise, would be able subsequently to restore dignity to them. Don Juan deceitfully married three of the four women he visited (surprisingly, Don Juan's polygamy has gone practically unnoticed by the critics). His necessary death enables his widows to marry their originally intended husbands. Hence, none of them is dishonored in the end. One could argue that secret marriages were frowned upon after the Council of Trent, but historian Renato Barahona demonstrates that the practice continued long after its apparent prohibition. Bruce W. Wardropper claims that in Scottish law, the practice lasted until 1935 ("*Burlador*" 63). Thus, marrying the male and female victims of Don Juan, making possible, therefore, the heterosexual continuity of the Symbolic Order, is in effect the King's most noble and necessary (sacramental) function in this play. Marc Vitse's reference to King Alfonso XI in this play as a "rey casamentero" ("a matchmaking king"), could not have been more appropriate (27).

The above constitutes an actantial reading of what happens dramatically in the first modality of the Don Juan myth, more specifically in Tirso's play.[5] When staging *El burlador de Sevilla*, one might depart slightly from the

---

[5]   In the second modality of the Don Juan myth, of which Zorrilla's *Don Juan Tenorio* would be iconic, Don Juan's Object of Desire is Doña Inés. Through her, Don Juan has the potential of being assimilated into the Symbolic Order by the expected promise of heterosexual continuity. The unforgiving statue of Don Gonzalo becomes the Opponent who blocks Don

text for reasons of exigency – as the Escuela de Arte Teatral of the Instituto Nacional de Bellas Artes (INBA) did in 1990 at the Chamizal Auditorium in El Paso, Texas – by using a woman as a monarch instead of a male;[6] but to reduce the monarchy purposely to an empty institution, or to show everybody in the play as corrupt, from the Castilian king down, as the Source Theater Company did in Washington, D. C., according to Mujica ("The End" 217), would in my opinion constitute a grave error in translating this playtext adequately into a performance text. It would also show a profound lack of understanding of the work in question and a remarkable disdain or disrespect for the text.

Nevertheless, a director has the right and obligation to interpret the text and make structural changes if necessary in the performance text in order to show a congruent and intelligible creative vision. This vision, of course, must respect the playtext and remain true in spirit and in close proximity to its original form and appropriately translated lexicon. Anne McNaughton's production of *Don Juan, The Trickster of Seville*, as performed by the Andak Stage Company on Saturday, 4 March 2006, at the Chamizal Auditorium, was not only an excellent production but the best rendition I have seen of Tirso de Molina's *El burlador de Sevilla* in any language. The production took some structural liberties and chose to start the play seemingly *in extremas res*, with actors dressed in black, singing the *Dies irae* in front of what appeared to be a statue of Don Juan (the actant Don Juan occupied the same pedestal to be used later by the dead Commander of Calatrava). Golden Age Spanish plays usually start *in medias res* to grab the public's attention immediately. But since everybody knows the story of Don Juan, it would certainly seem appropriate to start the plot *in extremas res*, precisely to catch the public's attention from the beginning. (In effect, something similar was done in the 1987 Radio Televisión Española [RTE] rendition of this play. Things must change to remain the same.) In the antepenultimate scene, three veiled women, dressed also in black, appeared and sang the moral of the play before the imminently damned Don Juan:

> Beware all you who think that God
> is slow to judge and punish you,
> for there's no bill that won't be paid,
> and there's no bill that won't come due.   (III.2771–4)

This song in effect put closure to the introduction to the play, the chorally

Juan. The final Judge or Arbiter is God, an actant who makes the figure of the king unnecessary.

6   To view the theatrical presentations listed in this essay, consult the web page for the Association for Hispanic Classical Theater, Inc. <http://www.comedias.org/>.

sung *Dies irae*, and served to reiterate the clear and unambiguous message of the work. The work was "framed" between these two musical interludes, as if in a baroque mirror. In this respect, the performance text was most effective.

Needless to say, in any staging of *El burlador de Sevilla*, four moments are paramount for congruency and intelligibility and cannot be excised or changed: (1) the Lisbon speech, (2) Tisbea's monologue, (3) the encounter of Don Juan with the Statue, and (4) the king's closure of the play. The omission or alteration of any of these elements would signal success or failure for any performance of this piece.

Of the four, the Lisbon speech is usually the least understood element of the work and the one scene that tends to disappear from performance texts. It consists of 137 lines (I.721–857) in *romance* meter delivered by the Spanish ambassador to Portugal, Don Gonzalo de Ulloa, to the Castilian King Alfonso XI. It is no doubt an encomium that reflects favorably on Lusitanian affairs during the time of the Dual Monarchy (1580–1640), an *ekphrasis*, and a speech that should make any eloquent actor stand out for a brief moment of glory. McNaughton, much to her credit, retained the speech in full. She positioned the king on the right center side of the stage, placing the Commander in the center. Brian George, as Don Gonzalo de Ulloa, recited his lines slowly and with conviction to Steve Peterson, the actor who played a pleasant and almost child-like and amused monarch. The illocution was as vivid as the one done in 1988 by René Buch of the Teatro Repertorio Español (TRE) of New York City, at the Chamizal Auditorium. Ironically, the same speech in abbreviated form was tedious, deadly, and static when it was done in 1990 by the Escuela de Arte Teatral, INBA, in the Chamizal Auditorium.

Apart from its rhetorical vividness, this speech is dramatically important for many reasons. First of all, it establishes a moral center (the Lisbon convents are stressed) by which to judge the subsequent description of the Seville brothels, inhabited, ironically, by Portuguese whores. Secondly, it gives depth, dignity, and dramatic time to Don Gonzalo, whose only other action (as a mortal) in the play is to die suddenly in his duel with Don Juan. The RTE 1987 presentation eliminated the Lisbon speech to the detriment of the character, whose hasty death simply lacked interest and intensity. The Lisbon speech also affects how one perceives the statue of the Commander. If the spectator has not had time to internalize or associate Don Gonzalo with the realm of the Elysian Fields (Ulisibona), she would be unable to care much for the statue when it appears on stage. In the 1990 INBA production, the abbreviated speech resulted in a statue not much different from Don Juan (the representative of the Seville brothels). In other words, the statue was not seen as having much moral weight. The 1986 Chamizal production of the Escuela de Bellas Artes, Universidad Autónoma de Chihuahua, Mexico (UAC), retained the full speech and presented an impressive and terrifying Commander. The 2000 Chamizal performance by AIET (Associació d'Investigació i Experimentació Teatral) of the Universidad de Barcelona under the direction of Isaac Benabu, a most experienced director, eliminated the speech; however, the statue was shown as a non-human entity that did not require the Commander to reappear as a corpse. The Lisbon speech, therefore, if reduced or cut, will have disastrous effects on other aspects of the performance text. It is by no means a filler.

If the Calatrava Commander associated with Portugal represents the visible moral element of the work, Tisbea represents Don Juan's only conquest. In almost all the productions I have seen of this play, Tisbea has been portrayed as a spectacularly beautiful, strong, and sensuous woman. She must also be shown as proud and arrogant, a *mujer esquiva* (*disdainful woman*) to offer Don Juan a meaningful challenge. To this day, the Tisbea of René Buch's production is still remembered fondly as the "perfect" Tisbea. Her feminine charm, sensuality, and passion were a good match for Don Juan's tricks. INBA's Tisbea was somewhat whorish, but she was able to match an older and vulgar Don Juan. The UAC production offered an attractive and proud Tisbea to match a cocksure trickster. Only in the AIET production was there a danger that the superbly sensuous Tisbea might overwhelm the beardless and puerile actor who played the rogue of Seville. In McNaughton's production, actress Maegan McConnell was exquisitely beautiful and sensuous. However, her apparent display of innocence or naïveté, as well as her small stature, produced a hapless victim instead of a challenge to the experienced lady killer. This was a serious mistake, although not as lethal as the RTE portrayal of Tisbea as an older and insecure woman. A strong, youthful, and passionate Tisbea must match an initially vulnerable professional scoundrel who has just been rescued from the sea. A mismatch of forces would produce pathos and make the protagonist of the work infinitely more detestable than he is already.

If Don Juan is to be punished for his sins, he needs to find not his match or an inferior but a superior force to destroy him. To show the avenging statue as a weak ghost is simply an error at the level of the performance text. This was the grave mistake of the RTE production, wherein the ghost is hardly able to move on its own. Don Juan's invitation to light his way home ("Aguarda, iréte alumbrando" [III.2459]; "My servant will light you back to your place" [III.2506]) becomes almost risible in this rendition. This was also the error of the 1977 Glyndebourne Festival Opera production of Mozart's *Don Giovanni*, wherein the ambulatory Commander (played by Pierre Thau) was no match for the intrepid and arrogant Don Giovanni (performed by Benjamin Luxon). The INBA production made the Commander into an equivalent of Don Juan, making the play into some sort of duel between equals, which it is not. That too was an error in judgment and a failure of understanding of the text. The UAC and TRE productions, both of which retained the Lisbon speech, presented hefty, dominant, ominous Commanders with deep and frightening voices. That was much to their credit. The McNaughton production presented an adequately somber Commander with an electronically altered voice, which gave an otherworldly quality to the statue. The use of a yellowish color, however, was by no means frightening and, at least for U.S. culture, it constituted an inadvertently equivocal sign (cowardice). The reddish design that simulated the flames of hell, however, compensated in part for the Commander's attire. In my estimation, the most effective representations of the statue have been done by Jan Blazek in Milos Forman's *Amadeus* (1984), wherein the Commendatore is shown in red as a malevolent and gigantic Darth Vader-like figure; and by the non-mimetic grotesque shape in white (whose appearance was accompanied by atonal music) used in Isaac Benabu's AIET production.

Finally, the kings, but especially the Castilian king, must be shown as effective in their only function, the administration of justice. In *El burlador de Sevilla*, as in many Spanish baroque works, the King acts as a *deus ex machina* figure. He is there to resolve problems. He can be played by a woman, as in the INBA production, or represented as a CEO, as in the TRE staging. He can even be mildly amusing, as in the McNaughton production, but he cannot be corrupt, ineffective, or superfluous. The king is present to bring closure to the work. Both monarchs in the RTE production were shown as older, dignified, and effective actants. That was much to the credit of this rendition, so weak in so many other respects. The kings of the UAC and TRE presentations had a remarkable sense of presence and serenity and were able to impose order and peace with a minimum of gestures and words, despite their appearance. The UAC king was beardless, but his charisma and crown gave him the dignity he needed. The TRE king was slender and mustached and did not look remarkably different from the other characters in this contemporarily attired production. But he had composure and was impeccably dressed in a dark business suit. There was no doubt he was in charge and could impose order. The McNaugton monarchs were shown as benevolent but bumbling heads of state for much of the performance, much like Emperor Joseph II in Forman's *Amadeus*. But in the end they were able to impose themselves as statesmen and function regally. This was much to the credit of the very tall and effective actor who played both roles, Steve Peterson. The INBA production used a woman who functioned royally and effectively throughout the performance. The crown she wore throughout the show also helped her to impose much-needed authority. However, in the end, Batricio occupied a down center position, in effect blocking the queen. He also uttered the last lines of the play, thus literally usurping not only the queen's place but her final words. The worst royal representation of this work was done by AIET, whose king was shown without dignity. The monarch looked absurdly like Cyrano de Bergerac with heavily greased hair. The king's final words, spoken either in exasperation or indifference, accompanied to boot with a gesture of disdain, were: "que se casen / todos" (III. 2856–7; "Now on with the weddings" [III.2907]). Batricio, likewise, as in the INBA production, uttered the final words of the play, thus supplanting the king. It was telling that these last two productions excised not only the play's epilogue, uttered by the monarch, but also the Lisbon speech. The consequences, of course, were dismal. The *deus ex machina* figure was unable to exercise adequately its only function in the play in the final two renditions. In the AIET case, in addition, the play became farcical, altering irremediably the performance and playtexts.

In sum, to be successful, a translation from one language or medium to another must approximate the form and lexicon of the original, be true to the spirit of the work, respect the original text, and offer a logical vision of it. In the case of the Spanish *Comedia*, the first two recommendations would apply more accurately to the playtext; the last two to the performance text. Anne McNaughton's staging of *Don Juan, The Trickster of Seville* was a successful accomplishment because she followed Dakin Matthews's superb translation. Her respect and understanding of the text, as well as its logical and persuasive presentation, made it clear that Tirso de Molina's original Don Juan, as evinced in *El burlador de Sevilla*, would become in her hands not only the famous trickster of Seville, but a rogue for all seasons.

# Aspectual, Performative, and "Foreign" Lope / Shakespeare: Staging *Capulets & Montagues* and *Peribáñez* in English and *Romeo and Juliet* in "Sicilian"

## SUSAN L. FISCHER

### Aspectual and Performative Lope

Jonathan Bate, in the final chapter of *The Genius of Shakespeare*, discerns two laws he believes all of Shakespeare's plays obey. The first concerns "the aspectuality of truth," the idea that "truth is not singular" (327); and the second has to do with "the performative truth of human 'being,'" radically the notion that "being and acting are indivisible." "All the world's a stage / And all the men and women 'wholly players'" is his reading of the topos (332).

Aspectuality is a key concept of diverse twentieth-century cultural fields. Albert Einstein recognized it in atomic physics; William Empson in literary criticism with his revolutionary *Seven Types of Ambiguity*; and Ludwig Wittgenstein in his later philosophy, when he adopted a "language game" method of arguing to attend to the particular function of words and, more to the point, when he reasoned, utilizing the familiar "duck/rabbit" drawing of Gestalt psychology, that both aspects are truths but cannot be seen both at one and the same time.[1] Shakespeare's "ambidextrous" (328) afterlife, the so-called "Shakespeare Effect" (321), Bate argues, can best be apprehended through a

---

[1]   Jonathan Miller's use of the perceptual drawing to describe Laurence Olivier's interpretation of Hamlet in relation to subsequent performances by other actors is revealing: "His brooding Dane monopolized the imagination of the mid-twentieth-century audiences and made it difficult to see any alternative figures in the part. The performance was so insistent and so charismatic that, like the inscription on the duck/rabbit figure which says 'see a duck', it may become impossible to see the equal and opposite claims for it to be a rabbit. When I cast Peter Eyre as Hamlet, however, an alternative figure did emerge. His 'duck' Hamlet supplanted the perception of Olivier's 'rabbit'. When Anton Lesser then played the part, in another subsequent performance, a third figure emerged from the author's composition" (*Subsequent* 112).

leap into a quantum world, where light has both wave and particle aspects, although each equation is incompatible with the other and cannot be specified at the same time. By extension, a text may have two or more contradictory meanings at once, but only one can be sensed in a given moment:

> Empson is Modernism's Einstein among literary critics. His 'both / and' is the twentieth century's most powerful understanding of Shakespeare because it is both a microscopic and a macroscopic way of seeing. It begins with ambiguous words and syntaxes – think of them as wavicles which are the literary work's smallest unit of energy – but it can be extended to the work as a whole. It enabled Empson to apply an 'uncertainty' principle to every aspect of Shakespeare. To a word as small as *not*: 'Shakespeare's use of the negative is nearly always slight and casual; he is much too interested in a word to persuade himself that it is "not" there, and that one must think of the opposite main meaning'. (316)

The law of aspectuality, as Bate notes, is the prerequisite of all good literary works but in and of itself does not make Shakespeare unique. What sets Shakespeare apart even from his most capable contemporaries, and makes him able to be reenacted again and again in different historical moments, is his so-called performativity.[2] The power of Shakespeare's characterization, Bate argues, comes from the *process* whereby he adapted his source narratives:

> Instead of being predetermined, identity is performed through action. At the same time, a vacuum is created in the space which belongs to motive; spectators and readers rush in to fill that vacuum, thus performing their own versions of the play. A greater variety of greatly different performances is thus possible than is the case with, say, the plays of Ben Jonson, which tend to be pre-scripted by character 'type'. Volpone is by nature

---

[2]    Bate's point of departure is J. L. Austin's approach to speech acts in *How to Do Things with Words*, despite Austin's (in)famous assertion that theatrical discourse is peculiarly hollow ("performative utterance will, for example, be *in a peculiar way* hollow or void if said by an actor on the stage") and uses language in ways that are "parasitic upon [language's] normal use – ways which fall under the doctrine of the *etiolations* of language" (22). Implicit in Bate's discussion, however, is an affirmation of W. B. Worthen's critique of Austin, drawing on Andrew Parker's and Eve Kosofsky Sedgwick's deconstruction of the opposition between "normal" and "etiolated" performance, the felicitously performative and the theatrical: "as Parker and Sedgwick imply, one of the problems of modeling theatrical performance on Austinian performativity is that it reduces performance to the performance of language, words, as though theatrical performance were merely, or most essentially, a mode of utterance, the (in-/felicitous) production of speech acts" (*Force* 8). The key point for Worthen is that "dramatic performance is not determined by the text of the play: it strikes a much more interactive, *performative* relation between writing and the spaces, places, and behaviors that give it meaning, *force*, as theatrical action" (*Force* 12).

cunning whereas Falstaff is no single thing by nature but potentially everything by performance. (332)

If drama is the most fully aspectual form of literature since it "disperses
the authorial voice," allowing each character to embody a different "aspect"
of the whole but only one character to speak at once, and no individual
character/aspect to be singled out as "the embodiment of 'the truth,'" it is
also the most fully performative because it "is premised on the act of imper-
sonation" (336). Bate, however, imposes a *caveat* on the perceptual game of
*both* "duck" *and* "rabbit" – the recognition of the different faces of the same
thing – insofar as inherent ambiguity does not mean "radical indeterminacy":
"Words have semantic range, but they also have semantic limits" (335).

   "Could any writer except Shakespeare have become the world-genius of
literature?" asks Bate (336), referring to the primary meaning of "genius" in
Shakespeare's own time, that is, "character disposition, bent, or inclination;
natural character or constitution" (5). His answer is embedded in what Keats
called *"negative capability"* – a willingness to accept "half knowledge," to
remain in uncertainty and doubt "without any irritable reaching after fact and
reason" (330–1). This "aspectual, negatively capable" dramatist will be

> equally at home in many different kinds: tragedy of honour, comedy of
> love-intrigue, historical play. The favoured form will be one which recog-
> nizes, on the duck-rabbit principle, the different faces of the same thing
> – it will therefore be a mingling of tragedy and comedy. This will allow
> for a mingling of high and low: the dramatist will be equally able in the
> representation of all ranks of men and women; the plays will appeal equally
> to all ranks. The dramatist's knowledge of the performativeness of things
> will require some kind of Fool-figure who is simultaneously inside and
> outside the action, who will frequently parody the language and habits of
> the serious characters. Devices such as disguises and plays-within-plays
> will also perform performativeness. (336–7)

   The only aspectual, negatively capable dramatist imbued with "a Shakespearean myriad-mindedness" (338), according to Bate, is that Spanish
monster of nature, Lope de Vega. The vast array of characters embraced
by his dramatic output is, according to Bate, testimony to his own Lopean
myriad-mindedness: "convicts, pimps, whores, parasites, conmen, vagrants,
astrologers, gangsters, friars, hired assassins, farmers, merchants, cooks,
travelers, wet-nurses, counts, dukes, princes, queens, kings, God, and the
devil. Moreover, his women are frequently rebellious, energetic and coura-
geous, whilst his men are more often on the make both sexually and socially"
(338). If, in his at once revolutionary and monarchy-conscious *Fuenteovejuna*, Lope was "wily in his aspectuality," in his comedies of intrigue (e.g., *El
perro del hortelano* [*The Dog in the Manger*]) he was "equally two-handed"

(339). With regard to the "aspectual vision" that characterizes Lope's tragedy, Bate fingers *El castigo sin venganza*, remarking that, as the title indicates, "this is punishment without revenge: Federico is put to death by due process of law, not by a carnal bloody act of private vengeance. But it is also revenge without punishment: Federico is punished for a crime which he did not intend to commit, in revenge for a crime which he did" (339). Unlike Shakespeare, Bate reminds us, Lope self-consciously and self-referringly encoded the notions of aspectuality and performativity in a formal manifesto.

In the same way that Lope's wily aspectuality on the page is being increasingly recognized by Shakespeareans engaged in the bardology industry, so his latent performativity, too long neglected by professional directors of the classics in England, is beginning to achieve its proper standing within the repertoire of canonical and non-canonical works mounted on the boards. *Castelvines y Monteses* (1606–12), a tragicomic *Romeo and Juliet* that in a minor key illustrates many of the aspectual engagements with romantic love, honor, and revenge found in Lope's more serious plays, had its UK première in a production directed by Heather Davies, 13–16 August 2006, in the Royal Shakespeare Company's open-air Dell Theatre (Stratford-upon-Avon) as part of a joint project between the Complete Works Festival Fringe and the CAPITAL Centre (Creativity and Performance in Teaching and Learning) at the University of Warwick, before transferring to the George Bernard Shaw Theatre in London. More by chance than by design, Nancy Meckler's star-crossed staging of *Romeo and Juliet* was playing concurrently in repertory in the Royal Shakespeare Theatre; it had been the kick-off production of the RSC's 2006–7 Complete Works Festival. For the first time in history, then, one could compare the two performance texts of those two dramatic works, whose respective plots turn, to greater or lesser degree, on the same Italian *novelle* if not also on their French translations. Lope's *Castelvines y Monteses*, staged from a faithful, if flowing and rather natural, English translation by Gwynne Edwards was, by comparison, a smashing success on the boards of the Festival Fringe. From a different, yet parallel, performance standpoint certain choices made in Tanya Ronder's English translation of *Peribáñez y el Comendador de Ocaña* (1608), which Rufus Norris directed at the Young Vic Theatre in London in 2003, will prove equally revealing, not so much because of faithfulness to the "original" but because of some explicit "textual tampering" that occurred with respect to the English translation.

## "Foreign" (Performance) Texts

Few productions of a Shakespeare play (or of a Spanish *comedia* by extension), as W. B. Worthen reminds us, "follow *any* single text of the play without emendation, adaptation, elimination, substitution, or addition of text" (*Authority* 62). This is the case, as well, with early modern drama that traverses national borders and becomes accessible to "foreign" audiences through (post)modern productions based on translations and/or new versions that interrogate the original textual authority. The very act of translation, of denying a classical author his or her language, presents a challenge to the universalizing tendency of traditional stage history with its essentialist assumptions that classical texts "are stable and authoritative, that meaning is immanent in them, and that actors and directors are therefore *interpreters* rather than *makers* of meaning" (Bulman 1). Yet post-structuralist forms of thinking about plays – whether based on issues relating to gender, to perform-ance, or to materialist interpretations of history – persist in initiating their inquiry with a central tenet of the old approaches: they start with the written text. Traditional stage history has long underscored the primacy of the text, as director John Barton reminds us with regard to Shakespeare:

> If the textual points are ignored, then it's pretty certain that Shakespeare's intentions will be ignored or at least twisted. [...] Shakespeare *is* his text. So if you want to do him justice, you have to look for and follow the clues he offers. If an actor does that then he'll find that Shakespeare himself starts to direct him. (167–8)

The universalizing belief in a stable and authoritative text is turned on its ear, however, by the mere fact of contemporary performance which, as John Russell Brown points out, always already involves some form of "adapta-tion, transposition, misrepresentation, spectacular simplification, or novel accretion" (22). With respect to foreign-language productions, then, the moti-vating question is perforce more extreme: What happens when Shakespeare (or Lope) is manifestly *not* his text? Whatever the linguistic equivalent of a particular passage, translation studies theorist Susan Bassnett (McGuire) reminds us that "a theatre text exists in a dialectical relationship with the performance of that text" (87). With this *caveat*, she is underscoring a central paradox in the overall process of translating theatre texts: first that "the two texts – written and performed – are coexistent and inseparable"; and second, that the translator is being asked to "treat a written text that is part of a larger complex of sign systems, involving paralinguistic and kinetic features, as if it were a literary text, created solely for the page, to be read off that page" (87). A linguistic rendering is but one element in the overall act of dramaturgical analysis, which, as Patrice Pavis theorizes, "consists of concretizing the text in order to make it readable for a reader/spectator. Making the text readable involves making it visible – in other words, available for concretization on stage and by the audience" ("Problems" 28). The passage from the source dramatic text to the target dramatic text is a series of concretizations estab-lished in terms not only of an exchange between "spoken *text* and speaking *body*" but also of "the interaction of cultures juxtaposed in the hermeneutic act of intercultural exchange" (33). If, from the perspective of the theatre semiotician, the text is merely one of the elements of performance, in the process of translation ideological and cultural dimensions are grafted onto it as well (41). Or, in Gideon Toury's formulation, translation is a "teleological activity" conditioned by the goals set by the prospective receptor system(s): "Translators operate first and foremost in the interest of the culture *into* which they are translating, and not in the interest of the source text, let alone the source culture" (19).

Dennis Kennedy makes it clear in *Foreign Shakespeare* that performances in a target tongue, by foregrounding non-verbal elements of production, can explore "scenographic and physical modes more openly than their Anglophone [or Hispanic] counterparts and often redefine the meaning of plays in the process" (6). Since, in the course of linguistic and cultural translation, an essential element of the original is made redundant, some foreign performances may even have a more immediate access to the power of early (modern) plays; paradoxically, Shakespeare may be easier to understand in French and German translation than in the original (Pavis, "Problems" 28). In alleviating the archaism and remoteness of language that can create difficulties for twenty-first-century audiences, the contemporaneity of the target idiom frequently works to bridge the gap between past text and (post)modern context. The dialectic between a work's origins in the past and its effects in the present, between "history" and "interpretation," is key for an understanding of the ways that foreign renderings of a play through translation can reassess the possibilities of the original.

### Treble Playbill: Sicilian Shakespeare and English Lopes

"Some imp inside me, half way through *Romeo and Juliet*, always wants to shout, 'Oh do get on and swig that poison!'" (Letts). This spectator shared that reviewer's feeling, insofar as she had also to endure Meckler's physical-and-other-than-verbal rendition of a play most renowned for "the incandescent brilliance of its language," where linguistic power actually figures thematically (Greenblatt, Commentary 866). Unfortunately, this essential aspect of the playtext was glossed over in performance. If *Romeo and Juliet* is not a piece that radically cries out for stage rediscovery or reinvestigation, Meckler's attempt to spare it from "gory cliché" produced precisely that effect (Billington). Framed as a play-within-a-play, it was as though two modern Mafiosi-like families were performing Shakespeare's tragedy in a Sicilian village square, for they all lay down their weapons in a public amnesty in the first moments of the production. A chorus of women clad in black chanted intermittently in a Sicilian dialect and so added authenticity to the Italianate

setting. The action unfolded on a rectangular wooden platform to which
things were added as needed; actors who sat on chairs on the side of the inner
stage observed until it was their turn to step into the center and perform. The
village square was dominated by a huge movie screen and arc lights from a
film set, no doubt meant to reinscribe Baz Luhrmann's unconventional adaptation of *Romeo + Juliet*. A bare, dead tree, which (arche)typically derives
from productions of *Waiting for Godot*, formed part of the backdrop. When
Capulets fought Montagues, there were no swords but stylized tap/clog and
quasi-flamenco footwork to the tune of wooden poles banging rhythmically
on the floorboards; the jackets of the dead were then dangled from a wire
that resembled a catwalk. The refashioning of the balcony scene was perhaps
the most disconcerting element of the set design for seasoned spectators of
Shakespeare: Juliet greeted her Romeo from a subterranean bedroom whence
she emerged to climb atop "a wobbly rectangle of a scaffolding that look[ed]
like a practice turret for firemen" (Letts). If the hero dangled above and
peered down upon the heroine, the scuttlebutt had it that the play was actually taking place in an underground bomb shelter. Be that as it may, the
"perpendicular cage" that was Juliet's balcony gave the impression that she
was "less a domestic prisoner than a precocious gymnast" (Billington), and it
was "touch and go" as to whether Juliet would fall off the thing (Letts).

What is at stake here can perhaps best be captured if we invoke Peter
Hall's distinction between "*theatre*, which is pure – although it occurs rarely
– and *theatricality*, which is technique, trick, custom, that which is easily
accepted" (204). This is not to say that technique does not have its place,
but technique alone is not enough. Jean Vilar also goes to the heart of the
matter in a chapter of *The Making of Theatre* entitled, "The Murder of the
Director":

> In blocking the point is to simplify and pare down. Contrary to the usual
> practice, the idea is not to exploit space, but to forget it or ignore it.
>     For a production to have its full power of suggestion, it is not necessary
> that a so-called scene of action should be "busy" (with acrobatics, fisti-
> cuffs, brawling and other "realistic" or "symbolic" activity). One or two
> gestures, and the text, suffice; provided that both are "right." (209)

If Meckler's RSC production of *Romeo and Juliet* overemphasized the
"theatrical," Davies's Fringe enactment of *Capulets & Montagues* took us
back to the beginnings of "theatre," recapturing the "lightness of foot" of an
ensemble traveling company as it mounted a platform stage in order to share
a story. The director put her intentions this way:

> I wanted the audience to experience the verve, the passion, the zest of the
> characters of that "Monster of nature" Lope de Vega, the instinctive way

that they could grab life. These were people acting from the heart and desirous of free will; women could take risks, survive, and flourish despite a serious brush with that matter of Spanish honor. The point was to get past the shadow of the tragic in order to capture the dynamism and passion of the characters; the feud was only there to complicate the plot. Tragedy and comedy were butted against each other, yet the danger was funny because we knew it was not real; it was a matter of those people trying to get on with their lives. We had to remove the labels and play the changes, the flip side of tragic and comic, in order to create different dynamics and be alive to the surprises of the story. One had to consider the roving attention of the audience and balance abstraction against action. (Davies)

Davies's production, which lasted roughly one hour and forty-five minutes without an interval, was fluid and continuous; in that sense, it emulated what was customarily done in the sixteenth-century *corral de comedias*. The fast – Lopean – pace was due in some measure to the octosyllabic line that prevailed in the translation, which, "in the interests of flow and relative naturalness in the language, [. . .] rejected stanza forms and rhyme schemes" (Edwards xlv). Both in style and in décor the production hearkened back, not so much to Lope de Rueda's more elaborate mountings of Italianate romantic drama at court, but to his earlier repertoire, which had been performed on a low, improvised stage of planks the itinerant company carried with them into courtyards hired for the occasion. Cervantes's commentary in the Prologue to his *Entremeses* (Interludes), which bears witness to the scarcity of costumes and props in the theatre he had witnessed as a youth, is a useful yardstick against which to measure Davies's Fringe production (although the latter had access to period costumes resurrected from RSC stock).

The set of *Capulets & Montagues* was indeed a low platform stage sheltered by a huge weeping willow and decorated with purple flowers. The two hours' traffic of houseboats and rowboats on the river Avon a few yards behind contributed to the natural backdrop. An irregularly shaped golden floorcloth demarcated the central playing area. Two vertical poles stood on the set: one functioned as a signpost to designate scenes taking place alternately in Verona, Ferrara, and the countryside; the second, with its moon and star on one side, and its sun image on the other, indicated night and day, respectively. Once the audience had settled in on blankets spread out on the grass in the walled-in garden space near Holy Trinity Church where Shakespeare is buried, the traveling troupe of actors entered from all directions, chanting the refrain "Montagues, Capulets, Hey" and bringing in moveable props for the set: a dozen or so wooden boxes decorated in orange and yellow and weighted with gold bars; velvet-cushioned drawing room chairs for the Capulet household; a wheelbarrow containing paper lanterns and small box trees of lemons and oranges to be hung on poles to signify metonymically the stifling interior space for the Capulet party in the first scene, or the secret garden space for the lovers' trysts. After setting up the acting area, the troupe ended their "pre-show" with rhythmic stomping and clapping (simulated vestiges of *flamenco* seem always to work themselves into English productions of *comedias*). Shakespeare's Romeo/Lope's Roselo (Vaughan Jacob) and his *gracioso*-servant Marín (Karl Niklas) moved offstage for their opening entrance, and the Capulets dispersed to their party space, enclosed by the hanging lanterns. The audience was continually aware of the ensemble element, for the actors executed the scene changes themselves, often to the musical accompaniment of violin, flute, and guitar.

Certain staging choices, however "theatrical," deserve mention here, because they remind us that this play, even if lacking in the success or popularity of many of his other works, clearly "Es de Lope." The production succeeded in underscoring the ways that, for example, the Spanish bard's plots tend to be complicated and action-packed; events are compressed and accelerated, emotions are intense if not exaggerated; and the tone is varied with comedy and danger "promiscuously rubbing shoulders" (McKendrick, *Theatre* 74). The audience was pulled into the fast-paced, double-entendre action from the start as they became onlookers, along with Roselo and Marín, at the masked ball thrown at the Capulet house. Julia (Lizzie Phillips) was clever and spirited in addressing her declarations of love to her cousin Ottavio (Oliver Turner). She was of course intending them for Roselo, who was standing behind and holding on to her extended hand as he echoed the scorned Capulet's words in a stichomythia rejoinder, which allowed them all to fix a nocturnal garden tryst (*BAE* 3c; GE 127–33).[3] There was some clever staging, too, in having Roselo's father Arnaldo (Sam Smallman) peddle in on small-sized bicycle (on whose handle bars sat a stuffed horse's head so as to suggest his arrival in Verona), wearing traveling clothes, and bearing spurs and an arquebus. The reference to the exterior view of a church in Verona at the beginning of Act II – the setting for a dispute in church between the warring families over a private family chair that the Capulets accuse the Montagues of abusing (the overriding point of honor that catalyzes the action of the play) – was minimalistically staged by having the actors pile boxes one above the other so as to represent a house of worship with a steeple atop in the shape of a cross. The churchgoers lined up on the ground to the left of the platform stage; they stood beneath the weeping willow with their backs toward us. The set design smartly made use of the ground space surrounding the raised acting space, thereby producing a sense of "total theatre" in the grassy round. When Roselo took refuge in a tower after having killed Ottavio (counterpart here to Tybalt) in a sword-fight, he stood inside the multi-purpose

---

[3]   References to the play are to the translation by Gwynne Edwards (cited as GE), except when they are to Lope's *Castelvines y Monteses* (cited as *BAE* and indicated by page and column).

wheelbarrow, positioned on the grass to one side of the platform. Act II came to a close as Roselo rode to Ferrara into exile with Marín along with the Count Paris (Ryan Shorthouse – in Lope's play, protector of Roselo turned rival for Julia's hand) astride steeds created by having the actors sit atop stacked boxes and sway rhythmically, while gripping onto poles with horses' heads mounted on them.

In Act III, the choice of having the same actor double as Ottavio and his alter ego peasant Fernando was apt; it was as though Ottavio had returned to avenge his death when Fernando declared ironically, "Then if / I were a Capulet, I'd seize / This opportunity to take / Revenge" (GE 199). The production negotiated well the ambiguous moment in Lope's text (*BAE* 16a), where a series of ellipses indicating missing lines problematizes Julia's motive in soliciting a potion from the apothecary Aurelio; she expresses not only a wish to die – "My death shall end this pain. / Give me the potion" (GE 196) – but also consternation when, upon downing the drink, it seems to have the effect of poison: "He must have been confused. This is poison" (GE 196). If Bate's summary in the Program Notes indicated with some certainty that Julia "attempts suicide by drinking a potion," both the written and performance texts revealed some ambiguity with regard to that issue. The heroine's subsequent resurrection was well wrought: emerging, to the audience's utter surprise, from inside one of those wooden boxes sitting on the set that served then as her sepulcher inside the family tomb, Julia fumbled about in feigned darkness. The hilarity of the scene escalated when she thought she heard the voice of Ottavio whom she presumed had also risen from the dead, although it was really that of Roselo, who had coincidentally arrived with Marín in order to rescue her. The Montague and his servant also contributed to the comedic confusion as they bumped into "corpses" of actors strategically positioned in stage darkness, so as to make the following verses of Marín ring more absurdly true: "No, just the neck / Of a stinking corpse!" (GE 214); "His great / Fat belly and his skull" (GE 215). Phillips's Julia showed the ingenuity due her character when, in pretending to be a spirit from the other world, she stood behind a willow tree and spoke to her father (Jeff Leach) from "off" in order to oblige him to accept Roselo as her husband. The production tied up loose ends hastily in typical Lopean fashion. In a simple finale, the cast engaged in a musical and dance sequence, tossed rose petals, and finished as they had begun, with a "Hey."

Noteworthy about this shoe-string production was its performative fidelity to Lope's text despite the classically absurd "caso de honor" on which the plot turns, which would not necessarily make sense in the cultural context of the twenty-first century. This degree of faithfulness, not simply to the letter but also to the spirit of the "original," stands in sharp contrast, for example, to Tanya Ronder's prose translation and adaptation of *Peribáñez* (styled *Peribanez* in her version), which was directed by Rufus Norris with London's

Young Vic Company in 2002 and studied in detail elsewhere (Fischer, "Staging"). Suffice it to say here that Ronder's translation did not merely adapt Lope's work in order to make it "playable"; rather the English version seemed to tamper with the text so as to render it "acceptable." One troubled reviewer said the following of the "moral manipulation" he thought had taken place: "I felt on reflection that director and translator had been over-afraid of contemporary moral squeamishness," that "a certain amount of moral clean-up had taken place. Making the text playable is one thing. Making it entirely acceptable is another" (Fenton). Ronder, for her part, makes some revealing comments about the perceived "challenges" of adapting a play such as *Peribáñez* for audiences of today:

> It's the concepts such as 'honour', 'peasant', 'God', 'Commander', 'King', that mean such different things to us now. It's finding a way to translate those ideas into a meaningful context for us today. Also finding a way to absorb the structure of their theatre, with their asides to audience, their stock comic characters etc., without trying to do those same things. We don't have the same relationship with an audience as they had in Spain at that time, or the same expectations from our audience. Also trying to keep it the acceptable side of melodrama, which we don't get along with at all these days. How to make three bloody murders on stage believable. How to get across the idea of power and the importance of 'the Commander', when we don't have such overlords any more. How to make 'peasant' life believable to us city-dwellers with disposable incomes. How to keep the directness and simplicity of the story without underselling it in our world full of subtleties and complexities. How to make it genuinely funny rather than funny because of its quaint archaic-ness. (Wild 39)

One of the ways Ronder handled these matters was to excise Casilda's callous justification of her husband's jealous, if excessive and brutal, mode of revenge expressed in these verses: "No hay sangre donde hay honor" ("When it is a matter of honor, blood does not count") (III.2895), and "Muy justo ha sido el castigo" ("The punishment has been just") (III.2897).[4] The performance translation cut and modified Lope's text in order for Peribanez to experience a kind of *crise de conscience* upon killing Inés, dramatized on stage by having him tearfully hug her before slitting her throat from behind. Moreover, the interpolated stage directions in Ronder's adapted translation make explicit the doffing of Peribanez's bloody captain's clothes, the symbol of his noble status ignobly conferred, and the donning of working clothes in their stead. On stage the actress playing Casilda did nothing more than

---

4   References to the Spanish text of *Peribáñez* are to the edition by Alonso Zamora Vicente.

stare down at Ines's corpse, utterly appalled at the sight, but unable to speak. Ronder's performance version of this scene follows:

LUJAN.            Oh God forgive me.
PERIBANEZ *kills* LUJAN *brutally and messily. He immediately goes off
            and drags* INES *back in.*
INES.            It's me Pedro. . . Pedro – why me?
PERIBANEZ.    Because you betrayed me!
INES (to PERIBANEZ). Why are you crying? (*PERIBANEZ moves behind
            her so he can't see her face.*) Casilda! Oh God, cousin,
            help me. Casilda! *(He cuts her throat.)*
PERIBANEZ.    That's it. That's it. It's done.
            *Silence.*
            I have to leave. Will you go with me Casilda?
            I'll wrap you up warmly, put you on the back of the horse
            and, before you know it you'll wake up in Toledo.
            My darling. We need to get away from this. It'll look
            different from far away. I need to change these clothes.
            CASILDA *stares down at* INES's *body.* PERIBANEZ
            *takes his bloody captain's clothes off and returns to his
            working clothes. He dresses quickly. When he's dressed, he
            leads* CASILDA *out.*
            *Time passes. Out of the silence comes* LEONARDO's
            *voice.*
LEONARDO.    Peribanez? Where are you? Where are you, butcher?
            *He enters with his sword drawn and sees the dead bodies
            of* INES *and* LUJAN.
LEONARDO.    Oh Christ ... (Ronder 75–6)

Hispanists have often remarked on Peribanez's disturbing distortions in his self-defense at the end; his version of the truth is correspondingly portrayed with greater or lesser fidelity in English translations. Ronder rendered the husband's own deformed discourse in order to depict rape as unequivocally a crime of violence rather than of passion. This exaggerated description of how the Commander took Casilda by force was graphically enacted in Norris's production in the "real" encounter between the two (III.2814ff), as a glance at the interpolated stage directions will confirm: *"The* COMMANDER *grabs hold of* CASILDA *and roughly gets most of her clothes off and some of his own so he can put himself in her"* (Ronder 73). If Lope first associates Casilda with the reflection of the Virgin in Toledo, he also shows the flip side of that "myth of woman as intuitive, interceding, home-loving, forgiving madonnas" by making her, however unwillingly and unconsciously, an Eve-like temptress upon whom the Commander projects his jealous desire (Evans 148). Casilda's self-defense against her assailant reveals an intelligence and a strength that finally cause the Commander to pardon Peribanez for having been the instrument of his death. It is not surprising that the actress who played Casilda in Norris's production appreciated the role because it allowed her "to act like a woman who has guts" (Feay).

One might argue, however, that the directorial decision to play up the physical aspect of rape by making Casilda a veritable victim of sexual abuse worked, not only to undermine the power of her self-defense to stay her aggressor, but also to problematize further (by making less problematic) Peribanez's self-justification before the King; his explanation turned out to be not so much a pretext as the accurate replay of a subtext turned performance text. One would have thought that, having been so physically abused, Casilda might have approved of Peribanez's attack on Ines for having allowed the Commander to enter, though her silence could also be construed as characteristic of a victim mentality. On the other hand, the fact that she was so appalled at her husband's bloody acts resounded in the audience response to the play. One critic remarked that Peribanez "ends up looking much more like a psychopath than the salt of the earth," with the further contextualization that "there are 'honour' killings of women in Britain today, and we're far less likely to admire them" (Feay). Ultimately, this production's focus lay on "not just the reconciliation of the central couple," but on "whether Peribanez can ever be reconciled to himself again" (Taylor).

Scene five and a half, appended to Act III, was testimony to Norris's attempt to reconcile Lope's ironic ending not so much with politics and economics as with the painful, emotional issues raised in the play. Changes had occurred in the couple's way of relating one to the other, and not necessarily for the best if one considers the implications of the *non-dit*:

> *A room in the palace. Hanging up there is a rich and beautiful dress, and a captain's uniform with boots.* PERIBANEZ *watches* CASILDA. *Slowly she begins to undress in front of him, taking off her peasant dress. For a moment it looks like she will move towards* PERIBANEZ, *but she doesn't. She takes her new dress down and looks at it.* PERIBANEZ *is filled with grief as he dresses in his captain's uniform.*
> *The End.* (Ronder 82)

The emotional isolation of wife and husband was captured in the directorial decision to distance the pair physically on stage in the final moment. Casilda did not move towards Peribanez but rather stared down at her own clothing as if she meant consciously to prevent their eyes from meeting. Visibly, then, Norris's sense of an ending seemed to imply that, as Jonathan Thacker observes, "in today's society such momentous events would perhaps be more likely to drive a wedge between a couple than to unite them" ("Review" 265).

## From Stage to Page and Page to (Foreign) Stage: Whose Text is it, Anyway?

In response to his question – "What ought we be doing with the theatre?" – Jonathan Miller states that, all the while that he as a director is in control of what he feels to be the text, he is at the same time controlled by it, not simply by reference to the distant past but also to the recent past of theatrical precedent: "the notion of the past which is referred to in the play, and the notion of the past in which the play has been subsequently performed" (Interview 164–5). Stagings, like translations, are inevitably carried out not by totally free agents but by constituent individualities that exist in one moment in history and that, despite themselves, are governed as much by the period of reconstruction as of production. What, in fact, ought to be the *modus operandi* when the sustained history of precedent, of what Miller means by "subsequent performances" especially with regard to Shakespeare, is lacking as it often is with *comedias*? And the issue is further complicated when the succeeding productions are foreign ones dependent on the translation of the original text into a target language. Along these lines, one might reappropriate one of the questions Pavis posed in his 1985 Questionnaire designed for students of theatre without background in semiotics – "what role is given to dramatic text in production" ("Theatre Analysis" 209) – and ask instead, "what role is given to translated text in production?"

The publication of Bassnett's *Translation Studies* (1980) can be said to mark the emergence of translation as a separate discipline, overlapping with linguistics, literary criticism, and philosophy, but also exploring problems of cross-cultural communication. Bassnett takes an historical approach to theoretical concepts and understands practical strategies in relation to specific cultural and social situations. Even though she stresses literary translation, her book underlines a key theoretical supposition of the period: the relative autonomy of the translated text. "Translation," as Lawrence Venuti puts it, "is viewed as an independent form of writing, distinct from the foreign text and from texts originally written in the translating language. Translating is seen as enacting its own processes of signification which answer to different linguistic and cultural contexts" (*Reader* 221). Although this view has persisted in translation traditions from classical antiquity forward, it is now developed systematically, with the result that the defining of "equivalence" becomes not so burning an issue in the overall movement of meanings.

In the final pages of *Shakespeare and the Authority of Performance*, Worthen (recalling Clifford Geertz) reiterates that the act of mounting a classic play perforce risks becoming an act of betrayal – and the stakes would certainly appear to be higher in the case of a classic play in translation – but only if we have a need to "legitimate" the author in order to "authorize" our own retelling of the story:

Performance is a way of interpreting ourselves to ourselves; performance of the "classics" necessarily threatens to become an act of transgression, in which the cultural tradition embodied by the work is forced to tell a new story. Of course, this act is transgressive only if we believe that there are other alternatives, if we think that both the work and the tradition it metonymically represents can be known apart from their performance, if we think that the past is not constantly being remade by – and remaking – the present. (191)

If Worthen cannot deny that performances are essentially unstable modes of signification, producing meaning intertextually in ways that deconstruct notions of intention, fidelity, authority, and presence, Michel Foucault could be said to be positing an analogous dynamic when he distinguishes between two methods of translation:

> It is quite necessary to admit that two kinds of translation exist; they do not have the same function or the same nature. In one, something (meaning, aesthetic value) must remain identical, and it is given passage into another language; these translations are good when they go "from like to same" […]. And then there are translations that hurl one language against another […] taking the original text for a projectile and treating the translating language like a target. Their task is not to lead a meaning back to itself or anywhere else; but to use the translated language to derail the translating language. (21)

Davies's production of Edward's (faithful) rendition of *Capulets & Montagues* that can be said to go "from like to same," and Norris's staging of Ronder's (unorthodox) prose adaptation of *Peribanez* that arguably "hurl[s] one language against another," may well exemplify the two methods of translation defined by Foucault. At the same time, the foregoing attempts to (re)assess Lope's (foreign) aspectuality by "re-performing performance," by "retelling telling to new listeners" and generating an archival record of one spectator's multiple viewings of opposing translation texts in performance is, as Carol Chillingworth Rutter puts it, admittedly partial and selective in its remembering. In that sense, it is hardly different from the practices of transla-tion and performance: "it intends to be rigorous, committed, grounded, but knows it is provisional, contingent, never definitive" (xiii). However provi-sional, contingent, and never definitive the two English *comedia* produc-tions under discussion, two factors remain incontrovertible: first, "[Son] de Lope"; and second, they now belong to the repertoire of "el gran teatro del mundo."

# Zayas's Comic Sense: The First Performance in English of *La traición en la amistad*

SHARON D. VOROS

Since its inception in 1975, the Siglo de Oro Spanish Drama Festival at the Chamizal National Memorial in El Paso, Texas, has become both a venue for *comedias* in translation and for less canonical Golden Age plays. However, until 2003, when director David Pasto and his cast from Oklahoma City University mounted their production of Catherine Larson's translation of María de Zayas's *La traición en la amistad,* entitled *Friendship Betrayed,* the only other woman dramatist's work on the Chamizal stage was that of Sor Juana Inés de la Cruz.[1] With this performance Zayas's comic sense took center stage. Known primarily for her narrative works, this writer is some-times characterized, and perhaps not unjustifiably, as pessimistic (Soufas 148): "ni comedia se representa, ni libro se imprime que no sea todo en ofensa de mujeres" ("there is no play performed or book printed that is not offensive to women") (Zayas, *Tres novelas* 205). Zayas's only extant play, however, presents a problematic view of women as transgressors and comics in a kind of subversion of any feminist project we might attempt to elicit from her, although her female characters initiate dramatic action and are responsible for its outcome (Wilkins 114). Pasto's production, a first for the Chamizal and a first for this translation,[2] endeavors to come to grips with the ways in which a comic sense works in favor of women.

---

[1]  With grants from the Spanish Ministry's Program for Cultural Cooperation, the Associa-tion for Hispanic Classical Theater has sponsored productions of Spanish Golden Age plays in English translation. Donald T. Dietz, first president and co-founder of the AHCT, Catherine Larson, and Susan Paun de García have been successful in obtaining production grants. See the on-line catalogue <www.comedias.org> for the video of *Friendship Betrayed,* ZS 03.

[2]  The importance of this 2003 production as a first is evidenced by a session at the AHCT's 2004 conference organized by Amy Williamsen. Participants were Constance Wilkins, Valerie Hegstrom, and Sharon Voros. Two articles include information on this production: see Lopez-Mayhew; A. Williamsen's forthcoming article includes still photos. The distortion of the cover photo for Michael J. McGrath's edition of *La traición en la amistad*, with Belisa dressed in red and Don Juan offering her his sword, does not do justice to the actors.

Zayas includes in her play a traditional *gracioso* role, León, and two female roles, Lucía and Belisa, who function in some sense as foils to him. The most important of these is Belisa, and she is my concern here. She is a lady, not a maid, unlike Lucía, servant to Fenisa, and though she is referred to as *discreta*, best translated as "wise" (Voros, "Fashioning" 161–2), Belisa is León's true female counterpart. Lucía, to be sure, does manage to get in choice comments on her mistress's multiple love interests, and in the end marries León, but Belisa assumes the role of comedic heroine, despite subservience to her cousin Marcia.

The latter is the initiator of the dramatic action that precipitates betrayal among women friends when she clashes with Fenisa over Liseo in a typical love triangle. To her credit, Marcia backs off when Laura, seduced and abandoned by him, appears in order to plead her cause. While the plot revolves around the rift between Marcia and Fenisa, Fenisa's brazen overtures to men have attracted the lion's share of scholarly commentary. Lopez-Mayhew contends that the "engrossing," "seductive" Fenisa upstages all other women on the boards (180), while Soufas calls Belisa, Marcia, and Laura merely conventional, Fenisa being the only female character who breaks with stereotypical female roles (152).

Despite her secondary status, Belisa is not overlooked in the Pasto production. Though she has her own story, it is intertwined with Marcia's. However, she is the first female character to confront male infidelity in her beau, Don Juan, a victim of Fenisa's charms. She is also the only character to challenge the *gracioso* León's misogynistic sarcasm and get the better of him (in a scene I consider her best), displaying in the process wit, humor, and erudition, qualities conveyed energetically and convincingly by María Solano, the actress who portrays her in this production.[3]

I will examine here three scenes in which Belisa has a key part, all of them played on the minimalist set used throughout the performance: a raised white octagon center stage, two benches stage left, and one bench and platform with stairs stage right.[4] The scenes focus on her anger at Don Juan, her attack on León, and her fight with Fenisa. In these Belisa not only manifests the complexity of the "figura de donaire," as José Montesinos calls the

---

[3]    The cast of characters is: Marcia, Erin Patricia Hicks; Fenisa, Suzanne Proctor; Belisa, María Solano; Laura, Susan Riley; Lucía, Jack Devon Beyer; Juan and Antonio, David Scott McLemore; Liseo and Fabio, Matt Morgan; León, JD Church; Gerardo, Tyler Mueggenborg; Félix, Adrian L. Finley. The role of Lauro was eliminated.

[4]    Such stripped-down sets are not uncommon at Chamizal, where performances typically play for only one night.

*gracioso*,[5] but intrudes into the arena of the main characters.[6] Since Fenisa, the donjuanesque *dama* (Stroud, "Demand" 164), resorts to violence, not erudition, to get the better of León, she shares some of the latter's physical brand of comedy.[7] Hence, we have two levels of female comic expression, the physical (Fenisa with León) and the verbal (Belisa with León). It is not surprising, then, that Fenisa and Belisa come to blows at the end of Act III, with León egging them on, for both ladies indulge in a more bodily form of comedy here. It will be important later to examine how David Pasto resolves the staging issues for this problematic scene.

Belisa begins her dramatic trajectory as Marcia's poor, probably orphaned, cousin.[8] She makes her appearance at the end of Act I on the balcony with Marcia, when the latter's beau of seven years, Gerardo, depicted in this production as a myopic buffoon, comes to serenade.[9] Had Belisa remained subservient, her dramatic range would have been limited, although she shares characteristics of maids' roles that Monica Leoni cites as the ancestor of the comic (10). Marcia and Gerardo do not have servants, so Belisa assumes an ambiguous role, subservient, yet independent, with a mind of her own. Thus, when she occupies center stage, she no longer follows the orders of a domi-neering relative. As a maid, Belisa would not have had the autonomy of stage action that she acquires as the play progresses. Her scenes of comic repartee or "self-propagating freeplay" (Elam 5) could be reduced, as apparently occurred in the Almagro production of *La traición,* in which the *gracioso* role was eliminated altogether (Lopez-Mayhew 185).

It is Marcia's attraction to Liseo and her disdain for the long-suffering Gerardo, whose cause Belisa champions, that truly sets the play in motion, rather than Fenisa's attempts to seduce all the *galanes* available. When Belisa appears at a window with Marcia (73), it is to hear Gerardo's serenade, although he lets others do the singing. Marcia, however, dismisses Belisa's attempts to draw attention to him. She treats her cousin harshly, using, in the original Spanish, the word *necia*, a term often used by masters in their

---

5   Monica Leoni also studies the development of the *gracioso* as a figure who takes center stage.

6   Amy Williamsen notes that Belisa has 13.5% of the lines and Fenisa 16.25%. The male *gracioso* León has the highest percentage of lines, 16.5%.

7   See Leoni's analysis of the *gracioso*'s base form of humor, also at work in Zayas's León when he evokes anxiety about the body, especially after losing a few teeth at Fenisa's hand (84). Leoni also points out Bergson's comments on the body language of the comic.

8   Laura, the fourth lady, is an orphan (91), seduced and abandoned by her lover Liseo, the cause of the split between Marcia and Fenisa, who both claim him.

9   Lopez-Mayhew discusses the eighteenth-century costuming as inappropriate and effemi-nate for male characters (180). This is particularly true for a Gerardo with glasses who, despite his constancy, is given to fainting, all part of a semiotic of male weakness.

disparagement of their servants: "Hush up, and do not make me mad, or I will tell you just how foolish you are" (75).[10]

Larson's verse translation of the serenade is one of the overlooked jewels of this production: "But my rabid suffering and sorry fate / only harden the heart of this lovely ingrate" (75), altogether only ten lines, beautifully performed here by David Scott McLemore and Matt Morgan, employing Italian accents to disguise the fact that they double as Juan and Liseo. Though Belisa responds affectionately to her cousin, Marcia, the ingrate of the song, at this point storms off the stage. Belisa now plays the intermediary between Gerardo and Marcia, a role typical of servant go-betweens. However, her role as a mediator does not limit her dramatic discourse, if we understand discourse in the general Shakespearean sense of "language in *use*" (Elam 1).

At the beginning of Act II, Belisa continues as a virtual housemaid who answers the door to visitors. Laura, Liseo's former lover, now enters. Since he had mumbled Marcia's name, and Fenisa's, in his sleep (81), Laura comes to plead her cause. Belisa says: "A beautiful lady wants to speak to you. Do you want me to let her in? Not only is she lovely, but she looks noble as well" (86). Marcia's reply, "Well, what does she want?" prompts Belisa to repeat the request, although she has already stated the visitor's intentions, something that makes evident Marcia's self-indulgence and Belisa's perseverance. Marcia, accustomed to giving orders, expects those of her entourage to cater to her whims.

The dual role of cousin and maid places Belisa in a position that Lope de Vega explores in *La prueba de los ingenios (Trial by Wits)*, that of servants who have nothing to lose by speaking their mind. "Tú que no puedes perder / ni la autoridad ni el nombre" ("You have nothing to lose – neither your authority nor your good name"), says Laura, Lope's female principal, to her maid Finea (302), sending her off to discover the true sexual identity of Florela. The latter, really a woman disguised as a man (Félix) disguised as a woman (Diana), reminds her love object (Laura) that she has said "Si fueras hombre / tú solo fueras mi dueño" ("If you were a man, you alone would be my love") (292). In Zayas's play Belisa's flattery of Laura, "If I were a man, I would put my faith in your love" (89), recalls Lope's words, which may also be viewed as an expression of same-sex desire, as are other terms of endearment, without the guise of cross-dressing (Delgado 388).

While Belisa is taken by Laura's beauty, Don Juan, infatuated with Fenisa, is now part of the plan to set everything right. Since Belisa still has not made any decisions of her own and has not really found her dramatic voice, Marcia gives instructions to win Don Juan back: "Cousin, get him to return to his past desire" (97). In her confrontation scene with Don Juan, though

---

[10] All quotations for the Spanish edition and English translation are from Hegstrom and Larson.

she still follows orders from Marcia, she learns to show anger. With Laura, as with other jilted characters, even Belisa, Zayas touches on the violence perpetrated on women by men, a darker side of heterosexual relationships that she explores with greater depth in her *novelas*. This is a comedy, and all love entanglements will turn out for the best, except for the transgressing Fenisa, who remains alone at the end, though León alludes to future entanglements (197).[11]

Belisa enjoys another convention of the *comedia nueva*, the sonnet soliloquy (Dixon, "Manuel Vallejo" 68). In a reminiscence of serious drama, she refers to jealousy as "the violent tyrant," to which Larson appends a phrase from *Othello*, familiar to English-speaking audiences: "the green-eyed monster" (99). The phrase is an addition to the text, but in keeping with Belisa's growing rage over her lover's betrayal. When Don Juan enters, oblivious to the falling out with Marcia, he has the insensitivity to inquire: "I may be a fool for asking you this, but is Fenisa here?" (99).

Although he has enough sense to approach her as "wise Belisa," Belisa, now anything but wise, goes on the attack.[12] Now Don Juan is the tyrant, not jealousy, and Belisa leaves him speechless, calling him "ingrate," "enemy," and "traitor," before concluding, "So, you have nothing to say?" (101). She claims her own dramatic voice here with her ability to put men in their place and silence them. Don Juan's infidelities are perplexing, since he promises undying love and praises her bewitching eyes, a line he also fed to Fenisa: "I came by to gaze at those beautiful eyes of yours" (47). He apparently falls for any beautiful woman once he is in her presence, but then falls out of love with her in her absence. Such emotional barrier-shifting constitutes the dramatic discourse in this play in which there is no older authority figure to point out the follies of love, only well-meaning servants or poor cousins with no real power.

Don Juan claims his dalliance with Fenisa was all a mistake, and that Belisa is his "phoenix, heaven, an April springtime" (105). He even proposes marriage: "My dear friend, lovely rose, carnation, give me your hand and I, at your feet and on my knees, will offer you a husband in return" (107). On his knees he offers her his sword, as seen in a photo on the cover of McGrath's edition. Belisa, dressed imposingly in red with black lace gloves, eventually accepts his proposal, still mindful that his words may be lies. Don Juan's aside ("No more tricks, Fenisa" [109]) shows that he is making an attempt to be honest here, for he has already seen Fenisa to be untrue. Eighteenth-

---

11 Julián Olivares argues that Zayas is more severe with deceitful women ("Introducción," 79n89), which explains Fenisa's status as an outcast at the play's conclusion.

12 Marcia calls Gerardo "discreto" (129). He is the only other character with this descriptor.

century costuming in this production empowers women just as it feminizes men, as this scene shows with Don Juan now in a position of subservience.

At the end of Act II, with Don Juan's marriage proposal to Belisa secure, Marcia follows her cousin's lead and begins to change her mind about Gerardo. Belisa makes a statement here that will carry over to her main scene, not her cat-fight with Fenisa, but her challenge to the *gracioso* León. Marcia now also appears to consider Belisa more of an equal: "Amazing things have been happening, cousin!" (127). To this Belisa responds, "So amazing, it is as if Aesop's fables were coming to life!"[13] Aesop's fables are indeed coming to life, for Cupid, the creator of chaos, much like Shakespeare's mischievous Puck, will be defeated by wit, wisdom, and women's collective effort (Wilkins 110).

For Linda Bamber, scholars make too much of dramatic conflict in comedy in the expectation of moral reality (121). While Zayas's male characters show little moral development (Soufas 158), the mention of Aesop, not only once but twice, when Belisa outwits León, suggests that Zayas's comic sense involves critical judgment of her characters. Both José Luis Suárez and Evangelina Rodríguez Cuadros argue that *comedias* have a moralizing intent, although moralists of the period considered their examples harmful, largely because of the presence of women on the stage (Suárez 116). Here conflict is resolved, as the edgy, unrepentant Fenisa remains a figure of chaos at the play's conclusion (Paun de García, "*Traición*" 383). An idea of a right and a wrong in matters of love comes to the fore when Belisa and Don Juan reconcile their differences at the close of Act II. I agree with Larson (137n34) that the biblical quote regarding "rendering unto Caesar the things that are Caesar's" alludes to loving the right person, for the restoration of order and even justice in love relationships is now underway.

Order restored after comic confusion provides the discursive underpinnings of comedy, which is for Bamber inherently feminine (129). For Wilkins, women triumph through collective, not individual, action (110). Zayas's comic sense privileges women on the stage as a site for female agency, even in roles that swing both ways, such as Belisa's ambiguous lady/maid, something Bamber says male authors like Cervantes do not do (129). Zayas enhances a role that could have been written for a servant, despite George Mariscal's claim that she shows disrespect toward maids and values blood and class over gender (61).

While Belisa's sonnet soliloquy appears before an important scene, she never opens an act. Laura has this privilege with a soliloquy opening Act III when her servant Félix interrupts with news – which is, in fact, mere rumor

---

[13] Lopez-Mayhew's edition assigns this line (1599) to Belisa and lines 1600–5, including the reference to Aesop, to Marcia.

– that Liseo has married Fenisa. Laura falls in a swoon, while her overzealous servant falls on top of her, an action that provoked laughter from the audience in Pasto's production, which in general avoids playing every scene as more farcical than intended, unlike the Almagro production (Lopez-Mayhew 185). Belisa is still a nurturer for Laura in this scene, and Laura continues speaking to her affectionately: "Oh, my dear Belisa" (141). Belisa again has a short soliloquy that seals Liseo's fate, for he signs a promise to marry Marcia (really Laura), and every line in it has a form of *engañar*, literally "to deceive" or "to trick": "Because you have lived by trickery, and she has been tricked by you, today you will pay for that deceit, and you will be tricked into becoming her husband, whether you like it or not" (163). Belisa is also the messenger to Liseo himself, and now the trap is set for him (161).

In Act III, Belisa's verbal sparring with the *gracioso* León (175–86) shows her ability to outwit him on his own terms, for this is her principal moment of comic repartee. León as master storyteller employs all the misogynistic rhetoric he can muster, typical of "figuras de donaire" (Montesinos 40). The actor, JD Church, a huge hulk of a fellow, stands in stark contrast to María Solano's slender figure. It is the Feast Day of San Miguel (29 September), and León approaches her stage left, with the central octagon separating them, and wonders out loud why a pretty girl like her is not out on the town. Belisa briefly reverts to her housemaid-like subservience, for she is sitting stage right embroidering. While she is the only female character to mention classical traditions, a characteristic she shares with Gerardo (77), her choice of Aesop is particularly telling. It not only allows her to display her wit, but moves her center stage and sets a moralizing tone. A book in hand may have been a better stage prop, yet Belisa with her embroidery needles catches León off-guard.[14] He approaches her almost as an equal, expecting a little fun. However, humble Belisa is no fool. León implies that her status is not equal to her cousin's, for she is left home alone. The comic banter begins when she retorts that women in love do not need silly diversions. León counters that no such women exist, and if one did she must be a phoenix. Belisa is such a phoenix, and indeed Don Juan has addressed her as such to show his devotion to her as one of a kind (105). Pasto's raised central octagon is particularly effective here; it allows for interesting blocking, as it does indeed throughout this production in which actors determine their own "bodied" space, to borrow Stanton Garner's term.[15]

Embroidery, a conventional activity for women, does not prepare the audience, or the *gracioso*, for what is to follow. Wise Belisa emerges here with

---

[14] To open Act II, Marcia reads her sonnet soliloquy from a book in this production.

[15] For a contrary opinion, see Lopez-Mayhew, who contends that the central octagon was "at times cumbersome and awkward" (181).

intellectual clout that leaves León speechless. She has already mentioned
Aesop in an allusion to events in which foolishness is punished and wisdom
rewarded, and she now uses the fable to beat León at his own game. León,
however, the master narrator of this play, moves center stage and adjusts
his clothing to keep Belisa in suspense, as he tells his tale of female hypoc-
risy fraught with references to ill-gotten goods and *busconas* (prostitutes),
typical misogynistic arguments about women and their lack of virtue and
constancy.

Belisa now goes on the counter-attack, beginning – unlike in her scathing
comments to Don Juan – unassumingly, with the concession that such women
are "filthy harpies" (175). Then, she compares León to the lion, vulnerable
to disease despite his "ferociousness" (181), and stands up to take her position of defiance on the octagon. Belisa as female comic puts the *gracioso*
in his place, actions that then explain her defiance of Marcia and her attack
on Fenisa (189). Her verbal battle with León prepares the audience for the
coming physical battle (189). Belisa also tells Marcia, "Leave me alone,
cousin" (189), a statement we would not have expected from her earlier on.
Belisa uses the term "fool" with reference to Fenisa (193), whom she also
calls "low-class villain" (189), for she becomes quite proficient at hurling
insults as the play closes.

Belisa the wise now tells León a tale and expects him to get the point of
her narrative. Aesop's fable does indeed come true for Belisa, who is well
acquainted with Wisdom Literature and its moral examples (Goldberg 75).
A lion's arrogant ways, she warns, can be brought down by fever. The fable
of the Lion, the Wolf, and the Fox, the basis for her story (Aesop 166),
appears in La Fontaine, who also addresses the destructive nature of courtiers
(356–9) and who was available to Zayas in several translations (Beardsley
113). The king of beasts is ill, and the "callous wolf" (183) convinces him
that the skin of the fox will save him. The fox, however, despite her female
gender, her small size, and her humble demeanor, outwits the wolf, whose
skin, she argues to the lion, is much larger than hers and will cure him quite
nicely. In this production, Belisa moves from a sitting position to standing
and makes clawing motions at León, while telling him that the wolf's fate is
what happens to people who speak in court. Silencing León is no easy task,
for his clear loud voice makes him overbearing and impossible to ignore.
Belisa, however, rises to the occasion, eggs León on, and outwits him, telling
him, with her final word, to "hush" (187). Dumbfounded and bewildered,
León is speechless, but only temporarily, since a *gracioso* without a voice
has no place on the stage.

While a book as prop could have enhanced Belisa's role, the embroidery work catches León and the audience off-guard. Belisa shows she is not
cowardly, as I believe she demonstrates in the fight scene with Fenisa, when

she abandons her subservient demeanor.[16] David Pasto quite appropriately picked up a sense of Belisa's enhanced role, when she insults Fenisa and warns her cousin Marcia not to meddle (189). While Belisa's name rhymes with rival Fenisa's and suggests equal status, the fight scene between them is overplayed with sword brandishing. Zayas, however, does not use sword play as a means of conveying a heightened level of rivalry, although this stage convention was available to her. An example of a woman taking up the sword in female attire, not as a cross-dresser, appears in Juan Pérez de Montalbán, whom she apparently knew (Paun de García, "Zayas as Writer" 40). In his *La más constante mujer*, Isabel defends her beloved husband Carlos with sword in hand, an action that causes the Duke of Milan to abandon his seduction of her. While Zayas does not indicate sword play in her text, she certainly could have known of this stage convention and may have seen Montalbán's play performed.[17]

Reactions to introducing sword brandishing as a dramatic device here have been mixed, mostly because it does not appear in Zayas. Williamsen in a forthcoming article argues persuasively in favor of sword play as a way to avoid a hair-pulling cat-fight scene that would convey negative impressions to audiences today. Lopez-Mayhew considers this device simply awkward (179). As a spectator on 7 March 2003, I admit that the sword-brandishing ladies certainly had an impact on the audience. However, when Fenisa removes the sword from Gerardo, his fainting spell brought the house down, just as a hair-pulling incident might have.[18] Belisa then takes Don Juan's sword, but Marcia upstages her cousin as she awkwardly takes the sword away from her and pushes her aside, thus reestablishing her stage authority. This flurry of stage action undercuts Belisa just as she is gaining prominence. She recovers some of her feistiness when she takes the sword away from Fenisa, whom both cousins then hold at bay.

While female sword play remains at variance with the text, it brings up the problematic nature of showing women fighting on the stage, for even by today's standards, female body action is arguably more limited than that of males. For example, Garner cites Iris Marion Young's notion that "women tend to make less use of their bodies than men" (201). Young's analysis of the phenomenon of "throwing like a girl" is part of a patriarchal system that represses feminine body movement (141–59). This play and this production,

[16] Montesinos (28) notes that the *gracioso*'s cowardice feeds into comic routines.

[17] Barbara Weissberger (44) argues that Isabel the Catholic caused concern as she brandished the sword in Segovia to begin her rule. Belisa is also a common anagram for Isabel (Montesinos 239).

[18] In this scene Marcia tells Gerardo to "be brave and do not pass out on me" (191). His fainting here has some textual basis, for he may have done so during their lengthy seven-year courtship.

however, depict women who dominate the physicality of performance (even had the problematical hair-pulling scene been included), while men stand on the sidelines or even faint.

Certainly by seventeenth-century standards for female body action, Zayas's hair-pulling scene renders the physical encounter between Belisa and Fenisa problematic. Enjoying the spectacle, León discourages any interruption of the fight: "Leave them alone; hush" (189). As Wilkins and Bamber have argued, comedy uses the tools of subversion as entertaining stage action. Here men make comments and women act. Horrified at their behavior, Don Juan blames Fenisa: "Have you ever seen such a thing! This is really shameful, Fenisa" (189). Marcia tries to put an end to the fight, as León comments: "By God, if Marcia had not come in, those two really would be going after each other with vigor; they were pulling each other's manes out" (189). Zayas at first blush appears to undercut her own feminist agenda in the hair-pulling scene, when two ladies debase themselves. Yet through the ambiguities of comedy, she still privileges female dramatic discourse: Belisa subverts the *gracioso*'s misogynistic story-telling in which he delights in demeaning women.

The sword play in this production attempts to establish dramatic space as a privileged space for women in comedy, although Zayas herself allows her women to come to blows in ways that appear unacceptable and degrading. Women writers, however, do not always say what we want them to say. If this is indeed a play essentially directed to a female audience (Delgado 385), Zayas challenges female conventions of limited stage movement with this cat-fight scene that the Pasto production wishes to put into perspective for today's audiences. But in lowering her characters to the status of brawling buffoons, Zayas at least offers some idea of a comic sense at just the point in the play's conclusion when the audience is called to make critical or moral judgments, despite the subversive devices at work (Wilkins 115; Voros, "Calderón's Writing Women" 126–8). The base humor typical of *graciosos* is commandeered by two *damas*, while León supplies the laugh track, a clue for how the audience is to react and perhaps a hint from Zayas that this scene is supposed to reinforce female freedom of action on the stage. Belisa's humble role at the outset does not mean she is a housemaid; she is not cowardly and Fenisa gets her just deserts. Such is the stuff of festive comedy. Yet such problematic scenes remind us that the social or moral reality of the play is the subject of Zayas's challenge to notions of comedy on the stage.

This first performance of *Friendship Betrayed* provides a staging that privileges women in comic roles. Even the eighteenth-century costuming gives the edge to women, making men appear foppish, fickle, and morally weak. As a secondary character Belisa finds her own dramatic voice: her last lines warn Fenisa not to expect anything from Don Juan as he is her (Belisa's) husband already, whereupon he calls her "wise Belisa" (193), the last description we have of her in the play. Thus, Belisa begins and ends her role as a kind of stabilizing force of wisdom in the play, although she moves from gentle, almost subservient cousin to jealous lover, all to defend her sense of justice. Indeed, it is difficult to portray a comedic heroine without having some scenes that border on ridiculing her, such as the cat-fight scene that this production's sword play attempts to dignify. Had the previous scene with León not been a triumph for Belisa, her final confrontation with Fenisa could have undercut her stage authority. Thus, Belisa's actions all interconnect: she claims Don Juan as her husband and establishes a kind of comedic justice through coming to blows with Fenisa. Zayas's portrayal of wise Belisa shows her attention to secondary roles that enrich and enhance the staging of this play. By placing a sword in her hand, the director understood the strength of Belisa's role in this project to privilege female dramatic discourse. Belisa's stage action as subservient, yet independent, gives rise to an idea of Zayas's comic sense that challenges stage conventions of her own time and ours. She widens dramatic roles for comic women, with immense delight for audiences seeing this play in English, for the first time ever in the United States.

# María de Zayas's *Friendship Betrayed* à la Hollywood: Translation, Transculturation, and Production

## BARBARA MUJICA

Every theatre production is a translation. The director must deconstruct and decode a written text and "translate" it into a body of auditory and visual signs that are intelligible to spectators. When the text is the product of a culture different from the spectators', either because it was produced at a different historical moment or by an author whose frame of reference is alien to the audience's, issues of transculturation arise. Carl Weber defines "transculturation" as "the deconstruction of a text/code and its wrenching displacement to a 'historically and socially different situation'" ("AC/TC" 35). When the play in question was written by a person marginal to the traditional power elite – as in the case of any seventeenth-century woman dramatist – the transculturation process is complicated by the possibility that familiar codes may operate in unexpected ways. The July 2006 production of María de Zayas's *Friendship Betrayed*,[1] directed by Karen Berman of Washington Women in Theater, is an example of how one director met successfully the challenges posed by an early modern woman-authored play. This essay focuses first on those aspects of the *comedia* that Berman had to deconstruct in order to accomplish the "wrenching displacement" essential to transculturation, and next on Berman's methods for transforming the work into a performance piece easily decodifiable for modern audiences.

## The Play

*Friendship Betrayed* is a silly play about silly people. Fenisa, the central character, is a man-hungry minx hell-bent on accumulating as many suitors

---

[1]    All English quotes from the play are from the Catherine Larson translation of *La traición en la amistad.*

as possible. When her friend Marcia shows up with a portrait of her new love interest Liseo, Fenisa immediately decides to pursue him. At the same time, she wants to hang on to her current *galán*, Juan, formerly the suitor of Marcia's cousin Belisa, and also goes after Gerardo, Marcia's long-time admirer, as well as Liseo's friend Lauro. During all these shenanigans Liseo's manservant León, the *gracioso*, and Fenisa's maid Lucía make cynical remarks about the childish, self-indulgent pursuits of their betters.

Before undertaking the production of a play from a different culture and period, a director must take the time to analyze the underlying themes and to identify which of these might be relevant to her audiences, since seemingly silly plays sometimes contain fierce social messages. One of Berman's most important tasks was to identify the social ambience in which the action takes place. Zayas paints a society in which a rich, idle aristocracy passes its time in the pursuit of pleasure. Devoid of religious commitment or moral concerns, this is the ultimate "me generation." In spite of their constant references to God, the characters are indifferent to Christian values. Church is a place for trysts, and the convent is a place to go – or pretend to go – when one's marriage options appear to dissipate.

León calls the audience's attention again and again to the vapidity of upper-class society. When Liseo speaks of being "lost" and "a dead man" because he has been duped by Fenisa, León mocks him: "Oh, my dear master, you are driving me crazy. You are not lost; you are right here. Dead? I see you alive right here in front of me" (157). By pretending to understand literally terms that Liseo has used figuratively, León calls attention to the empty hyperbole that characterizes the talk of these vapid nobles who blow up every setback into a tragedy. He rebukes Liseo for his "terrible silliness" and tells him he is getting exactly what he deserves: "Look at the betrayal of the King of Cheats! Holy God, you make me laugh!" (157). Later on he remarks that, "It has been a long time since the days when holy innocence and truth have passed from the Golden Age" (177), a comment on rampant duplicity among the idle aristocracy. Betrayal rages everywhere. Not only has Fenisa betrayed Marcia, but she has also betrayed Juan, who has in turn betrayed Belisa. At the same time, Marcia has betrayed Gerardo to pursue Liseo, who has betrayed Laura to pursue Marcia. León laments living in an age "so poor and lacking in friendship [that] evil betrayal has flourished" (177). All of the characters are quick to accuse others of immorality while at the same time clothing their own base actions in moralistic rhetoric.

However, *Friendship Betrayed* is more than a comedy of manners or a spoof on the aristocracy's inane and stultifying pursuit of pleasure. Fenisa, the play's central character, is full of ambiguities, and to portray her effectively the director had to form a coherent concept of her personality in order to "translate" it into a modern context. On the one hand, Fenisa is immoral and catty, but on the other, she is strong, determined, feisty, and cunning.

Like the protagonists of many of Zayas's narratives, she is an autonomous female who exerts agency. She not only breaks with the norm of the passive, obedient young woman promoted by moralists, but also differs from the models provided by the female protagonists of the *comedia de capa de espada*, who sneak around behind the backs of their male guardians. Unlike in most male-authored comedies, in *Friendship Betrayed* fathers or brothers are conspicuously absent. The only mention of Fenisa's upbringing refers to her mother. Don Juan remarks that Fenisa knows enough to wear a *mantilla* when she goes out, since "her mother always taught her to cover herself, just like a hairpiece covers a bald head" (133) – a snide suggestion that Fenisa's mother snuck around *tapada* just like her daughter.

What is the audience supposed to feel for Fenisa? It is with regard to this question that the author's gender becomes relevant. Since Zayas's use of traditional codes is atypical enough to create ambiguity, the director herself must form a cohesive notion of her character and then decide how to portray her. Are we supposed to admire this brazen woman who refuses to play the submissive female? Is Fenisa simply an empty-headed floozy whose only concern is having a good time, or is she a rebel against a repressive patriarchal society that offers women no intelligent pastimes? In *Three Uses of the Knife: On the Nature and Purpose of Drama,* David Mamet observes that what defines a hero is resistance: "The power to resist makes the hero's journey affective" (18). To the extent that Fenisa resists society's expectations, it is possible to see her as a hero. It is true that at the end of the play she loses control of herself and flails at everyone, but until then, she comes across as a clever maneuverer who juggles several lovers at the same time. But does Zayas approve of Fenisa or offer her as an example of societal decay? Is juggling several lovers at the same time a skill we should admire or a sign of degeneracy – or both? Any director wishing to mount *Friendship Betrayed* successfully must recognize the ambiguity of the central character, whether to exploit or to conceal it.

And what are we to make of the end of the play? It is a truism of the Spanish *Comedia* that the closing must appear to restore order, which explains why Fenisa winds up without a man and ostracized from her group of girlfriends. This is her punishment for betraying Marcia. However, the ending is not as clear-cut as it might seem. As a woman, Zayas had to proceed with caution when depicting for the stage a female protagonist whose behavior challenged existing norms. Constance Wilkins notes that "the fact that plays are the most public form of literature makes them especially subject to influence by internal or external censorship" (109). For women writers, the need to reinstate the standard was especially keen: "when one considers the degree to which play-writing reaffirms the patriarchal order, the obstacles facing women dramatists are staggering" (109). Thus, Zayas duly punishes her wayward protagonist. However, just how serious is Fenisa's punishment?

Fenisa is still standing and presumably capable of continuing her escapades as the play closes. She is not lying dead on the floor, and she is not being carried down to hell by a talking statue. León's remarks to the men in the audience suggest that Fenisa's adventures are far from over: "My lords, as you can see, Fenisa is left alone without a single lover. If one of you is interested, let me know and I will pass on her address" (197). The final pairing of the couples further complicates the question. Marcia, Liseo, and Juan have all committed betrayals and yet are "rewarded" with matrimony, albeit, in the case of Liseo, with some coercion. (And we cannot help but wonder, in spite of the dictum about never "reading beyond the end," how the marriages of these flighty youngsters will fare.)

Research on Zayas's novellas sheds considerable light on the ambiguity of her protagonists. Although scholars do not agree on whether Zayas was an early modern feminist or a conservative defender of conventional morality, most recognize her as one of the few writers of her period to examine feminine desire. Zayas's novellas contain numerous examples of women who, like Fenisa, pursue men openly. Jacinta, for example, protagonist of "Aventurarse perdiendo" ("Everything Ventured"), not only has an affair right in her father's house but later continues it in the convent as a tertiary, with the collusion of the prioress.[2]

The paradoxes and tensions that fill *Friendship Betrayed* are also evident in the novellas. Some of these stem, as Margaret Greer notes, from the difficult situation in which Zayas finds herself: "that of defending the moral and intellectual equality and capacity of women while maintaining a conservative aristocratic ideology and upholding the very concepts of social propriety and obligation, class distinction, institutional rectitude, and the patriarchal honor code that held women in a subordinate position," which Greer sees as an "insurmountable antithesis" for Zayas (*María de Zayas* 350). Although she "vigorously asserts women's capacities and attacks the educational disadvantages and social practices that restrict their development," in Greer's view Zayas "devises no new plots that demonstrate those assertions" (350). But the play *does* offer something new: a plot that revolves almost entirely around women and a rare look at the workings of female social interaction in seventeenth-century Spain from a woman's point of view.

Whether they see *Friendship Betrayed* as a celebration of female desire or as a condemnation of upper-class licentiousness, most critics stress the play's feminist aspects, as exemplified by the solidarity between Marcia, Belisa, and Laura. Although all the women in the play have problematic relations with men, only Laura has lost her virginity. When she confides her dishonor to Marcia and Belisa, the other women rally to her aid immediately, even though

---

[2]  Tertiaries did not take vows and often were not cloistered. On the Church's efforts to cloister tertiary nuns, see Elizabeth A. Lehfeldt, *Religious Women in Golden Age Spain*.

remedying her situation requires that Marcia renounce her claim to Liseo. In the homosocial environment that Zayas portrays, women bond together and help one another. Although many male-authored *comedias* offer examples of women scheming together, Zayas provides the example of a female group in which an outsider is accepted simply because she is a woman in need. Fenisa, the one woman who betrays the trust of the others, is excluded in the end, more for her lack of solidarity than for her polygamous desire. Lisa Vollendorf remarks that Fenisa is "[d]emonized for her sexual choices as well as for her refusal to make sacrifices that other women have been shown making for each other" (83). All the other women have either been inconstant or lax in their dealings with men; what really sets Fenisa apart is her devaluation of friendship, which results in the betrayal of another woman: "Sorry, Friendship, but Love has my fancy" (61). Surprisingly, Belisa shows a certain loyalty even to her: "She would not do such crazy things [...] if she just knew how to act right [...]. But we should be patient with her condition" (135). This unexpected generosity serves to underscore Fenisa's treachery by juxtaposing it with the other women's loyalty to one another.

In contrast, the men are loners. With the exception of Gerardo, each one is a wolf on the prowl, anxious to accumulate kills. Don Juan, like his Tirsian predecessor, is a typical *galán*, "conquering women all over the place" (49). Liseo is another lecher who, having already dishonored Laura, goes after Marcia and Fenisa at the same time. "Quite a life, if you marry half a dozen women!" remarks León (109). His pursuit of Marcia is serious, Liseo explains, but he is courting Fenisa "with deception, tricks and lies, and only to satisfy my desire [...]. Fenisa is a joke" (109). Significantly, early in the play, Fenisa describes Liseo as "a mirror image of the men at court" (51). Men like Don Juan and Liseo are not the exception, but the rule. Although men are always talking of love, complains Belisa, they "have a hundred women, without really loving any of them" (177). What makes these male characters different from the Tirsian prototype, notes Valerie Hegstrom, is that all are ultimately controlled by women. Don Juan is deceived by Fenisa, Liseo is dumped by Marcia, and Gerardo is so docile Hegstrom calls him an "hombre mujeril" ("womanly man") (62–3).

In contrast, Fenisa is a "mujer varonil*"* ("manly woman"). Perhaps Fenisa's real crime, in society's eyes, is that she behaves like a man. She collects suitors as men collect girlfriends. Constance Wilkins notes: "Fenisa's expression of her sexuality approaches or enters male terrain [...]. With her unrestrained sexuality Fenisa represents a threat to difference and maintenance of hierarchy, thus provoking turmoil in her world" (111). Fenisa is different from the men because she does not sleep with lovers one after the other and then abandon them. Nevertheless, her blatant insatiability jeopardizes a patriarchal order obsessed with female chastity.

Several critics have compared Zayas's predatory Fenisa with Tirso's Don

Juan; however, there are essential differences between Fenisa and Don Juan that stem from the specific expectations for men and women in the Spanish seventeenth century. Don Juan's objective is sexual conquest. He repeatedly uses verbs such as "burlar" ("deceive," "take advantage of") and "gozar" ("enjoy," "take pleasure in") when speaking of his plans to seduce women. He never speaks of love except when he is trying to dupe women into having sex with him. For Don Juan, seduction is a means of asserting his power not only over women, but also over other men. By seducing women, he humiliates the men who are responsible for them. Don Juan is the embodiment of the insecure male who needs a steady diet of conquests in order to affirm his manliness. Like Fenisa, he betrays friends (Octavio, Mota), thereby converting the seduction game into a kind of sexual one-upmanship. But, unlike her, he is not interested in maintaining ties with his partners after he has slept with them.

Fenisa's objective is not to bed her prey, but to accumulate admirers. In spite of her predatory behavior, she never speaks of compromising her virginity. It is precisely her ability to maintain her honor intact that allows her to stay in the game – flirting, trysting, and stealing her girlfriends' boyfriends. The text is ambiguous enough so that, as we shall see shortly, in performance Fenisa's chastity can be called into question, but as the play is written, dishonor is Laura's problem, not Fenisa's. Unlike Don Juan, she does not speak of "goces" ("pleasures") and "burlas" ("deceptions"), but of "amor." She camouflages her desire in a romanticized image of munificence, describing her affection in almost spiritual terms. She is so bountiful that countless men fit in her "soul." She insists over and over that she loves them all. When Lucía counters, "you really did not love a single one of those men" (165), Fenisa becomes indignant.

But Lucía is right. The kind of superficial, immature attachment that Fenisa feels is not love at all; significantly, Catherine Larson sometimes uses the word "crush" in her translation. It is not until nearly the end of the play, when her whole scheme begins to unravel, that Fenisa admits that "no hay gloria como andar / engañando pisaverdes" ("there is nothing greater than deceiving these dandies" [126–7]). She can no longer even pretend to love them; she has to admit to simply toying with them. Like Don Juan, Fenisa seems an insecure, vulnerable adolescent whose exploits allow her to feel superior to her peers. She is like a teenage girl constantly craving attention. Belisa observes shrewdly, "to women like her, it is punishment enough not to pay attention to them" (135). But in seventeenth-century Spain, what tools does a young woman have to attract notice besides her pretty face and figure?

## The Performance

For Karen Berman, the challenge was to bring the court and its inhabit-
ants – shallow, yet fraught with ambiguity – onstage in a way meaningful to
American audiences. Maria Aitken stresses the importance of actors' famil-
iarizing themselves with the period they are playing, since the actor is the
link between the text and the performance. She suggests that the actor study
paintings, costumes, furniture and everyday paraphernalia in order to fill in
the spaces for the audience (85). The actor must know, for example, what a
seventeenth-century Spanish woman might be doing with her hands when she
is relaxing. Would she fold them? Would she sew a garment or fan herself?
This familiarization process is even more essential for the director, who must
guide her actors' movements. Aitken is quick to clarify that the purpose of
historical research is to enrich the cast's and director's understanding of the
play; it does not imply period *mises en scène*.

Today, most dramatic theorists warn against what Peter Brook called
"deadly theatre" – boring, irrelevant theatre that preserves historical plays as
though they were museum pieces (*Empty Space* 9–41). Patrice Pavis notes
that any *mise en scène* that simply reproduces archeologically the historical
context of a play is destined to fail; the purpose of historical research is
to help the director create a new, germane social context for her material
(*Crossroads* 38). Knowing whether an early modern woman would fold her
hands or occupy them with sewing is essential not because the actress must
perform those movements, but because such knowledge reveals certain attitudes toward women and toward leisure that will be pertinent to the new *mise
en scène*.

The obstacles facing Berman might at first seem enormous. The early
modern Spaniard's obsession with honor and chastity are largely meaningless
for today's spectators, and references to life at Court are lost on them. Zayas's
young women are in their twenties, judging from Gerardo's seven-year courtship of Marcia. Yet their behavior corresponds more to what modern audiences might expect of young adolescents – kids who push things almost to the
limit, but usually without going "all the way." Today's young women, especially in workaholic Washington, D. C, where the play was performed, have
more in their heads than chasing men. They may crave attention like Fenisa
or fret over lost lovers like Laura, but the obsessive fussing over "who loves
whom" seems too reminiscent of junior high school behavior to be meaningful to a contemporary public.[3] Thus, Berman had to find some model in
American society by which she could meaningfully translate Zayas's characters. She had to ask herself: What constitutes aristocracy in the United

---

[3]   And, in fact, the David Pasto production at the Chamizal produced just this reaction
among some spectators, who complained that the play was "juvenile" and "pointless."

States? What component of our social fabric consists of rich, spoiled, shallow people for whom sexual conquest is a primary pastime? And how can such empty-headed characters be made interesting? Fortunately, Berman hit on just the right answers.

We do have such an aristocracy in America, of course. The American "court" is Hollywood. Berman reconstructed Fenisa as a spoiled celebrity, not by dressing her in sunglasses and stilettos or by creating a glitzy setting, but by vaguely suggesting, through movement, costume, and props, a recognizably Hollywood environment. "In this age we are living in," Berman explains, "many of our female icons from pop culture behave in a manner similar to Fenisa. We read in the tabloids about the constant stream of men flowing through the lives of such women as Britney Spears and Paris Hilton. Characters in the television shows *Sex and the City* and *Desperate Housewives* are not unlike those in *Friendship Betrayed*" (Mujica, "Zayas" 219). The parallels are striking. Seventeenth-century moralists such as Juan de Mariana condemned young Spanish aristocrats for their decadence, finding in their values, clothes, leisure activities, and penchant for frivolity signs of moral decay. Today, we deplore the lifestyles of our celebrities. We judge their behavior to be outrageous, irresponsible, infantile, and stupid. And yet, like the public in Zayas's time, we are fascinated by our moneyed elite.

We know that Zayas's novellas, which she often presented as *romans à clef,* reached huge audiences of readers hungry for scandal and gossip. Marina S. Brownlee notes in her study of the publishing industry in the seventeenth century that, thanks to mass production, many more people than previously had books, and reading became a popular pastime. People especially enjoyed *romans à clef,* gossipy stories, supposedly true, about the goings-on at court. Around the same time, *relatos de sucesos* – "scandal sheets" similar to today's tabloids – included news of murders and other crimes, as well as gossip and innuendo (Brownlee 77). Zayas exploited this taste for the sensational in her stories, and often added an assurance that the events depicted are true, just as she does at the end of *Friendship Betrayed*: "it is such a true story that a year has not even passed since it happened at court" (195). No matter what kinds of social, political, or moral statements Zayas may have been trying to make with her writing, there is no denying their entertainment value.

Zayas's readers loved trash, and so do we. As scholars, we are reluctant to admit watching *Desperate Housewives* – although some of us not only watch it, but read the secrets of Eva Longoria in the supermarket check-out line. And as scholars, we know we should be analyzing Zayas's play for the moral, sociological, and political implications rather than chortling at Fenisa's exploits. But what draws us in to Berman's production and holds our attention is not the intellectual content, but the naughty thrill of watching a Paris Hilton look-alike snare man after man and almost get away with it. Maybe we shouldn't love her, but we do.

In order to make the transculturation process work, Berman chose a multi-racial, multi-ethnic cast of beautiful actors whose demeanor and body language identified them as hip, young Americans. Mundy Spears, in the role of Fenisa, suggested the crass sexiness and coy dizziness of Paris Hilton. With her long, blond, tied-back hair, svelte figure, and spectacular legginess, she conveyed perfectly the notion of Hollywood glamor. Valeka Nichols, in the role of Belisa, transformed her character into a strong, determined black woman whose striking good looks and self-assured stance suggested a young Angela Bassett. In contrast, Lucía, Fenisa's maid, played by Taisha Cameron, came across as a down-to-earth Hispanic woman who is bored to tears with her mistress's antics, but is shrewd enough to humor her. As Fenisa becomes more and more frenzied over her unmanageable love life, Lucía offers help while at the same time conveying aloofness by always engaging in some activity – eating, filing her nails – while speaking to Fenisa.

Washington audiences are used to "race-blind casting," in which characters are assigned roles irrespective of their ethnicity. This means that directors choose actors of different races without calling attention to the individual actor's color or culture; a black actor might play the role of Friar Lawrence in *Romeo and Juliet*, but he plays it as though he were white. In contrast, Berman calls attention to her actors' cultural identities. For example, Nichols plays Belisa as a tough, black, street-smart sister, the kind of strong, glamorous woman made popular with audiences through the Blaxploitation films of the 1970s, such as Melvin van Peeble's *Sweet Sweetback's Baadasssss Song.* "I did want a modern urban feel to the play," explains Berman, "and I think the multicultural cast achieved that. Belisa's lines seemed to match well with the [image of the] confident black woman [...]. I encouraged my cast to bring their own personalities to the forefront in these roles. Primarily, I was interested in the multi-cultural sisterhood which brought women of all races and ethnicities together" (Mujica, "Zayas" 227–8). To this end, Berman deliberately sought a racially and ethnically diverse cast, although she did not have specific roles destined for members of particular groups. An added benefit of Berman's casting was that the play attracted a large, culturally diverse audience.

Another of Berman's innovations was the modernization of the sexual theme. In her production, Fenisa is clearly sleeping with the men she seduces. "The coy Paris Hilton who is caught on sex tapes and making the nightclub scene with different men each night is an icon of today's voyeurism," says Berman (Mujica, "Zayas" 221–2). Similarly, her Fenisa appeals to the voyeuristic impulses of not only the other characters, who seem to derive a shocked pleasure from her antics, but also of the audience. The director achieves this modification without changing either the text or Fenisa's psychological make-up. Whenever Fenisa speaks of a man entering her "soul," the actress pauses slightly, and through suggestive facial expressions and body movements, imbues the phrase with an alternate sense. For example, when Lucía announces that Lauro is at the door, Fenisa responds, "I have already let him enter my soul" (169). While it would be perfectly possible to utter this sentence matter-of-factly, thereby eliminating the double entendre, Fenisa makes it deliciously suggestive by pausing and smiling wickedly before "soul."

Of course, ways of gleaning public approval have changed. While women in Zayas's time had to keep up appearances, wearing *mantillas* when they went out to protect their reputations, today's celebrities make a spectacle of their sexuality. (Think Paris, Madonna, Britney, and Ellen De Genees.) These public figures become role models for our young people, who see glamour in experimentation. Berman comments: "I think the sexuality of today's youth is similar to that portrayed in Zayas's society." For Berman, today's attitudes toward sex provided a cultural link between Zayas's world and our own. For a director mounting an early modern play, especially one from a foreign culture, the identification of such links is essential. Berman explains: "I've always felt that it was important to make a play relevant for a current-day audience attending. A play only exists in the moment of its playing and for the audience attending. There is no way to recreate the dynamic of Golden Age society and ensure the same reception. Instead, every play must be interpreted for its time, and within the context of the society receiving the play – certainly a postmodern sensibility" (Mujica, "Zayas" 221). Thus, the director must be cognizant not only of the codes embedded in the play that must be "translated" into visual and auditory signs, but also of the receptive capacity of a particular audience.

Berman uses costuming to highlight her characters' sexuality. Rather than period costumes, she opted for a look that would convey "historical" and "modern" as well as "Spanish" and "international" at the same time. She hit upon a fetching combination of bustled skirts and Madonna-like bustiers, with black pants, suggesting underbritches, for Fenisa. Rather than looking to seventeenth-century painters such as Velázquez for ideas, Berman and her costume designer, Martin Schnellinger, found their inspiration in Goya, whose colors are brighter and more sensuous. "The women were somewhat underdressed," explained Berman, "in pieces of underwear, to represent that they were at home – the domain of women – and sexually available. The corseting of the women was particularly important to me as the undergarments of women express society's expectations of the physical shape and freedom, or lack thereof, for women in that culture" (Mujica, "Zayas" 223–4). In both early modern Spain and modern America, says Berman, "women who are molded and cinched at the waist – either by corsets, diet, or liposuction – are considered appealing" (Mujica, "Zayas" 224). Through costuming Berman was able to convey both the women's sexual drive and society's imposition of restraints. In contrast with the women, the men wear suits, also inspired by Goya, since they "navigate the exterior landscape," says Berman (Mujica, "Zayas" 224). The fact that the men are fully clothed, while the women are partially undressed, also conveys through strong visual cues the women's position as quarry.

In order for Berman to develop the notion that women are both predators and prey, it was essential that she lay bare both Fenisa's rapacious sexuality and her vulnerability. As Mundy Spears darts around the stage, one senses Fenisa's growing edginess, which will explode into hysteria toward the end of the play. In order to convey these contradictory internal forces – calculated predacity and frightening vulnerability – the actress has to control every movement and facial expression. Berman achieves her goal by alternating stasis and movement with great precision. Stasis conveys cerebral activity through a scowl, a raised eyebrow, a sigh, or a snarl. But stasis dissolves with increasing frequency into a flurry of seemingly uncontrolled activity.

When Fenisa begins to rant that her extraordinary capacity for love increases her suffering, thereby turning her into a Christ figure, we can only wince at her twisted logic:

> I have lovers by the dozens. Blind god, you are really putting me to the test, especially if you consider the fact that if one man causes suffering, I am suffering ten times over […]. I bow to every one of the men I love; I love them, esteem and adore the ugly and the handsome ones, young boys and old men, rich and poor, and only because they are male. I have the same disease that heaven has, because since God has room for everyone near him, I can make room for all those men inside my heart. (169)

Lucía points out that Fenisa may be demonic rather than godly, perhaps an oblique reference to *El burlador:* "There is also plenty of room in hell, and it is fuller than heaven. Following that line of reason, you must also be in the inferno of love" (169). Fenisa's hyperbolic suffering calls to mind that of celebrity nervous breakdowns. But stars who break down and wind up in rehab programs are not necessarily pretending. They *are* vulnerable because their superficial, publicity-hungry lives do not provide them with the grounding they need to deal with disappointment. When Fenisa senses her male harem slipping away from her, she has the baroque equivalent of an emotional collapse. Berman's depiction of Fenisa suggests that, like today's stars, Zayas's female predator is profoundly lacking, not because she needs a man to give her direction, but because those whose only satisfaction lies in the admiration of others will be devastated when that admiration evaporates.

Berman develops three visual metaphors to convey the nature of her characters' interpersonal relationships: the hunt, the game, and the dance. For Zayas's characters as for today's celebrities, life is a continual chase, a hunt for the next love affair that will provide prestige or publicity. Zayas's women remark repeatedly that the men they pursue are "honorable," meaning that these men have the social standing necessary to make the pursuit worthwhile. A good "catch" for a starlet would be a man as celebrated as she, or more so, a man whose name, when coupled with hers, will assure front-page coverage. Both Zayas's characters and today's celebrities are driven by a kind of basic predatory instinct, which Berman conveys through animal skins strewn over the set, animal masks, prowling movements, clawing gestures, and props such as bows and arrows and darts. When Fenisa gives Liseo the note with which she intends to "catch" him (61–3), she lowers it on a fishing pole. Later, thinking she has "caught" Lauro, she pets him like a dog. By constantly exchanging masks with one another, the characters suggest their interchangeability and also their superficiality and volatility. "Everyone in the play is pursuing the opposite sex," remarks Berman, noting that the text is full of animal references: León refers to a "clawing cat" and Belisa, to "wild beasts," a "lion's cruelty," the "proud and arrogant wolf," and a "fox." Lucía says that she has "a recipe for domesticating wild animals," and Liseo calls Laura a "wild beast." Fenisa calls herself a "lion" (Mujica, "Zayas" 223).

While Zayas's upper-class characters often veil their animal instincts in the language of love, the servants are more open about their appetites. León mocks his master's glorification of chastity, expressing candidly his lust for bawdy serving maids. He celebrates sexual hunger, insisting that women love men who "eat meat" and scorn as "capons" those who are abstinent (59). Berman underscores León's unrestrained sexuality by transforming him into a bisexual for whom desire is not limited by sex or gender. She builds on the traditional master–servant relationship, with its intrinsic element of male bonding, by depicting León as a tease who repeatedly comes on to Liseo. Although Berman says she sees potential homosexuality in the relationship among the women as well,[4] it is León's lust for Liseo that she explored more clearly in this production.[5]

Berman conveys the childish, game-like quality of the characters' behavior through visual metaphors suggesting play. At times the characters' movements hint of tag or leap-frog. The implication is that these are people who are caught in a whirlwind of shallow emotions, with no moral foundation or psychological grounding. A see-saw stage left on which different pairs of actors balance and bob and from which they occasionally fall suggests not only immaturity but also instability. These are people, the visual metaphor suggests, who constantly "tip" reality through deception, but sometimes their ploys backfire and land them in the mud.

---

4  For an exploration of this aspect of the play, see María José Delgado, "Lesbiagrafisis."

5  Berman suggested after the July 2006 production that she might develop this aspect of the women's relationships between themselves in a future production of the play.

The most spectacular use of game imagery is the finale, which consists of an elaborate musical chairs dance. Berman incorporates music and dance throughout the play, using them to imbue the work with a contemporary feel. For example, she transforms Gerardo's servants' songs into blues numbers, which Antonio[6] croons Elvis-style, complete with guitar and hip gyrations. Other songs integrate Spanish guitar and country rock melodies. In addition, Marcia sings her long monologues. The stunning musical chairs dance that closes the play reintegrates not only these musical themes, but also the animal motif. An erotic, celebratory wedding dance that fuses classical flamenco and contemporary American guitar with beast-like writhing, stalking, and heavy breathing, the finale suggests both a monumental gender battle and a recon-ciliation. "It's a partner dance in which each person settles in with a lover, only to change partners, which mirrors the action of the show," explains Berman. "Just as each pairing gets comfortable, each woman literally kicks her partner away in order to find another man" (Mujica, "Zayas" 229–30). At the end of this sexually charged musical chairs dance, Fenisa is left alone, while all the other characters are paired.

In the past three decades debates have arisen over whether or not it is really possible to communicate the essence of one culture to another through theatre, that is, whether or not theatre produced at a particular time for a particular audience is really intelligible to a different public in a different context.[7] Peter Brook defends theatrical interculturalism, asserting that theatre audiences are always confronted with specific as well as universal truths, and that although they may miss particular references, they will grasp sweeping generalities. For Brook, theatre makes possible communication between members of different societies (*Open Door*). At the other extreme, new historicists question the very notion of universality, arguing that ideals traditionally promoted as universal are actually those of the power elite. For Berman, transcultural communication is not only a possibility, but one of the most stimulating aspects of the directing experience. Making the play meaningful for the "ephemeral here and now" is one of the attractions of directing: "It is certainly an exciting part of a director's task to conceptu-alize any play. Translating a play from one culture to another, and one era to another, creates additional joys and challenges" (Mujica, "Zayas" 222). But in order to conceptualize Zayas's play successfully, Berman had to nego-tiate a script that was already a mediation between early modern Spain and contemporary America.

For her production Berman used *Friendship Betrayed,* Catherine Larson's translation of the Valerie Hegstrom edition of *La tradición en la amistad.* Larson's translation, in contemporary American prose, shows a keen sensi-

---

6   Sung by Antonio and Fabio in Zayas's original.
7   We actually do not know whether Zayas's play was performed in her own time.

tivity to the original and a sharp ear for idiomatic English. Occasionally, one might quibble with her choice of words: "self control" is an inaccurate and misleading translation of "voluntad" (44–5); "que coja clavelinas" might have better been translated as "to hell with him" instead of "let him go pick flowers" (175); and "they'd have really knocked the hell out of each other" captures the spirit of "con hermoso brio, / se asían de las melenas," better than "those two really would be going after each other with vigor" (189). Larson writes in her introduction to the translation that the editor's nixing of contractions (can't, don't) had certain drawbacks (28). The most obvious of these is the unnatural sound of parts of the dialogue. However, in spite of these difficulties, the translation as a whole is truly inspired – accurate, colloquial, and fluent.

As a script, Berman finds the translation "very contemporary, very readable, and very playable" (Mujica, "Zayas" 219). She appreciates that Larson did not attempt to render Zayas's stanzas into English verse, which might have resulted in an even more stilted text, but instead used prose, thereby heightening "the contemporary flavor" and "making it audience-friendly" (Mujica, "Zayas" 219). In her production Berman drew attention to the Spanish source by inserting snippets of the original text into the English translation. María Aitken notes that when viewing classical comedies in English, such as Shakespeare's *A Midsummer Night's Dream* or *As You Like It*, most English-speaking spectators do not react to the cleverness of the wordplay, but to the actor's apparently spontaneous response. The repartee often depends on linguistic games and contextual references too distant from spectators to be immediately grasped, but audiences do react to the dynamic onstage. That is why Aitken insists that a witty script is not enough: "If the audience has to pant after us, we are doing something wrong. But if we understand the game and communicate not only the meaning but our relish for the form, the audience will keep up with us, and the experience will make *the audience* witty" (59). This is precisely what Berman achieved. Although most of her audience probably did not understand the Spanish fragments, the actors' vitality and perfect timing kept the viewers engaged.

Through a clever, innovative use of Catherine Larson's *linguistic* translation, an in-depth analysis of the aspects of the play that lend themselves to *cultural* translation, and the meticulous transformation of these two translations into the language of performance, Karen Berman achieved a clever, engaging, meaningful production of Zayas's *Friendship Betrayed*.

# WORKS CITED

PRIMARY SOURCES CITED: PLAYS

Miscellaneous Collections
*Diez comedias del Siglo de Oro* [*La Numancia* (Cervantes); *Fuenteovejuna* (Lope de Vega); *La Estrella de Sevilla; El burlador de Sevilla* (Tirso de Molina); *Las mocedades del Cid* (Guillén de Castro); *El esclavo del demonio* (Mira de Amescua); *La verdad sospechosa* (Ruiz de Alarcón); *La vida es sueño* (Calderón); *Del rey abajo, ninguno* (Rojas Zorrilla); *El desdén con el desdén* (Moreto)]. Eds. José Martel and Hymen Alpern. Rev. Leonard Mades. 2nd edn. New York: Harper & Row, 1968.
*Eight Spanish Plays of the Golden Age* [*The Gallant, the Bawd, and the Fair Lady* (Juan Ruiz); *The Mask* (Lope de Rueda); *Peribáñez and the Comendador of Ocaña* (Lope de Vega); *Pedro, the Artful Dodger* (Cervantes); *The Jealous Old Man* (Cervantes); *The Playboy of Seville* (Tirso de Molina); *The Mayor of Zalamea* (Calderón); *The Mystery Play of Elche*]. Trans. and ed. Walter Starkie. New York: Modern Library, 1964.
*Spanish Drama* [*The Olives* (Lope de Rueda); *The Vigilant Sentinel* (Cervantes); *Fuente Ovejuna* (Lope de Vega); *The Rogue of Seville* (Tirso de Molina); *The Truth Suspected* (Ruiz de Alarcón); *Life Is a Dream* (Calderón); *When a Girl Says Yes* (Moratín); *The Great Galeoto* (Echegaray); *The Bonds of Interest* (Benavente); *Blood Wedding* (García Lorca)]. Ed. and introd. Angel Flores. New York: Bantam, 1962.
*The Theatre of Don Juan: A Collection of Plays and Views, 1630–1963*. Ed. Oscar Mandel. Lincoln: U of Nebraska P, 1963.
*Three Spanish Golden Age Plays* [*The Duchess of Amalfi's Steward* (Lope de Vega), *The Capulets and Montagues* (Lope de Vega)], *Cleopatra* (Rojas Zorrilla). Trans. and introd. Gwynne Edwards. London: Methuen, 2005.
Tuke, Samuel. *The Adventures of Five Hours*, reprinted from the folio of 1663 and the third impression of 1671, together with Coello's *Los empeños de seis horas*. Ed. A. E. H. Swaen. Amsterdam: Swets & Zeitlinger, 1927.

Plays by Author
Calderón de la Barca, Pedro
*La dama duende*. Ed. Fausta Antonucci. Introd. Marc Vitse. Barcelona: Crítica, 1999.
*Las dos versiones dramáticas primitivas del Don Juan: El burlador de Sevilla*

*y convidado de piedra y Tan largo me lo fiáis*. Reproducción en facsimile de las ediciones *princeps*. Ed. Xavier A. Fernández. Madrid: Revista Estudios, 1988.

*Eight Dramas of Calderón* [*The Painter of His Own Dishonour; Keep Your Own Secret; Gil Perez, the Gallician; Three Judgments at a Blow; The Mayor of Zalamea; Beware of Smooth Water; The Mighty Magician; Such Stuff as Dreams Are Made Of*]. Trans. Edward FitzGerald. 1853/1902. Foreword Margaret R. Greer. Urbana: U of Illinois P, 2000.

*Four Comedies* [*From Bad to Worse; The Secret Spoken Aloud; The Worst Is Not Always Certain; The Advantages and Disadvantages of a Name*]. Trans. Kenneth Muir. Notes Ann L. Mackenzie. Lexington: UP of Kentucky, 1980.

*The Great Stage of the World*. Trans. George W. Brandt. Manchester: Manchester UP, 1976.

*The Last Days of Don Juan*. Adapt. Nick Dear. Bath: Absolute, 1990.

*Life Is a Dream*. Trans. and introd. John Clifford. London: N. Hern Books, 1998.

*Life's a Dream*. Trans. Michael Kidd. Boulder: UP of Colorado, 2004.

*Love Is No Laughing Matter (No hay burlas con el amor)*. Eds. and trans. Don Cruickshank and Seán Page. Warminster: Aris & Phillips, 1986.

*The Mayor of Zalamea, Life's a Dream, The Great Theatre of the World: Three Plays by Pedro Calderón de la Barca*. Trans. Adrian Mitchell and John Barton. Bath: Absolute, 1990.

*El médico de su honra*. Ed. Don Cruickshank. Madrid: Castalia, 1987.

*The Painter of Dishonour*. Trans. David Johnston and Laurence Boswell. Bath: Absolute, 1995.

*The Painter of His Dishonour / El pintor de su deshonra*. Ed. and trans. Alan K. G. Patterson. Warminster: Aris & Phillips, 1991.

*Le Prince Constant / El príncipe constante*. Ed. and trans. Bernard Sesé. Paris: Aubier, 1989.

*The Schism in England*. Eds. and trans. Kenneth Muir and Ann L. Mackenzie. Warminster: Aris & Phillips, 1990.

*Six Plays* [*Secret Vengeance for Secret Insult; Devotion to the Cross; The Mayor of Zalamea; The Phantom Lady; Life Is a Dream; The Crown of Absalom*]. Trans. Edwin Honig. New York: IASTA Press, 1993.

*Six Plays* [*Life Is a Dream; The Wonder-Working Magician; The Constant Prince; The Devotion of the Cross; Love after Death; Belshazzar's Feast*]. Trans. Denis Florence MacCarthy. Rev. Henry W. Wells. New York: Las Américas, 1961.

*The Surgeon of His Honour*. Trans. Roy Campbell. Introd. Everett W. Hesse. Madison: U of Wisconsin P, 1960.

*Three Comedies* [*A House with Two Doors is Difficult to Guard; Mornings of April and May; No Trifling with Love*]. Trans. Kenneth Muir and Ann L. Mackenzie. Lexington: UP of Kentucky, 1985.

*La vida es sueño*. Ed. José M. Ruano de la Haza. Madrid: Clásicos Castalia, 1994.

Castro, Guillén de
  *Las mocedades del Cid*. Ed. Stefano Arata. Introd. Aurora Egido. Barcelona: Crítica, 1996.
Cervantes, Miguel de
  *Eight Interludes*. Trans. Dawn Smith. London: J. M. Dent, 1996.
  *Entremeses*. Ed. Nicholas Spadaccini. Madrid: Cátedra, 1982.
  *The Interludes of Cervantes*. Trans. Edwin Honig. New York: New American Library, 1964.
  *The Interludes of Cervantes*. Trans. Sylvanus Griswold Morley. 1948. New York: Greenwood, 1969.
  *Pedro, the Great Pretender*. Trans. Philip Osment. London: Oberon, 2004.
Claramonte, Andrés de
  *Andrés de Claramonte y "El burlador de Sevilla."* Ed. Alfredo Rodríguez López-Vázquez. Teatro del Siglo de Oro 3. Kassel: Reichenberger, 1987.
Cruz, Sor Juana Inés de la
  *Festejo de* Los empeños de una casa. *Obras completas de Sor Juana Inés de la Cruz*. Vol. 4. Ed. Alberto G. Salceda. Mexico, D. F.: Fondo de Cultura Económica, 1957.
  *House of Desires: A Play by Sor Juana Inés de la Cruz*. Trans. Catherine M. Boyle. London: Oberon, 2004.
Moreto, Agustín
  *El desdén con el desdén*. Ed. Vern Williamsen. 1995. <http://www.comedias.org/moreto/Desden.pdf>.
  *Spite for Spite*. Trans. Dakin Matthews. Lyme, NH: Smith and Kraus, 1995.
  *Spite for Spite*. Trans. Dakin Matthews. Acting Edition. Los Angeles: Andak Theatrical Services, 2004.
Pérez de Montalbán, Juan
  *La más constante mujer. Drámaticos contemporáneos de Lope de Vega*. Ed. Ramón de Mesonero Romanos. Biblioteca de Autores Españoles. Vol. 45. Madrid: Rivadeneyra, 1858. 495–511.
Ruiz de Alarcón, Juan
  *Las paredes oyen. Parte primera de las comedias de don Juan Ruiz de Alarcón*. Madrid: Juan González, 1628. Ed. Vern Williamsen. 1998. <http://www.comedias.org/alarcon/Pareoy.html.>
  *The Proof of the Promise*. Trans. Dakin Matthews. Acting Edition. Los Angeles: Andak Theatrical Services, 2001.
  *La prueba de las promesas. Parte segunda de las comedias de don Juan Ruiz de Alarcón*. Barcelona, 1634. Ed. Vern Williamsen. 1998. <http://www.comedias.org/alarcon/Prupro.html>.
  *The Truth Can't Be Trusted*. Trans. Dakin Matthews. New Orleans: UP of the South, 1998.
  *The Truth Can't Be Trusted*. Trans. Dakin Matthews. Acting Edition. Los Angeles: Andak Theatrical Services, 2000.
  *La verdad sospechosa*. Ed. Vern Williamsen. 1986. <http://www.comedias.org/alarcon/Versos.html>.

*The Walls Have Ears*. Trans. Dakin Matthews. New Orleans: UP of the South, 1998.

Tirso de Molina [Gabriel Téllez]

*El burlador de Sevilla*. Ed. Américo Castro. 5th edn. Madrid: Espasa Calpe, 1952.

*El burlador de Sevilla*. Ed. James A. Parr. 1994. Ashville, NC: Pegasus, 2000.

*El burlador de Sevilla*. Ed. Vern Williamsen. 2001. <http://www.comedias.org/tirso/Bursev.html>.

*El burlador de Sevilla, atribuída tradicionalmente a Tirso de Molina*. Ed. Alfredo Rodríguez López-Vázquez. Kassel: Reichenberger, 1987. 7th edn. Letras Hispánicas. Madrid: Cátedra, 1995.

*El burlador de Sevilla y convidado de piedra*. Ed. Luis Vázquez. Madrid: Revista Estudios, 1988.

*El condenado por desconfiado*. Ed. Daniel Rogers. Oxford: Pergamon, 1974.

*Don Gil of the Green Breeches*. Trans. Gordon Minter. Warminster: Aris & Philips, 1991.

*Don Juan, Ladykiller of Seville*. Trans. Michael Kidd. Unpub. ms.

*Don Juan, The Trickster of Seville*. Trans. Dakin Matthews. Los Angeles: Andak Theatrical Services, 2006.

*Las dos versiones dramáticas primitivas del Don Juan:* El burlador de Sevilla y convidado de piedra *y* Tan largo me lo fiáis. Reproducción en facsimile de las ediciones *princeps*. Ed. Xavier A. Fernández. Madrid: Revista Estudios, 1988.

*Marta la piadosa; Don Gil de las calzas verdes*. Ed. Ignacio Arellano. Kassel: Reichenberger, 1988.

*Obras dramáticas completas*. Ed. Blanca de los Ríos. 2nd edn. Vol. 3. Madrid: Aguilar, 1968.

*The Playboy of Seville, or Supper with a Statue*. Trans. Adrienne M. Schizzano and Oscar Mandel. *The Theatre of Don Juan. A Collection of Plays and Views, 1630–1963*. Ed. Oscar Mandel. Lincoln: U of Nebraska P, 1963. 47–99.

*The Rape of Tamar*. Trans. Paul Whitworth. London: Oberon, 1999.

*Tamar's Revenge*. Trans. and ed. John Lyon. Warminster: Aris & Phillips, 1988.

*Tamar's Revenge*. Trans. James Fenton. London: Oberon, 2004.

*The Trickster of Seville and the Stone Guest (El Burlador de Sevilla y el convidado de piedra)*. Trans. Gwynne Edwards. 1986. Warminster: Aris & Phillips, 1992.

*Two Plays: Damned for Despair, Don Gil of the Green Breeches*. Trans & adapt. Laurence Boswell, Jonathan Thacker, and Deirdre McKenna. Bath: Absolute, 1992.

*La venganza de Tamar*. Ed. Alan K. G. Paterson. Cambridge: Cambridge UP, 1969.

Vega Carpio, Lope Félix de
   *A Bond Honoured.* Trans. and adapt. John Osborne. London: Faber & Faber,
      1966.
   *El caballero de Olmedo.* Ed. Joseph Pérez. Madrid: Castalia, 1983.
   *El castigo sin venganza.* Ed. José María Díez Borque. Madrid: Espasa Calpe,
      1987.
   *Comedias escogidas de Frey Lope Félix de Vega Carpio.* Biblioteca de Autores
      Españoles. Vol. 52. Madrid: Atlas, 1952.
   *La dama boba.* Ed. Diego Marín. Madrid: Cátedra, 1987.
   *The Dog in the Manger (El perro del hortelano).* Trans. Victor Dixon. Ottawa:
      Dovehouse, 1990.
   *The Dog in the Manger.* Trans. David Johnston. London: Oberon, 2004.
   *The Duchess of Amalfi's Steward (El mayordomo de la duquesa de Amalfi).*
      Trans. Cynthia Rodriguez-Badendyck. Ottawa: Dovehouse, 1985.
   *Es de Lope. Texto Integro de* El perro del hortelano *de Lope de Vega en versión
      de Emilio Hernández.* Madrid: Ayuntamiento de Madrid, 2003.
   *Five Plays* [*Peribáñez; Fuenteovejuna; The Dog in the Manger; The Knight
      from Olmedo; Justice without Revenge*]. Trans. Jill Booty. New York: Hill
      & Wang, 1961.
   *Fuente Ovejuna.* Ed. and trans. Victor Dixon. Warminster: Aris & Phillips,
      1989.
   *Fuente Ovejuna; Lost in a Mirror (El castigo sin venganza).* Adapt. Adrian
      Mitchell. Introd. Nicholas Dromgoole. Bristol: Absolute, 1989.
   *The Great Pretenders. The Gentleman from Olmedo. Two Plays by Lope de
      Vega.* Trans. David Johnston. Bath: Absolute, 1992.
   *Peribanez.* Trans. Tanya Ronder. London: Nick Hern, 2003.
   *Peribáñez and the Comendador de Ocaña.* Ed. and trans. James Lloyd. Warm-
      inster: Aris & Phillips, 1990.
   *Peribáñez y el comendador de Ocaña / La dama boba.* Ed. Alonso Zamora
      Vicente. Clásicos Castellanos. Madrid: Espasa Calpe, 1978.
   *El perro del hortelano.* Ed. Victor Dixon. London: Tamesis, 1981.
   *El perro del hortelano / El castigo sin venganza.* Ed. A. David Kossoff.
      Madrid: Castalia, 1993.
   *La prueba de los ingenios. Obras de Lope de Vega.* Ed. Marcelino Menéndez
      Pelayo. Biblioteca de Autores Españoles. Vol. 246. Madrid: Atlas, 1971.
      277–338.
   *El villano en su rincón.* Ed. Juan María Marín. Madrid: Cátedra, 1987.
Zayas y Sotomayor, María
   *La traición en la amistad.* Ed. Bárbara López-Mayhew. Newark, DE: Juan de
      la Cuesta, 2003.
   *La traición en la amistad.* Ed. Michael J. McGrath. Newark, DE: Cervantes
      & Co. / European Masterpieces, 2006.
   *La traición en la amistad / Friendship Betrayed.* Ed. Valerie Hegstrom. Trans.
      Catherine Larson. Lewisburg, PA: Bucknell UP, 1999.

Other Primary Sources

Aesop
    *Fables.* Trans. George Fyler Townsend. Garden City, NJ: Doubleday, 1968.
Anonymous
    "Camiñaba Don Galán." *Don Juan y su evolución dramática.* Ed. Arcadio
        Baquero. 2 vols. Madrid: Nacional, 1966.
Covarrubias, Sebastián de
    *Tesoro de la lengua castellana o española según la impresión de 1611, con
        las adiciones de Benito Remigio Noydens publicadas en la de 1674.* Ed.
        Martín de Riquer. Barcelona: Horta, 1943.
Cruz, Sor Juana Inés de la
    *Poems, Protest, and a Dream: Selected Writings.* Trans. Margaret Sayers
        Peden. London: Penguin, 1997.
    *Sor Juana's Love Poems.* Trans. Joan Larkin and Jaime Manrique. Madison:
        U of Wisconsin P, 2003.
Horace [Quintus Horatius Flaccus]
    *Satires, Epistles and Ars Poetica.* Trans. H. Rushton Fairclough. The Loeb
        Classical Library. Cambridge, MA: Harvard UP, 1970.
La Fontaine, Jean de
    *The Complete Fables of Jean de la Fontaine.* Ed. and trans. Norman B. Spector.
        Evanston, IL: Northwestern UP, 1988.
López Pinciano, Alonso
    *Philosophía antigua poética.* Ed. Alfredo Carballo Picazo. 3 vols. Madrid:
        CSIC, 1973.
Mariana, Juan de
    *Obras.* Biblioteca de Autores Españoles. Vol. 30. Madrid: Rivadeneyra,
        1854.
Ovid [Publius Ovidius Naso]
    *The Art of Love, and Other Poems.* Trans. J. H. Mozley. The Loeb Classical
        Library. London: Heinemann, 1962.
Shelley, Percy Bysshe
    "To Thomas Love Peacock." *The Letters of Percy Bysshe Shelley.* Vol. II:
        *Shelley in Italy.* Ed. Frederick L. Jones. Oxford: Clarendon, 1964.
Vega Carpio, Lope Félix de
    *Arte nuevo de hacer comedias en este tiempo.* Madrid: Espasa Calpe, 1967.
    *The New Art of Writing Plays.* Trans. William T. Brewster. Introd. Brander
        Matthews. New York: Dramatic Museum of Columbia U, 1914.
Zayas y Sotomayor, María de
    *The Enchantments of Love: Amorous and Exemplary Novels.* Trans. H. Patsy
        Boyer. Berkeley: U of California P, 1990.
    *Tres novelas amorosas y tres desengaños amorosos.* Ed. Alicia Redondo
        Goicoechea. Madrid: Castalia, 1989.

REVIEWS OF PERFORMANCES

Benach, Joan-Antón. "El Tirso trágico y gritado de Plaza." Rev. of *La venganza de Tamar*, by Tirso de Molina. Compañía Nacional de Teatro Clásico. Barcelona. *La Vanguardia* 5 Oct. 1997.

Billington, Michael. Rev. of *The Dog in the Manger*, by Lope de Vega. Royal Shakespeare Company. Stratford-upon-Avon. *Guardian* 22 Apr. 2004.

——. Rev. of *House of Desires*, by Sor Juana Inés de la Cruz. Royal Shakespeare Company. Stratford-upon-Avon. *Guardian* 9 Jul. 2004.

——. Rev. of *Life Is a Dream*, by Pedro Calderón de la Barca. Royal Lyceum Theatre Company. Edinburgh Festival. *Guardian* 20 Aug. 1998.

——. Rev. of *Life's a Dream*, by Pedro Calderón de la Barca. Royal Shakespeare Company. The Other Place. Stratford-upon-Avon. *Guardian* 1 Dec. 1983.

——. Rev. of *The Mayor of Zalamea*, by Pedro Calderón de la Barca. National Theatre. London. *Guardian* 13 Aug. 1981.

——. Rev. of *Romeo and Juliet*, by William Shakespeare. Royal Shakespeare Company. Stratford-upon-Avon. *Guardian* 19 Apr. 2006.

Brantley, Ben. "Metaphysical Wrestling, With No Holds Barred." Rev. of *Life Is a Dream*, by Pedro Calderón de la Barca. Royal Lyceum Company. Harvey Lichtenstein Theater of the Brooklyn Academy of Music. *The New York Times* 14 Oct. 1999.

Bravo, Julio. Rev. of *La venganza de Tamar*, by Tirso de Molina. Compañía Nacional de Teatro Clásico. Madrid. *ABC* 11 Dec. 1997.

Bruckner, D. J. R. "Mocking Social Custom since the 17th Century." Rev. of *The Phantom Lady*, by Pedro Calderón de la Barca. Pearl Theater Company. New York. *The New York Times* 24 Jan. 2002.

Chaudhuri, Una. "Populist Mechanics." Rev. of *Fuente Ovejuna*, by Lope de Vega. The National Asian American Theatre Company. Intar Theatre. New York. *The Village Voice* 23–29 Oct. 2002.

Christiansen, Rupert. Rev. of *Spite for Spite*, by Agustín Moreto. Writer's Theatre. Glencoe, IL. *The Chicago Tribune* 12 Sept. 2000.

Clapp, Susannah. Rev. of *The Dog in the Manger*, by Lope de Vega. Royal Shakespeare Company. Stratford-upon-Avon. *Observer* 25 Apr. 2004.

de Jongh, Nicholas. Rev. of *Life's a Dream*. Royal Shakespeare Company. The Other Place. Stratford-upon-Avon. *Guardian* 5–7 May 1984.

Escarré, Josep. Rev. of *La venganza de Tamar*, by Tirso de Molina. Compañía Nacional de Teatro Clásico. Teatre Victòria. Barcelona. *La Vanguardia* 2 Oct. 1997.

*Evening Standard*. Rev. of *Fuente Ovejuna*, by Lope de Vega. National Theatre. Cottesloe. London. Jan. 1989.

Feay, Suzanne. Rev. of *Peribáñez*, by Lope de Vega. Young Vic. London. *Independent on Sunday* 18 May 2003.

Fenton, James. "Honour Bound." Rev. of *Peribanez*, by Lope de Vega. Young Vic. London. *Guardian* 24 May 2003.

Fletcher, Jackie. Rev. of *Life's a Dream*, by Pedro Calderón de la Barca. Blue Elephant Theatre. London. *British Theatre Guide* Sept. 2004.

Galindo, Carlos. "Tirso reflexionó sobre la violencia y la venganza, algo que cobra triste actualidad." Rev. of *La venganza de Tamar,* by Tirso de Molina. Compañía Nacional de Teatro Clásico. Madrid. *ABC* 17 Jul. 1997.

Gardner, Lyn. Rev. of *The Gentleman from Olmedo*, by Lope de Vega. Watermill Theatre. Newbury. *Guardian* 28 Apr. 2004.

Gussow, Mel. Rev. of *Life Is a Dream,* by Pedro Calderón de la Barca. Intar. New York. *The New York Times* 4 June 1981.

Guzmán, Almudena. "Por goleada." Rev. of *Tamar's Revenge*, by Tirso de Molina. Royal Shakespeare Company. Madrid. *ABC* 1 Nov. 2004.

Haro Tecglén, Eduardo. "Melodrama de gritos." Rev. of *La venganza de Tamar,* by Tirso de Molina. Compañía Nacional de Teatro Clásico. Madrid. *El País* 13 Dec. 1997.

Kelly, Kevin. Rev. of *Life Is a Dream*, by Pedro Calderón de la Barca. American Repertory Theatre. Cambridge, MA. *Boston Globe* 2 June 1989.

Kendt, Rob. "Ageless Confection Is Still Sweet." Rev. of *Spite for Spite*, by Agustín Moreto. Andak Stage Company. NewPlace Theatre Center. N. Hollywood. *Los Angeles Times* 26 Mar. 2004.

Letts, Quentin. Rev. of *Romeo and Juliet,* by William Shakespeare. Royal Shakespeare Company. Stratford-upon-Avon. *Daily Mail* 19 Apr. 2006.

Ley, Pablo. "Perdidos de Tamar." Rev. of *La venganza de Tamar*, by Tirso de Molina. Compañía Nacional de Teatro Clásico. Madrid. *El País* 6 Oct. 1997.

Lohrey, David. Rev. of *The Phantom Lady*, by Pedro Calderón de la Barca. Pearl Theatre Company. New York. *CurtainUp.com* 23 Jan. 2002.

———. Rev. of *The Wonder*, by Susanna Centlivre. Gloria Maddox Theatre. New York. *CurtainUp.com* 27 Jan. 2002.

López Sancho, Lorenzo. Rev. of *La venganza de Tamar* by Tirso de Molina. Compañía Nacional de Teatro Clásico. Madrid. *ABC* 14 Dec. 1997.

Macaulay, Alastair. Rev. of *The Wonder* by Susanna Centlivre. The Other Company. The White Bear. London. *Financial Times* 8 Nov. 2006.

"Nariz Azul." Rev. of *The Mayor of Zalamea*, by Pedro Calderón de la Barca. Everyman Playhouse. Liverpool. *bbc.co.uk* 24 Feb. 2004.

Pasto, David. Rev. of *Life Is a Dream,* by Pedro Calderón de la Barca. American Repertory Theatre. Boston. 10 June 1989. *Theatre Journal* 42 (May 1990): 251–2.

Pérez de Olaguer, Gonzalo. "El grito por encima de la razón." Rev. of *La venganza de Tamar*, by Tirso de Molina. Compañía Nacional de Teatro Clásico. Madrid. *El Periódico* 12 Oct. 1997.

Shuttleworth, Ian. Rev. of *The Gentleman from Olmedo*, by Lope de Vega. Watermill Theatre. Newbury. *The Financial Times* Apr. 2004.

Taylor, Paul. "Enter a New Bard." Rev. of *Peribanez*, by Lope de Vega. Young Vic. London. *Independent Review* 24 Apr. 2003.

Thacker, Jonathan. Rev. of *Peribanez*, by Lope de Vega. Young Vic. London. *Comedia Performance* 1 (2004): 260–5.

Walker, Lynne. Rev. of *The Mayor of Zalamea*, by Pedro Calderón de la Barca. Everyman Playhouse. Liverpool. *The Independent* 2 Mar. 2004.

Wechter, Aleksei. Rev. of *Peribáñez*, by Lope de Vega. Company B. Sydney, Australia. *SydneyStageOnline* 27 Jul. 2006.

Weimer, Christopher. Rev. of *Tamar's Revenge*, by Tirso de Molina. Royal Shakespeare Company. Stratford-upon-Avon *Comedia Performance* 2 (2005): 234–7.

Weiss, Hedy. Rev. of *Spite for Spite*, by Agustín Moreto. Writers' Theatre. Glencoe, IL. *Chicago Sun Times* 12 Sept. 2000.


SECONDARY SOURCES


Aitken, Maria. *Style: Acting in High Comedy.* New York: Applause, 1996.

Allen, Ned B. "The Sources of Dryden's *The Mock Astrologer.*" *Philological Quarterly* 36 (1957): 453–64.

——. *The Sources of John Dryden's Comedies.* 1935. New York: Gordian, 1967.

Allison, A. F. *English Translations from the Spanish and Portuguese to the Year 1700. An Annotated Catalogue of the Extant Printed Versions (excluding Dramatic Adaptations).* [London]: Dawson of Pall Mall, 1974.

Alvarez, Román, and M. Carmen-Africa Vidal, eds. *Translation, Power, Subversion.* Clevedon: Multilingual Matters, 1996.

Arnott, Peter D. *The Theater in Its Time.* Boston: Little, Brown, 1981.

Austin, J. L. *How to Do Things with Words.* Eds. J. O. Urmson and Marina Sbisà. Cambridge, MA: Harvard UP, 1975.

Bal, Mieke, ed. *The Practice of Cultural Analysis: Exposing Interdisciplinary Interpretation.* Stanford: Stanford UP, 1999.

Bamber, Linda. *Comic Women, Tragic Men. A Study of Gender and Genre in Shakespeare.* Stanford: Stanford UP, 1982.

Baquero, Arcadio. *Don Juan y su evolución dramática.* 2 vols. Madrid: Editora Nacional, 1966.

Barahona, Renato. *Sex Crimes, Honour, and the Law in Early Modern Spain: Vizcaya, 1528–1735.* Toronto: U of Toronto P, 2003.

Barnstone, Willis. *The Poetics of Translation: History, Theory, Practice.* New Haven: Yale UP, 1993.

Barthes, Roland. *Image, Music, Text.* Trans. Stephen Heath. London: Fontana, 1977.

Barton, John. *Playing Shakespeare.* London: Methuen, 1984.

Bassnett-McGuire, Susan. "Ways Through the Labyrinth: Strategies and Methods for Translating Theatre Texts." *The Manipulation of Literature: Studies in Literary Translation.* Ed. Theo Hermans. New York: St. Martin's, 1985. 87–102.

Bate, Jonathan. *The Genius of Shakespeare.* New York and Oxford: Oxford UP, 1998.

Baudrillard, Jean. "On Seduction." *Selected Writings.* Ed. Mark Poster. Stanford: Stanford UP, 1988. 149–65.

Beardsley, Jr, Theodore S. *Hispano-Classical Translations Printed Between 1482–1699.* Pittsburgh: Duquesne UP, 1970.

Benabu, Isaac. *Reading for the Stage: Calderón and His Contemporaries.* London: Tamesis, 2003.

——. "Reading the Opening of a Play: Tirso's *El burlador de Sevilla.*" *Bulletin of the Comediantes* 47 (1995): 191–200.

Benedetti, Jean. *Stanislavski and the Actor.* London: Routledge, 1998.

Bénichou, Paul. *Romancero judeo-español de Marruecos.* Madrid: Castalia, 1968.

Bentley, Eric. "The Universality of the *Comedia.*" *Hispanic Review* 38 (1970): 147–62.

Bentley, Gerald Eades. *The Jacobean and Caroline Stage.* 7 vols. Oxford: Clarendon, 1941–68.

Besterman, Theodore, ed. *Voltaire on Shakespeare.* Studies on Voltaire and the Eighteenth Century. Vol. 54. Geneva: Institut et Musée Voltaire, 1967.

Bevis, Richard W. *English Drama: Restoration and Eighteenth Century, 1660–1789.* London and New York: Longman, 1988.

Boase-Beier, Jean, and Michael Holman, eds. *The Practices of Literary Translation: Constraints and Creativity.* Manchester: St Jerome, 1999.

Bowers, Fredson, gen. ed. *The Dramatic Works in the Beaumont and Fletcher Canon.* 10 vols. Cambridge: Cambridge UP, 1966–96.

Bowman, James. *Honor: A History.* New York: Encounter, 2006.

Brook, Peter. *The Empty Space.* New York: Atheneum, 1968.

Brown, John Russell. "Foreign Shakespeare and English-speaking Audiences." *Foreign Shakespeare: Contemporary Performance.* Ed. Dennis Kennedy. Cambridge: Cambridge UP, 1993. 21–35.

Brownlee, Marina S. *The Cultural Labyrinth of María de Zayas.* Philadelphia: U of Pennsylvania P, 2000.

Bulman, James C. "Introduction: Shakespeare and Performance Theory." *Shakespeare and Performance.* Ed. James C. Bulman. London: Routledge, 1996. 1–11.

Burling, William J. *New Plays on the London Stage, 1700–1810.* Version 1.3 January 2006. <http://www.faculty.missouristate.edu/W/WilliamBurling/Research/Complete%20New%20Cat%201700–1810%201.1.doc>.

Bushee, Alice H. "The Greatest Spanish Dramatists." *Hispania* 17 (1934): 51–8.

Butler, Judith. *Excitable Speech. A Politics of the Performative.* London: Routledge, 1997.

*The Cambridge Companion to English Restoration Theatre.* Ed. Deborah Payne Fisk. Cambridge: Cambridge UP, 2000.

Cañadas, Ivan. *The Public Theaters of Golden Age Madrid and Tudor-Stuart London: Class, Gender, and Festive Community.* Aldershot, Hampshire: Ashgate, 2005.

Carlson, Marvin. "Theatrical Performance: Illustration, Translation, Fulfillment, or Supplement?" *Theatre Journal* (1985): 5–11.

Casines, Gisela. "Private Sins, Public Penance: Poetic Justice in Some Restoration Plays with Spanish Sources." *South Atlantic Review* 53 (1988): 27–39.

Certeau, Michel de. *Heterologies. Discourse on the Other.* Minneapolis and London: U of Minnesota P, 1986.

Clifford, James. *Travel and Translation in the Late Twentieth Century.* Cambridge, MA: Harvard UP, 1997.

Cohen, Walter. "Calderón in England: A Social Theory of Production and Consumption." *Bulletin of the Comediantes* 35 (1983): 69–77.

——. *Drama of a Nation: Public Theatre in Renaissance England and Spain.* Ithaca and London: Cornell UP, 1985.

Conlon, Raymond. "Amón: the Psychology of a Rapist." *Bulletin of the Comediantes* 45 (1993): 41–52.

Cooke, William. *Memoires of Samuel Foote, esq. With a collection of his genuine bon-mots, anecdotes, opinions, &c. mostly original. And three of his dramatic pieces, not published in his works.* New York: Mesier, 1806.

Corman, Brian. "Comedy." *The Cambridge Companion to English Restoration Theatre.* Ed. Deborah Payne Fisk. Cambridge: Cambridge UP, 2000.

Darby, Trudi. "Cervantes in England: The Influence of Golden-Age Prose Fiction on Jacobean Drama, c1615–1625." *Bulletin of Hispanic Studies* [Liverpool] 74 (1997): 425–41.

Davies, Heather. Personal interview with Susan L. Fischer. Stratford-upon-Avon. 11 Aug. 2006.

Davis, Ann. "Don Juan and Foucauldian Sexual Discourse: Changing Attitudes to Female Sexuality." *European Studies: A Journal of European Culture, History, and Politics* 17 (2001): 159–70.

de Armas, Frederick A. "Rosaura Subdued: Victorian Readings of Calderón's *La vida es sueño.*" *South Central Review* 4 (1987): 43–62.

de Armas, José. *Ensayos críticos de literatura inglesa y española.* Madrid: Vitoriano Suárez, 1910.

Defourneaux, Marcelin. *Daily Life in Spain in the Golden Age.* Trans. Newton Branch. London: Allen, 1970.

Delgado, María-José. "Lesbiagrafisis. Exposición y expansión del deseo femenino en *La traición en la amistad* de María de Zayas y Sotomayor." *Lesbianism and Homosexuality in Early Modern Spain.* Eds. María-José Delgado and Alain Saint-Saëns. New Orleans: UP of the South, 2000. 379–94.

Déprats, Jean-Michel. "Translation at the Intersections of History." *Shakespeare and Modern Theatre.* Eds. Michael Bristol and Kathleen McLuskie, with Christopher Holmes. London: Routledge, 2001. 73–92.

Dixon, Victor. "*Beatus ... nemo: El villano en su rincón*, las 'polianteas' y la literatura de emblemas." *Cuadernos de Filología* 3, 1–2 (1981): 279–300.

——. "*El castigo sin venganza*: The Artistry of Lope de Vega." *Studies in Spanish Literature of the Golden Age presented to Edward M. Wilson.* Ed. R. O. Jones. London: Tamesis, 1973. 63–81.

——. "Manuel Vallejo. Un actor se prepara: Un comediante del siglo de oro ante un texto (*El castigo sin venganza*)." *Actor y técnica de representación del teatro clásico español.* Ed. José María Díez Borque. London: Tamesis, 1989. 55–74.

———. "The Study of Versification as an Aid to Interpreting the *Comedia*: Another Look at Some Well-known Plays by Lope de Vega." *The Golden Age* Comedia: *Text, Theory and Performance.* Eds. Charles Ganelin and Howard Mancing. West Lafayette: Purdue UP, 1994. 384–402.

———. "Translating Spanish Plays for Performance: Toward a Model Approach." *Prologue to Performance: Spanish Classical Theatre Today.* Eds. Louise Fothergill-Payne and Peter Fothergill-Payne. Lewisburg, PA: Bucknell UP, 1991. 93–112.

———. "*El villano en su rincón*: otra vez su fecha, forma, fuentes y sentido." *Bulletin of the Comediantes* 50 (1998): 5–20.

Dobson, Michael. "Adaptations and Revivals." *The Cambridge Companion to English Restoration Theatre.* Ed. Deborah Payne Fisk. Cambridge: Cambridge UP, 2000.

Duffy, Dennis. Rev. of *Grief Lessons: Four Plays by Euripides.* Trans. Anne Carson. *Globe and Mail* [Toronto] 5 Aug. 2006: D5.

Dunn, Peter N. "Some Uses of Sonnets in the Plays of Lope de Vega." *Bulletin of Hispanic Studies* 34 (1957): 213–22.

*Early American Playbills: Guide.* Houghton Library, Harvard College Library. MS Thr 479. <http://oasis.harvard.edu:10080/oasis/deliver/~hou01711>.

Eco, Umberto. *Mouse or Rat? Translation as Negotiation.* London: Weidenfeld & Nicolson, 2003.

Edwards, Philip and Colin Gibson, eds. *The Plays and Poems of Philip Massinger.* 2 vols. Oxford: Clarendon, 1976.

Egido, Aurora. "Sobre la demonología de los burladores (de Tirso a Zorrilla)." *Iberoromania* 26 (1987): 19–40. Rpt. *Cuadernos de Teatro Clásico* 1.2 (1988): 37–54.

Elam, Keir. *Shakespeare's Universe of Discourse: Language-Games in the Comedies.* Cambridge: Cambridge UP, 1984.

Elliott, J. H. *Spain and Its World, 1500–1700.* New Haven: Yale UP, 1989.

Empson, William. *Seven Types of Ambiguity.* 1930. London: Penguin in association with Chatto and Windus, 1965.

Erickson, Martin E. "A Review of Scholarship Dealing with the Problem of a Spanish Source for *Love's Cure.*" *Studies in Comparative Literature.* Ed. Waldo F. McNeir. Baton Rouge: Louisiana State UP, 1962. 102–19.

Evans, Peter. "*Peribáñez* and Ways of Looking at Golden Age Dramatic Characters." *Romanic Review* 72 (1983): 136–51.

Fauconnier, Giles and Mark Turner. *The Way We Think: Conceptual Blending and the Mind's Complexities.* New York: Basic Books, 2002.

Ferrán Graves, Natalia. "Adrian Mitchell y su versión de *Fuenteovejuna.*" *Traducir a los clásicos. Cuadernos de Teatro Clásico* 4 (1989): 175–80.

Fischer, Susan L., ed. *"Comedias del Siglo de Oro" and Shakespeare.* Lewisburg: Bucknell UP, 1989.

———. "Historicizing *Painter of Dishonour* on the 'Foreign' Stage: A Radical Interrogation of Tragedy." *Bulletin of Spanish Studies* 77 (2000): 183–216.

——. "'Some are Born Great' and 'Have Greatness Thrust Upon Them': Staging Lope's *El perro del hortelano* on the Boards of the Bard." *Comedia Performance* 2 (2005): 9–68.

——. "Staging Lope de Vega's *Peribáñez*: The Problem of an Ending." *Bulletin of Spanish Studies* 82 (2005): 159–79.

Fothergill-Payne, Louise and Peter Fothergill-Payne, eds. *Parallel Lives: Spanish and English National Drama, 1580–1680.* Lewisburg, PA: Bucknell UP, 1991.

Foucault, Michel. "Les Mots qui saignent." *L'Express* 29 Aug. 1964: 21.

Franzbach, Martin. *El teatro de Calderón en Europa.* Madrid: Fundación Universitaria Española, 1982.

García Lorenzo, Luciano. "Tirso de Molina en escena: de los años cuarenta a la Compañía Nacional de Teatro Clásico." *Cuadernos de Teatro Clásico* 18 (2003 [2004]): 21–36.

Garner, Stanton B. *Bodied Spaces: Phenomenology and Performance in Contemporary Drama.* Ithaca: Cornell UP, 1994.

Gaw, Allison. "Tuke's *Adventures of Five Hours* in Relation to the 'Spanish Plot' and to John Dryden." *Studies in English Drama. First Series.* Ed. Allison Gaw. University of Pennsylvania Studies in Philology and Literature. Vol. 14. New York: Appleton, 1917.

Gaylord, Mary Malcolm. "How to Do Things with Polymetry." *Approaches to Teaching Early Modern Spanish Drama.* Eds. Laura R. Bass and Margaret R. Greer. New York: MLA, 2006. 76–84.

Gennep, Arnold van. *The Rites of Passage.* Trans. Monika B. Vizedom and Gabrielle L. Caffee. Chicago: U of Chicago P, 1960.

Giesekam, Greg. Rev. of *New British Drama in Performance on the London Stage, 1970–1985,* by Richard Allen Cave. *Theatre Journal,* 41.3, *Performance in Context* (1989): 413–14.

Giles, Anthony. "Mining the Golden Age." *American Theatre* (June 1985): 15–17, 42.

Gitlitz, David. "Confesiones de un traductor." *Traducir a los clásicos. Cuadernos de Teatro Clásico* 4 (1989): 45–52.

Goldberg, Harriet, ed. and introd. *El jardín de nobles doncellas.* By Fray Martín de Córdoba. Chapel Hill: North Carolina Studies in Romance Languages and Literatures, 1974. 11–126.

Goldmann, Lucien. *Le Dieu caché: Étude sur la vision tragique dans Les Pensées de Pascal et dans le théâtre de Racine.* Paris: Gallimard, 1955.

González-Cruz, Luis F. "El soneto: esencia temática de *El perro del hortelano,* de Lope de Vega." *Lope de Vega y los orígenes del teatro español: Actas del I congreso internacional sobre Lope de Vega.* Ed. M. Criado de Val. Madrid: Edi-6, 1981. 541–5.

González-Gerth, Miguel. "The Image of Spain in American Literature, 1815–1856." *Journal of Inter-American Studies* 4. 2 (1962): 257–72.

Green, Jeffrey M. *Thinking Through Translation.* Athens: U of Georgia P, 2001.

Greenblatt, Stephen. Introduction. *Romeo and Juliet. The Norton Shakespeare.*

Eds. Stephen Greenblatt, Walter Cohen, Jean E. Howard, Katharine Eisaman Maus. New York: Norton, 1997. 865–71.

——. *Shakespearean Negotiations: The Circulation of Social Energy in Renaissance England*. Berkeley: U of California P, 1988.

Greer, Margaret Rich. *María de Zayas Tells Baroque Tales of Love and the Cruelty of Men*. University Park: Pennsylvania State UP, 2000.

——. "The (Self)Representation of Control in *La dama duende*." *The Golden Age Comedia: Text, Theory and Performance*. Eds. Charles Ganelin and Howard Mancing. West Lafayette: Purdue UP, 1994. 87–106.

Gumbrecht, Hans Ulrich. *In 1926: Living at the Edge of Time*. Cambridge, MA: Harvard UP, 1997.

Hall, Peter. "Is the Beginning the Word?" *The Making of Theatre: From Drama to Performance*. Ed. Robert W. Corrigan. Glenview, IL: Scott, Foresman, 1981. 198–208.

Hegstrom, Valerie. "The Fallacy of False Dichotomy in María de Zayas's *La traición en la amistad*." *Bulletin of the Comediantes* 46 (1994): 59–68.

Hesse, Everett W. *Tirso's Art in* La venganza de Tamar: *Tragedy of Sex and Violence*. York, SC: Spanish Literature, 1991.

Hills, Elijah Clarence. "English Translations of Spanish Plays." *Hispania* 3 (1920): 97–108.

Hogan, Floriana T. "Notes on Thirty-One English Plays and Their Spanish Sources." *Restoration and 18th Century Theatre Research* 4–6 (May 1965–November 1967): 56–9.

Holloway, James E. "Lope's Neoplatonism in *La dama boba*." *Bulletin of Hispanic Studies* 49 (1972): 236–55.

Hughes, Derek. *English Drama, 1660–1700*. Oxford: Clarendon Press, 1996.

Hume, Robert D. "Diversity and Development in Restoration Comedy 1660–1679." *Eighteenth-Century Studies* 5 (1972): 365–97.

Hutton, Ronald. *Charles the Second, King of England, Scotland, and Ireland*. Oxford: Clarendon, and New York: Oxford UP, 1989.

*Index to the London Stage, 1660–1800*. Ed. Ben Ross Schneider, Jr. Carbondale: Southern Illinois UP, 1979.

Johnston, David. "Securing the Performability of the Text." *Drama Translation and Theatre Practice*. Eds. Sabine Coelsch-Foisner and Holger Klein. Frankfurt: Peter Lang, 2004.

——. "Spain's New Golden Age." *Plays and Players* 430 (1989).

——. Introduction and ed. *Stages of Translation*. Bath: Absolute, 1996.

——. "Translation, Performance and the New Historicism." *Theatre and Translation: Contact Stages*. Porto: Campo das Letras, 2007.

Jonas, Susan. "Aiming the Canon at Now: Strategies for Adaptation." *Dramaturgy in American Theatre: A Source Book*. Eds. Susan Jonas, Geoffrey S. Proehl, and Michael Lupu. Fort Worth: Harcourt, 1997. 244–65.

Jörder, Otto. *Die Formen des Sonnetts bei Lope de Vega*. Halle: Max Niemeyer, 1936.

Jurado Santos, Agapita. *Obras teatrales derivadas de las novelas cervantinas (siglo XVII): para una bibliografía*. Kassel: Reichenberger, 2005.

Kamen, Henry. *Golden Age Spain*. London: Macmillan, 1988.

Karttunen, Frances. *Between Worlds: Interpreters, Guides and Survivors*. New Brunswick: Rutgers UP, 1994.

Kennedy, Dennis, ed. *Foreign Shakespeare: Contemporary Performance*. Cambridge: Cambridge UP, 1993.

Knight, G. Wilson. *The Wheel of Fire*. London: Methuen, 1949.

Lancaster, Henry Carrington. *A History of French Dramatic Literature in the Seventeenth Century*. 5 pts. in 9 vols. Baltimore: Johns Hopkins UP, 1929–42.

Larson, Catherine. "Gender, Reading, and Intertextuality: Don Juan's Legacy in María de Zayas's *La traición en la amistad*." *INTI: Revista de literatura hispánica* 40–41 (1994–95): 129–38.

——. "Translator's Note." *La traición en la amistad / Friendship Betrayed*. Ed. Valerie Hegstrom. Trans. Catherine Larson. Lewisburg, PA: Bucknell UP, 1999.

Larson, Donald R. *The Honor Plays of Lope de Vega*. Cambridge, MA: Harvard UP, 1977.

Lehfeldt, Elizabeth A. *Religious Women in Golden Age Spain: The Permeable Cloister*. Aldershot: Ashgate, 2005.

Leoni, Monica. *Outside, Inside, Aside: Dialoguing with the* Gracioso *in Spanish Golden Age Theater*. New Orleans: UP of the South, 2000.

Leyva, Juan. "Métrica y teatralidad en Lope de Vega: *Las bizarrías de Belisa*." *Texto, espacio y movimiento en el teatro español del Siglo de Oro*. Ed. Aurelio González. Mexico, D. F.: Colegio de México, 2000. 91–112.

Loftis, John. "La comedia española en la Inglaterra del siglo XVII." *La comedia española y el teatro europeo del siglo XVII*. Eds. Henry W. Sullivan, Raúl A. Galoppe, and Mahlon L. Stoutz. Woodbridge, Suffolk: Tamesis, 1999. 101–19.

——. "Spanish Drama in Neoclassical England." *Comparative Literature* 2 (1959): 29–34.

——. *The Spanish Plays of Neo-Classical England*. New Haven: Yale UP, 1973.

*The London Stage, 1660–1800. Parts I–V*. 11 vols. Ed. William Van Lennep. Introd. Emmett L. Avery and Arthur H. Scouten. Carbondale: Southern Illinois UP, 1960–8.

Lopez-Mayhew, Barbara. "From Manuscript to 21st Century Performances: *La traición en la amistad*." *Comedia Performance* 1 (2004): 174–91.

Lundeberg, Olav K. "The True Sources of Robert Dodsley's *The King and the Miller of Mansfield*." *Modern Language Notes* 39 (1924): 394–7.

Lynch, John. *Spain Under the Habsburgs*. 2nd edn. Vol. 2. *Spain and America 1598–1700*. Oxford: Blackwell, 1981.

Mamet, David. *Three Uses of the Knife: On the Nature and Purpose of Drama*. New York: Vintage, 2000.

Mandel, Oscar. "The Legend of Don Juan." *The Theatre of Don Juan: A Collection of Plays and Views, 1630–1963*. Lincoln: U of Nebraska P, 1963. 3–33.

Marañón, Gregorio. "Don Juan." *The Theatre of Don Juan: A Collection of Plays and Views, 1630–1963*. Ed. Oscar Mandel. Lincoln: U of Nebraska P, 1986. 637–41.

Mariscal, George. *Contradictory Subjects: Quevedo, Cervantes, and Seventeenth-Century Spanish Culture*. Ithaca: Cornell UP, 1991.

Matthews, Dakin. "A Note on the Text and the Verse." *Don Juan. The Trickster of Seville*. By Tirso de Molina. Trans. Dakin Matthews. N. Hollywood: Andak Theatrical Service, 2006.

McGaha, Michael. "Hacia la traducción representable." *Traducir a los clásicos. Cuadernos de Teatro Clásico* 4 (1989): 79–86.

McKendrick, Melveena. "Communicating the Past." *Approaches to Teaching Early Modern Spanish Drama*. Eds. Laura R. Bass and Margaret R. Greer. New York: MLA, 2006. 29–38.

——. *Theatre in Spain, 1490–1700*. Cambridge: Cambridge UP, 1989.

*Memoirs of Ann, Lady Halkett and Ann, Lady Fanshawe, The*. Ed. and introd. John Loftis. Oxford: Clarendon, 1979.

Metford, J. C. J. "Tirso de Molina's Old Testament Plays." *Bulletin of Hispanic Studies* 27 (1950): 149–63.

Miller, Jonathan. *The Afterlife of Plays*. San Diego: San Diego State UP, 1992.

——. Interview. *In Contact with the Gods? Directors Talk Theatre*. Eds. María M. Delgado and Paul Heritage. Manchester: Manchester UP, 1996. 158–74.

——. *Subsequent Performances*. London: Faber & Faber, 1986.

Montesinos, José F. *Estudios sobre Lope de Vega*. Salamanca: Anaya, 1976.

Moore, Frank Harper. *The Nobler Pleasure: Dryden's Comedy in Theory and Practice*. Chapel Hill: U of North Carolina P, 1963.

Moreland, James. "The Theatre in Portland in the Eighteenth Century." *The New England Quarterly* 11 (1938): 331–42.

Morley, Sylvanus Griswold. "Objective Criteria for Judging Authorship and Chronology in the *Comedia*." *Hispanic Review* 5 (1937): 281–5.

Morley, Sylvanus Griswold and Courtney Bruerton. *Cronología de las comedias de Lope de Vega*. Madrid: Gredos, 1968.

Mountjoy, Kathleen. "Interview with Laurence Boswell." *Comedia Performance* 2 (2005): 171–92.

——. E-mail to Dawn L. Smith. 5 May 2006.

Muir, Kenneth. "Translating Golden Age Plays: A Reconsideration." *Translation and Literature* 1 (1992): 104–11.

Mujica, Barbara. "María de Zayas on the Washington Stage: Interview with Karen Berman." *Comedia Performance* 4 (2007): 217–32.

——. "The End: Modern Production of *El Burlador de Sevilla*, with Special Attention to Closings." *Bulletin of the Comediantes* 47 (1995): 201–22.

Muñoz Carabantes, Manuel. "Cincuenta años de teatro cervantino." *Anales Cervantinos* 28 (1990): 155–90.

Nicholson, Florence. "Spanish Drama on the American Stage, 1900–1938." *Hispania* 22 (1939): 135–44.

Nicoll, Allardyce. *A History of Restoration Drama, 1660–1700*. 3rd edn. Cambridge: Cambridge UP, 1940.

O'Brien, Robert. *Spanish Plays in English Translation. An Annotated Bibliography.* New York: Las Americas, 1963.

Olivares, Julián. Introduction. *Novelas amorosas y ejemplares de María de Zayas y Sotomayor.* Madrid: Cátedra, 2000. 11–47.

Orgel, Stephen. *The Authentic Shakespeare.* London: Routledge, 2002.

Pane, Remigio Ugo. *English Translations from the Spanish. 1484–1943. A Bibliography.* New Brunswick: Rutgers UP, 1944.

Parker, Andrew and Eve Kosofsky Sedgwick. Introduction. *Performativity and Performance.* Eds. Andrew Parker and Eve Kosofsky Sedgwick. London: Routledge, 1995. 1–18.

Parr, James A. *Don Quixote, Don Juan, and Related Subjects: Form and Tradition in Spanish Literature, 1330–1630.* Selinsgrove, PA: Susquehanna UP, 2004.

Paterson, Alan K. G. "Reflexiones sobre una traducción de *El pintor de su deshonra.*" *Traducir a los clásicos. Cuadernos de Teatro Clásico* 4 (1989): 113–32.

Paun de García, Susan. "*Traición en la amistad* de María de Zayas." *Anales de Literatura Española* 6 (1988): 377–90.

——. "Zayas as Writer: Hell Hath No Fury." *María de Zayas: The Dynamics of Discourse.* Eds. Amy R. Williamsen and Judith A. Whitenack. Madison, NJ: Associated UP, 1995. 40–51.

Pavis, Patrice. "Problems of Translation for the Stage: Interculturalism and Post-Modern Theatre." *The Play Out of Context: Transferring Plays from Culture to Culture.* Eds. Hanna Scolnicov and Peter Holland. Cambridge: Cambridge UP, 1989. 25–44.

——. "Theatre Analysis: Some Questions and a Questionnaire." *New Theatre Quarterly* 1–2 (1985): 208–12.

——. *Theatre at the Crossroads of Culture.* Trans. Loren Kruger. London: Routledge, 1992.

Péristiany, J. G., ed. *Honour and Shame: The Values of Mediterranean Society.* Chicago: U of Chicago P, 1966.

*Platform Papers.* London: Royal National Theatre, 1992.

Praag, Jonas Andries van. *La comedia espagnole aux Pays-Bas au XVII et XVIIIe siècle.* Amsterdam: H. J. Paris, 1922.

Pratt, Mary Louise. "The Traffic in Meaning: Translation, Contagion, Infiltration." *Profession* (2002): 25–36.

Prettiman, C. A. "Calderón, Richard Savage, and Christopher Bullock's *A Woman Is a Riddle.*" *Philological Quarterly* 68 (1985): 25–36.

*Princeton Encyclopedia of Poetry and Poetics.* Eds. Alex Preminger, Frank J. Warnke, with O. B. Hardison, Jr. Princeton: Princeton UP, 1974.

Pym, Anthony. *Method in Translation Theory.* Manchester: St Jerome, 1998.

Rabassa, Gregory. *If This Be Treason: Translation and Its Dyscontents.* New York: New Directions, 2005.

Randall, Dale B. J. *The Golden Tapestry. A Critical Survey of Non-chivalric Spanish Fiction in English Translation (1543–1657).* Durham, NC: Duke UP, 1963.

Reed, Cory A. *The Novelist as Playwright: Cervantes and the* Entremés nuevo. New York: Peter Lang, 1993.

Reichenberger, Arnold. "The Uniqueness of the *Comedia.*" *Hispanic Review* 27 (1959): 303–16.

Rennert, Hugo. *The Spanish Stage in the Time of Lope de Vega.* New York: The Hispanic Society of America, 1909.

Rice, Warner G. "The Sources of Massinger's *The Renegado.*" *Philological Quarterly* 2 (1932): 65–75.

Richards, I. A. *Complementarities. Uncollected Essays.* Manchester: Carcanet, 1976.

Roach, Joseph. *Cities of the Dead: Circum-Atlantic Performance.* New York: Columbia UP, 1996.

Robinson, Douglas. *Performative Linguistics: Speaking and Translating as Doing Things with Words.* London: Routledge, 2003.

——, ed. *What is Translation? Centrifugal Theories, Critical Interventions.* Kent, OH: Kent State UP, 1997.

Rodríguez Cuadros, Evangelina. "Registros y modos de representación en el actor barroco: datos para una teoría fragmentaria." *Actor y técnica de representación del teatro clásico español.* Ed. José María Díez Borque. London: Tamesis, 1989. 35–53.

Rozas, Juan Manuel. *Significado y doctrina del arte nuevo de Lope de Vega.* Madrid: SGEL, 1976.

Rozik, Eli. "Framing, Decoding and Interpretation: On the Spectator's Vital Role in Creating Theatrical Meaning." *Gestos* 17 (2002): 9–27.

Ruano de la Haza, José. "Trascendencia y proyección del teatro clásico español en el mundo anglosajón." *Proyección y significados del teatro clásico español.* Eds. José María Díez Borque and José Alcalá-Zamora. Madrid: SEACEE, 2004. 233–44.

Rudder, Robert S. *The Literature of Spain in English Translation.* New York: Frederick Ungar, 1975.

Ruiz Ramón, Francisco. *Historia del teatro español (desde sus orígenes hasta 1900).* 10th edn. Madrid: Cátedra, 2000.

Rundle, James Urvin. "D'Avenant's *The Man's the Master* and the Spanish Source." *Modern Language Notes,* 65 (1950): 194–6.

——. "More about Calderón, Boursault, and Ravenscroft." *Modern Language Notes* 62 (1947): 382–4.

——. "The Source of Dryden's 'Comic Plot' in *The Assignation.*" *Modern Philology* 45 (1947): 104–11.

——. "Wycherley and Calderón: *A Source for Love in a Wood.*" *Publications of the Modern Language Association* 64 (1949): 701–7.

Russell, P. E. "A Stuart Hispanist: James Mabbe." *Bulletin of Hispanic Studies* 30 (1953): 75–84.

Rutter, Carol Chillingworth. *Enter the Body: Women and Representation on Shakespeare's Stage.* London: Routledge, 2001.

Saglia, Diego. "Tirso y la literatura inglesa: Modalidades de la apropiación del siglo XVII al XIX." *Tirso de Molina: textos e intertextos*. Eds Laura Dolfi and Eva Galar. Pamplona: Instituto de Estudios Tirsianos, 2001. 327–50.

Santoyo, J. C. "Traducciones y adaptaciones teatrales: ensayo de tipología." *Traducir a los clásicos. Cuadernos de Teatro Clásico* 4 (1989): 95–112.

Schevill, Rudolph. "On the Influence of Spanish Literature upon English in the Early Seventeenth Century." *Romanische Forschungen* 20 (1905–6): 603–34.

Siliunas, Vidmantas. "Calderón en Rusia y Unión Soviética en el siglo XX." *Calderón en escena: siglo XX*. Eds. José María Díez Borque and Andrés Peláez Martín. Madrid: Comunidad de Madrid, 2000. 181–9.

Sloman, Albert E. *The Dramatic Craftsmanship of Calderón*. Oxford: Dolphin, 1969.

——. "The Two Versions of *El burlador de Sevilla*." *Bulletin of Hispanic Studies* 42 (1965): 18–33.

Smith, Dawn L. "Crossing Generic Boundaries: the Case of *The Rape of Tamar*." *Indiana Journal of Hispanic Literatures* 10–11 (1997): 37–44.

——. "El envés del tapiz: recreando los entremeses de Cervantes en versión inglesa." *Romance Languages Review* 5 (1993): 513–17.

——. "El reto de las maravillas: el traductor ante los *Entremeses* de Cervantes." *Traducir a los clásicos. Cuadernos de Teatro Clásico* 4 (1989): 159–70.

——. Rev. of *The Novelist as Playwright*, by Cory A. Reed. *Cervantes* 15 (1995): 171–3.

——. "El teatro clásico español en Inglaterra en los últimos quince años." *Cuadernos de Teatro Clásico* 8 (1995): 299–309.

Snell-Hornby, Mary. *Translation Studies: An Integrated Approach*. Amsterdam: John Benjamins, 1988.

Sontag, Susan. *Susan Sontag Reader*. Harmondsworth: Penguin, 1983.

Soufas, Teresa. "María de Zayas's (Un)Conventional Play, *La traición en la amistad*." *The Golden Age* Comedia*: Text, Theory, and Performance*. Eds. Charles Ganelin and Howard Mancing. West Lafayette: Purdue UP, 1994. 148–64.

Souriau, Étienne. *Les deux cent mille situations dramatiques*. Paris: Flammarion, 1950.

Spadaccini, Nicholas and Jenaro Talens. *Through the Shattering Glass: Cervantes and the Self-Made World*. Minneapolis: U of Minnesota P, 1993.

Steiner, George. *After Babel: Aspects of Language and Translation*. 3rd edn. Oxford: Oxford UP, 1998.

Stoye, John Walter. *English Travellers Abroad 1604–1667: Their Influence in English Society and Politics*. London: Jonathan Cape, 1952.

Stroud, Matthew. "The Demand for Love and the Mediation of Desire in *La traición en la amistad*." *María de Zayas: The Dynamics of Discourse*. Eds. Amy R. Williamsen and Judith A. Whitenack. Madison, NJ: Fairleigh Dickinson UP, 1995. 155–69.

——. "Love, Friendship, and Deceit in *La traición en la amistad*, by María de Zayas." *Neophilologus* 69 (1985): 539–47.

Suárez García, José Luis. *Teatro y toros en el Siglo de Oro español: Estudios sobre la licitud de la fiesta*. Granada: U of Granada, 2003.

Suckling, Norman J. "Molière and English Restoration Comedy." *Restoration Theatre*. Eds. John Russell Brown and Bernard Harris. London: Edward Arnold, 1965. 92–107.

Sullivan, Henry. *Calderón in the German Lands and the Low Countries: His Reception and Influence, 1654–1980*. Cambridge: Cambridge UP, 1983.

Sullivan, Henry W., Raúl A. Galoppe, and Mahlon L. Stoutz, eds. *La comedia española y el teatro europeo del siglo XVII*. Woodbridge, Suffolk: Tamesis, 1999.

ter Horst, Robert. "The True Mind of Marriage: Ironies of the Intellect in Lope's *La dama boba*." *Romanistisches Jahrbuch* 27 (1976): 347–63.

Thacker, Jonathan. "Sex, Treachery, and Really Big Moustaches: Cervantes's *Entremeses* at the Edinburgh Fringe Festival." *Comedia Performance* 3 (2006): 185–99.

———. "'Puedo yo con sola la vista oír leyendo:' Reading, Seeing and Hearing the *Comedia*." *Comedia Performance* 1 (2004): 143–73.

Thomas, Henry. "Shakespeare and Spain." *Studies in European Literature, Being the Taylorian Lectures*. Second Series, 1920–30. Oxford: Oxford UP, 1930.

Tietz, Manfred, ed. *Teatro calderoniano sobre el tablado: Calderón y su puesta en escena a través de los siglos: XIII Coloquio Anglogermano sobre Calderón*. Stuttgart: Steiner, 2003.

Totzeva, Sophia. "Realizing Theatrical Potential: The Dramatic Text in Performance and Translation." *The Practices of Literary Translation: Constraints and Creativity*. Eds. Jean Boase-Beier and Michael Holman. Manchester: St Jerome, 1999. 81–90.

Toury, Gideon. "A Rationale for Descriptive Translation." *The Manipulation of Literature: Studies in Literary Translation*. Ed. Theo Hermans. New York: St. Martin's, 1985. 16–41.

Tracy, Clarence. *The Artificial Bastard. A Biography of Richard Savage*. Cambridge, MA: Harvard UP, 1953.

Turkevich, Ludmilla Buketoff. *Spanish Literature in Russia and in the Soviet Union, 1735–1964*. Methuen, N. J.: Scarecrow, 1967.

Tymoczko, Maria, and Edwin Gentzler, eds. *Translation and Power*. Amherst: U of Massachusetts P, 2002.

Umpierre, Gustavo. *Songs in the Plays of Lope de Vega: A Study of their Dramatic Function*. London: Tamesis, 1975.

Venuti, Laurence. *The Translator's Invisibility*. London: Routledge, 1995.

———, ed. *The Translation Studies Reader*. London: Routledge, 2000.

Vernon, P. F. "Wycherley's First Comedy and Its Spanish Source." *Comparative Literature* 18 (1966): 132–44.

Vidler, Laura L. "Coming to America: Translating Culture in Two U.S. Productions of the Spanish *Comedia*." *Comedia Performance* 2 (2005): 69–98.

Vilar, Jean. "Murder of the Director." *The Making of Theatre: From Drama to Performance*. Ed. Robert W. Corrigan. Glenview, IL: Scott, Foresman, 1981. 208–13.

Vitse, Marc. "La descripción de Lisboa en *El burlador de Sevilla*." *Criticón* 2 (1978): 21–41.

Vollendorf, Lisa. *The Lives of Women: A New History of Inquisitional Spain.* Nashville: Vanderbilt UP, 2005.

Voros, Sharon D. "Calderón's Writing Women and Women Writers: The Subversion of the *Exempla.*" *Looking at the* Comedia *in the Year of the Quincentennial.* Eds Barbara Mujica and Sharon D. Voros. Asst. ed. Matthew D. Stroud. Lanham, MD: UP of America, 1993. 121–32.

——. "Fashioning Feminine Wit in María de Zayas, Ana Caro, and Leonor de la Cueva." *Gender, Identity, and Representation in Spain's Golden Age.* Eds. Anita K. Stoll and Dawn L. Smith. Lewisburg, PA: Bucknell UP, 2000. 156–77.

Wandor, Michelene. *Drama Today. A Critical Guide to British Drama 1970–1990.* London and New York: Longman, 1993.

Wardropper, Bruce W. "*El burlador de Sevilla*: A Tragedy of Errors." *Philological Quarterly* 36 (1957): 61–71.

——. "*Fuente Ovejuna: el gusto* and *lo justo.*" *Studies in Philology* 53 (1956): 159–71.

Weber, Carl. "AC/TC: Currents of Theatrical Exchange." *Interculturalism and Performance.* New York: PAJ, 1991. 27–37.

——. "Foreign Drama in Translation: Some Reflections on Otherness, Xenophobia, the Translator's Task, and the Problems They Present." *Dramaturgy in American Theatre: A Source Book.* Eds. Susan Jonas, Geoffrey S. Proehl, and Michael Lupu. Fort Worth: Harcourt, 1997. 266–75.

Weiner, Jack. *Mantillas in Muscovy: the Spanish Golden Age Theater in Tsarist Russia, 1672–1917.* Lawrence: U of Kansas P, 1970.

Weissberger, Barbara. *Isabel Rules: Constructing Queenship, Wielding Power.* Minneapolis: U of Minnesota P, 2003.

Welles, Marcia L. "The Anxiety of Gender: The Transformation of Tamar in Tirso's *La venganza de Tamar* and Calderón's *Los cabellos de Absalón.*" *Bulletin of the Comediantes* 47 (1995): 341–72.

Wilcox, John. *The Relation of Molière to Restoration Comedy.* New York: Columbia UP, 1938.

Wild, Kate. "Resource Pack, *Peribáñez.*" Ed. Sue Emmas with contributions from Nizar Zuabi. London: Young Vic, 2003. 1–47.

Wilkins, Constance. "Subversion through Comedy? Two Plays by Sor Juana Inés de la Cruz and María de Zayas." *The Perception of Women in Spanish Theater of the Golden Age.* Eds. Anita K. Stoll and Dawn L. Smith. Lewisburg, PA: Bucknell UP, 1991. 102–20.

Williamsen, Amy. "From Page to Stage: Readers, Spectators, Expectations and Interpretations of María de Zayas's *La traición en la amistad.*" *Heroines of the Golden Stage. Women and Drama in Spain and England, 1500–1700.* Eds. Rina Walthaus and Marguérite Corporaal. Estudios de Literatura 105. Kassel: Reichenberger, forthcoming.

Williamsen, Vern G. "A Commentary on 'The Uses of Polymetry' and the Editing of the Multi-strophic Texts of the Spanish *comedia.*" *Editing the Comedia.* Eds. Frank P. Casa and Michael D. McGaha. Michigan Romance Studies. Vol. 5. Ann Arbor: U of Michigan, 1985. 126–45.

——. "The Critic as Translator." *Prologue to Performance: Spanish Classical*

*Theater Today.* Eds. Louise Fothergill-Payne and Peter Fothergill-Payne. Lewisburg, PA: Bucknell UP, 1991. 136–52.

Wilson, E. M. "Did John Fletcher Read Spanish?" *Philological Quarterly* 30 (1948), 187–90.

Wilson, Margaret. *Spanish Drama of the Golden Age.* Oxford: Pergamon, 1969.

Worthen, W. B. *Shakespeare and the Authority of Performance.* Cambridge: Cambridge UP, 1997.

——. *Shakespeare and the Force of Modern Performance.* Cambridge: Cambridge UP, 2003.

Young, Iris Marion. *Throwing Like a Girl and Other Essays in Feminist Philosophy and Social Theory.* Bloomington: Indiana UP, 1990.

# INDEX

*A secreto agravio, secreta venganza* (*see under* Calderón de la Barca, Pedro)

*Absalom's Hair* (*see under* Calderón de la Barca, Pedro)

Acadia University 99n11

actants 207–9, 212

*A House with Two Doors is Difficult to Guard* (*see under* Calderón de la Barca, Pedro)

*A Midsummer Night's Dream* (*see under* Shakespeare, William)

*A Woman is a Riddle* (*see under* Bullock, Christopher)

Advanced Acting Master's Program (University of Wisconsin, Milwaukee) 155

*Adventures of Five Hours, The* (*see under* Tuke, Samuel)

Aesop 234, 235, 236

AHCT (*see* Association for Hispanic Classical Theater, The)

Aitkin, Maria 246, 253

Alarcón (*see* Ruiz de Alarcón, Juan)

*alcalde de Zalamea, El* (*see under* Calderón de la Barca, Pedro)

Alemán, Mateo
  *Guzmán de Alfarache* 6

Alfonso XI 111n4

*All Accounts Must Be Settled, All Debts Paid and the Stone Guest* (*see under* Zamora, Antonio de)

Allen, Ned B. 12n27

Allison, A. F. 6n15

Almagro, Festival de Teatro Clásico 84, 88n9, 97, 231, 235

Alpern, Hymen 38n1

Alvarez Quintero, Joaquín and Serafín 19–20n40

Alvarez, Lynne 110n2

*Amadeus* 212

American Repertory Theatre 24

Andak Stage Company 26, 27, 29, 140, 141, 190, 209

Antaeus Company 26, 27, 144

Ark Theatre 30

Armfield, Neil 29

*Ars Poetica* (*see under* Horace)

*Arte nuevo de hacer comedias* (*see under* Vega Carpio, Lope Félix de)

*As You Like It* (*see under* Shakespeare, William)

asides 4, 136

Asociación de Escritoras de España y las Américas (AEEA) (*see* Grupo de Estudios sobre la Mujer en España y las Américas)

aspectuality 214–17, 228

*Assignation; or, Love in a Nunnery, The* (*see under* Dryden, John)

Associació d'Investigació d'Experimentació Teatral, Universidad de Barcelona (AIET) 211, 212, 213

Association for Hispanic Classical Theater, The (AHCT) 29, 87, 97, 98n7, 209n6, 229n1

Aston, Lord 6

*astrólogo fingido, El* (*see under* Calderón de la Barca, Pedro)

Austin, J. L. 56, 215n2

*Aventurarse perdiendo* (*see under* Zayas y Sotomayor, María de)

*Bagnios of Algiers, The* (*see under* Cervantes, Miguel de)

Bal, Mieke 70

Bamber, Linda 234, 238

*Banditti, The* (*see under* Durfey, Thomas)

*baños de Argel, Los* (*see under* Cervantes, Miguel de)

Baquero, Arcadio 208